Traumatic Brain Injury:
Rehabilitation for Everyday Adaptive Living

Jennie Ponsford
Chief Neuropsychologist,
Bethesda Hospital, Melbourne, Australia

with

Sue Sloan
Chief Neuropsychologist,
Ivanhoe Manor Private Rehabilitation Hospital,
Melbourne, Australia

Pamela Snow
Speech Pathologist,
Department of Communication Disorders, LaTrobe
University, Melbourne, Australia

LAWRENCE ERLBAUM ASSOCIATES, PUBLISHERS
Hove (UK)   Hillsdale (USA)

Copyright © 1995 by Lawrence Erlbaum Associates Ltd.
   All rights reserved. No part of this book may be reproduced in any form,
by photostat, microform, retrieval system, or any other means without the
prior written permission of the publisher.

Lawrence Erlbaum Associates Ltd., Publishers
27 Church Road
Hove
East Sussex, BN3 2FA
UK

British Library Cataloguing in Publication Data

A catalogue record for this book is available from the British Library

   ISBN 0-86377-376-1 (Hbk)
   ISBN 0-86377-377-X (Pbk)

Cover design by Joyce Chester
Printed and bound in the United Kingdom by Redwood Books Ltd., Trowbridge, Wilts.

This book is dedicated to those traumatically brain-injured individuals and their families, who have taught us so much.

Contents

Acknowledgements

This book is borne of a very special colleagueship, which has spanned more than ten years as members of the Head Injury Team at Bethesda Hospital. Although Sue and Pamela have been directly involved in writing only two chapters each, we have spent many hours collaborating on the themes and content of all chapters. I have greatly appreciated the depth of experience and expertise this has brought to the book. Both Sue and Pamela have also assisted me with some case and reference material for other chapters.

We also owe a great deal to many fellow team members from the Head Injury Unit at Bethesda Hospital, Melbourne, who have, over the past 12 years, participated in the evolution of the approach to traumatic brain injury rehabilitation which is recommended in this book.

Heather Granger provided much inspiration and energy along the way, in facilitating our collaborative efforts and assisting us to formulate our "direction". We all thank her deeply for her time given so generously.

Elizabeth Cameron and Carolyn Curran gave invaluable assistance with typing, referencing and proof-reading, as well as an enormous amount of moral support. I would also like to acknowledge the tolerance of other members of the Bethesda Psychology Department, who had to work so hard through my long absences. I particularly thank Ann Parry and Lyn Boag for their personal support and assistance. Alison Stewart-Scott and Margaret Mealings also gave a great deal of support and encouragement.

Ann Parry, Jacinta Douglas, Alison Stewart-Scott and Margaret Mealings gave helpful feedback on particular chapters. I also gratefully acknowledge the contribution of a case study by the staff of the Bethesda Hospital Transitional Living Centre. Richard O'Sullivan kindly contributed reproductions of CT and MRI studies. Janet Cockburn and Ian Robertson provided invaluable feedback which helped shape the final draft.

Finally, we all acknowledge the love, support and, above all, tolerance of our respective husbands, Lew, Rick and Stuart. Without our children, Isabelle and Alice, William and Jack, and Alexandra and Katie, the book may have been written much more quickly, but our labours would be far less worthwhile. Our parents have also provided enormous practical and moral support, for which we are eternally grateful.

Preface

Over the past two decades there has been a growing awareness of the needs both of those who experience traumatic brain injury and of their families. Initially the emphasis was on defining the nature of sequelae. More recently, there has been much written regarding rehabilitative strategies. A number of different approaches to management have been advocated, based on the development of some excellent model rehabilitation programmes, most notably those of Yehuda Ben-Yishay and colleagues, George Prigatano and colleagues, Peter Eames and Rodger Wood, and McKay Moore Sohlberg and Catherine Mateer. These programmes target different types of problems at different levels. Whilst these approaches have much to offer clinicians, we felt there was a need for more comprehensive guidelines, covering a broader spectrum, in terms of severity, problems and time frames.

With the burgeoning growth of services for those with traumatic brain injury, increasing numbers of rehabilitation professionals are being employed in traumatic brain injury rehabilitation programmes, often with limited education and experience in this area. There was, therefore, a perceived need for a book which provided comprehensive and practical guidelines for psychologists and therapists in training, and practitioners working in this complex and stressful area.

When we actually set about doing this, there was a growing realisation that it would not be possible to cover every aspect of traumatic brain injury. Reflecting the expertise of the authors, this book focuses on the psychological consequences of traumatic brain injury, rather than the medical or physical consequences. This should not imply that medical or physical consequences are less important or significant in their impact on certain traumatically brain-injured individuals. However, these have been explored comprehensively elsewhere. Moreover, there is now substantial evidence to show that, in the majority of cases, the psychological consequences of traumatic brain injury have the most significant and pervasive impact on the rehabilitation process and, more importantly, on the lifestyle of the person who is injured.

Whilst it is acknowledged that some of those who sustain mild traumatic brain injury will have ongoing difficulties and require interventions along the lines outlined in this book, those who sustain moderate and severe injuries more commonly have ongoing problems. Hence, greater emphasis has been placed on dealing with the difficulties presented by those who sustain moderate and severe injuries.

Chapter 1 discusses the epidemiology, pathophysiology, sequelae and psychosocial consequences of traumatic brain injury. Using this as a basis, it also outlines the principles of the approach recommended to rehabilitation following traumatic brain injury. We have termed this the REAL approach, signifying Rehabilitation for Everyday Adaptive Living.

Chapter 2 covers assessment and management of individuals with impaired consciousness, incorporating both coma and post-traumatic amnesia. Chapters 3 and 4 provide guidelines for the assessment and management of cognitive problems. Chapter 5 deals with communication and interpersonal difficulties, and Chapter 6 with behaviour problems. The emphasis in managing all of these problems, both within a rehabilitation setting and in the community, is on effective teamwork, focusing on the real world, involving the injured person and family in therapy, and taking a long-term view.

In Chapter 7, issues involved in returning to the community are explored. These include return to independent living, work, study, avocational interests and driving. Chapter 8 explores the nature of and methods of assisting with emotional and social problems, which tend to arise or have a greater impact after return to the community, including problems with self-awareness and self-esteem, depression, anxiety, anger control, relationship problems and sexual difficulties.

Chapter 9 addresses the impact of traumatic brain injury on the families, caregivers and others close to the person who is injured. It outlines methods of minimising this impact, with emphasis on the need for their involvement in all aspects of the rehabilitation process, and the need for support to continue indefinitely.

The impact of traumatic brain injury on children is, in some respects, different from that in adults. Chapter 10 explores these differences and discusses approaches to assessment and rehabilitation which take account of the special needs of children. Detailed guidelines for return to school are also provided in this chapter.

A significant challenge in writing this book has been to strike a suitable balance between research findings and clinical practice. Every effort has been made to base our recommendations on evidence from research studies. We cannot overemphasise the need to evaluate the effectiveness of interventions. We also acknowledge that there is a significant need for further research into many aspects of traumatic brain injury, particularly the development of better methods of measurement, exploration of long-term sequelae and scientific evaluation of the impact of different methods of intervention in terms of their effectiveness in alleviating disability and handicap in individuals with different types of injury and impairment.

However, given the perceived need for detailed and practical guidelines for those working with traumatically brain-injured individuals, the book is essentially clinically driven. The content is largely based on our experience in clinical practice over a period of 12 years as members of the Head Injury Rehabilitation Team at Bethesda Hospital, Melbourne, Australia. As such, not all the recommendations have been scientifically evaluated, although ongoing attempts are being made to do this. Every effort has been made to illustrate guidelines with case material. Whilst the majority of these case descriptions are based on real interventions, we have tried to preserve confidentiality by using pseudonyms and altering certain details.

It is important to acknowledge that the extent to which the guidelines recommended in this book may be implemented will be largely determined by the institutional, social, and, above all, financial resources available to traumatically brain-injured individuals, their families, and clinicians. In many cases these are very limited, and significant adaptations will need to be made accordingly. It is, unfortunately, something of a paradox that these resources tend to diminish over time, whilst some of the problems experienced, or the injured person's receptivity to intervention, may actually increase over time. Rehabilitation professionals have an obligation to draw this to the attention of funding bodies, so that models of service delivery may be adjusted. A significant, unresolved issue within the existing framework of services is that of how services should be co-ordinated over the longer term. It is not desirable to maintain the dependency of traumatically brain-injured individuals and their families on hospitals or rehabilitation centres. This is an area which policy-makers need to address.

Traumatic brain injury can have a devastating impact on those who are injured, and on their relatives. It creates complex and stressful challenges for those involved with any aspect of their rehabilitation or long-term care. We hope that this book will, in some way, alleviate the burden of traumatically brain-injured people, their families, and the rehabilitation professionals assisting them.

Melbourne, April, 1995.

How to Get There

"How to Get There" by Leunig.
(Reprinted from *A Bunch of Poesy* with permission of the publishers,
Collins Angus & Robertson Publishers Pty. Ltd.; Sydney, Australia.)

Mechanisms, recovery, and sequelae of traumatic brain injury: A foundation for the *REAL* approach

Jennie Ponsford

INTRODUCTION

In recent years there has been an enormous growth of interest in the study of traumatic brain injury. The literature now abounds with studies of its epidemiology, pathophysiology, neuropsychology and outcome, and there have been a large number of comprehensive texts written on the subject. In spite of this, rehabilitation professionals remain uncertain in dealing with the challenging and complex problems presented by those who have sustained traumatic brain injury, and most find it highly stressful. Moreover, recent outcome studies suggest that in spite of rehabilitative efforts, many severely traumatically brain-injured people remain significantly handicapped, often causing great stress to their families. The reasons for this lie largely in the unique epidemiological, pathophysiological and neuropsychological characteristics of this population.

Before examining these characteristics more closely, it is important to be clear as to what is meant by the term "traumatic brain injury". The National Head Injury Foundation (NHIF) in the USA has described a traumatic brain injury as "an insult to the brain caused by an external force that may produce diminished or altered states of consciousness, which results in impaired cognitive abilities or physical functioning" (NHIF, 1989). Such an injury may result from a blow to the head from a relatively blunt object or from blunt impact of the head with a stationary object. Traumatic brain injuries may also result from penetration by a sharp instrument or a missile. However, penetrating injuries result in a somewhat different pattern of neurological deficit. The present text will deal with the consequences of traumatic brain injury (TBI) which have resulted from blunt impact.

EPIDEMIOLOGY

Most studies suggest that around 70% of traumatic brain injuries result from motor vehicle accidents. Other causes include bicycle accidents, assault, falls, and sports injuries. It is difficult to obtain precise data regarding the incidence of TBI, due to variations in definition and methods of data collection. Jennett and MacMillan (1981) cited estimates of the incidence of hospitalisation following head injury in Britain and the United States as between 200 and 300 per 100,000 of the population. The most recent estimates from Australia suggest figures in a similar range (Health Department of Victoria, 1991). The majority of these head injuries have resulted in a duration of post-traumatic unconsciousness of less than one hour. Jennett and MacMillan (1981) estimated that probably only around one in five of those admitted to hospital have sustained moderate or severe head injuries. Nevertheless, this represents a sizeable number. Moreover, many of those who sustain mild head injuries suffer ongoing cognitive difficulties (Levin et al., 1987c).

Most estimates indicate that two to three males sustain TBI for every female. More than two-thirds of those who sustain TBI are aged under 30 years, the majority occurring in those 15 to 24 years of age (Anderson & McLaurin, 1980; NHIF, 1984; Health Department of Victoria, 1991).

A number of studies focusing on other characteristics of the population of those who sustain TBI have suggested that a greater than average proportion have pre-existing maladaptive problems, such as a history of psychopathology, substance abuse, particularly heavy alcohol consumption, and poor academic performance (Bond, 1984; Haas, Cope, & Hall, 1987; Rimel & Jane, 1984). TBI has been shown to occur more commonly in the lower socioeconomic classes and amongst those who are unemployed (Rimel & Jane, 1984).

Thus, typically, TBI occurs in young working class males, who may have had limited educational attainment and who may not have had a stable work history prior to injury. Improvements in the acute management of TBI, particularly more rapid transfer to hospital and the use of measures to monitor and reduce intracranial pressure, have resulted in reduced mortality rates in recent years (Eisenberg, Weiner,

& Tabaddor, 1987). This, together with the relative youth of those who sustain TBI, has led to a rapid growth in the number of survivors of TBI in the community. They will be confronting their disabilities for decades in a society where most services for the disabled have traditionally catered to the elderly or those with congenital intellectual disabilities.

PATHOPHYSIOLOGY

Blunt trauma to the head associated with acceleration or deceleration forces results in a combination of translation and rotation, which may cause laceration of the scalp, skull fracture and/or shifting of the intracranial contents.

Skull fracture

Skull fractures result from deformation of the skull at the time of impact. The majority of skull fractures are linear fractures, in which the area of impact is bent inwards and the surrounding skull is bent outwards (Levin, Benton, & Grossman, 1982a). Fractures of the base of skull are common in the most severe head injuries, and carry a risk of intracranial infection via the sinuses or the middle ear. In a depressed skull fracture the bone has been pushed inwards beyond the level of the skull, and in a comminuted fracture the bone has broken into fragments. Both of these fractures may result in laceration of the cerebral cortex and a possible focus for post-traumatic epilepsy and/or infection (Richardson, 1990). Fractures over the middle meningeal groove or the sagittal sinus may lead to the formation of an extradural haematoma.

It is useful to distinguish between primary and secondary brain injury resulting from blunt trauma to the head. *Primary injury* occurs at the moment of impact, being caused directly by the blow. As such, it is irreversible. *Secondary injury* occurs as a result of systemic complications, which are potentially treatable.

Primary brain injury

The mechanisms of primary brain injury may be classified as follows:

Cerebral contusion.
Cerebral contusions result when a sharp blow is dealt to the head, causing it to accelerate or decelerate rapidly. This results in differential movements between the brain and the skull. Contusions are haemorrhagic lesions usually found on the crests of the gyri of the cerebral hemispheres, although they may extend into the subcortical

white matter (Adams et al., 1985). They may occur at the site of impact, referred to as a "coup" injury, if local deformation has been sufficiently severe. However, the frontal and temporal regions of the brain adjacent to the sphenoidal ridge are by far the most common sites of surface contusions, irrespective of the site of impact (Adams et al., 1985; Levin et al., 1987a). Contusions may also be found on the medial surfaces of the cerebral hemispheres and along the upper surface of the corpus callosum (Adams, Doyle, Graham, Lawrence, & McLellan, 1986). As Teasdale and Mendelow (1984) have pointed out, cortical contusions are of less clinical significance than previously thought. They can result in secondary complications, such as brain swelling, oedema and local ischaemia, but they do not cause the initial loss of consciousness.

Diffuse axonal injury.

Diffuse axonal injury, produced at the moment of impact, is now thought to be the primary mechanism of traumatic brain injury and loss of consciousness, and an important determinant of the quality of recovery. Holbourn (1943) postulated that rotational acceleration of the brain resulted in shearing strains which led to neural tearing throughout the deep portions of the brain. Strich (1956) first documented ventricular enlargement and diffuse white matter degeneration in the brains of patients with severe closed head injuries, who had survived for at least several months in a persistent vegetative state. She found large numbers of nerve fibres with retraction balls, indicative of widespread axonal transection, thought to have occurred at the time of injury.

The work of Ommaya and Gennarelli (1974) suggests that the shearing strains resulting from blunt trauma decrease in magnitude from the cortical surface to the centre of the brain, so that the central diencephalic and mesencephalic structures are only affected in the most severe injuries. Ommaya and Gennarelli have also postulated that the shearing strains are enhanced along interfaces between substances of different densities. Thus, shearing lesions, although diffuse, occur most commonly in the grey–white matter junctions around the basal ganglia, the periventricular zone of the hypothalamus, the superior cerebellar peduncles, the fornices, the corpus callosum, fibre tracts of the corpus callosum, and in the frontal and temporal poles (Pang, 1985).

Diffuse axonal injury is more likely to be incurred in motor vehicle accidents than as a result of falls. Experimental studies have suggested that critical causative factors are the type and duration of acceleration/ deceleration, and the direction of head movement (McLellan, 1990). In examining the effects of angular acceleration in non-human primates, Gennarelli et al. (1982) identified three grades of severity of diffuse axonal injury, which were closely correlated with the clinical state of the affected animals. A similar grading of diffuse axonal injury in humans was described by Blumbergs, Jones, and North (1989). It is now clear that lesser degrees of diffuse axonal injury also occur in mild head injuries, where there may be as little as five minutes' loss of consciousness (Pilz, 1983).

Secondary brain injury

Both intracranial and extracranial complications may result in secondary brain injury, either as a consequence of cerebral ischaemia or distortion and/or compression of the brain/mass effect. *Intracranial complications* may include the following:

Intracranial haematoma

Tearing of blood vessels at the time of impact leads to bleeding inside the skull and the formation of a clot, which can eventually cause compression of the brain. This may lead to the development of coma after a delay, or to a deterioration in conscious state, necessitating prompt surgical intervention to stop the bleeding and evacuate the haematoma. Intracranial haematomata are classified according to their anatomical location.

An *extradural haematoma* results from bleeding between the skull and outer covering of the brain, known as the dura mater. This is most commonly a complication of a skull fracture, where meningeal vessels have been torn. A *subdural haematoma* is a collection of blood between the dura mater and the arachnoid mater. It may result from damage to arteries and veins in the cerebral cortex, from tearing in the bridging veins which extend from the surface of the brain to the dural venous sinuses, or from direct injury to a sinus. A *subdural hygroma* is a collection of cerebrospinal fluid in the subdural space through a tear in the arachnoid mater. It develops days or weeks after injury, and may form after the evacuation of an acute subdural haematoma (Jennett & Teasdale, 1981). A *subarachnoid haemorrhage* refers to bleeding between the arachnoid and pia mater. This may cause arterial spasm, leading to ischaemic brain damage. It can also lead to obstruction of the flow of cerebrospinal fluid, resulting in communicating high pressure hydrocephalus (Teasdale & Mendelow, 1984). An *intracerebral haematoma* is an accumulation of blood within the brain. As with other pathological consequences of TBI, intracerebral haematomata occur most commonly in the frontal and temporal lobes.

Brain swelling

Two mechanisms lead to an increase in the volume of the brain following TBI. The first is an increase in the cerebral blood volume, termed hyperemia, caused by hypoxia, hypercapnia, or obstruction of major cerebral veins as a result of cerebral oedema. The second is cerebral oedema, resulting from an increased volume of intra- or extracellular fluid in the brain tissue. Cerebral oedema may be caused by damage to the walls of cerebral blood vessels, accumulation of fluid within the cell as a result of ischaemia, increased intravascular pressure, or an obstruction to the flow of cerebrospinal fluid. These mechanisms may result in brain swelling of either a localised or a diffuse nature. Damage to the brain tends to be caused by a mass effect, with brain shift and/or raised intracranial pressure, leading to hypoxia/ischaemia.

Infection

Infection, which may develop in the subacute phase after TBI, is a complication associated with skull fracture. It can manifest itself in two forms: meningitis and cerebral abscess, causing raised intracranial pressure and/or brain shift.

Raised intracranial pressure

Increases in intracranial pressure are a common consequence of the abovementioned intracranial complications, causing impairment of brain function in two ways: reduction in cerebral blood flow and brain shift. According to Bowers and Marshall (1980), the monitoring and treatment of elevated intracranial pressure has had a significant impact on mortality following severe TBI. Uncontrolled intracranial pressure frequently causes diffuse ischaemic brain damage (Graham, Adams, & Doyle, 1978). Another potential consequence of raised intracranial pressure, haematoma and/or brain swelling is herniation. "Subfalcine herniation" occurs when one cingulate gyrus herniates across the midline. A more serious type is "transtentorial herniation", where there is downward displacement of the parahippocampal gyrus and uncus of one or both temporal lobes through the tentorial hiatus into the posterior fossa. Compression of the oculomotor nerve, as well as mid-brain dysfunction, commonly result from tentorial herniation. Unchecked tentorial herniation leads to a deterioration in brain stem functioning, with consequent respiratory abnormality, hyperventilation, decerebration and, eventually, death (Levin et al., 1982a). "Tonsillar herniation" occurs when the cerebellum is forced through the foramen magnum, leading to symptoms of vagus nerve compression, hypoxia, oedema of the medulla, and, eventually, respiratory arrest and death.

Extracranial complications may occur where there is multiple trauma, and the brain is only one of a number of organs or body parts injured. Injuries to other parts of the body may cause hypoxia or hypotension, causing further brain damage as follows:

Respiratory failure

Inadequate movement of air into and out of the lungs may result from chest injuries, aspiration of vomit, asphyxiation during an epileptic seizure or respiratory rhythm abnormalities. This results in a reduced oxygen content in the arterial blood passing to the brain and consequent hypoxia (Teasdale & Mendelow, 1984).

Hypotension

A fall in blood pressure may be caused by blood loss associated with splenic or skeletal injuries. Other effects of the head injury may prevent the brain from compensating for the drop in blood pressure.

Ischaemic brain damage

Cerebral ischaemia, as a result of inadequate blood flow and consequent tissue hypoxia, is usually the ultimate cause of secondary brain damage associated with TBI. Either a reduction in systemic arterial blood pressure or an elevation of intracranial pressure may lead to cerebral ischaemia. Reductions in cerebral blood flow result, progressively, in coma, loss of cerebral electrical activity, increased potassium in the extracellular space and, ultimately, death of nerve cells. According to Adams (1988), hypoxic damage is frequently found in the border zones of areas supplied by the major cerebral arteries, particularly in the parasagittal cortex. The hippocampus and the thalamus are also differentially sensitive to hypoxia. Graham et al. (1989) reported ischaemic damage to the hippocampus and the basal ganglia in around 80% of fatal head injury cases. Tentorial herniation may lead to infarction in the brainstem and the territory supplied by the posterior cerebral artery (Graham, Lawrence, Adams, Doyle, & McLellan, 1987). Diffuse cortical damage like that associated with status epilepticus or cardiac arrest has been seen in 30–40% of fatally head-injured cases (Graham et al., 1989).

Delayed complications of TBI

Post-traumatic epilepsy

Jennett (1979) estimated the overall incidence of post-traumatic epilepsy following non-missile head injury at 5%. He distinguished between early post-traumatic epilepsy, which occurs within the first week after injury, and in the first 24 hours in about 50% of cases, and late post-traumatic epilepsy, which typically occurs more than three months post-injury. Focal motor seizures and partial complex "temporal lobe" seizures are seen most commonly. Predisposing factors include the length of coma and post-traumatic amnesia, the presence of a focal brain lesion as a result of a depressed skull fracture, or an intracranial haematoma and the presence of focal neurological signs (Jennett, 1979). Children are more susceptible to early epilepsy. Late epilepsy occurs in about 20% of those who experience early epilepsy.

Hydrocephalus
Communicating hydrocephalus, which occurs in 1–2% of cases, results from obstruction to the flow of cerebrospinal fluid by blood in the subarachnoid space. This leads to ventricular enlargement and a consequent decline in cognitive function, gait disturbance and incontinence (Granholm & Svendgaard, 1972). Ventricular enlargement can also occur without signs of communicating hydrocephalus, as a result of a general reduction in the bulk of the cerebral white matter (Adams, Mitchell, Graham, & Doyle, 1977).

Summary of pathophysiological evidence
To summarise the pathophysiological evidence, the factors causing TBI are complex and numerous, resulting in wide variations in the quantity and distribution of damaged brain tissue. As Teasdale and Mendelow (1984, p.24) have pointed out, "It is...extremely difficult to correlate sequelae of head injury with specific structural brain damage, as the combination of the various factors so modify the original lesion that the final outcome may be totally different, given identical starting points in different patients." In spite of the apparent heterogeneity of brain injury resulting from blunt trauma to the head, and the difficulties in its delineation, it seems clear from the neuropathological evidence available that diffuse injury is common, and that damage occurs most frequently in the frontal and temporal lobes, the hippocampus and the basal ganglia. The neurobehavioural significance of this will be discussed in a later section of this chapter.

NEUROIMAGING AND TBI

It is usually not possible to gain an accurate picture of the extent of damage to the brain using any of the techniques currently available for studying regional brain morphology and function. Computer-assisted tomography (CT) is useful in the detection of intracranial haematomata, large contusions, cerebral abscess, ventricular enlargement and atrophy (see Fig. 1.1a). It also has the advantage of a relatively rapid scanning time, and greater ease of patient monitoring, which are important factors in the acute management phase (Siegel & Alavi, 1990). However, it does not have sufficient resolution to detect smaller areas of contusion or the diffuse white matter lesions which so frequently occur (Wilson & Wyper, 1992; Zimmerman, Bilaniuk, & Gennarelli, 1978).

Since its introduction in the early 1980s, Magnetic Resonance Imaging (MRI) has been found to be more sensitive, particularly to non-haemorrhagic grey and white matter lesions (Snow, Zimmerman, Gandy, & Deck, 1986) (see Fig. 1.1b). Levin et al. (1987a) compared CT and MRI findings in 20 survivors of mild or moderate head injury. Nearly five times as many lesions were apparent on MRI as on CT, and lesions were generally larger in volume on MRI. However, MRI also lacks sensitivity to the microscopic lesions, which are commonly associated with TBI.

Positron Emission Tomography (PET) is used to study regional metabolic rates for oxygen and glucose. A comparative study by Langfitt et al. (1987) showed that PET detected regions of brain dysfunction, manifested by decreased glucose metabolism, not visualised by CT or MRI. However, PET studies are not routinely available to neurosurgical units, the costs still being extremely high.

An alternative measure of cerebral function is the mapping of regional cerebral blood flow using the radiopharmaceutical 99mTc hexamethyl propylene amine oxime. Uptake of this compound reflects relative regional perfusion and can be imaged using a rotating gamma camera, or the more sensitive dedicated Single Photon Emission Computer Tomography (SPECT) scanner. The relationships between structural lesions (CT or MRI), SPECT lesions and neuropsychological performance have yet to be clearly delineated (Wilson & Wyper, 1992). However, studies by Newton et al. (1992) and Nedd et al. (1993) have found SPECT to be more sensitive to lesions in TBI individuals than CT or MRI, taken alone or in combination. PET and SPECT have the potential to measure the distribution of specific neurotransmitters and receptors, as well as blood flow and regional metabolism.

Computer-averaged evoked potentials have supplanted the EEG for studying the functional integrity of neural networks, but little is known of the relationship between evoked potentials and the patient's functional abilities. Neurological, neuropsychological and functional assessment thus play an important role in delineating the nature and extent of impairment and disability resulting from TBI.

RECOVERY FROM TBI

The mechanisms set in motion when TBI occurs are extremely complex, taking place over hours, days or weeks following injury. They affect not only the neurons directly injured, but also areas of the brain far removed from the lesion site, through processes such as transneuronal

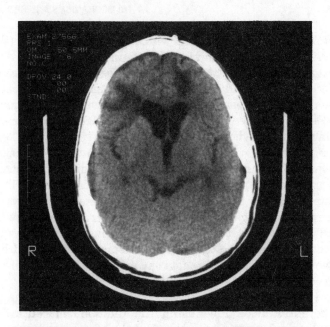

FIG. 1.1a. Non-contrast CT scan taken two months after severe TBI, showing frontal contusions and generalised atrophy. Left internal capsule shearing injury not evident.

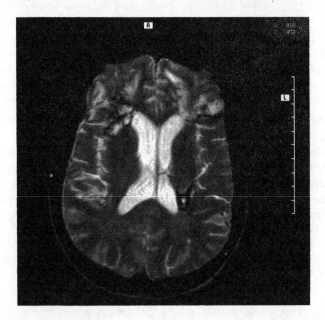

FIG. 1.1b. Axial T2 MRI taken two months after severe TBI in same individual as Fig. 1a, showing extensive frontal haemorrhagic contusion and left internal capsule haemorrhagic shear injury.

degeneration, neurochemical alterations, oedema, raised intracranial pressure, and vascular disruption due to haemorrhage or ischaemia (Almli & Finger, 1992; Schoenfeld & Hamilton, 1977).

Recovery following TBI generally tends to follow a negatively accelerating curve, which is most rapid in the first 3 to 6 months, but may continue for several years after injury (Groswasser, Mendelson, Stern, Schecter, & Najenson, 1977; Thomsen, 1984). There is, however, a great deal of individual variability in recovery curves, so that it is extremely difficult to predict the pattern, time course or ultimate extent of recovery in a given individual (Brooks & Aughton, 1979).

The process of recovery is exceedingly complex. Various functions may follow different time courses of recovery because of differing physiological and structural substrates; specific mechanisms may be pertinent to some functions, but irrelevant to others; individual differences in cerebral organisation may influence recovery, as may factors such as the age, intelligence and motivation of the person sustaining the injury. Other potential sources of variability include the specific aetiology of the lesion(s), their severity and location (Powell, 1981).

The mechanisms underlying recovery of function are, as yet, relatively poorly understood. There are a number of proposed mechanisms of recovery, which have been reviewed by Laurence and Stein (1978), Finger and Stein (1982), and Miller (1984). Some of these support the concept of restitution of function to damaged areas, that is, the notion that spontaneous physiological recovery occurs in the damaged area, enabling neural pathways to resume activity and the functions subserved by them to be restored. Others suggest that recovery occurs through the substitution or reorganisation of neural structures and/or functions.

Theories supporting restitution of function

A great deal of the early spontaneous recovery after TBI is probably explained by the resolution of temporary physiological changes, such as oedema, vascular disruption, intracranial pressure changes, and biochemical alterations, which have caused functional, rather than structural axonal disruption. This results in the return of temporarily suppressed functions or areas of the brain to normal within the first few hours, days or weeks after injury (Schoenfeld & Hamilton, 1977).

Beyond this period it is difficult to find scientifically proven physiological explanations for the resumption of neural activity and restoration of function in the damaged area. The presence of regenerative and collateral sprouting into denervated areas has been investigated quite extensively. Evidence from animal studies suggests that the new connections that form are operational (Steward, 1989). However, the significance of such growth as far as recovery of function is concerned remains unclear (Almli & Finger, 1992). There is, for example, great difficulty inherent in experimental attempts to determine whether sprouting is the cause of recovery, or the result of it. At this point in time there is no evidence that axonal sprouting is of functional significance in behavioural terms, certainly in adults (Marshall, 1984).

Theories supporting substitution or reorganisation of function

There are two main classes of substitution theory—those that postulate *anatomical reorganisation*, and those that postulate *behavioural compensation* or *functional adaptation* as mechanisms of recovery.

Anatomical reorganisation

A number of related theories predict that intact areas of damaged neural systems may adequately mediate the functions previously subserved by the system as a whole. These include the theories of redundancy, equipotentiality, and hierarchical representation. Finger and Stein (1982) argue that such explanations do not adequately account for recovery of function, although they do contribute to our understanding as to why certain abilities are spared from damage in some individuals.

Other theories postulate that anatomical reorganisation occurs by virtue of cerebral plasticity, that is, other parts of the brain take over the damaged function. Whilst it was once assumed that the immature brain displayed considerable potential for plasticity, evidence from more recent studies, such as those of Johnson and Almli (1978) and Goldman (1974), has cast considerable doubt on this. There is even less evidence of plasticity in mature subjects (Miller, 1984). As Finger and Stein (1982) point out, it is, in reality, very difficult to draw conclusions regarding the reorganisation of functions, due to limitations in the technology available to study brain–behaviour relationships. Inferences regarding localisation of functions are generally based on behavioural observations. However, an improved ability to perform a task cannot be accepted as evidence that another part of the brain has taken over the function required to perform that task. It may, alternatively, reflect a change in strategy on the part of the injured individual.

Behavioural compensation and functional adaptation

Behavioural compensation or functional adaptation is the final explanation of recovery of function. Instead of re-routing connections, brain-injured individuals may develop new solutions to problems using intact structures, that is, they adapt. In order to view this as a possible means of recovery, it is necessary to conceive a function in terms of goals, rather than the means used to attain these goals (Laurence & Stein, 1978). Qualitative analysis of the subject's performance will frequently reveal that alternative strategies are being brought into play to make up for the loss of function associated with the brain lesion. It is the nature of these alternative "means" of performing a task that are of particular interest in understanding behavioural compensation as a process of recovery.

There are many examples of spontaneous functional adaptation to be found in the literature, both from animal studies (Gentile, Green, Niebergs, Schmelzer, & Stein, 1978) and from human studies (Gazzaniga, 1978; Holland, 1982a). Luria (1963) has described a number of cases where brain-injured individuals were trained to use alternative modalities in order to perform tasks. As with other theoretical explanations for recovery, there is certainly a need for more carefully controlled and detailed investigation in this area. Whilst improved technology may provide evidence to the contrary, there does appear, however, to be more support for the notion of functional adaptation as a means whereby recovery occurs beyond the first few weeks after injury. This has significant implications for the rehabilitation of cognitive deficits, which will be explored in detail in Chapter 4.

IMPAIRMENT OF CONSCIOUSNESS

Blunt trauma to the head usually results in immediate loss or impairment of consciousness. The duration and degree of that impairment of consciousness is of major significance in indicating the severity of injury. In the case of mild head injury there may be a clouding of consciousness, where the person is confused and disoriented for a period of time, which they subsequently do not clearly remember. In the case of more severe injuries, coma may persist for days, weeks or months. The essential feature of *coma* is decreased behavioural responsiveness to external stimuli and inner need.

Coma is graded by measuring the degree of decrease in observable responsiveness to external stimuli. The measure which is most frequently used to grade the depth of coma is the Glasgow Coma Scale (GCS), devised by Teasdale and Jennett in 1974 and revised in 1976 (Teasdale & Jennett, 1974, 1976). This scale, which allows for the assessment and grading of the patient's eye opening, verbal and motor responses, is used at regular intervals to monitor the progress and recovery of comatose individuals. According to Teasdale and Jennett (1974), coma is defined as the absence of eye opening, a failure to obey commands, and a failure to give any comprehensible verbal response. This corresponds to a total score of 8 or less on the amended GCS. This definition of coma has been widely used in studies of TBI. Further detail regarding the assessment and management of comatose TBI individuals is contained in Chapter 2.

In a small percentage of cases the TBI person passes from coma into what is termed a "persistent vegetative state". In this state the person typically shows eye opening, with sleep and wake cycles, and sometimes the ability to "track" (albeit briefly) with the eyes. There may be an ability to make reflex postural adjustments with the limbs, and a range of primitive reflexes may be evident (e.g. bite, grasp). However, there is no evidence to suggest that these people are responsive to their environment (Jennett & Teasdale, 1981). The persistent vegetative state will also be discussed further in Chapter 2.

Following emergence from coma, the person who has sustained TBI usually remains confused and disoriented for a period of time, having no capacity to remember ongoing events. This may last for hours, days, weeks or months. The period from the time of injury to the return of the capacity to form new memories is termed *post-traumatic amnesia* (PTA). The duration of PTA has also been used as a measure of severity of TBI. The assessment and management of patients in PTA will also be discussed in detail in Chapter 2.

ONGOING SENSORIMOTOR IMPAIRMENTS

Depending on the location and extent of injury to the brain, a broad range of sensorimotor impairments may result from TBI. Motor deficits can take the form of weakness or paralysis on one or both sides of the body, incoordination of muscle movements (ataxia), a loss of fine and gross motor dexterity, poor balance and reduced physical endurance. Injury to the nerves which supply the motor apparatus responsible for the production of speech is not uncommon, resulting in a reduced capacity to articulate speech sounds and/or difficulties with phonation, resonance and prosody (dysarthria), and impaired motor programming of articulation (dyspraxia). Swallowing disorders (dysphagia) may also occur.

A broad range of sensory disturbances may be caused by cranial nerve lesions, or injury to subcortical or cortical sensory pathways. Diminished sense of smell can result from olfactory nerve lesions. Visual impairment is particularly common due to a range of causes. Damage to the optic nerve may result in blindness or loss of visual acuity, lesions in the optic pathways in the temporal, parietal or occipital lobes may result in visual field defects, and cranial nerve lesions may lead to a range of eye movement disorders, with blurring of vision or diplopia occurring commonly. Eye movement disorders may also result from damage to the frontal lobes and/or the basal ganglia. Hearing loss occurs in a smaller percentage of cases. It tends to be sensorineural, often bilateral, and associated with transverse petrous fractures. The lesion is most often in the Organ of Corti, which is believed to be damaged by concussion. Conductive deafness may be caused by blood in the middle ear system or disruption of the ossicular chain. Tinnitus occurs frequently, especially following mild head injuries (Jennett & Teasdale, 1981). Vertigo may follow diffuse injury of, or bleeding into, the labyrinth. Injury to the glossopharyngeal nerve, associated with fracture of the base of skull, may produce difficulty in swallowing and loss of taste on the posterior one-third of the tongue, as well as paralysis of some of the pharyngeal muscles. Tactile sensation (pain, temperature and texture) and proprioception (the ability to feel the position of joints and limbs in space) may be impaired as a result of sensory pathway lesions.

COGNITIVE AND BEHAVIOURAL SEQUELAE

Following the return of consciousness and orientation, most of those who sustain TBI exhibit a range of ongoing cognitive and behavioural sequelae. These occur in various permutations and combinations, and vary widely in their nature and severity, depending on the location and extent of injury, as well as premorbid characteristics of the injured individual.

Sequelae of mild TBI

In the case of mild TBI, where loss of consciousness has been less than 20 minutes, or post-traumatic amnesia less than one hour, neurological deficits are rarely apparent. However, the person may experience a range of symptoms, including headache, dizziness, sensitivity to noise and/or bright lights, tinnitus, blurred or double vision, restlessness, insomnia, reduced speed of thinking, concentration and memory problems, fatigue, irritability, anxiety and depression (Dikmen, McLean, & Temkin, 1986; Gronwall & Wrightson, 1974; Kay, 1992; Levin et al., 1987c; Rimel, Giordani, Barth, Boll, & Jane, 1981). Typically, those who have sustained mild TBI and have no other injuries return home within a few days, with the expectation of resuming their normal activities. In many cases these so-called post-concussional symptoms subside over a period of days or weeks. Most neuropsychological studies, such as those cited above, have indicated that cognitive deficits resolve within three months of the injury. In some instances, however, the symptoms persist. In a prospective study of 66 males who had sustained mild TBI, Wrightson and Gronwall (1981) found that 13 still had post-concussional symptoms 90 days after their injuries. The main problems in ten of the cases related to memory, concentration and coping at work, and in the other three cases they related to fatigue and irritability. Of eight of these people followed up two years post-injury, four still reported mild symptoms.

For many years these symptoms were assumed to have a psychogenic basis, related to the trauma of the accident, pre-existing psychological problems and/or the seeking of compensation (Miller, 1961, 1966). However, there is now clear evidence that microscopic diffuse axonal injury can result from mild TBI, providing some organic basis for the difficulties experienced (Pilz, 1983). Levin et al. (1987a) found evidence of injury on MRI in some mildly head-injured subjects. Moreover, MacFlynn, Montgomery, Fenton, and Rutherford (1984) found evidence of significantly delayed evoked potential responses to auditory stimuli in the brain stem in nearly half of a sample of 24 mildly head-injured patients, tested 48 hours and six weeks after injury.

Gronwall and Sampson (1974) found significantly reduced speed of information processing, as measured by performance on the Paced Auditory Serial Addition Test (PASAT), in a group of mildly concussed subjects, with PTA lasting less than one hour, when tested 48 hours after injury. Their performance had returned to normal when they were reassessed four weeks post-injury. Moreover, Gronwall and Wrightson (1974) found that impairment of performance on the PASAT was related to the presence of post-concussional symptoms, and Gronwall (1976) reported that scores on the PASAT improved as the symptoms resolved. Gronwall and Wrightson (1974) suggested that reduced speed of information processing formed the basis of the post-concussional syndrome, causing poor concentration on tasks involving a high information load.

A similar pattern of memory impairment, which tends to have resolved within four weeks of injury, has also been demonstrated in mild TBI subjects. For example, Levin et al. (1987c) studied a group of 57 individuals with mild TBI, whose loss of consciousness was less than 20 minutes, comparing their performance on verbal and visual memory tasks with that of a healthy control group. They were found to be impaired on all tasks at the initial assessment, conducted one week post-injury, but not at reassessment a month later. Richardson and Barry (1985) presented evidence suggesting that the basis of memory difficulties following mild TBI was an inability to use strategies, such as mental imagery, to aid encoding and retrieval.

The issue as to why post-concussional symptoms sometimes persist beyond the first few weeks or months after mild TBI is still somewhat controversial. The results of a number of studies have shown that compensation factors are not responsible for the development or persistence of post-concussional symptoms (McKinlay, Brooks, & Bond, 1983; Rimel et al., 1981). Factors influencing poor outcome have not been clearly established, although several authors have postulated that the problems are more likely to occur in those who have had a previous head injury, pre-existing personality disorder and adjustment problems, drug and alcohol abuse and/or psychiatric disorder. Driven, hard-working individuals in demanding occupations, students, those with other concurrent stresses in their lives, and those who are older also appear to be at risk (Gronwall, 1991; Kay, 1992).

Van Zomeren and van den Burg (1985) and Hinkeldey and Corrigan (1990) studied residual complaints of head-injured subjects several years post-injury, examining how these complaints related to severity of injury. Whilst there were some differences between the studies in terms of the factor structures of patients' complaints, both identified two broad classes of complaints: (1) those that were related to severity of head injury, which included slowness, poor concentration, difficulty doing two things at once, and, in the van Zomeren and van den Burg (1985) study, forgetfulness; and (2) those not related to severity, which included crying, dizziness, irritability, headache, fatigue, hypersensitivity to noise, bustle or light, anxiety, and depression. This latter group of symptoms bears strong resemblance to descriptions of the post-concussional syndrome. Both sets of authors presented evidence suggesting that this latter group of complaints is present in the victims of mild, moderate and severe head injury, and is strongly associated with the presence of anxiety.

Van Zomeren and van den Burg (1985) proposed that these post-concussional symptoms resulted from the chronic effort required to cope with persisting cognitive deficits, most particularly reduced speed of information processing. In the case of mild TBI, where there is no visible handicap, the expectations of the patient and others are that there will be a resumption of previous activities. The presence of ongoing limitations in information processing may create difficulties in this respect. An inability to understand the basis of such difficulties may lead to the development of feelings of frustration, anxiety and guilt. There may be criticism from family, friends, or employers when responsibilities are not met. Jobs may be lost and relationships may deteriorate. It is sometimes only after a period of time, and the development of more serious anxiety and depression, that professional help is sought. The extent to which such anxiety develops may also depend on the demands placed on the person who has sustained the injury, and the previous personality and adaptive abilities of the injured individual, causing the associations noted earlier.

Whether or not it is true that persistent post-concussional symptoms following mild TBI have both organic and functional determinants, it would appear that the development of serious, ongoing post-concussional problems may be circumvented, or significantly curtailed, by early screening, the provision of information, and follow-up assessment, as well as support and assistance in developing more adaptive coping strategies (Gronwall, 1991; Ponsford, 1990). Models of such management protocols have been established at centres in the USA (Kay, 1992; Mateer, 1992) and New Zealand (Gronwall, 1986). Further evaluation of appropriate methods of assisting those with mild TBI is needed, however.

Neurobehavioural consequences of moderate and severe TBI
In the case of moderate and severe TBI, where coma has persisted for more than 20 minutes, and PTA for more than one hour, cognitive and behavioural changes are more extensive and persistent than in the case of mild head injury. The nature and degree of these changes varies widely, according to the site and extent of injury. Disorders of language, perception or praxis may result from lesions disrupting the systems responsible for these neuropsychological functions. However, because of the high incidence of diffuse axonal injury, and damage to the frontal and temporal lobes, problems in the following areas are particularly common. Whilst some would be termed "cognitive" and some "behavioural" problems, they will be considered together.

Attentional deficits and fatigue
Follow-up studies have indicated that one of the most universal and persistent cognitive, as well as physical problems reported following mild, moderate, and severe TBI is fatigue (e.g. Dikmen et al., 1986, 1993; Ponsford, Olver, & Curran, 1995a; van Zomeren & van den Burg, 1985). These studies, and others, have indicated that attentional problems also occur very frequently at all levels of severity of injury, although there are significant problems in the definition and measurement of attentional deficits. Attentional difficulties commonly reported include reduced speed of information processing, leading to a reduced information processing capacity, with consequent difficulties in focusing on more than one thing at once, or coping with complexity. Poor selective attention (the capacity to focus on some things and screen out others), which can manifest itself as distractibility or poor attention to detail is also reported, along with problems in sustaining attention over time,

and difficulty in the allocation of attentional resources in a goal-directed fashion (Ponsford & Kinsella, 1991).

There is ample experimental evidence of a reduction in speed of information processing following TBI and resulting difficulties in coping with increased task complexity (Ponsford & Kinsella, 1992; van Zomeren & Brouwer, 1994). The findings of Ponsford and Kinsella (1992) suggest that, where possible, TBI subjects sacrifice speed of performance on neuropsychological tasks to maintain accuracy. However, it has been more difficult to demonstrate other attentional problems experimentally in groups of TBI subjects. For example, they do not make significantly more focused attention errors, as measured on the Stroop Color Word Test. On the Tower of London Task, designed as a measure of the capacity to allocate attentional resources in a goal-directed fashion, they perform more slowly, but do not make significantly more errors than controls (Ponsford & Kinsella, 1992). Whilst TBI subjects show no greater decline in performance on vigilance tasks than controls (Brouwer & Van Wolffelaar, 1985; Ponsford & Kinsella, 1992), the findings of Stuss, Stethem, Hugenholtz, Picton, Pivik and Richard (1989) suggest greater inconsistency of performance on attentional tasks over time in TBI subjects. For further discussion of attentional deficits associated with TBI, see Chapter 3.

Learning and memory problems

It has already been noted that TBI patients usually have a period of confusion, disorientation and inability to remember ongoing events immediately following their emergence from coma, lasting for days, weeks, or, in the most severe cases, months. This is known as *post-traumatic amnesia* (PTA). There is also frequently impairment of memory for events which immediately preceded the injury, termed *retrograde amnesia*. The period of retrograde amnesia is variable, being broadly related to the period of unconsciousness. There may be "islands of memory" within the period over which retrograde amnesia extends, and the period of retrograde amnesia tends to "shrink" over time (Russell & Nathan, 1946). The period of persistent retrograde amnesia is usually too brief for it to give a reliable indication of the severity of injury or probable outcome (Long & Webb, 1983).

After they have emerged from PTA, many people who have sustained TBI report ongoing difficulties with learning and memory. Indeed follow-up studies conducted from 6 months up to 7 years after injury have found this to be the most frequent subjective complaint of TBI individuals and/or their relatives (Brooks, Campsie, Symington, Beattie, & McKinlay, 1987a; Brown & Nell, 1992; Oddy, Humphrey, & Uttley, 1978a,b; Ponsford et al., 1995a; van Zomeren & van den Burg, 1985).

Although there is some doubt as to the reliability of subjective reports, there is also ample evidence from neuropsychological studies of the presence of persistent memory difficulties in TBI subjects. These have been demonstrated across a wide range of tasks, involving learning, recall and recognition of both verbal and non-verbal material (Baddeley, Harris, Sunderland, Watts, & Wilson, 1987; Brooks, 1984a). As with attentional difficulties, there is potential heterogeneity in the nature and severity of memory difficulties experienced by TBI individuals, depending on the site and extent of injury. Where there is bilateral hippocampal damage, there may be a severe amnesic syndrome, affecting the ongoing storage and retrieval of all types of material. In the case of unilateral temporal lobe injury, there may be a material-specific learning difficulty with either verbal or non-verbal material. Injury to the frontal lobes, which occurs very frequently, may result in a problem in "maintaining a stable intention to remember" and in the use of organisational strategies to aid learning and recall (Walsh, 1991). In many cases, poor performances on memory tasks may result primarily from attentional difficulties (Newcombe, 1982). Whatever the nature of the problem, there is usually a marked contrast between the capacity to remember events and skills learned prior to the injury, and the ability to learn and retain new material since the time of injury, the former being relatively preserved.

Impaired planning and problem-solving
The high frequency of damage to the frontal lobes associated with TBI means that many of those who have sustained TBI have difficulties in analysing, planning and executing the solutions to problems or complex tasks. They may perform well in structured activities, which require little initiative or direction. However, although there may be a willingness and ability to perform each component of a task, and assurances may be given as to their competence, those with planning and problem-solving deficits are frequently unable to generate strategies for efficient task performance, to follow through with the organisation and implementation of complex tasks, or to check for and correct errors. TBI individuals often have difficulty in sustaining performance on tasks. Complex behaviours may dissolve into inert stereotypes. There can be a tendency to lose track of the task at hand, responding to distractions or inappropriate cues in the environment. There also tends to be a failure to look ahead, using past experience to prepare for anticipated events. TBI people can have particular difficulty in adapting to new situations.

Concrete thinking

Difficulties in forming or dealing with abstract concepts are very common. This can result in an inability to generalise from a single instance, or distil the essence of a situation or a conversation, with a tendency to focus on specific, concrete aspects, or be "stimulus-bound". There may also be difficulties in understanding humour or other forms of indirect language. An inability to understand the implications of situations or events is common. There may be problems in benefiting from experience. Alternatively, there may be an inability to think creatively and generate different solutions to a given problem, with a tendency to repeatedly apply an old, unworkable solution, resulting in failure and frustration (Vogenthaler, 1987).

Lack of initiative

Some of those who have sustained TBI show a lack of initiative or drive in some or all aspects of their behaviour and thought processes. In severe cases there may be a complete inability to initiate speech or any activity without prompting. At a more subtle level, there may be a tendency to lack spontaneity, to be somewhat passive in conversation, to fail to move on to the next task once one is completed, or to move from one step to another within tasks. It is frequently reported by relatives that the TBI person who was previously active achieves very little in a day and may sit for hours in a chair watching television.

Inflexibility

Inflexibility in thought processes and behaviour may be manifested as difficulty in switching from one task to another, in changing train of thought or shifting "mental set". This may lead to frequent repetition or "perseveration" of the same responses, comments, demands or complaints. There may be an inability to see other people's points of view and a tendency to rely on rigid adherence to routines. Sudden changes in routine may cause the TBI individual to become upset.

Dissociation between thought and action

It is frequently reported that there is a dissociation between what people who have sustained TBI know or say, and how they actually behave. This results in an inability to follow through with instructions, to correct errors or modify behaviour in the light of feedback. This, together with the next few problems, appears to result from a reduced capacity to control, regulate and monitor thought processes and behaviour.

Impulsivity

A reduced capacity to control and monitor behaviour commonly results in impulsivity. There is a difficulty in inhibiting the tendency to respond to problems or situations before taking account of all relevant information, and before thinking of all the possible consequences of one's actions.

Irritability/ temper outbursts

One of the most commonly reported problems following TBI is a low tolerance for frustration. Those who have sustained TBI are prone to become irritable and to lose their temper easily. The anger may be completely out of proportion to the situation, and there may be physical aggression.

Communication problems

Whilst aphasia is uncommon following TBI, discourse problems are frequently encountered. These can include excessive talking, with poor turn-taking skills, a tendency to repeat oneself or have difficulty keeping to the point. Word-finding difficulties and impaired auditory processing are also common. Communication problems following TBI will be discussed in detail in Chapter 5.

Socially inappropriate behaviour

Lack of behavioural control can also lead to an inability to inhibit inappropriate responses, such as swearing, sexual disinhibition, tactlessness or other socially inappropriate behaviours. There may be a failure to respond to non-verbal cues given by others, which normally let a person know when it is time to finish a conversation or move onto another topic, or when someone else is feeling uncomfortable with a certain behaviour.

Self-centredness

Those who have sustained severe TBI can be very egocentric. This results in a tendency towards demanding, attention-seeking and sometimes manipulative behaviour. It can also lead to jealousy, and insensitivity to the feelings or emotional needs of others, as well as a failure to see other people's points of view. This is the source of many relationship problems following TBI.

Changes in affect

TBI can result in a flatness of affect, where there is little emotional response at all, or an elevation of affect, with euphoria. It is commonly reported by relatives that they are surprised how "accepting" the injured person is of the disabilities, or how happy they are. Those who develop depression tend to do so more after they have returned home and become aware of the consequences of the injury for their lifestyle. Reduced emotional control can also lead to a tendency to laugh or cry for no apparent reason, or to show emotions which are quite out of proportion, or inappropriate, to the situation.

Lack of insight/self-awareness

Severe TBI frequently results in an inability to perceive, or a lack of awareness of, changes in cognitive function and behaviour. This leads to a tendency to attempt work or other tasks which are beyond their capabilities. There may also be a failure to recognise how impulsive, irritable, childish or demanding they are in certain situations, with disastrous consequences for interpersonal relationships (Prigatano, 1991). This results in a degree of perplexity in the TBI person, who fails to understand the reasons for failure at work or in social relationships. Occasionally, one sees the emergence of frank delusions (Prigatano, O'Brien, & Klonoff, 1988). Another unfortunate consequence of lack of insight is the inability to understand the need for rehabilitation or other forms of assistance in overcoming limitations.

The cognitive and behavioural changes described above frequently coexist in a complex fashion, being difficult to disentangle in an individual, particularly as they are imposed upon varying premorbid personality characteristics. Planning and problem-solving, abstract thinking, initiative, mental flexibility, and control and regulation of thought processes and behaviour have been termed "executive functions" by Lezak (1983), Baddeley (1986) and Stuss and Benson (1986), and this term is now commonly used. Walsh (1991) referred to such problems as a "loss of adaptive abilities". Broe, Tate, Ross, Tregeagle, and Lulham (1981) have collectively termed the most common cognitive and behavioural sequelae of TBI "organic psychosocial deficit". Lezak (1978), who has so ably described the problems of those who have sustained TBI, referred to the "characterologically-altered" brain-injured patient.

Whilst these deficits are most commonly thought to be associated with injury to the frontal lobes (Stuss & Benson, 1986; Walsh, 1991), some of them have also been associated with lesions to other parts of the brain which may be injured as a result of TBI. For example, Prigatano (1991) noted evidence to suggest that self-awareness or insight may also be affected by lesions in the anterior temporal and parietal lobes, although there may be qualitative differences in the nature of loss of self-awareness.

As with attentional problems, it is frequently difficult to demonstrate difficulties with "executive" or "adaptive" functions in the relatively structured neuropsychological assessment situation (Shallice & Burgess, 1991). This is certainly the case when such assessment consists only of intelligence tests, such as the WAIS-R, which have been widely reported as lacking sensitivity to deficits associated with frontal lobe injury (Stuss & Benson, 1986; Walsh, 1991). Issues in the assessment of the TBI individual will be explored in greater detail in Chapters 3 and 5.

CONSEQUENCES OF NEUROBEHAVIOURAL SEQUELAE FOR REHABILITATION AND OUTCOME

The changes in cognition and behaviour outlined in the previous section have been documented in numerous follow-up studies involving moderate and/or severe TBI (Bond, 1975; Brooks & McKinlay, 1983; Brooks et al., 1986, 1987a; Brown & Nell, 1992; Dikmen et al., 1993; Jacobs, 1988; Klonoff, Snow, & Costa, 1986b; Levin & Grossman, 1978; McKinlay, Brooks, Bond, Martinage, & Marshall, 1981; Oddy et al., 1978a; Oddy, Coughlan, Tyerman, & Jenkins 1985; Ponsford et al., 1995a; Thomsen, 1984; van Zomeren & van den Burg, 1985). It is clear that they have a significant impact on the TBI individual's capacity to participate in and benefit from rehabilitation, and to resume previous activities and relationships.

Attentional problems place constraints on the person's capacity to participate in therapy, and memory problems may result in little being retained from one therapy session to the next. The commonly seen dissociation between thought and action can mean that in spite of good participation in therapy sessions, and apparent willingness to follow instructions or suggestions, there is little carry over into other settings. Lack of initiative may necessitate constant prompting. Behavioural changes can be so difficult to handle that the staff become highly stressed and the patient receives insufficient rehabilitative therapy. Above all, the TBI individual may be so lacking in awareness of changes in cognition or behaviour as to lack motivation for therapy, and in some instances to precipitate discharge. These problems, in combination, frequently result in TBI people receiving inadequate rehabilitation, either because the treating staff feel they are unable to benefit from therapy or are too difficult to handle, or because the injured person refuses to participate.

Many outcome studies have documented the difficulties of those who have sustained moderate or severe TBI in attempting to return to their previous lifestyle (Brooks, McKinlay, Symington, Beattie, & Campsie, 1987b; Brown & Nell, 1992; Dikmen et al., 1993; Jacobs, 1988; Klonoff et al., 1986b; Malec, Smigielski, DePompolo, & Thompson, 1993; Oddy et al., 1985; Ponsford et al., 1995a; Tate, Lulham, Broe, Strettles, & Pfaff, 1989; Vogenthaler, Smith Jr, & Goldfader, 1989). Whilst figures for return to employment vary widely, according to the severity of injuries studied, definition of employment, and consideration of pre-injury employment status (Crepeau & Scherzer, 1993), it appears that the majority of individuals with severe TBI are unable to return to employment. The study by Brooks et al. (1987b), for example, found that of a group of 98 severely head-injured patients, 86% of whom were employed prior to injury, only 29% were employed seven years after injury. Difficulties in making and maintaining relationships, with consequent social isolation and loss of leisure activities, are also common (Oddy et al., 1985). Tate et al. (1989) followed up a series of 87 severely head-injured subjects three to nine years post-injury, looking at psychosocial reintegration in terms of employment, interpersonal relationships, functional independence, social contacts and leisure interests. Three-quarters of the series were classified as demonstrating major disability, having either a "Poor" or "Substantially Limited" reintegration. Many of those who have sustained severe TBI remain financially and socially dependent.

In the majority of cases it is the cognitive and behavioural, rather than the sensorimotor or physical impairments, which are most disabling (Bond, 1975, Broe et al., 1981; Brooks et al., 1987a; Ponsford et al., 1995a). Indeed most TBI people make a relatively good physical recovery. In a follow-up study of 60 survivors of severe head injury, Broe et al. (1981) found that 63% had no physical defect more than a year after injury, but 71% of these patients, who demonstrated no abnormality on standard neurological examination, showed what Broe et al. termed "organic psychosocial deficit", with or without cognitive impairment. Ponsford et al. (1995a) found that, by two years after injury, 97% of a group of 175 moderate to severe TBI individuals were able to walk independently, whereas more than 70% reported ongoing cognitive and/or behavioural difficulties.

It is the relatives who often provide the only ongoing support for those who have sustained moderate or severe TBI (Kozloff, 1987). Jacobs (1988) found that the majority of TBI individuals live with their families in the longer term. Studies focusing on the impact of TBI on family life have shown that it creates an enormous burden, which increases, rather than decreases over time (Brooks et al., 1986). They have also indicated that it is the changes in behaviour and personality, rather than physical disabilities, which are the major source of family disruption and distress

(McKinlay et al., 1981; Brooks et al., 1987a). These issues will be discussed further in subsequent chapters.

SUMMARY AND CONCLUSIONS

Traumatic brain injury presents unique problems to its survivors, their relatives, and those faced with the task of assisting their rehabilitation. It occurs predominantly in young adults, most commonly males, many of whom may have had limited educational attainment and an unstable work history. Some are still at school or undergoing tertiary training or apprenticeships. Those who are working have not had very long to establish their skills. They may have only recently attained independence from their parents, and are establishing new long-standing relationships. These young people will be confronting their disabilities for decades in a society which most commonly associates disability with the elderly or those with congenital intellectual disabilities.

Above all, however, it is the nature and complexity of the disabilities resulting from TBI which are most challenging. Neuropathological evidence suggests that there are a number of mechanisms of brain injury, some operating at the moment of impact (primary brain injury) and others as a consequence of intracranial or extracranial complications (secondary brain injury). This results in marked heterogeneity of injury across individuals. Limitations in the sensitivity of various imaging techniques make delineation of the precise nature and extent of injury in an individual very difficult. However, it is apparent from the neuropathological evidence available that diffuse axonal injury is common, and that damage occurs most frequently in the frontal and temporal lobes, the basal ganglia and hippocampus also being commonly affected in severe cases.

TBI usually results in immediate loss or impairment of consciousness, followed by a period of confusion, known as post-traumatic amnesia. The depth or length of coma, and the duration of post-traumatic amnesia may be used as measures of severity of TBI. Following the return of orientation, most of those who sustain TBI exhibit a range of ongoing sensorimotor, cognitive and behavioural sequelae, which vary widely in their severity. Mechanisms of recovery are poorly understood, and there is considerable variability in patterns of recovery. However, recovery from moderate or severe TBI tends to follow a negatively accelerating curve, which is most rapid in the first 3 to 6 months, but may continue for several years. In the case of mild TBI, recovery takes place within a couple of months, although some have symptoms which persist beyond this period.

In the majority of cases it is the cognitive, behavioural, and emotional changes which are most disruptive and disabling in the long term. These may include deficits of attention, speed of information processing, memory, planning and problem-solving, abstract thinking, initiative, flexibility, and control and regulation of behaviour and thought process, egocentricity, changes in affect, and lack of self-awareness. These problems, which occur in differing combinations and in varying degrees of severity, have been shown to have a significant impact on the TBI individual's capacity to participate in and benefit from rehabilitation, and to resume previous activities and relationships. As a consequence, a majority of those who sustain severe TBI are unable to return to employment. Social isolation, loss of leisure activities, and difficulty in forming or sustaining relationships are also common. Such disabilities, occurring in young people in the prime of their life, can have a catastrophic impact, not only on the life of the person who has sustained severe TBI, but also on that of their relatives, on whom there may be dependency for the rest of their lives.

It is for these reasons that TBI represents such a unique and complex challenge for rehabilitation professionals, a challenge which in many cases they have not been trained to meet, and which some may wish to avoid. This text aims to provide some practical guidelines to assist rehabilitation professionals in dealing with some of these challenges and an opportunity to gain the satisfaction of ameliorating at least some of the difficulties faced by those who have sustained TBI and their families.

PRINCIPLES UNDERLYING SUCCESSFUL REHABILITATION FOLLOWING TBI— THE *REAL* APPROACH

The approach recommended has been termed the REAL approach, signifying *Rehabilitation for Everyday Adaptive Living*. The fundamental principles of this approach are discussed below. Practical guidelines for the implementation of the REAL approach are outlined in detail in the following chapters.

Rehabilitation
Rehabilitation stands for the team structure and processes mediating intervention which are most likely to result in successful outcomes for TBI individuals. The essential ingredients are interdisciplinary teamwork, involvement of the injured individual and family, and a recognition of the need to evaluate the effectiveness of interventions.

Interdisciplinary teamwork.
Good teamwork is essential in the rehabilitation of TBI individuals. The sequelae of TBI impact significantly on one another. In particular, the cognitive, behavioural and emotional changes can affect all aspects of the injured person's rehabilitation. Those participating in the rehabilitation of people who have sustained TBI need to approach their task from a broad and long-term perspective, sharing information, expertise and goals, which, in turn, must be shared with the injured person and the family. The focus of the team's endeavours should be on individuals in the context of their role in the community, rather than on the performance of specific tasks or skills. In this respect, the rehabilitation process needs to be "person-focused", rather than "discipline-focused". This is the essence of what is termed interdisciplinary teamwork, the cornerstone of successful TBI rehabilitation. Clinicians working with TBI individuals need to have a sound understanding of all aspects and implications of TBI. It is important that they have a flexible attitude and are not concerned with role-boundaries, as there will inevitably be considerable overlap in the therapy process. Indeed, this is considered essential to the success of rehabilitation following TBI, especially as TBI individuals have such difficulty in generalising what is learned in one setting to another.

Working with TBI individuals and their families can be a very stressful and thankless task. Interdisciplinary teamwork may alleviate this stress, by providing a supportive network for discussing the uncertainties and frustrations which are encountered. There will, inevitably, be conflicts within the team. Ideally, staff should be given regular opportunities and encouragement to discuss concerns, both with regard to those they are treating and with regard to the team. Burnout is a common problem in such complex and demanding work. Whilst a sound understanding of all the problems associated with TBI, combined with good team communication and support should alleviate this feeling, it may, from time to time, be necessary to encourage clinicians to take a break from working with TBI individuals.

In dealing with these issues, good team co-ordination is essential. The professional background of the team co-ordinator is less important than personal qualities of maturity, good interpersonal skills and an ability to put the goals and development of the team ahead of one's own goals, together with breadth of experience in working with TBI. Team co-ordination is concerned not with directing, but with facilitating and maximising co-operation between team participants, and ensuring that contributions are made by all members of the team. Decisions should be made on a consensus basis, involving input from all team members, and implemented accordingly. An alternative to having a single team co-ordinator is that of assigning individual team members as "case managers" or "key persons". Their roles may include the facilitation, documentation and review of goals, co-ordination of meetings and liaison with the TBI individual and the family. Each rehabilitation team must find what works best for them in this respect. However, it is vital that those who perform these roles have the necessary expertise and personal qualities. The essence is in maintaining good communication between staff, the TBI individual and the family.

Involvement of the injured individual and family

The injured individual and the family must be seen as equal members of the rehabilitation team, being involved actively, wherever possible, in the processes of assessment, goal-setting, therapy, evaluation, and long-term planning. All too frequently these processes are conducted by hospital or rehabilitation staff, with minimal consultation with the injured person and family, who are simply informed of decisions. The negotiation of realistic therapy goals and plans for the future is not always easy, but it needs to be recognised that it is these individuals who will be confronting and dealing with the long-term consequences of the injury directly, not the rehabilitation team. There is no doubt that the motivation and involvement of the injured individual and family in the rehabilitation process will be enhanced by their active participation, and that they will be better prepared to deal with the challenges they will face in the future.

Evaluating the effectiveness of interventions

Whilst evaluation of the effectiveness of interventions is an essential element of the rehabilitation process, it is, for a variety of reasons, also one of the most difficult. A myriad of methodological difficulties face clinicians and researchers in the rehabilitation setting. There is a lack of agreement over definitions and established criteria for measurement. Heterogeneity of injury makes it difficult to study groups. The multifocal nature of the rehabilitation process poses problems for assessment of the impact of specific forms of therapy. It is also difficult to separate effects due to the therapist from those due to the therapy itself, spontaneous recovery or practice effects on repeated measures. Another difficulty is the general lack of research training received by most rehabilitation staff. For all of these reasons there is a significant lack of data regarding the effectiveness or otherwise of specific forms of intervention following TBI. Many of the studies which have been conducted to date have neglected to assess the impact of the intervention on the daily life and psychosocial adjustment of the injured individual, which is most important.

Maintaining the focus of therapy on the individual in the context of everyday life is likely to facilitate evaluation of its effectiveness. The use of single-case designs will also overcome some of the problems involved. As Wilson (1987b) has pointed out, single-case designs enable the therapist to tailor therapy to the individual's particular needs, and to alter it if it is not working. It is possible to evaluate continuously the person's responses to the intervention, whilst controlling for the effects of practice or spontaneous recovery. It is also possible to ascertain reasons for failure to respond to treatment, and thus establish sources of variability, such as in procedures, patient background, nature and severity of injury, nature of other strengths and weaknesses, and so on. There will be further discussion of methods of evaluating the impact of different forms of therapy throughout this text.

Everyday
Everyday emphasises the need to focus assessment and treatment on the individual in the context of everyday life and roles in the community. Many of those who sustain TBI have impaired executive or adaptive functions. As a consequence of this there is difficulty in generalising or adapting what is learned in one situation to another. It is therefore particularly important to focus goals and therapeutic intervention in a very practical way directly on activities performed in their everyday life. As impaired self-awareness is also common, a focus on everyday living should also maximise the likelihood of the injured individual participating in goal-setting and seeing the relevance of rehabilitation activities.

This focus on everyday life necessitates an understanding of individuals in the context of their previous lifestyle, relationships, abilities, values, personality and behavioural patterns, life goals and roles in the community. This is particularly important in the case of TBI, where the manifestations are heterogeneous and complex, and cannot be divorced from the qualities of the individual who has sustained the injury. Assessment, goal-setting, and intervention need to be conducted within this framework.

Adaptive
Adaptive signifies the need to recognise that, whilst there is usually a substantial degree of spontaneous recovery following TBI, there are, following moderate or severe injuries, frequently residual impairments which have a significant impact on the lifestyle of the injured individual. It is unrealistic to imagine that these impairments can all be cured or restored to normal through any rehabilitation process. Rehabilitation should aim to facilitate and maximise the extent of recovery, but it should also assist those who are injured to adapt to whatever limitations affect their ability to function in the community. Such adaptation may

involve learning new ways of performing tasks or interacting with others: obtaining prompting, supervision or assistance from other people or devices, or modification of tasks, roles or the environment.

Emotional adaptation to the changes imposed by the injury is just as important as practical adaptation. There is substantial evidence that many TBI individuals have significant ongoing psychological adjustment difficulties. A need for a greater emphasis on ameliorating these problems and providing psychological support to the injured person is needed. Such interventions will usually be required over many years. In particular, it is important that the injured individual is given assistance in coming to terms with changes and rebuilding a positive sense of self. Similarly, families and other caregivers deserve active support and assistance in adapting to the impact of the injury and developing a new identity.

Living

Living signifies the ongoing and long-term nature of the experience of living with the consequences of TBI in the community. This experience will be unique to the individual, depending not only on the nature and severity of ongoing disability, but also on the previous personality, relationships, values, resources, skills and goals, as well as emotional factors. The extent to which a person with TBI is able to play a meaningful role in the community is also likely to be determined by the availability of practical and emotional supports.

In planning rehabilitation following TBI it is important from the outset, to consider all of these background factors, and to take a long-term view. In setting goals, the rehabilitation team should give careful consideration to the probable needs of the individual in the longer term. As numerous follow-up studies have shown, the recovery process extends over many years. Some problems, particularly those of a psychological nature, do not manifest themselves, or become accessible to intervention until several years after injury. Simply training a person to be independent in activities of daily living and setting them up in work, study, or avocational activities does not guarantee successful adaptation. The needs and difficulties of these predominantly young individuals will alter as they face a myriad of changes in their lives. The time frame of rehabilitation should therefore be a very lengthy one, with follow-up support available indefinitely. It is for this reason that involvement of the family in the rehabilitation process from the early stages is so essential. It is, in many instances, the family who provide most ongoing assistance, both practical and emotional, and carry the burden associated with that. They need to be supported in this role over an extended period and every attempt should be made to alleviate their burden.

CHAPTER TWO

Assessing and managing impairment of consciousness following TBI

Pamela Snow and Jennie Ponsford

INTRODUCTION

The periods when the brain-injured individual is comatose, or is emerging from coma represent possibly the most challenging and stressful stages after injury, both for relatives, and for the staff caring for the injured person. At no other stage in the recovery process is there so much uncertainty, both regarding the injured person's current level of awareness, and what the future will hold. The purpose of this chapter is to describe the features of impaired consciousness at different stages following TBI, together with approaches to assessment and management. The importance of close involvement of family members will be emphasised throughout.

As depicted in Fig. 2.1, there are several possible outcomes following coma resulting from severe TBI. Bricolo, Turazzi, and Feriotti (1980) reported that 30% of their series of TBI subjects who entered coma had died at one year follow-up. Death may occur in the acute stages after injury, or many months later, in which case cause of death is not necessarily recorded as brain injury. As Jennett and Teasdale (1981) observed, statistics in this area are complicated by the fact that in cases of multitrauma, the exact cause of death may be difficult to determine. This is particularly so where death occurs prior to the injured person reaching hospital. Those who die in the early days after injury may do so after being declared brain dead. Between one and seven percent of survivors pass into what is termed a vegetative state, and either

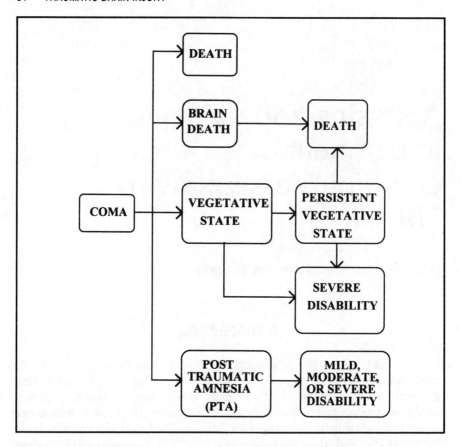

FIG. 2.1. Evolution from coma.

subsequently recover with residual disabilities, or enter a persistent vegetative state. The majority of survivors will, however, progress from coma to post-traumatic amnesia (PTA), and go on to recover with varying degrees of disability. This framework will be used as the basis for discussion of emergence from coma throughout this chapter.

ASSESSING AND MONITORING THE COMA-EMERGING BRAIN-INJURED PERSON

The essential feature of coma is decreased behavioural responsiveness to external or internal stimuli. Plum and Posner (1972) observed that consciousness may be impaired either by widespread damage to the cerebral hemispheres and/or suppression of brainstem activating mechanisms. The two essential elements of consciousness, then, are arousal and awareness. These rely on intact cortical and subcortical functioning.

It is essential that coma-emerging people at all levels of severity and chronicity are carefully investigated and monitored over time, both medically, and in terms of their responsiveness. This will enable medical conditions which may be compromising cognitive status to be treated. It also provides an objective basis for decisions regarding clinical management, as well as a means of conveying information to families which is as accurate as possible, both diagnostically and prognostically. Those caring for the coma-emerging person are, to some extent, constrained by a lack of uniform guidelines for the assessment and monitoring of progress and response to interventions over time. In the absence of a specific code of diagnostic criteria, clinicians need to engage in a process of hypothesis testing, using both behavioural and neurodiagnostic measures.

The Glasgow Coma Scale

As noted in Chapter 1, coma is graded by measuring the reduction in observable responsiveness to external stimuli. The measure most commonly used for this purpose is the Glasgow Coma Scale (GCS). The GCS was devised by Teasdale and Jennett in 1974 and revised in 1976 (Teasdale & Jennett, 1974, 1976). It utilises the injured person's eye-opening, and verbal and motor responses, in order to regularly monitor progress and/or deterioration over time. Responses in each category are ranked and assigned a numerical value, yielding a total score between 3 (a person showing no response) and 15 (a person who is alert and well oriented). Teasdale and Jennett (1974) defined coma as the absence of eye-opening, failure to obey commands, and failure to give any comprehensible verbal response. This corresponds to a total score of eight or less on the amended GCS, and constitutes a widely-used definition of coma in studies of TBI.

Table 2.1 displays the scores associated with each parameter of the GCS. For a detailed description of how to administer the scale, the reader is referred to Chapter 4 of Jennett and Teasdale (1981).

GCS scores in the first 24 hours after injury are frequently used to grade severity of injury and to predict outcome. Scores of 3 to 8 have been said to indicate severe injury, 9 to 12 moderate injury, and 13 to 15 mild injury (Jennett & Teasdale, 1981). Because of the potential for deterioration in conscious state within the acute period, however, there has been some debate as to the optimal time after injury at which the GCS should be derived, i.e. whether this should be at the time of admission to hospital (Levin & Eisenberg, 1979a,b), following non-cranial resuscitation (Marshall et al., 1983), six hours after injury

TABLE 2.1
Glasgow Coma Scale (Teasdale & Jennett, 1974, 1976).
(Reprinted with the authors' permission.)

Eye Opening	
Spontaneous	E4
To speech	3
To pain	2
Nil	
1	
Best Motor Response	
Obeys	M6
Localises	5
Withdraws	4
Abnormal flexion	3
Extensor Response	2
Nil	
1	
Verbal Response	
Oriented	V5
Confused conversation	4
Inappropriate words	3
Incomprehensible sounds	2
Nil	
1	

Coma Score: (E + M + V) = 3 to 15

(Teasdale & Jennett, 1976) or as the best score in the first 24 hours after injury (Vogenthaler et al., 1989). There is also evidence that the scale is best administered by trained raters (Rowley & Fielding, 1991). Regardless of the time of administration, it is important to note that the GCS does have some limitations. Ocular swelling may prevent eye-opening, the insertion of an endotracheal tube prevents the injured person from responding verbally, and the use of barbiturates and paralysing drugs to lower intracranial pressure immobilises the person (Levin et al., 1982a). A number of follow-up studies have shown initial GCS scores to be significant predictors of outcome on a range of measures (Bishara, Partridge, Godfrey, & Knight, 1992; Klonoff, Costa, & Snow, 1986a; Ponsford, Olver, Curran, & Ng, 1995b). However, it must be noted that GCS scores, by themselves, have accounted for less than a third of the variance in these studies.

Neuroimaging techniques

Despite the limitations of CT and MRI scans outlined in Chapter 1, they play an important role in early medical/surgical management, and in detecting causes of deterioration in conscious state (e.g. hydrocephalus). CT scans can provide a useful basis for explaining structural changes to family members. As noted in Chapter 1, however, conscious state may be impaired in the absence of significant changes being evident on CT. For this reason, the limitations of CT scans need to be explained to relatives. Information derived from PET and SPECT scans regarding metabolism of oxygen and glucose within the brain and regional cerebral blood flow, may also assist in elucidating the extent of brain dysfunction, assuming a relationship exists between metabolic requirements and functional status of cortical tissue (see Levy et al., 1987; Newton et al., 1992, for expansion).

Neurophysiological measures

As noted in Chapter 1, the electroencephalogram (EEG) has a limited role in the management of the coma-emerging person, due to the numerous sources of artefact, and inconsistencies between EEG data and behavioural indices (see Ganes & Lundar, 1988; Higashi et al., 1981; Hughes, 1978; Oboler, 1986; Papanicolaou, 1987).

Evoked potentials (EPs) have, however, been studied extensively as predictors of outcome from coma or vegetative states of varying aetiologies. They have gained a place in the assessment of the coma-emerging brain-injured person by virtue of their ability to provide information about the integrity of various sensory modalities in people unable to give a behavioural response. Rappaport (1986) suggested that EPs have four main uses in the evaluation of individuals who are comatose or vegetative following TBI: (1) to assess sensory functioning and identify probable sensory deficits; (2) to monitor sensory and CNS changes over time; (3) to document current status from an electro-physiological perspective; and (4) to help predict degree of recovery and future level of disability. A review of the literature dealing with the use of EPs in coma-emerging people suggests that it is easier to predict the likelihood of either death or survival using multimodality EP data than it is to predict the quality of survival (Ying, Schmid, Schmid, & Hess, 1992). Brainstem EPs are generally regarded as weaker predictors of quality of survival than measures of cortical activity, such as the somatosensory EP (Alter, John, & Ransohoff, 1990; Papanicolaou, Loring, Eisenberg, Raz, & Contreras, 1986; Rappaport, 1986).

HELPING THE FAMILY OF THE COMATOSE
BRAIN-INJURED PERSON

The time that the injured person spends in coma is frightening and confusing for family members. There is likely to be a high degree of distress and anxiety displayed by relatives, largely over whether or not the injured person is going to survive. During this time families may feel compelled to spend many hours each day at the injured person's bedside, and will eagerly await signs of lightening of conscious state. It is most important that, wherever practicable, families are made to feel welcome and useful, as familiar, reassuring figures in the injured person's unfamiliar environment. Family members should be encouraged to spend as much, or as little time at the bedside as they wish, and should also be encouraged to touch and speak to the injured person.

Throughout this time of enormous stress and confusion, a great deal can be done to achieve the trust of family members. Whilst not all members of the treating team have a particular role to play in terms of managing the injured person at this stage, those who will soon become involved can introduce themselves to the family, and provide opportunities for relatives to simply talk about their loved one. It will be important for families to talk about the injured person as the spouse, sibling or parent he or she is, not merely as a patient being kept alive in a sophisticated intensive care unit. There may be a number of pressing practical and financial issues which need to be addressed for the next of kin, and social work assistance should be available to deal with these. The need for readily available counselling and emotional support for families at this stressful time cannot be overemphasised. This is discussed further in Chapter 9.

During the period of coma there may be disagreement between staff and families as to the injured person's level of awareness. It must be acknowledged that familiar faces and voices may evoke more responses than staff will observe during routine care. It is important to involve family members in the assessment process. Staff should not discuss, in the presence of the injured person, any negative views regarding prognosis. The need for consistency in the information conveyed by team members cannot be overemphasised. Because this information is both complex and emotionally charged, inconsistencies merely perpetuate confusion, and do little to engender trust in the expertise of the treating team as a whole.

As confidence about survival increases, questions regarding the quality of that survival may begin to emerge in the minds of staff. For family members, however, this tends to be a period of enormous relief and renewed hope. Signs of a lightening of conscious state are greeted with excitement and optimism. It is wise to prepare relatives for the fact that consciousness is likely to be regained gradually, with fluctuations and the possible emergence of agitated behaviours. Great care needs to be taken to provide family members with information which is clear, and care needs to be taken with the use of terms such as "recovery". Clinicians may use this as a synonym for survival, whilst family members, will, quite justifiably, interpret this to mean return to pre-accident level of functioning. Family members may bring considerable pressure to bear on staff in their efforts to be reassured about their loved one's prognosis. In such circumstances, it is wise to resist the temptation to "guesstimate" outcome. Staff need to explain why they do not know the answers to the questions they are being asked, and outline a process by which the relevant issues will be monitored and reviewed. This information will need to be rephrased and repeated many times, and will need to be amended according to changes which occur in the injured person's condition. Family members are likely to have lasting memories of the way information was conveyed to them in these early stages, and this may have important implications for the way they view future communications from those caring for their loved one.

THE VEGETATIVE STATE

The term "persistent vegetative state" was proposed by Jennett and Plum in 1972, to describe the small percentage of brain-injured people (variously described as between one and seven percent), who remained in what they termed a state of "wakeful unresponsiveness". Jennett and Plum stressed a number of common characteristics of this condition, in particular:

- The emergence of eye-opening, initially only in response to pain, but later spontaneously. It was noted that although the person may appear to visually track moving objects, careful observation reveals that this is not sustained beyond a few seconds.
- The presence of abnormal motor responses, such as decerebrate rigidity. Primitive reflexes, such as grasping, sucking and rooting may also be present. Chewing movements and teeth grinding (bruxism) may occur. A noxious stimulus may initially elicit an abnormal extensor response; however, delayed flexion generally occurs. Jennett and Plum noted that "untrained or optimistic" observers are wont to interpret this reflex activity as purposeful behaviour.
- The absence of communication, either verbal or non-verbal, although grunting and groaning noises may be heard.

The term "vegetative" was selected by Jennett and Plum because it refers to the fact that the person's life-sustaining mechanisms (e.g. respiration, digestion, blood pressure regulation) do not require artificial support. Non-vegetative functions, (i.e. those indicative of cortical activity, most notably communication), are absent. Jennett and Plum noted that although the person in a vegetative state may spend long periods of the day with eyes open, the need for 24-hour nursing care can make it difficult to determine whether a diurnal rhythm is present. They stressed that a key feature of this condition is the absence of adaptive responses to either the internal or external environment.

An understanding of the pathophysiology of the vegetative state forms an important basis for the provision of appropriate and sensitive care. There is now a large body of evidence attesting to the belief that the vegetative state occurs when brainstem functions are relatively patent, but there is profound cortical damage (Bates, 1993; Cranford, 1988; Jennett & Plum, 1972; Multi-Society Task Force on PVS, Part One, 1994; Papanicolaou et al., 1986). Papanicolaou et al. summarised this thinking when they observed that "An intact brainstem...only increases the likelihood of the patient's survival and has little relevance to the quality of this survival, which depends on hemispheric function" (1986, p. 173).

This raises the question of the distinction between arousal (a mesencephalic brainstem function) and awareness (a cortical function). Whereas arousal reflects a primitive brainstem function in response to internal or external stimuli, awareness reflects integration of cognitive processes via cortical activity. According to Berrol, "...a patient demonstrates awareness through goal-directed or purposeful motor behaviour and by seeming to comprehend language, even if he or she does not speak" (1990, p. 561). Consciousness, then, implies the presence of both arousal and awareness and, more than anything else, is signalled by the presence of some communication ability (receptive and/or expressive). The absence of this vital combination of arousal and awareness sets the vegetative state apart from other severely compromised levels of functioning following brain injury.

Unfortunately, both the nature and number of terms used to describe minimally responsive brain-injured people serves to confuse, rather than clarify clinicians' understanding of this condition. Terms which have been used to describe the person in a vegetative (or similar) state include: prolonged coma, akinetic mutism, coma vigile, apallic syndrome, de-afferented state and, most recently, post-comatose unawareness (Sazbon, Costeff, & Groswasser, 1992), and reflexive state (Andrews, 1993). It is, however, most important that the *locked-in syndrome* be clearly distinguished from the vegetative state. This rare syndrome has been discussed in some detail in the literature (e.g. Maguire, Hodges, Medhat, & Redford, 1986; Oboler, 1976; Pearce, 1987; Plum & Posner, 1972) and usually results from a lesion (infarction, haemorrhage, or demyelination) in the ventral pons or medulla. The person is typically quadriparetic and mute, but is able to demonstrate significantly preserved cognitive abilities via vertical eye movements and/or blinking. Unlike the person in a vegetative state, the person in a locked-in state is able to give clear signs of awareness of self and the environment. It is also important to differentiate the vegetative state from *brain death*, which results in the absence of both brainstem and supratentorial function. Brain death is confirmed by the presence of various combinations of coma, apnoea, dilated pupils, absent cephalic reflexes, and electrocerebral silence on EEG recording. It is also important that *minimally responsive* survivors are differentiated from those in a vegetative state. As Cranford and Zasler (1994) have noted, these individuals display intermittent evidence of awareness and/or ability to follow commands.

The vegetative state is not merely a stage of recovery through which severely injured survivors are expected to pass. Entry into a vegetative state carries with it an extremely poor prognosis for recovery to any significant degree of independence (Berrol, 1986; Jennett et al., 1977). As Fig. 2.1 indicates, some individuals who pass from coma into a vegetative state will remain in this condition until death (sometimes many years later). Others, however, will progress to the "severe disability" category of the Glasgow Outcome Scale (Jennett & Bond, 1975). Jennett et al. (1977) found that, of the individuals in the International Data Bank who were diagnosed as vegetative at 3 months post-injury, approximately one-third had progressed to the severe disability category by 12 months post-injury. For this reason there is a strong body of opinion that the adjective "persistent" should not be used until a year has passed following the injury (Berrol, 1986; Bricolo et al., 1980; Jennett, 1992). Life-expectancy is generally significantly reduced in these individuals. Death may be caused by infection, generalised systemic failure, respiratory failure, or other disease-related factors (Multi-Society Task Force on PVS, Part Two, 1994).

Factors determining who will eventually display clear signs of awareness (e.g. age, type and severity of injury) are not, however, well understood. For this reason, painstaking efforts need to be made to observe the injured person for signs of awareness. This was emphasised by Whyte and Glenn (1986), who observed that "A patient who can respond or communicate to any extent is likely to have a better prognosis than one who cannot, but without extensive observation and examination can be difficult to distinguish from someone in PVS" (p. 40). It is also important that vigilant medical care be provided, in order to ensure that the common medical complications of the vegetative state (for example decubitus ulcers, urinary tract infections, chest infections, epilepsy, limb contractures, and/or heterotopic ossification) are not compromising cognitive functioning. The management of these medical conditions plays a central role in maximising the injured person's capacity to benefit from treatment aimed at improving conscious state. Such management is beyond the scope of this text, however further detail is provided by Andrews (1990) and Bontke, Baize, and Boake (1992).

ASSESSING AND MONITORING THE PERSON WHO IS COMA-EMERGING OR IN A VEGETATIVE STATE

Whilst during the 1970s the rehabilitation community recognised the need for a common language in the study of outcome, the early 1980s saw energetic efforts to improve the clinical utility of such measures. Hence, the emergence of tools such as the Disability Rating Scale for Severe Head Trauma (DRS) (Rappaport, Hall, Hopkins, Belleza, & Cope, 1982) and the Levels of Cognitive Functioning Scales (LOCF, also known as the Rancho Los Amigos Scale) (Hagen, 1982). The Glasgow Outcome Scale (GOS) (Jennett & Bond, 1975) is well known as a broad index of outcome and has been used in a number of large outcome studies. It comprises the following five categories: (1) death; (2) persistent vegetative state; (3) severe disability; (4) moderate disability; and (5) good recovery. Whilst the GOS has been widely adopted as a research tool, it lacks clinical sensitivity, both in terms of its ability to distinguish between subjects within one category, and in its ability to reflect change within a given individual over time. In general, the scales outlined above are not sensitive to many of the behavioural indices of concern to clinicians working with minimally responsive injured people.

A number of recent scales have been published in an attempt to provide a more sensitive means of assessing and monitoring coma-emerging and/or vegetative people over time. These include, amongst others, the Coma Recovery Scale (Giacino, Kezmarsky, DeLuca, & Cicerone, 1991), the Sensory Stimulation Assessment Measure (Rader & Ellis, 1989), the Coma–Near Coma Scale (Rappaport, Doughtery, & Kelting, 1992), the Western Neuro Sensory Stimulation Profile (Ansell & Keenan, 1989), and a scale developed by Horn, Shiel and co-workers (Horn, Shiel, McLellan, Campbell, Watson, & Wilson, 1993; Shiel, Wilson, Horn, Watson, & McLellan, 1994).

These scales all attempt to describe and objectively measure behaviours which may signal small increments of improvement in conscious state. This is generally achieved by examining each sensory modality (e.g. sight, hearing, touch, taste) in terms of spontaneous and/or criterion-referenced behaviours (i.e. responses which occur in response to a particular stimulus, such as a command). For example, earlier non-verbal, predominantly visual items on the scale proposed by Shiel et al. record responses to naturally occurring stimuli, or stimuli presented by a therapist (e.g. "Eyes following the person moving into the line of vision"; "Moving a cloth placed over the face"). As recovery progresses, behaviour becomes more interactive, (e.g. "Frowning to show dislike" or "Alerting to a voice outside"). More spontaneous behaviour items are included at the higher levels, (e.g. "Seeking eye contact"). This is followed by the beginning of verbal communication. Items relevant to day-to-day orientation and memory are then included on the scale.

The Sensory Stimulation Assessment Measure (SSAM; Rader & Ellis, 1989) builds on the three response modalities of the GCS (eye-opening, verbalisation, and ability to follow commands) in its assessment of the individual's response to specific stimulation. This scale utilises five sensory modalities (vision, hearing, touch, taste, and smell) and provides a detailed six-point scoring system to define the injured person's response to specific stimulation in each of the three response modalities. In the eye-opening category, for example, raters note which of the following occurred after the administration of a specific stimulus to one of the five sensory modalities: (1) no change in eye opening; (2) eye opening in response to stimulation only; (3) visual tracking < three seconds; (4) visual tracking > three seconds; (5) blinks, opens or closes eyes in response to commands; (6) correctly responds to simple requests (e.g. "Blink if you are male"). The SSAM is designed to be administered by both a scorer and a rater, in order to minimise problems of observer bias or inaccuracy. This scale allows for the recording of spontaneous movements and responses, as well as those which occur following a command or other stimulus. Rader and Ellis noted that the SSAM was not designed as a stand-alone measure in the assessment of severely injured TBI individuals. Like all such measures, it should be used alongside traditional means of monitoring these people, such as neuroimaging techniques, electrodiagnostic measures and vigilant attention to overall medical condition.

Horn et al. (1993) have cautioned that whilst these scales have greater sensitivity than, for example, the GCS, they do have methodological limitations, including subjectivity, poor intra- and inter-rater reliability, and the inappropriate summing of data relating to different behavioural parameters. Notwithstanding these limitations, it is important that staff caring for people in a vegetative state select and consistently utilise a measure of behavioural responsiveness. This should remove at least some of the guesswork inherent in *ad hoc* observations over time, and form a basis for discussions with family members. The very fact that a behavioural measure is being applied may, in itself, reassure family members that staff take seriously the need to monitor cognitive functioning in a vigilant manner.

THE USE OF SENSORY STIMULATION PROGRAMMES WITH COMA-EMERGING AND VEGETATIVE TBI INDIVIDUALS

Closely related to the question of behavioural assessment of the person in a vegetative state is the issue of sensory stimulation, i.e. the use of more or less systematic therapeutic procedures designed to improve the injured person's level of arousal and/or awareness. Sensory stimulation has received increasing attention in the last five years, and a variety of theoretical justifications have been proposed for its use in the management of severely injured TBI survivors. These vary with respect to their acknowledgment of scientific models of recovery in the damaged nervous system. A number of workers in this area have referred to the detrimental effects of environmental deprivation on the recovering nervous system (e.g. Ansell, 1993; Mitchell, Bradley, Welch, & Britton, 1990), or have speculated about so-called "spare capacity" in the brain (e.g. Baker, 1988; Freeman, 1987, 1991). Similarities between recovery in the damaged brain and development in the normal brain have also been postulated (e.g. Ansell, 1993; Johnson & Roethig-Johnson, 1989; Mitchell et al., 1990). Others have emphasised the economic and humanitarian benefits of attempting to effect a functional change in the status of people in a vegetative state, particularly given that they are predominantly young people (e.g. Pierce et al., 1990). At a theoretical level, it might be postulated that the use of structured sensory stimulation programmes could help determine the characteristics of the subgroup of people who do emerge from the vegetative state.

It must be stressed that the evidence in favour of structured sensory stimulation with this population is, at present, equivocal (Hall, Macdonald, & Young, 1992; Horn et al., 1993; Mitchell et al., 1990; Pierce et al., 1990; Rader, Alston, & Ellis, 1989; Wilson, McCranny, & Andrews, 1992b; Wilson, Powell, Elliot, & Thwaites, 1991). Notwithstanding the lack of evidence for the effectiveness of sensory stimulation programmes, there may be reasons for incorporating them into an overall management regime. First, the use of structured sensory stimulation techniques can be a means whereby staff and family members can work together to systematically determine whether a pattern exists in the injured person's behavioural repertoire, and whether there are changes in response to environmental contingencies. Incorporating structured sensory stimulation programmes may be psychologically important to relatives, who may not be able to resolve their grief about their loved one's condition until reasonable efforts have been made to improve responsiveness in this way. Furthermore, without systematic ways of monitoring the vegetative person, staff may become poorly motivated, which can lead to the provision of less than optimal care.

In designing a structured sensory stimulation programme, a number of factors need to be considered. First and foremost are the expectations which staff and family members have of such programmes. It is important that staff promote discussion of not only the role, but also the limitations of sensory stimulation, so that unrealistic hopes are not engendered in relatives. It is helpful to agree on a timeframe for trialling and reviewing stimulation programmes, so that confusion does not develop between staff and families. Decisions need to be made about which modality or modalities will be utilised. In making this decision, staff need to consider both clinical and neurodiagnostic evidence regarding the relative patency of different sensory pathways, as well as the evidence in favour of multimodal, as opposed to unimodal stimulation (e.g. Wilson et al., 1991). Single-case methodology has a number of advantages as both a research and a clinical tool to evaluate the impact of such programmes. In addition to overcoming artefact associated with heterogeneity, it allows the impact of a number of stimuli to be compared over time, and provides a means of objectively assessing whether change is actually occurring.

If sensory stimulation techniques are used, it is important, as Watson and Horn (1991) have pointed out, that stimuli which are personally salient to the injured person are employed. This may be the tape-recorded sound of a familiar voice or a favourite piece of music, or the use of photographs of familiar people. Familiar people such as relatives may elicit the most favourable responses from severely injured TBI individuals. Family members who wish to participate in sensory stimulation programmes should be encouraged to do so, working alongside therapy staff. Participating in this way may alleviate relatives' feelings of helplessness, although it is important to ensure that overoptimism is not engendered by the use of these programmes, and that there are no feelings of guilt if they are not effective.

Staff need to decide which behaviours will be recorded, and whether criterion-referenced responses only will be noted, or whether spontaneous behaviours will be included in the response checklist. Naturally, choosing to use one of the published measures noted above obviates the need to make this decision. Either way, it must be remembered that there is scope for subjectivity and observer bias/expectancy in rating what is sometimes a very limited behavioural repertoire. For this reason, it is important that the injured person is rated by at least two staff and that videotaping is used as a means of objectively recording responses over time. Even where inter-observer agreement is adequate, it is not always possible, on the basis of motor activity, to distinguish reflex from purposeful behaviour. For this reason, it is important that the distinction between arousal and awareness is constantly borne in mind and discussed with family members. Ultimately, the purpose of these programmes is to determine whether the injured person is reaching some sort of "rehabilitation readiness" (see Ansell, 1993) and this is the perspective that must be constantly brought to bear on discussion of response patterns.

All of these factors need to be considered in the context of the injured person's day-to-day environment. As Wood and his co-workers (e.g. Wood, 1991; Wood, Winkowski, & Miller, 1993; Wood, Winkowski, Miller, Tierney, & Goldman; 1992) have speculated, the almost constant background noise present in most ward environments may interfere with the brain-injured person's habituation and dishabituation mechanisms. These workers have stressed that everything done to, or in the presence of, the injured person needs to be considered a form of sensory stimulation. For this reason, they advocated a conceptual shift away from sensory stimulation to sensory regulation (i.e. limiting the use of television and radio, reducing noise levels, and avoiding situations where habituation is likely to occur). These factors may need to be considered in the design, implementation, and evaluation of sensory stimulation programmes.

Sensory stimulation programmes, and the monitoring of coma-emerging or vegetative people using behavioural measures such as those outlined above, form only part of the management of these severely injured survivors of TBI. Good medical and nursing care are vital to minimise medical complications associated with this condition, and physiotherapy should be provided to maximise limb mobility. It is essential that the injured person be maintained in an optimal state of general health, in order to maximise opportunities to benefit from structured sensory stimulation programmes.

HELPING THE FAMILY OF THE INJURED PERSON WHO ENTERS A VEGETATIVE STATE

Whilst the period that the injured person spends in coma is fearful and distressing, it does carry at least an implicit expectation of improvement to a more independent and responsive level of functioning. This hope is usually realised through family members' observations of their loved one and other injured people in the acute care setting, as they begin to show definite signs of awareness. For some families, however, the initial relief in seeing a lightening of conscious state is short-lived, as the injured person has entered a vegetative state. These families face the prospect of long-term despair, confusion, and anger, as they struggle to understand a condition which seems to parody awareness.

Lay people cannot be expected to easily understand or accept explanations from staff that their injured relative's movements, groans, or apparent eye-contact are not purposeful events, particularly as these are the very behaviours that they and the staff had recently greeted as signs of emergence from coma. The term "vegetative" may be a convenient form of medical shorthand, but it does little to comfort or inform family members about their loved one's condition. Indeed this term has very negative connotations and is arguably unsuitable for use in communicating with families. Regardless of the terminology employed, it is important to explain what the condition means, and to outline the possible outcomes, both within 12 months, and beyond. Family members will need many months, or even years, to come to terms with the diagnosis and prognosis associated with the vegetative state. Whilst this may, to some extent be assisted by the provision of CT, MRI, and evoked potential data, it may be difficult for relatives to reconcile what they are hearing from staff, with what they observe in the injured person from day to day.

It is common for family members to feel that the injured person is aware of their presence and/or is communicating via behaviours such as eye closure or groaning. On the other hand, the injured person's failure to communicate may be interpreted by family members as stubbornness, withdrawal or depression. Differences between the assessment of the injured person by staff, and that of the family need not be a source of conflict or hostility, particularly if continued efforts are being made to monitor the injured person, and provide an optimal management environment. It is helpful if treating staff are not only consistent in their input to family members, but show a genuine interest in, and make use of, the perceptions of relatives about the injured person's level of responsiveness. The injured person who is capable of demonstrating awareness may be more likely to do so with those familiar to him or her, rather than to one of several strangers who appear periodically at the bed-side.

If good staff–family relationships are cultivated, relatives can be gently educated about the distinction between arousal and awareness and can be asked to monitor signs they see as evidence for either or both of these.

Staff need to be receptive to concerns expressed by family members and, where possible, accommodate their suggestions regarding approaches to the care of the injured person. This demands personal and professional maturity of staff, who may, because of their own sense of frustration, sadness, and despair about the injured person's condition, find communicating with family members particularly difficult and stressful. Team members need opportunities to discuss their feelings of inadequacy with each other, so that they can continue to provide empathic support to relatives. Family members commonly feel confused and angry about their loved one's condition: angry that the accident occurred, angry that progress is not occurring, angry with staff for not doing a better job, and, consciously or unconsciously, angry with the injured person. The latter applies particularly in circumstances where the accident involved excessive alcohol consumption or other types of risk-taking behaviour.

It is normal for family members to want to investigate all options which hold some promise of improvement in their loved one's condition. It is most important in these circumstances that staff do not become resentful of relatives for what they may label as "shopping around". Few of us, in such catastrophic circumstances, would turn our backs on the possibility, no matter how remote, of effecting change in a severely injured relative's condition. Treating staff can assist relatives by inviting open discussion of alternative, sometimes controversial treatments, and by not rejecting family members (overtly or covertly) for their decision to explore one or more of these.

ASSESSMENT AND MANAGEMENT DURING POST-TRAUMATIC AMNESIA

The majority of TBI individuals do emerge from coma, over widely varying periods of time. Following this, the injured person typically passes through a phase of generalised cognitive disturbance, termed post-traumatic amnesia (PTA). People in this state may be partially or fully conscious, but are confused and disoriented, absorbing little from the environment. There is an inability to store and retrieve new information, and a period of retrograde amnesia is also common. Speech content may be quite confused. Awareness of circumstances is limited. Perception of the new environment, and incoming stimuli in general may be distorted, which serves to increase confusion, perplexity, and sometimes fear. As a result of lack of awareness of the nature of their condition, there is a failure to understand the reasons for being in hospital. Restlessness, agitation, physical and/or verbal aggression are common. If physically capable, people in PTA may wander. The problems may be worse at night, when there are fewer environmental cues to decrease confusion. The person in PTA may experience delusions and hallucinations. People do not recall this period afterwards, although they may have "islands" of memory. Some describe it as like being in a dream.

The term "post-traumatic amnesia" was first used by Symonds (1940, p.77) to refer to "...a general defect of cerebral function after consciousness has been regained". However, subsequent definitions have tended to focus on the injured person's disorientation in time, place and person, and/or inability to remember new experiences in an ongoing fashion (Artiola i Fortuny, Briggs, Newcombe, Ratcliff, & Thomas, 1980; Russell & Nathan, 1946; Russell & Smith, 1961; Schacter & Crovitz, 1977; Symonds & Russell, 1943). PTA has been said to terminate with the return of continuous memory. Its duration is generally taken to include the full period of coma. The duration of PTA therefore dates from the time the injury was incurred until the return of the capacity to store and retrieve new information (Russell & Nathan, 1946).

Russell and his colleagues used the person's retrospective reports to determine the duration of this period of PTA (Russell & Nathan, 1946). However, Symonds (1942) pointed out that the presence of "islands of memory" may distort the TBI individual's estimate, resulting in a period shorter than the actual length of PTA. The results of a prospective study of PTA by Gronwall and Wrightson (1980) indicated that retrospective assessment of the length of PTA by the injured person agreed with their own prospective assessment of the person's level of orientation and capacity to store ongoing memories in 75% of cases, and remained relatively constant over time. In most instances, the TBI individual gave longer estimates of PTA duration than had been apparent from objective assessment. Whilst this result suggested that the estimates of those who are injured may be correct more often than not, it is clearly impossible to establish the accuracy of their reports without objective monitoring. In view of the fact that PTA duration is commonly used as an estimate of injury severity, the use of more standardised and objective measures for the determination of its duration is very important.

Assessment of the person in PTA

A number of standardised scales have been developed for measuring the duration of PTA. The first was published by Levin and his colleagues in 1979 (Levin, O'Donnell, & Grossman, 1979). It was known as the Galveston Orientation and Amnesia Test (GOAT). The GOAT requires the person to give basic biographical information (name, address, and birthdate), and assesses orientation for time and place, recollection of events surrounding the accident and admission to hospital, and asks for a description of the first recollection after the injury. The total number of error points is deducted from 100. Scores below 65 are considered to be defective, those from 66 to 75 borderline, and those above 75 normal (Levin et al., 1982a). The test was designed to be administered at least once daily. Levin et al. (1982a) reported significant associations between the length of PTA, as measured by the GOAT, and both acute neurological impairment, as measured by the Glasgow Coma Scale, and the level of overall social and vocational recovery, as rated on the Glasgow Outcome Scale (Jennett & Bond, 1975).

The GOAT has, however, subsequently been criticised by several authors. Gronwall and Wrightson (1980) asserted that recovery of orientation, as assessed on the GOAT, did not necessarily mean that the person had emerged from PTA. Shores, Marosszeky, Sandanam, and Batchelor (1986) pointed out that a normal score could be recorded even if the injured person could not answer the specific amnesia questions, thus arguing that the scale was sensitive only to disorientation, and not the amnesia which may also be present in PTA. Indeed Saneda and Corrigan (1992) have more recently confirmed the potential for a temporal dissociation between the recovery of orientation and new learning ability in PTA. Wilson, Baddeley, Shiel, and Patton (1992a) have also correctly pointed out that people both in and out of PTA are frequently unable to answer questions about the last memory before the accident, or the first memory after the accident.

Shores et al. (1986) extended the earlier work of Artiola i Fortuny et al. (1980) to produce the Westmead PTA Scale as a clinical test of orientation, and the ability to lay down memories from one day to the next. As shown in Fig. 2.2, the test requires injured people to give their age and date of birth, assesses orientation in time and place, the capacity for recall of the examiner's face and name, and for identification, from an array, of which three pictures of common objects they have been shown the day before. If injured people do not respond spontaneously to the questions asked, they are presented with a multiple choice. For example, if they do not respond to the question, "What is the name of this place?", they may be asked, "Is it home, is it Westmead Hospital or is it Parramatta Hospital?".

In the case of failure to spontaneously recall the pictures, a choice is given from the three target pictures and six distractor pictures. From the first day on which a score of 12 is recorded, the three target pictures are changed daily. The procedure is repeated until a perfect score of 12 is obtained on three successive days. The period of PTA is said to have ended on the first of these three days.

Shores et al. (1986) assessed a group of 20 subjects with severe brain injuries who were still in PTA, as judged by their performance on the Westmead PTA Scale. They performed significantly worse than a group

WESTMEAD P.T.A. SCALE

Westmead and Parramatta Hospitals
and Community Health Services

P.T.A. may be deemed to be over on the first
of 3 consecutive days of a recall of 12

Title	Family Name	M.R.N.
Given Names		C.M.O.
Address	Street	Age	Sex	H.I.S.
Suburb	Postcode	Adm. date

A = Answer   S = Score (1 or 0)

DATE													
1.	How old are you ?	A											
		S											
2.	What is your date of birth ?	A											
		S											
3.	What month are we in ?	A											
		S											
4.	What time of day is it ? (morning, afternoon or night)	A											
		S											
5.	What day of the week is it ?	A											
		S											
6.	What year are we in ?	A											
		S											
7.	What is the name of this place ?	A											
		S											
8.	Face	A											
		S											
9.	Name	A											
		S											
10.	Picture I	A											
		S											
11.	Picture II	A											
		S											
12.	Picture III	A											
		S											
	TOTAL													

FIG. 2.2. Westmead PTA Scale. (Reprinted with permission of the Department of Rehabilitation Medicine, Westmead Hospital, Westmead, NSW, Australia.)

51

of severely brain-injured subjects who were out of PTA on an independent test of learning ability, the Selective Reminding Test (Buschke & Fuld, 1974). The performance of both of these groups was significantly impaired relative to that of a group of 20 hospitalised orthopaedic patients. Shores et al. concluded that even people with extremely severe brain injuries, and experiencing some ongoing learning difficulties, were able to carry out the requirements of the standardised PTA scale. They also found that the scale showed a high level of inter-rater reliability and could be used, with only a small amount of training, by medical staff, nurses or therapists, as well as psychologists. It is important to stress, however, that it is preferable that the scale is administered by the same individual from one day to the next, because of the requirement to remember the examiner's face and name.

Forrester, Encel, and Geffen (1994) have recently developed a modified version of the Westmead Scale, termed the Julia Farr Centre PTA Scale. Based on the assumption that recovery of orientation always precedes recovery of memory, this scale separates the assessment of orientation and memory, allowing for assessment of orientation only initially. The examiner is required to record different scores according to the amount of assistance or cueing needed to give correct responses, rather than the simpler binary scoring procedure used in administration of the Westmead Scale. The predictive validity of this scale is currently under investigation. However, the assumption that recovery of orientation invariably precedes that of memory may be premature. Moreover the scoring system appears to be quite complex, it being unclear what level of assistance is indicative of a person still being in PTA.

Whilst the Westmead PTA Scale is probably the preferred measure available for use in assessing people in PTA, there are a number of issues pertaining to the assessment of PTA which have yet to be resolved. As Wilson et al. (1992a) have pointed out, there are a small number of TBI individuals who remain so severely amnesic that they never obtain a perfect score on the Westmead PTA Scale. This raises the question as to when PTA should be redefined as the presence of a severe and chronic amnesic syndrome. In our experience, people who have remained disorientated and amnesic for more than 6 months after their emergence from coma, are likely to exhibit ongoing amnesic difficulties, and therapy should be planned accordingly.

There are also other cognitive and behavioural disturbances associated with PTA, which are not assessed on any of the currently available PTA scales, but which may assist in differentiating this phase of recovery. There has been relatively little documentation of these disturbances, studies of PTA having tended to focus on impairment of memory. Symonds (1937) noted that PTA was characterised by defects of perception, judgement and speech functions, perseveration of thought processes, elation of mood, and talkativeness, in addition to disorientation in space and time, and memory impairment. Mandleberg (1975) found a group of severely brain-injured people in PTA to be impaired across all subtests of the WAIS, more so on the Performance subtests than the Verbal subtests, relative to a group of severely brain-injured people out of PTA. They concluded that PTA was characterised by a general disorder of cognitive ability.

More recently, Wilson et al. (1992a) compared the performance of a group of subjects in PTA with that of groups of amnesic, memory impaired and orthopaedic controls on a range of tests of memory and attention. Most of the measures which differentiated the performances of the PTA subjects from those of the other groups, namely simple reaction time, speed and accuracy of comprehension, verbal fluency, backward digit span, and delayed recall of prose, placed demands on attention, and particularly information processing capacity, speed and accuracy. It would appear that these functions are also significantly impaired in PTA, and that they should be monitored in addition to orientation and memory.

It remains to be seen whether recovery of these functions occurs rapidly and concurrently with the resolution of the disorientation and amnesia, or more gradually. Corrigan and Mysiw (1988) and Corrigan, Mysiw, Gribble, and Chock (1992) have found the relationships between cognition, agitation, and attention to be by no means straightforward, there being a temporal dissociation in recovery on each of these dimensions. Further study in this area would be fruitful. Future developments in the assessment of people during the phase of PTA will need to consider assessment of behaviour and cognitive function in a more general sense, particularly measures of attention, and speed and capacity of information processing.

There have been a number of studies examining the nature of the memory impairment in PTA. Several authors have argued that PTA is characterised by a failure of consolidation of new information into long-term memory (Benson & Geschwind, 1967; Shores et al., 1986; Yarnell & Lynch, 1970). Richardson (1990) has suggested, on the other hand, that the memory disorder in PTA may represent a retrieval problem, resulting from inefficient encoding of memories. He argues that this may explain the phenomenon of "islands" of memory. Unfortunately, studies which have tested this hypothesis have had methodological limitations, so there is no definitive evidence to support or refute this argument (Brooks, 1984a). Given the fairly generalised nature of the cognitive impairment associated with PTA, it seems arguable that the memory disorder may be characterised by failure of both consolidation and retrieval mechanisms, as well as poor organisation in the encoding of material.

Other studies have focused on the relative preservation of motor (procedural) learning skills in PTA (Ewert, Levin, Watson, & Kalisky, 1989). Such findings are similar to those in subjects with an amnesic syndrome of a more permanent nature, such as that associated with Korsakoff's syndrome. Gasquoine (1991) found that TBI subjects in PTA, who were unable to learn verbal material, showed some capacity to retain information regarding spatial location, although this learning was well below normal levels. They suggested that, using this information, people in PTA may be assisted in achieving spatial orientation within the hospital setting.

PTA duration as a measure of severity of TBI

The duration of PTA has frequently been used by clinicians and researchers as an index of severity of TBI. Both Moore and Ruesch (1944) and Russell and Smith (1961) found an association between longer periods of PTA and other clinical signs indicative of serious brain injury, including skull fracture, intracranial haemorrhage, raised intracranial pressure, and the presence of residual neurological deficits, such as motor and language disorders. A number of studies have also demonstrated a significant relationship between the duration of PTA and eventual outcome, as measured by the Glasgow Outcome Scale (Bishara et al., 1992; Jennett, 1976), persistent memory disturbance (Brooks, 1975, 1976; Brooks & Aughton, 1979), psychosocial dysfunction (Bond, 1975, 1976), or occupational status (Russell & Smith, 1961). The classification originally proposed by Russell and Smith (1961) and expanded by Jennett and Teasdale (1981) was as follows:

- Less than 5 minutes—very mild
- 5 to 60 minutes—mild
- 1 to 24 hours—moderate
- 1 to 7 days—severe
- 1 to 4 weeks—very severe
- More than 4 weeks—extremely severe

The majority of studies have used this classification, which was established on the basis of clinical experience rather than outcome data. Using residual complaints and return to work two years after injury as outcome criteria, van Zomeren and van den Burg (1985) suggested that 13 days may be more appropriate than seven days as a cut-off point between the severe and very severe categories. Similarly, Brooks et al. (1987a) found that ongoing problems were most likely to be reported when PTA exceeded two weeks. Bishara et al. (1992) found that no subject with a PTA duration of more than eight weeks showed a good outcome as measured on the Glasgow Outcome Scale at 12 months. On the other hand, eight of the ten TBI individuals with a PTA duration between four and eight weeks did show a good recovery. This led them to suggest that a more appropriate cut-off for the extremely severe category might be a PTA duration of eight weeks. No studies to date have clearly established clinically useful criteria at the mild end of the spectrum. It would appear that some revision of the guidelines for classification of injury severity using PTA duration may be appropriate on the basis of the results of comprehensive outcome studies. However, continuing problems in the selection of appropriate measures of outcome render this task extremely difficult.

Unfortunately, variable criteria have been used for measuring PTA duration in outcome studies conducted to date, some having relied on questioning of the injured person, others on hospital records, and others having used standardised scales. This places some limitations on the validity and comparability of findings. Whilst the relationship of PTA duration with outcome may have been demonstrated as statistically significant, and stronger than that of many other individual variables, in most studies it explains little more than a third of the variance in outcome. For example, Bishara et al. (1992) found that PTA duration alone explained only 36% of the variance in outcome as measured on the Glasgow Outcome Scale at 12 months post-injury. Van Zomeren and van den Burg (1985) found a correlation of 0.52 with outcome measured in terms of return to work. Outcome following TBI is influenced by many variables, relating not only to injury severity, but also to social and demographic factors and the post-injury environment. It is therefore difficult to predict outcome with accuracy in any individual case (Ponsford et al., 1995b; Vogenthaler et al., 1989). It is certainly unwise for clinicians to convey a definite prognosis based on PTA duration to the injured person and/or family in the early stages of recovery.

Management of the person in PTA

TBI individuals in PTA can present a significant management problem for nurses, therapists, and families, causing considerable disruption in hospital or rehabilitation wards. As a consequence, it is not uncommon for such individuals to be sedated. However, this tends to have the effect of further reducing the person's level of arousal, potentially increasing confusion and hence prolonging agitation, as well as exacerbating problems with attention, initiation and fatigue (Cope, 1987). Major tranquillisers may increase the likelihood of post-traumatic epilepsy, and the results of some studies have suggested that they may have a deleterious impact on recovery (Cope, 1987). Whilst behavioural principles should be adhered to in interactions with people in PTA, as in other stages of recovery (see Chapter 8), the institution of formal behaviour modification programmes is also inappropriate at this stage.

The recommended approach to the management of brain-injured people in PTA involves the creation of an environment which minimises agitation. Physical restraint, or lying between the bars of cot sides, tends to compound feelings of agitation and fear. It is preferable that restless or physically active individuals who are in PTA be nursed on the floor, with padding around the bed, so they can move about freely without harming themselves. The "Craig Bed", designed by the staff of Craig Hospital in Denver, USA., is ideal for this purpose (Fig. 2.3).

Noise and overstimulation also tend to exacerbate agitation in those who are in PTA. It is therefore important to maintain an environment that is as quiet as possible, as well as being safe and secure. It is best for individuals in PTA to have a room to themselves and remain there as much as possible, to enable the development of familiarity with surroundings. Moving around may only serve to increase confusion. However, individuals who are physically mobile and want to wander around the ward should be allowed to do so, with appropriate supervision. They should not, however, be allowed to leave the ward area. It is helpful to have an enclosed courtyard area to enable them to spend time outdoors. Electronic surveillance systems represent the ideal method of monitoring the movements of people in PTA, although most units do not have such equipment. If the unit cannot be locked, an alternative may be the use of a bracelet system, whereby a designated staff member takes responsibility for monitoring the whereabouts of the injured person for a specified period, during which a bracelet is worn. This is handed from one staff member to another as each takes responsibility for surveillance of the person concerned.

It is a good idea to have the same staff dealing consistently with the person in PTA. The presence of family, and familiar photographs and possessions around the bed, may also be reassuring, as may frequent reminders as to what has happened, where they are, the time of day, and so on. The number of visitors should be limited, again to avoid over stimulation. It is best to have only one or two visitors at a time, for short periods only, and no visitors if there is obvious fatigue or distress. People in PTA generally fatigue easily, and need much more sleep than usual.

Physiotherapy may be necessary at this stage. If at all possible, this should be conducted on the ward. Taking a person in PTA to a busy physiotherapy department is likely to exacerbate confusion and

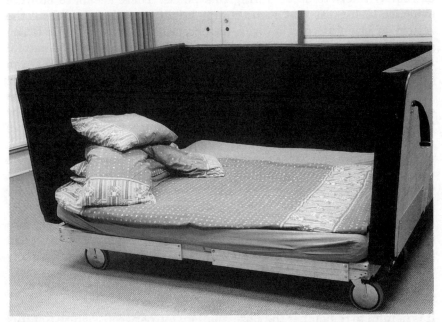

FIG. 2.3. The Craig Bed. (Photographed with permission of Craig Hospital, Englewood, Colorado, USA.)

agitation. It may be helpful for other therapists to establish a supportive relationship through regular, but brief contacts on the ward. However, it is very important to realise that, whilst in PTA, people will benefit little from therapy which requires active participation, although it is conceivable that there may be some carry over from physiotherapy if motor learning skills remain relatively intact (Ewert et al., 1989).

The question as to whether individuals in PTA might benefit from "Reality Orientation Therapy" is somewhat controversial. According to Moffat (1984, p.82), Reality Orientation Therapy, which was designed to assist in the care of confused elderly patients, "...aims to maintain or retrain a person's awareness of time, place and current events by incorporating this information in staff interactions with the patient. This structured conversation may be assisted by classroom sessions, the use of external aids, repetition and possibly by specific behavioural training". Whilst there have been reports of improvement in the cognitive function of TBI individuals in PTA when they were participating in Reality Orientation groups (Corrigan, Arnett, Houck, & Jackson, 1985), no controlled studies have been conducted to date. As

Corrigan et al. have acknowledged, spontaneous improvement is extremely likely to occur during this phase. There seems to be little evidence to suggest that such therapy might actually bring about the return of orientation. However, participation in Reality Orientation groups and other Reality Orientation methods are likely to be helpful at the point at which the person is beginning to emerge from PTA, in order to assist in, or expedite the reorientation process.

Attempts at assessment of language and other cognitive functions during PTA, and, to a lesser extent, physical abilities, are likely to be thwarted by restlessness, poor concentration, a fluctuating level of arousal, and reduced control over thought processes and behaviour. A picture of severe and generalised impairment may emerge, bearing little resemblance to the pattern of ongoing deficits which is apparent following emergence from PTA. This may result in an unnecessarily gloomy prognosis being conveyed to family members. Many TBI individuals show a rapid improvement in mental state on emergence from PTA. It is, therefore, usually misleading to attempt to assess and prognosticate during PTA. Formal assessment and treatment is likely to serve only to distress the injured person.

Maximising communication skills during PTA

It is helpful to remember the close relationship between cognitive status and communication ability during the period of PTA. As GCS scores increase, it is usual to see improvements in both the form and content of verbal output, together with improvements in information processing skills. Communication needs will probably change quite rapidly as the person emerges from PTA. It is important that the relationship between cognition and communication is explained to families, in order to allay anxieties about the sometimes bizarre manifestations of this. The term "aphasia" should not be used to describe the verbal difficulties displayed by the person in PTA. Whilst certain features of these difficulties may resemble aphasia, it is common for many of them to dissipate rapidly following emergence from PTA.

There are a number of ways in which communication with the injured person may be enhanced during the period of PTA. These are summarised below:

- Keep instructions and explanations to a minimum, and deliver them slowly. Allow additional time for the person to respond.
- Establish a reliable yes/no response as early as possible. All staff should take care in framing yes/no, as opposed to forced-choice questions. A yes/no question, for example, might be "Would you like a drink?", where an example of a forced choice question is

"Would you like juice or water?" A range of modalities may need to be available to the person to communicate at this level. These include speech, head nodding/shaking, yes/no boards, thumbs up/down, and any or all combinations which appear to be successful for the person concerned.

- Because of their close relationship with the injured person, family members may be the first to establish a means of communication. Team members need to respect this and build on the work of families.
- Consistently reinforce any communication attempts the injured person makes, however no attempt should be made to modify content or articulation at this time.

It may be distressing and confusing for family members whose relative swears or uses language otherwise uncharacteristic of their previous communication style. Staff should explain that these behaviours reflect the person's reduced control over what is being said, and that as far as possible, they are best ignored at this stage. Other verbal behaviours which may be inadvertently reinforced by family members include perseveration, confabulation and echolalia. Again, these need to be explained in terms of the person's brain injury, and strategies (such as distraction) should be suggested for dealing with them as they arise. It should also be explained to family members that emergent communication skills are likely to fluctuate.

Summary of principles of management of the person in PTA

- Keep noise and stimulation to a minimum.
- Maintain a safe, secure and familiar environment.
- Avoid restraint.
- Allow freedom to wander around the ward area under surveillance.
- Avoid taking the person from the ward.
- Keep staff changes to a minimum.
- Limit the number of visitors and their length of stay.
- Allow frequent rest times.
- Reinforce any attempts at communication and keep instructions simple.
- Provide regular reassurance regarding circumstances.

- Except for specific needs, do not attempt to assess the injured person.

- Do not prognosticate.

- Keep therapy contact brief.

- Do not allow person to go home.

Helping the family of the person in PTA

Families are usually very anxious at this stage to obtain information about the nature of deficits and the likely prognosis. Staff should resist pressure to make predictions. Instead they should use this as an opportunity to explain what PTA is, how the family can assist in appropriate management of the injured person during this phase, and that further assessment and therapy will be conducted following emergence from PTA. Not uncommonly, families ask the same questions over and over, and staff need to be patient with this, being prepared to reiterate information many times. Understandably, families may also be very keen to see their injured relative being treated intensively, and may even attempt to do this themselves. It is important, therefore, to maintain constant communication between staff and family, so that energies can be harnessed in as appropriate a way as possible.

Families may also wish to take their TBI relative home. However, it is unwise to send a person in PTA home for visits, let alone to allow discharge. Although it may seem helpful for the injured person to be in the familiar home environment, such visits lead, more often than not, to overstimulation. On return to hospital, the injured person may be more confused, agitated, fatigued, and unsettled. Often, people in PTA cannot see the reason for being in hospital, and taking them home for brief visits only unsettles them further. It is also usually extremely stressful for families to try to manage a person in PTA in the home environment. This is not to say that TBI individuals should not spend time at home—indeed this is to be actively encouraged, once there is consistent orientation and awareness of circumstances, and the family seem able to cope appropriately.

MAKING THE TRANSITION TO ORAL FEEDING

Because of factors such as fatigue, agitation, and fluctuating awareness, it is common for TBI individuals to receive a combination of artificial and oral nutrition during PTA. Many of the principles outlined below refer to brain-injured people across the disability spectrum who are progressing from artificial to oral feeding. Some, however, have particular relevance to those who are severely disabled as a result of their injuries.

It is important that eating difficulties following TBI are not viewed simply in terms of mechanical breakdown. There is a need to consider cognitive, communicative, and behavioural skills as well as oromotor functioning, as ultimately it is the person's overall level of cognitive functioning, and ability to co-operate in the eating process which will underpin successful transition to oral feeding. This transition requires the skills, expertise and co-operation of all team members, including the family. Everybody involved in the process needs to have realistic expectations and be prepared to set achievable short-term goals. Staff need to be prepared to stop and start eating programmes according to the person's overall progress, and the occurrence of medical setbacks, such as urinary tract infections. It is not always possible to fully wean a brain-injured person off artificial feeding. Under these circumstances, staff and family need to develop and accept a workable compromise.

The person who does not exhibit reliable signs of awareness (e.g. a yes/no response, or the ability to follow simple commands at a better than chance level), is not a candidate for oral feeding. In order for the transition to oral feeding to be a meaningful rehabilitation milestone, the injured person should be actively participating to some extent, e.g. in choice of foods, timing of mouthfuls, or quantity to be consumed at any one sitting. Primitive oral reflexes should not be mistaken for purposeful, volitional participation in the eating process. Their presence and physiology needs to be carefully and simply explained to family members, who may be very eager, on the basis of these reflexes to commence oral feeding. At the very least, family members need to understand the risks if they choose to proceed.

In some cases (for example when the injured person appears to be in a vegetative state), prolonged periods of artificial nutrition will be necessary, either via a nasogastric (NG) tube or percutaneous endoscopic gastrostomy (PEG). The use of NG tubes is increasingly limited to about three months, because of complications such as oesophagitis, ulceration, and displacement. PEG has a number of advantages over NG feeding, most notably the reduced risk of excoriation of the nasal cavity, pharynx, and oesophagus, the reduced risk of aspiration, and the greater ease with which weight can be maintained.

Ongoing assessment and management of eating difficulties
If the injured person displays any capacity to participate in the mealtime process, this should be encouraged and facilitated, e.g. via the provision of modified utensils, and allowing greater time and spillage rates. Although invariably slow at first, this is a significant step towards

independence in self-care. To accommodate a tendency to fatigue rapidly, a regime of frequent short meals may need to be implemented. Regardless of the means by which nutrition is provided, it should be noted that certain medications may interfere with the absorption of nutrients. These have been reviewed by Haynes (1992) and include psychotropic drugs, antidepressants, antispasticity agents, anticonvulsants and broad-spectrum antibiotics. The injured person should be weighed weekly until optimal weight has been achieved and thereafter monthly, once staff are confident that weight has been stabilised.

As far as possible, people need to be assessed for oral feeding in the setting in which they are likely to be eating, as staff need to determine the extent to which they can deal with visual and auditory distractions. Assessment in a quiet setting, free of all distractions may artificially elevate expectations of the person's performance.

The person should be sitting up straight or slightly reclined, either in bed supported by pillows, or in a chair, and should remain in an upright position for 15–30 minutes following oral feeding. The head needs to be upright and midline. Before attempting formal assessment, a number of behavioural observations should be made. These are summarised below. It is helpful to substantiate these observations by liaising with other staff and family members, and also by observing the person at different times of day, following different activities (e.g. bathing as opposed to physiotherapy).

Factors to consider prior to the commencement of oral feeding

- The position of the mouth at rest.
- The presence of drooling (bi/unilateral) and the patient's level of awareness of this.
- Ability to maintain head in an upright position.
- Ability to establish and maintain eye-contact.
- Intelligibility and content of any verbal responses, and/or ability to use non-speech communication aids.
- Yes/no response and how this is indicated.
- Presence of behavioural disturbance.
- Occurrence of spontaneous (reflex) cough.
- Voice quality (normal/wet/hoarse).

- Response to verbal input from staff member.

- Dentition (own/false teeth, missing teeth, general condition of oral cavity).

If the injured person is able to actively participate in assessment, dysarthria and cranial nerve examinations may be necessary. The presence of bi/unilateral weakness and the occurrence of any primitive reflexes which may interfere with eating should be noted. Although voluntary cough and gag reflex should be checked, their importance for oral feeding has probably been overstated in the past, at the expense of evaluating reflex cough, general level of awareness, and ability to co-operate.

Before introducing any food, it is important to determine the person's likes and dislikes by discussing these with family members and, where possible, the injured person. If this is not done, it may be difficult to determine the significance of behaviours such as lip pursing and turning the head away from the spoon. Staff should consider not only the taste, but also the texture and the temperature of the food to be presented, in order that optimal stimulation is provided. When preparing to feed a person who has hitherto relied on artificial nutrition, staff should use verbal cueing before, during and after each mouthful, in order to ensure a state of readiness, adequate movement of the bolus within the mouth, and the clearing of any debris via a second swallow (and/or a sip of fluid) before another mouthful is introduced. Because the injured person may be distractable and/or impulsive, it is wise to minimise the number of items on the tray, and to verbally label each food before a spoonful is introduced. Staff should be vigilant for signs of fatigue (such as difficulty maintaining head posture, increased drooling), and cease feeding when these emerge.

In general, thin liquids are the most difficult for TBI individuals to control, thus the eating assessment usually commences with about half a teaspoon of pureed fruit, (thickened with infant rice cereal if necessary). Dairy products, such as ice cream and milkshakes are also avoided in the early days of oral feeding as they tend to increase secretions and may form a bolus of mixed consistency, thus requiring two swallows in quick succession (one for the liquid component, one for the solid). Upon introducing puréed fruit, the person's response should be closely observed, noting the presence and effectiveness of masticatory movements, time taken to initiate and execute the swallow, the presence of debris after the swallow and the occurrence of any coughing or choking noises. It should be noted that apparent successful swallowing of small amounts of pureed food does not preclude silent aspiration, and does not mean that in practical terms the person is ready to proceed to an upgraded oral diet. If the person eats too slowly or fatigues rapidly, it will not only be impossible to achieve an adequate fluid intake, but will make unreasonable demands on staff time.

Because it is not always possible to determine by clinical measures alone which people are ready to proceed to oral feeding, it may be necessary to perform a *Modified Barium Jelly Swallow* (MBa+JS). This radiological technique is the only objective means of observing all three stages of the swallowing process (oral, pharyngeal, and oesophageal), and determining the relative strengths and weaknesses of each of these. During this technique, staff evaluate the person's response to varying bolus consistencies and volumes, and may also introduce some treatment measures (e.g. postural modifications) to evaluate their impact on the swallowing process. The diagnostic information yielded by the MBa+JS not only provides a less equivocal diagnosis about underlying neuromuscular dysfunction and/or structural changes, but also assists in the formulation of individually tailored treatment programmes. Common difficulties identified by this procedure include delayed or absent triggering of the swallow reflex, reduced tongue control, and diminished or absent cough reflex.

CONCLUSIONS

At all stages following TBI it is essential that the conscious state of the injured person is carefully monitored, as objectively as possible. Information regarding changes or otherwise in conscious state is used as a basis for medical management, for implementing therapy programmes, and for communicating with family members. It must be stressed that impairment of consciousness, at any stage after injury is a stressful and confusing time for relatives. Staff can alleviate this stress by involving family members as much as possible in the care of the injured person, by being available to listen to their concerns, and providing clear, simple explanations about the person's progress. Much can be done to minimise the effects of agitation and confusion associated with impairment of conscious state, and every effort should be made to provide an environment that maximises opportunities for improved responsiveness over time, and minimises the development of ongoing behaviour problems.

CHAPTER THREE

Assessment of cognitive difficulties following TBI

Sue Sloan and Jennie Ponsford

INTRODUCTION

Due to the high frequency of diffuse axonal injury, combined with localised frontal and temporal lobe damage, TBI tends to result in a characteristic range of cognitive impairments. These include deficits of attention and speed of information processing, learning and memory, executive function and the ability to think in abstract terms, reduced initiative, inflexible thought processes, and impairment of the ability to control and monitor thoughts and behaviour. The precise nature and extent of these problems varies widely, as a function of the location and severity of injury, as well as premorbid factors. As many follow-up studies have demonstrated, they may affect the TBI individual's capacity to perform many of the activities that are necessary and relevant in daily life. It has also been demonstrated that they have a more significant impact on psychosocial outcome than physical disabilities.

Many of these cognitive impairments are, however, not always readily apparent on standardised psychometric assessment. Moreover, it is frequently difficult to predict how those problems that are apparent will affect the individual's daily life and roles in society. As a consequence of this, the assessment of cognitive difficulties following TBI presents a significant challenge to psychologists and therapists involved in the rehabilitation process, requiring a more direct focus on the skills needed in everyday living. Following the principles of the REAL approach, outlined in Chapter 1, the aim of this chapter is to provide guidance in attaining an understanding of the nature of cognitive difficulties, as well as residual strengths, and their impact on the life of the injured individual, as a basis for intervention. The use of this assessment information to set goals and plan treatment will be discussed and expanded in Chapter 4.

Concepts of impairment, disability and handicap, as outlined by the World Health Organization (WHO) (1980), provide a useful framework for understanding the manifestations of cognitive difficulties associated with TBI. According to this conceptual structure, injury is seen to result in impairments, which affect the structure or function of brain areas (e.g. verbal memory impairment), disabilities, which are the resulting difficulties in performing practical daily tasks (e.g. difficulty recalling instructions), and handicaps, which are defined as the social disadvantages for the individual in their valued roles and responsibilities (e.g. failure to hold down a job). Due to their nature and complexity, it is important to assess the manifestations of cognitive sequelae associated with TBI on each of these dimensions. Assessment methods relevant to impairment, disability and handicap are outlined in the sections below. Assessment of the TBI person who is emerging from coma and/or exhibits very severe disabilities has been covered in the previous chapter.

ASSESSMENT OF COGNITIVE IMPAIRMENT

The World Health Organization (1980, p.27) defines impairment as "any loss or abnormality of psychological, physiological, or anatomical structure or function". Cognitive impairments are deficiencies of neuropsychological function that can be related to damage in specific areas of the brain. Neuropsychological assessment is the method most commonly used to delineate the nature and severity of cognitive impairment following TBI. Whilst neuropsychological assessments should not be used to define disability or handicap, they do provide a relatively standardised and objective means of delineating the specific nature of the cognitive impairments which may underlie disabilities, and thereby provide clues as to the basis of everyday difficulties and possible methods of overcoming these.

A distinction has been drawn between cognitive assessments that employ a fixed battery of neuropsychological tests (Reitan & Wolfson, 1985), and approaches which emphasise flexibility in test selection (Walsh, 1991). Typically, in the former approach the psychologist relies on test scores alone to identify impairments. In the latter approach, qualitative features of task performance are taken into consideration, in an effort to understand how the score was obtained (Lezak, 1983). Whilst it is important to maintain standard methods of obtaining test scores, for a number of reasons the latter approach is seen to be particularly useful in the examination of TBI individuals. Many of the difficulties characteristic of disorders of attentional and executive function most commonly associated with TBI, such as distractibility and impulsivity, are more easily documented qualitatively. Behavioural observations of the injured person's approach to the task, as well as subjective reports as to the cognitive strategies employed during task performance, provide a context within which test scores can be interpreted.

In practice, the assessment usually comprises a number of key tests that are administered to establish the injured person's previous level of ability, detect the presence of deficits commonly found following TBI, such as those of memory, attention, and executive function, and obtain a profile of the person's strengths. Additional tests are selected on the basis of the TBI individual's test performance and other neuropathological evidence. Following standardised administration, from which the score is derived, the neuropsychologist may systematically alter components of the test to gain further understanding of the nature of the person's difficulties (Walsh, 1991). In interpreting test performance, the clinician must also take into account the individual's age, cultural background, education, past history of drug abuse, psychiatric or neurological disorder, level of anxiety and fatigue, emotional state, motivation, frustration tolerance, level of insight, and premorbid ability at the task in question. Principles of neuropsychological assessment of TBI individuals have been comprehensively covered in a number of sources, including Walsh (1991) and Morse and Montgomery (1992). Lezak (1994) provides detailed guidelines regarding test selection and administration. They will not, therefore, be covered in great detail in this chapter. Assessment of language and communication skills is covered in Chapter 5. Whilst the discussion in this chapter will focus on assessment of the most common areas of cognitive impairment associated with TBI, it must be understood that impairment of any aspect of cognitive function may occur.

Taking a history

As Walsh (1991, 1994) and Saling (1994) have cogently argued, it is essential to have a comprehensive history prior to commencing the neuropsychological assessment. This should provide vital information on which to base test selection and interpretation of performance. All available information regarding the brain injury and other injuries sustained, surgical intervention, complications, Glasgow Coma Scale scores, scan results and PTA duration should be gathered. Estimation of PTA duration may be extremely difficult in cases where the injured person underwent surgery, had severe internal injuries and/or was heavily sedated. The injured person's recall of events is likely to be poor under these circumstances, potentially inflating PTA estimates. Further details regarding the estimation of PTA duration are outlined in Chapter 2.

At the initial interview it is important, first, to establish that the person being assessed has emerged from PTA, along the lines suggested in Chapter 2. Neuropsychological assessment is likely to be inconclusive and distressing for the person who is still in PTA, and is therefore not recommended during this phase. It will be necessary to carefully monitor the performance of those who have ongoing problems with attention and fatigue, perhaps conducting the assessment over a series of short sessions. The neuropsychologist should explain the nature of and reasons for the assessment to the injured person. The person's recall of events prior to and including the accident, as well as events subsequent to the accident needs to be determined.

Details regarding age, personal, medical and social history, educational and occupational background, and leisure interests should also be obtained. It is important to establish whether the individual has had a previous brain injury or any other neurological disorder, has a history of emotional or psychiatric disturbance or substance abuse. All of these factors may significantly influence the test results, making differential diagnosis difficult. The injured individual's subjective perception of changes in cognitive, behavioural and physical function, and the impact of these changes on their ability to fulfil everyday roles and responsibilities should also be obtained, using both general and specific questioning. In the early stages after injury it is common to find awareness of physical disabilities, but failure to report significant changes in cognition and behaviour.

If there is such an awareness, the individual may be anxious or depressed. It is important to explore the injured person's psychological reaction to the injury and coping strategies. Methods of assessing the injured person's psychological state are outlined in Chapter 8. The presence of significant emotional disturbance is likely to have an impact on the assessment results. The clinician must apply considerable care and skill in distinguishing organic impairments from those with a functional basis [see Walsh (1991, 1994) for further discussion of this issue]. This distinction is likely to be particularly difficult in the case of mild TBI. Finally, it is useful at the initial interview to discuss the injured person's goals and expectations of rehabilitation. Such information is useful, not only in designing the rehabilitation plan, but also in tailoring feedback on completion of the assessment to the individual's level of insight, areas of concern and overall goals.

Wherever possible, an attempt should be made to speak with a family member to check the accuracy of the information given by the injured individual, hear their account of the person's emergence from coma and PTA, discuss premorbid personality and behaviour patterns, abilities and interests, obtain their perceptions of cognitive and behavioural change since the injury, and the impact this has had on daily activities and relationships. Previous school records should also be obtained.

Establishing premorbid level of ability

In order to make accurate interpretations of test performances it is necessary to establish the injured person's premorbid level of intelligence. Measures traditionally used to determine premorbid IQ include the Wechsler Adult Intelligence Scale-Revised (WAIS-R) Vocabulary subtest score or best WAIS-R subtest score (Lezak, 1983, Wechsler, 1981), the New Adult Reading Test (NART) (Nelson & O'Connell, 1978), and demographic estimates, such as that developed by Wilson, Rosenbaum, Brown, Rourke, Whitman, and Grisell (1978). In the early stages of recovery there may be fairly generalised impairment of cognitive function, including word-finding difficulties, so that all WAIS-R subtest scores, including Vocabulary, may underestimate the injured person's previous level of ability. Blurred vision or previous learning disability affecting reading skills may preclude administration of the NART.

Under these circumstances, and for those whose native language is not English, there may be a need to rely on a demographic estimate. However, there are obvious limitations in using such estimates, and any conclusions drawn from this must be backed up with as much historical information as can possibly be obtained, particularly regarding previous school performance. Those with a history of poor academic performance may demonstrate a long-standing discrepancy between Verbal and Performance scores, the latter being significantly higher. In such cases, the WAIS-R Vocabulary subtest score is clearly not going to give an accurate indication of non-verbal intelligence. In many instances the neuropsychologist will need to integrate information from a number of sources (test results, cultural, social, educational and occupational background and demographic formulae) in order to estimate the injured person's premorbid level of ability. In some instances a realistic picture of this may only emerge over time.

Assessment of attention

The assessment of attention following TBI is not a straightforward task for a number of reasons. First, attention is clearly not a unitary concept. There is little agreement as to definitions of aspects of attention and there are few established criteria for measurement. Nevertheless, problems with attention, concentration and slowness are amongst the most common cognitive problems reported by TBI individuals and their relatives in follow-up studies (e.g. McKinlay et al., 1981; van Zomeren & van den Burg, 1985).

In a study by Ponsford and Kinsella (1991), therapists were asked to rate the attentional difficulties of people with moderate and severe TBI, based on clinical observations in the context of therapy. The most frequently reported problem was, in all instances, "slowness in performing mental tasks". Other commonly reported difficulties included "being able to pay attention to more than one thing at a time", "making mistakes because he/she wasn't paying attention properly", "missing important details", and "having difficulty concentrating". Whilst these therapists' responses were limited by the nature of the items presented in the rating scale, it would appear that a variety of attentional problems are observed clinically. Therefore, in conducting the neuropsychological assessment of TBI individuals, it is important to observe and record, both quantitatively and qualitatively, a broad range of attentional behaviours. These might include information processing speed, the ability to focus attention and avoid distraction, the ability to divide attention across more than one task or aspect of a task, attention to visual and auditory detail, and the ability to sustain attention. Unfortunately, there is no commonly available neuropsychological test or tests which uniquely taps these behaviours. Rather, the assessment of attentional behaviour will need to be derived from performance across a number of tests. The Test of Everyday Attention, developed by Robertson, Ward, Ridgeway, and Nimmo-Smith (1994) may be particularly useful, as it has been shown to be sensitive to a range of attentional difficulties in TBI individuals.

Van Zomeren and Brouwer (1994) have presented a detailed review of studies of aspects of attention following TBI, many of which they have conducted. The reader is referred to this text. They concluded that the most conspicuous phenomenon was "a nonspecific slowing of perceptual–motor and cognitive processes, approximately equal to task difficulty" (van Zomeren & Brouwer, 1994, p. 93). Results of a study by Tromp and Mulder (1991) suggested that task novelty had a crucial influence on speed of information processing, less familiar tasks being performed more slowly by TBI individuals. They hypothesised that an important causal mechanism was a problem in the activation of information stored in memory.

According to the findings of Ponsford and Kinsella (1992), a number of tests of speed of information processing may differentiate between TBI individuals and controls. These include the WAIS-R Digit Symbol subtest, the oral and written versions of the Symbol Digit Modalities Test (Smith, 1973), choice reaction time (van Zomeren, 1981) and the Paced Auditory Serial Addition Test (Gronwall & Sampson, 1974). Ponsford and Kinsella (1992) found the Symbol Digit Modalities Test to be the best of these measures in differentiating TBI subjects from controls.

From the review of van Zomeren and Brouwer (1994) it appears that there is little empirical evidence of deficits of focused, divided or sustained attention following TBI. In the experimental situation, TBI individuals appear to be able to ignore irrelevant stimuli that provoke conflicting responses as well as controls (Ponsford & Kinsella, 1992; Stuss et al., 1985). Distraction effects evident on a reaction time task conducted by van Zomeren and Brouwer (1987) appeared to be proportional to the additional time required to process the distracting stimuli. Van Zomeren and Brouwer (1994) concluded that performance on divided attention tasks was affected only by reduced processing speed, and that there were no specific impairments of the ability to divide and shift attention. There is no evidence of a greater decline in performance over time on vigilance tasks in severe TBI subjects compared to controls, although the TBI subjects do respond more slowly overall (Brouwer & von Wolffelaar, 1985; Ponsford & Kinsella, 1992).

Experimental studies have also failed to demonstrate impairment of the ability to allocate attentional resources in a goal-directed fashion. Ponsford and Kinsella (1992) used the Tower of London task as a measure of this ability. They found that severe TBI subjects performed more slowly than controls, but did not make significantly more errors.

This is not to say, however, that these tests may not be sensitive to deficits in individual cases. Summarised scores, in the form of group data, may be affected by heterogeneity across TBI individuals. Trexler and Zappala (1988) found significant differences in attentional functioning when TBI subjects were classified into different clinicopathological groups. Stuss and his colleagues have suggested that there may also be a need to focus more on variability in performance within tasks (Stuss et al., 1989). Test scores may not reveal qualitative aspects of performance, which enhance the clinician's understanding of attentional problems in the individual case. There is clearly a need for further work in the development of more sensitive tests of aspects of attention. As Ponsford and Kinsella (1992) concluded, it seems that some attentional problems may only be manifested in more complex settings and over longer periods of time than exist in the structured assessment situation. Recent work by Whyte and his colleagues has added support to this contention (Whyte, Polansky, Cavallucci, Fleming, & Coslett, submitted). They have demonstrated behavioural evidence of increased distractibility in TBI subjects relative to controls whilst performing a range of tasks (e.g. shape-sorting, jig-saw) over a 45-minute period.

Memory assessment

Ongoing learning and memory difficulties, evidenced once the individual has emerged from PTA, are commonly observed following TBI. These have been described in detail by a number of authors, and the reader is referred to those sources for a detailed discussion of research in this area (e.g. Baddeley et al., 1987; Brooks, 1984a; Richardson, 1990). As outlined in Chapter 1, the specific nature of the problems will vary between individuals, and over time within the same individual. Information on the person's ability to learn and remember is vital for planning rehabilitation programmes, so it is important that this area be thoroughly assessed and monitored.

Where the TBI person has suffered temporal lobe damage, the memory disturbance may be characterised by difficulty storing or consolidating new information. Depending on the site of injury, this may take the form of a general amnesic syndrome, or, if there is greater injury in one hemisphere, it may be worse for one class of material (i.e. verbal or non-verbal) than another.

More typically, the head-injured person's learning of all new material (both verbal and non-verbal) is slower and imperfect (Brooks, 1984a, Walsh, 1991). Walsh (1991) has suggested that this learning deficit may be due to the person's difficulty in adequately monitoring performance, detecting errors, and using this error information to modify (i.e. improve) subsequent responses. Those with frontal lobe impairment following TBI are also less likely to take an active approach to organising and structuring the material to be learnt. Questioning of the person on completion of a task often reveals an absence of strategies or an unsystematic approach to the learning task. These memory deficits may be seen as secondary to the dysexecutive syndrome described below.

The TBI individual with such a memory problem will commonly perform better when recall is tested via recognition as compared to free recall (Shimamura, Janowsky, & Squire, 1991). This suggests that more is stored in memory than can be spontaneously retrieved on demand. Memory for the temporal order of events may also be disturbed. In this case the person may be able to remember the individual item, but be unable to accurately state when it occurred, suggesting that the contextual information surrounding that item is lost or unavailable (Shimamura et al., 1991).

The clinician must also examine aspects of attention when making an assessment of memory function. Slow information processing, reduced selective attention, fatigue and other attentional difficulties may contribute significantly to poor performances on memory tasks.

Neuropsychological assessment of memory function should encompass the following areas:

- Ability to recall past events; information, both biographical and general knowledge; and skills.
- Ability to acquire and recall new information that is of varying complexity and nature, i.e. verbal/non-verbal, declarative/procedural, discrete or lengthy information, presented over one trial or a series of trials.
- Ability to recall material following varying periods of delay, with and without interference, using free recall and recognition.
- Subjective accounts as to the approach used to acquire material.

There are many standardised memory tests available. These include the Wechsler Memory Scale-Revised (Wechsler, 1987), the Selective Reminding Test (Buschke & Fuld, 1974), the Rey Auditory–Verbal Learning Test (Rey, 1964), the Rey–Osterrieth Complex Figure (Osterrieth, 1944; Rey, 1959), the RANDT (Randt & Brown, 1983) and the California Verbal Learning Test (Delis, Kramer, Kaplan, & Ober, 1987). The clinician's choice should be determined by the questions being asked, the complexity of the task relative to the injured person's level of functioning and the clinician's experience with the instrument. Miller and Berenguer (1994) have pointed out that the Wechsler Memory Scale-Revised has no normative data for the age groups 18–19 and 25–34 years, in which TBI is heavily represented.

Executive functions

Executive functions are defined as those cognitive abilities that encompass the generation, selection, planning and regulation of responses that are goal-directed and adaptive, given the demands placed on the individual. According to Lezak (1983, p.38), who first coined the term, executive functions "enable a person to engage in independent, purposive, self-serving behaviour successfully." As outlined in Chapter 1, executive functions are thought to be largely dependent on the integrity of the prefrontal regions of the brain and are therefore commonly impaired following TBI.

Executive deficits include "impaired initiative and planning, inability to make structure with attendant structure dependence, and inability to carry out complex plans or complex activities" (Lezak, 1982, p.53), problem-solving difficulties (McCarthy & Warrington 1990), reduced regulation of responses (Luria, 1973), lack of initiative (Stuss & Benson, 1986) and difficulty making decisions (Shallice & Burgess, 1991). Baddeley (1986) refers to this collection of cognitive disorders as the dysexecutive syndrome. Fryer and Haffey (1987) identified "planning" and "self-initiation" as the abilities which were most strongly associated with continuing psychosocial disability in a group of severe TBI subjects.

For the TBI individual executive difficulties are frequently pervasive, but variable, as their manifestation is influenced by factors related to the individual, the injury and the task being performed. The structure inherent in the task, the novelty of the task and the presence or absence of contextual cues, as well as the intelligence and level of motivation of the injured individual, will interact to influence the level of competence displayed at any point in time. These factors need to be borne in mind when conducting the neuropsychological assessment of executive function. Subtle variations in cognitive demands may lead to variations in performance that are difficult to account for if the examiner relies solely on test scores.

Neuropsychological assessment of executive functions should include tests where the material and problems posed are novel to the individual. Additionally, varying levels of task complexity should be administered, and the person's performance interpreted in the light of the degree of complexity they were capable of managing premorbidly. Tests should incorporate components demanding planning, problem solving, abstract thinking, idea generation, and response control, including the ability to inhibit well-learned stereotyped responses. Qualitative observations of the individual's level of initiative, self-monitoring, error detection and utilisation, and perseverance should be integrated with quantitative information.

Tests which may be sensitive to executive dysfunction include the WAIS-R Similarities, Picture Arrangement, and Block Design subtests (Wechsler, 1981); the Porteus Maze Test (Porteus, 1965); the Austin Maze (Walsh, 1991), tests of discursive problem-solving, such as Luria's arithmetical problems (Christensen, 1984); the Tower of London Task (Shallice, 1982); the Wisconsin Card Sorting Test (Milner, 1963); the Stroop Color Word Naming Test (Stroop, 1935); Reitan's Trail Making Test Part B (Reitan & Wolfson, 1985); and the Controlled Word Association Test (Benton & Hamsher, 1989). It must be stressed, however, that these tests are multifactorial in nature, performance also being affected by other cognitive deficits. For example, performance on the Block Design subtest will be affected by visuoconstructional difficulties, and on the Austin Maze, by visuospatial and non-verbal learning problems. Furthermore, these tests may fail to elicit executive problems, which are nevertheless apparent in the performance of daily activities (Damasio, 1985). Indeed, as mentioned earlier in the discussion of attentional assessment, some group studies have failed to differentiate the performance of severe TBI subjects from that of controls on the Tower of London Task and aspects of the Stroop (Ponsford & Kinsella, 1992).

The role of neuropsychological assessment in the rehabilitation process

Neuropsychological assessment provides a means of measuring, relatively objectively, the injured person's cognitive impairments. Reassessment at intervals allows for objective measurement of recovery. Results of impairment assessment can help to tease out the underlying nature of the injured person's difficulties in everyday activities. Through the identification of specific strengths, as well as weaknesses, assessment results may be used to assist in the formulation of appropriate management strategies (Morse & Morse, 1988). They may also provide valuable clues as to the aetiology of difficulties, which, in turn, influences treatment. For example, the management of a memory problem related to depression is likely to differ from that of an organically based memory difficulty.

However, as already mentioned, neuropsychological tests may fail to capture more complex disturbances, particularly those underlying problems with attention, executive function and social behaviours (Prigatano, 1991). Moreover, some tasks which are initially sensitive to impairments of, for example, executive function, lose their novelty, and hence their sensitivity, as the person is tested repeatedly over time. This frequently happens through the lengthy course of rehabilitation, and possibly also with repeated assessments for legal proceedings (Maddocks & Sloan, 1993). Another very important issue is that of the power of neuropsychological assessment to predict the nature of disability and handicap. Although many of the cognitive functions tapped by the tests are also required to perform everyday tasks, neuropsychological tests clearly do not sample the full range of skills related to everyday living.

Relationship between neuropsychological impairment and disability

Ecological validity is a term frequently used in the rehabilitation literature which, according to Tupper and Cicerone, "is concerned with assessing the relationship between test performances and the ability to function in the real world" (1990, p.6). There have been many studies examining the ecological validity of neuropsychological tests (e.g. Acker,

1986; Acker & Davis, 1989; Searight, Dunn, Grisso, Margolis, & Gibbons, 1989; Klonoff et al., 1986a; Tabbador, Mattis, & Zazula, 1983). A comprehensive review of these studies is available in Acker (1986, 1990). Findings have been mixed. Most researchers have reported global, modest relationships between test results and gross functional measures. That is, lower test scores tend to be associated with poorer functional outcome (e.g. Acker, 1986; Acker & Davis, 1989; Searight et al., 1989). However, it is clear that prediction from test scores regarding performance in specific daily activities is less certain (Acker, 1986; Searight et al, 1989). For example, Acker (1986) found that psychology test scores at six months post-injury were significantly correlated with scores on the Rappaport Disability Rating Scale at one year, and Social Status Outcome at two years post-injury. However, correlations of test scores with occupational therapists' ratings of community skills at one year post-injury were not significant. Such findings have led some authors to caution that the functional relevance of test scores is tenuous, particularly in the TBI population, where problems are typically more pronounced in demanding real-life environments than they are in the structured test situation (Hart & Hayden, 1986).

An understanding of the individual's disability clearly requires more than the identification of the neuropsychological deficits (Hart & Hayden, 1986; Heaton & Pendleton, 1981; Naugle & Chelune, 1990). As pointed out by Heaton and Pendleton, no two brain-injured people are exactly alike. They differ not only in their patterns of impairments and strengths, but also in the requirements of their daily lives, the environment in which they live, their past experiences, and other factors, such as the degree of family and financial support available. It is important to understand the interplay between these individual or environmental factors and neuropsychological deficits, including identifying the circumstances in which a deficit is likely to appear, and how various environmental factors define the way specific deficits interact (Naugle & Chelune, 1990). Neuropsychological tests do not sample the full range and combination of behaviours involved in independent living. Predictions are also likely to be limited by a lack of understanding of the nature of everyday tasks and the environments in which they are performed.

A number of researchers have attempted to address the limitations of current impairment assessments by devising simulated functional tests. Like neuropsychological measures, the construction and administration of the simulated functional test is psychometrically sound, but the test items and materials are modelled on everyday demands. Some examples of simulated functional assessment batteries include the Rivermead Behavioural Memory Test (Wilson, Cockburn, &

Baddeley, 1985), the Behavioural Inattention Test (Wilson, Cockburn & Halligan, 1987), the Test of Everyday Attention (Robertson et al., 1994), the Bay Area Functional Performance Evaluation (Bloomer & Williams, 1979; Houston, Williams, Bloomer, & Mann, 1989), the Allen Cognitive Level Test (Allen, 1985) and the Allen Cognitive Level Test-Problem Solving version (Josman & Katz, 1991), the Everyday Memory Interview (West, 1985, cited in Little, Williams, & Long, 1986), computerised tests designed to simulate everyday memory performance (Crook & Larrabee, 1992; Youngjohn, Larrabee, & Crook, 1991), the Six Element Test and the Multiple Errands Test (Shallice & Burgess, 1991).

These tests and test batteries have greater face validity than conventional neuropsychological tests, and they offer standardised procedures not available when directly observing individuals performing everyday activities. Some are more sensitive to impairments that are difficult to demonstrate on traditional tests (e.g. Shallice & Burgess, 1991). By virtue of their greater similarity to everyday tasks, they are likely to be more accurate predictors of functional performance. Wilson (1993) reported significant correlations of performances on the Rivermead Behavioural Memory Test and the Behavioural Inattention Test both with neuropsychological measures and with therapists ratings of everyday functioning.

However, these measures retain properties of standard neuropsychological assessment which are not present in natural settings. The tests are, by and large, still administered in a quiet, one-to-one, structured settings over a limited time frame, and performance is initiated by the examiner. By virtue of their standardised nature, these tests cannot be adapted to account for the requirements of the individual's daily life, past experiences, motivation, etc. So although simulated functional tests represent an important and essential move towards improving the ecological validity of neuropsychological impairment assessments, they cannot replace the need for direct assessment of the injured person's performance of everyday activities.

ASSESSMENT OF DISABILITY

Disability is defined as "any restriction or lack (resulting from an impairment) of ability to perform an activity in the manner or within the range considered normal for a human being" (WHO, 1980, p.28). Disability is concerned with "compound or integrated activities expected of the person or of the body as a whole, such as are represented by tasks, skills or behaviours" (p.28). Assessment of disability involves the identification of the individual's functional strengths and limitations in activities of everyday life, both as they present initially, and as they change following time and intervention.

Use of behaviour rating scales and checklists

One method of assessing the nature of everyday cognitive difficulties is the use of behaviour rating scales or checklists. These may be completed by therapists observing the injured person's behaviour in the therapy setting (e.g. Ponsford & Kinsella, 1991; Wilson, 1984). However, there are relatively few such scales which have been properly validated. The findings of Ponsford and Kinsella (1991) suggest that although good correlations may be found between such assessments and neuropsychological test results, correlations between ratings made by different raters in different contexts may be much lower. This points to the potential influence of context and the frame of reference of the rater, which may reduce the reliability of these ratings.

Alternatively, ratings may be obtained from TBI individuals themselves or their relatives using questionnaires such as the Memory Failures Questionnaire developed by Sunderland, Harris, and Baddeley (1983). Unfortunately, a number of studies have found the reliability of self-assessments on scales such as this to be extremely limited (Bennett-Levy & Powell, 1980; Sunderland et al., 1983; Sunderland, Harris, & Gleave, 1984). Sunderland et al. (1984) assessed the ratings of relatives as more reliable than those of the patients themselves, but Heaton and Pendleton (1981) have suggested that the ratings of family members and others may be influenced by emotional factors, or by the degree of opportunity to observe relevant behaviours. A great deal of further work is required to evaluate the use of these assessments. There is no doubt that self-report is important in evaluating problems from the injured person's point of view. However, there is also a significant need for direct behavioural observation of performance of everyday activities.

Assessment of activities of daily living (ADL)

A distinction is commonly drawn between performance of routine self-care activities such as bathing, dressing, eating, and toileting (ADL), and those tasks that are more complex. The latter are referred to as instrumental activities of daily living (IADL) and include domestic tasks such as cooking, laundry and cleaning, as well as shopping and financial management (Law, 1993). There have been many scales developed to assess activities of daily living, some of which are standardised. Therapists supplement or replace the use of standardised measures with observations of the person performing daily tasks. In the following sections, studies that have examined disability in ADL and IADL in traumatically brain-injured individuals will be discussed. Limitations of the current assessment tools will be outlined and alternative approaches proposed.

Activities of daily living

Some of the more commonly used measures of self-care ADL, for which information on reliability and validity is available, include the Barthel Index (Mahoney & Barthel, 1965), the Index of ADL (Katz, Ford, Moskowitz, Jackson, & Jaffe, 1963), The Kenny Self-Care Evaluation (Schoening, Anderegg, Bergstrom, Fonda, Steinke, & Ulrich, 1965), the Klein–Bell ADL Scale (Klein & Bell, 1982), PULSES Profile (Granger, Albrecht, & Hamilton, 1979) and the Functional Independence Measure (Granger & Hamilton, 1987). However, there have been few studies employing assessments such as these to document self-care ability in TBI individuals.

Nevertheless, it is clear from a number of follow up studies that most TBI individuals do not demonstrate long-term difficulties with personal care tasks. Panikoff (1983) reported that, by 12 months post-injury, 90% of a group of 78 TBI subjects were independent in feeding, bed mobility, and grooming, and 80% were independent in dressing. Where ongoing disability was present, it was classified as mild and restricted to subjects with a coma length of greater than 14 days. Jacobs (1988), Brown and Nell (1992) and Ponsford et al. (1995a) had similar findings. Where difficulties with ADL are identified, they tend to occur in those who are more severely injured, and who have significant physical impairments, suggesting that dependence is not primarily due to cognitive deficits (Jacobs, 1988; Tuel, Presty, Meythaler, Heinemann, & Katz, 1992; Warnock et al., 1992). These findings are not surprising, as basic activities of daily living are typically well-learned and performed within familiar environments studded with contextual cues. These factors may mitigate against the effects of residual executive impairments.

For those individuals who experience long-term difficulties with self-care activities due to cognitive–behavioural impairments, common problems include lack of initiative or poor attention to detail in personal care, resulting in failure to shower regularly, clean the teeth or brush the hair. Such individuals may require verbal cues or encouragement from a spouse in order to satisfactorily complete self-care tasks. Otherwise they may present as unkempt. Conversely, changes in personality, such as rigidity or obsessive attention to detail, may lead to the individual spending an excessive amount of time over personal care. Although such a person will present as well-groomed, the time spent in the activity may disrupt the normal family routine. Poor self-regulation of behaviour, manifested as impulsivity, may compromise safety in tasks, such as regulating water temperature or using appropriate transfer techniques to compensate for physical disabilities. Difficulty making decisions may be apparent in clothing selections that fail to take account of the weather or activities to be undertaken during the day. These functional difficulties will necessitate a higher level of assistance from the spouse/carer than would be predicted on the basis of physical limitations alone.

The unfamiliarity of the hospital setting may add to the TBI person's difficulties in performing personal tasks. Toiletries and towel will be located in unusual places, and the bathroom layout may be unfamiliar. This may result in the level of independence in the familiar home environment being underestimated. On the other hand, the strict daily routine and degree of supervision and prompting available in a structured hospital environment may facilitate performance. On return home, when these cues are no longer available, performance may decline. It is important, therefore, to document not only performance of the ADL task itself, but also cues that facilitate performance, and the extent to which novel demands compromise independence. Observations must be made in the home, as well as the hospital setting.

Instrumental activities of daily living
Measures available to assess performance of more complex daily activities (IADL) within the domains of domestic and community function include the Frenchay Activities Index (Holbrook & Skilbeck, 1983; Wade, Legh-Smith, & Hewer, 1985), the Comprehensive Evaluation of Basic Living Skills (Casanova and Ferber, 1976), the Functional Life Scale (Sarno, Sarno, & Levita, 1973), the Canadian Occupational Performance Measure (Department of National Health & Welfare and Canadian Association of Occupational Therapists, 1983, cited in Law, Baptiste, McColl, Opzoomer, Polatajko, & Pollock, 1990), and the Intellectual Housework Assessment (Soderback, 1988). However, there have been no controlled studies reported to date which have used standardised assessments to document TBI individuals' performance of instrumental activities of daily living.

Clinical experience and evidence from follow-up studies indicate that people who have suffered TBI experience a much greater level of ongoing disability in more complex daily activities than is evident in self-care tasks (Brown & Nell, 1992; Jacobs, 1988; McNeny, 1990; Panikoff, 1983; Ponsford et al., 1995a). It tends to be the ongoing cognitive and behavioural impairments, rather than physical limitations, which underlie these problems. Jacobs (1988) found that only 63% of his sample were independent in higher order tasks such as shopping, caring for personal health and safety and money management. Jacobs reported on levels of ability hierarchically within each skill area, ranging from basic processes, such as understanding of money, through to more complex ones, such as budgeting. Levels of dependency were greatest for the more complex tasks.

There have been no group studies reporting in detail on the specific nature of difficulties experienced in these activities of daily living. However, in a series of case reports focusing on executive dysfunction, Shallice and Burgess (1991) described the difficulties experienced by three individuals who had sustained TBI. These included untidiness, failure to initiate personal care or domestic activities, failure to purchase all the items on a shopping list, impulse buying, and failure to organise social events or plan spare time activities.

Limitations of current measures of ADL

There is increasing recognition that the scales currently available to assess performance of IADL have serious limitations (Christiansen, 1993; Law, 1993), As a consequence therapists appear to be reluctant to use them in daily practice, tending to use unstandardised assessments combining tests and daily activities. ADL scales are not generally based on a conceptual framework that is appropriate to the specific needs of the individual who has sustained TBI. Most instruments have been validated on populations of stroke patients and are heavily weighted towards assessment of physical aspects of basic self-care activities. This is not typically an area of long-term difficulty for people with TBI (e.g. Jennett, Snoek, Bond, & Brooks, 1981; Brooks et al., 1987a). This renders the scales relatively insensitive to the problems TBI individuals experience. Validity is further compromised by the fact that IADL instruments, in particular, are neither comprehensive nor client-focused. Rather, they sample a small range of preselected tasks, which may or may not be relevant to the specific life roles of a given individual. As Law (1993) has argued, the assessment process should be tailored to the daily living skills identified by the client as relevant.

Standardised ADL assessments usually focus on individual tasks performed in the hospital environment in isolation from normal routines and settings. The imposition of structure and simplification of demands also inherent in these assessments may render them insensitive to the executive deficits associated with TBI. These factors are likely to elicit individuals' best performances, and may not reflect their capacity to perform the same tasks in their own home or local community. Consistency of performance over an extended period of time is another aspect not covered. Fluctuations in initiative, mood, motivation, fatigue and concentration, commonly associated with TBI, may lead to variations in the level of assistance required in daily activities. Such variables need to be isolated through systematic and structured observations in both hospital and home settings.

A further problem with current scales is the insensitivity of ratings. Ratings generally encompass between three and five points, reflecting "levels of independence". These judgements are essentially based on the type of assistance required to perform the task, that is, individuals are rated as more independent if they require only the use of an adaptive device, less independent if they require supervision, and less independent again if they require physical help from another person. Such categories do not necessarily enable therapists to measure the effectiveness of interventions, since quite small but possibly significant improvements in function may not be reflected in ratings. Additionally, such ratings do not accurately reflect the actual nature and degree of assistance required in an individual case. The category of "supervision" can encompass a broad range of interventions, from support and encouragement to begin a task, through to step-by-step cueing throughout the activity. Overall, these are serious limitations, which point to a need to refine and extend these measures to ensure they are more relevant to the TBI individual.

The absence of an accepted scale to measure daily living skills has resulted in a lack of information on the levels and nature of the disability experienced by TBI individuals. It has posed problems for researchers attempting to monitor recovery and evaluate the effectiveness of interventions. The majority of follow-up studies have used either neuro-psychological measures or subjective reports. Review of the rehabilitation literature highlights the bias of outcome studies towards impairment assessment. As already noted, neuropsychological measures sometimes lack sensitivity to the cognitive difficulties associated with TBI (Shallice & Burgess, 1991). This potentially results in under-estimation of the actual level of disability. In order to evaluate the effectiveness of rehabilitation, functional skills need to be measured directly, rather than inferred from performance on neuropsychological tests.

Guidelines for the assessment of disability

For the purposes of programme evaluation and research it is important for clinicians to utilise an existing, standardised measure of disability, despite the limitations discussed. For the purposes of treatment planning, however, a more detailed and accurate understanding of the specific nature of the injured person's difficulties and strengths in daily tasks is required. Therefore, standardised scores need to be supplemented with systematic and structured behavioural observations. The outcome of assessment of disability should be a knowledge of injured individuals' ability to perform the full range of functional activities necessary in their daily life. It is vital that this information is supplemented by a knowledge of the "means" by which these "ends" are achieved, that is, the skills and strategies used by the person to facilitate performance. Furthermore, a knowledge of the skills the person lacks, and the level and nature of the input required to complete the task must be obtained. This information, combined with the results of neuropsychological assessment of impairment and an understanding of handicap, will form a basis for treatment planning, and serve as a baseline for the purposes of evaluating its effectiveness.

Assessment of disability should commence with semi-structured interviews of the injured person and relevant family members, preferably conducted in the home. Information needs to be obtained regarding the lifestyle and specific activities performed by the injured individual in the daily routine in the home and the community prior to injury. The level of skill, methods of carrying out activities, and strategies used to facilitate performance, as well as the nature of any assistance required before injury must be ascertained. This information should be interpreted within the context of a knowledge of the roles and responsibilities of the individual within the household. It is against this background of what was "normal" and "achievable" for the person premorbidly, that current performance will be evaluated.

Both a family member and the injured individual should be questioned about the activities the person currently performs (i.e. since the injury) in hospital, at home and/or in the community. Areas where assistance is given may be identified through subjective reports and compared with patterns of premorbid behaviour. It is also important to identify the nature and degree of ongoing support and assistance that is likely to be available.

The specific tasks of daily living assessed by the therapist will depend on what was relevant to the individual before and since the injury. For example, an adolescent living within a family unit may never have been required to engage in laundry or cooking activities, or house and garden maintenance, and may not in the foreseeable future. These activities are better assessed at the time they are needed. The person may, however, have been a student. So, the activities involved in this role will need to be comprehensively assessed.

The tasks for assessment may include those listed below, although this list is by no means exhaustive. Whilst they are very important activities of daily living, assessment of skills related to driving, work and study have not been included in this list. They are discussed in detail in Chapter 7 (return to work, tertiary study, and driving) and Chapter 10 (return to school).

Assessment of activities of daily living

- Showering/bathing, including washing and drying self and hair.
- Dressing, including selecting, taking off, and putting on clothing, shoes, and accessories.
- Grooming, including cleaning teeth, shaving, applying make-up, and nail care.
- Toileting.
- Mobility and transfers, including walking inside and out, using stairs, elevators, etc., transferring from one position to another.

Assessment of instrumental activities of daily living

Daily organisation of activities

- Getting up at the appropriate time in the morning (state method, e.g. alarm clock).
- Taking all necessary items when leaving the house (e.g. money, keys).
- Ensuring windows and doors are secured, and turning on/off relevant appliances as appropriate.
- Leaving and arriving punctually.
- Using a diary or other system (specify) to organise daily, weekly, monthly activities.
- Completing scheduled activities for the day.
- Keeping appointments.
- Rescheduling timetable to deal with unexpected events or demands.

Domestic activities

- Cooking, including preparation of breakfast, lunch, dinner, and snacks (hot and cold).
- Mealtime activities, including setting/clearing of table, feeding self and taking medication.
- Housekeeping, including daily (light) household tasks such as washing dishes, making beds, as well as weekly (heavy) household tasks, such as changing bed linen, vacuuming.

- Laundry, including sorting, washing, drying, folding and putting away clothes.

- Home maintenance, including carrying out repairs, changing light bulbs and fuses.

- Garden maintenance, including mowing grass, weeding, planting and pruning.

- Car maintenance, including maintaining car with petrol, water and oil, as well as carrying out repairs.

Child-care activities

- Activities within the home, including cleaning and organisation of children's clothes, feeding, bathing and dressing, changing nappies, structuring a safe, healthy, and stimulating environment, discipline, organising to leave the house, assisting in school-related tasks, etc.

- Activities outside the home, including transport to and from activities such as school, outings, sports, visiting friends, communication with people relevant to child (e.g. teachers, other parents) and shopping with children.

Community activities

- Transport, including using private and public forms of transport, road safety, and use of maps and timetables.

- Shopping for household needs and services, both locally and at large shopping complexes.

- Financial management, including managing money in the community (e.g. recognising coins/notes, checking change, taking care with cash), utilising bank account(s), paying bills, budgeting for daily/weekly/long-term financial needs.

- Use of community resources, including awareness and access of local resources such as library, local government facilities, community groups.

Communication and social interaction

- Reading for leisure (e.g. books, magazines, newspapers), and for community access (e.g. signs). Writing (e.g. signs name, deals with correspondence, fills out forms).

- Telephoning, including answering the telephone, taking and passing on messages, using the telephone for social contact and community-related needs, using telephone book/teledex.

- Social interaction, including face-to-face interaction with support staff, family, friends, acquaintances.

- Recreation and leisure activities (e.g. sport, hobbies, entertainment).

Recording qualitative observations

It is vital to conduct this evaluation within the home or other environment in which the task is normally performed. Identification of the components of the specific tasks selected for assessment can be undertaken using the process of activity analysis (e.g. Pedretti, 1985). The ability of the TBI individual to perform each of these components should be assessed. The therapist should observe the individual's performance on the task from the point of view of skill competency, rather than identification of impairments. It is usually extremely difficult to make accurate interpretations of underlying impairments, particularly on the basis of observations of the person performing multifaceted functional tasks. Responses should be recorded in terms of behavioural observations, rather than interpretations of underlying problems. For example, "John commenced dressing after a verbal prompt", rather than "John lacks initiative". This method of assessment is very similar to that recommended for behaviour problems outlined in Chapter 8.

The assessment should be extended to ascertain whether the TBI individual is reliably able to demonstrate the same level of task competence in the context of a normal daily routine, as when tasks are performed individually. For example, personal care should be evaluated, not only as a series of separate skills, such as putting on clothing, but also as a routine, beginning with getting up in the morning, showering, etc., and finishing with tidying up. Frequently the difficulty experienced by the injured person does not relate to performance of the individual task, but to the scheduling of multiple tasks within functional constraints, such as time factors (Mayer, Keating, & Rapp, 1986).

Observations of behaviour may be structured and recorded under the following headings, allowing for premorbid abilities and requirements:

Timing

- Able to get started on the task.

- Allows enough time to complete task.

- Performs task at an appropriate speed.

- Schedules different elements of the task sequentially or simultaneously as required.

- Stays focused on the task.

- Gets going on the task at the appropriate time within the context of an ongoing behavioural routine.

- Consistently demonstrates an adequate level of competence day-in, day-out despite fluctuations in mood, stress, and fatigue.

Preparation

- Makes appropriate choices when selecting the activity or the content of it.

- Considers all relevant information in making choices.

- Obtains all relevant equipment and materials.

- Organises the work area.

- Takes and/or gives instructions.

Execution

- Uses equipment, tools and materials appropriately.

- Is aware of safety issues as they arise and takes necessary precautions.

- Detects and corrects mistakes as the activity proceeds.

- Solves problems as they arise.

- Deals with frustration adaptively.

- Seeks help appropriately.

- Completes all relevant aspects of the task.

- Uses strategies, methods and systems that allow the task to be performed with greater efficiency.

Completion

- Realistically appraises performance.

- Cleans the work space.

- Monitors (e.g. waits for something to cook, set, dry, and comes back to the task and finishes off).
- Follows up (e.g. putting an ingredient on a shopping list).
- Reports back or goes on with the next activity.

The therapist should also seek to identify those contextual factors within the injured person, the environment or the therapist/carer that cause variations in performance from one task or setting to another. The following are examples of the variables which should be carefully considered when assessing disability.

Environment

- Quiet or distracting.
- Contextual cues to prompt performance.
- Presence of others.
- Time of day task is performed.
- Weather.

Person

- Motivation and interest in activity (e.g. whether person perceives the task as relevant to their specific goals).
- Premorbid skill level, influencing familiarity with task.
- Level of anxiety, depression, etc.
- Level of insight, which will interact with motivation and interest.
- Level of fatigue and stress.

Therapist/Carer

- Assistance provided by therapist/carer (e.g. physical, verbal).
- Relationship with injured person (including level of trust).
- Approach to injured person (e.g. encouraging, condescending).

Obtaining quantitative information

Qualitative observations should be supplemented with quantitative information that forms a component of the baseline record of performance. This may include the following:

- Time taken to complete task, or components of it.
- Number of errors made.
- Number of times specific prompts were given (verbal, written, physical).
- Number of steps initiated by the injured person (identified by task analysis).

This assessment provides much necessary detail from which to gain an understanding of the injured person's difficulties, as a basis for planning treatment. There are, however, a number of limitations inherent in this form of behavioural assessment. Due to its subjectivity, it is intrinsically less reliable, potentially affecting the accuracy of assessments from one reporter or therapist to another, and reassessments. In this respect, the use of quantitative observations becomes extremely important. Due to the individualised nature of such an assessment, it is difficult to make comparisons across individuals and thereby establish patterns of disability. The authors are currently attempting to establish the validity and reliability of this form of assessment, particularly as it relates to the assessment of executive difficulties. There is also a need for studies examining the relationship between this form of assessment and measures of impairment and handicap.

HANDICAP FOLLOWING TBI

Handicap is defined as "a disadvantage for a given individual, resulting from an impairment or a disability, that limits or prevents the fulfilment of a role that is normal (depending on age, sex, and social and cultural factors) for that individual" (WHO, p.29). What distinguishes a handicap from a disability is that the person or his peers attaches value to the departure from the performance norm. Individuals are handicapped relative to others within their own cultural/social context. Handicap is thus "a social phenomenon" (p.28). The consequences of handicap are that "the individual will be unable to sustain the roles to which he is accustomed or to attain those to which he might otherwise aspire" (p.41).

There is frequent confusion between the concepts of disability and handicap. There is a tendency to presume or predict handicap based on an assessment of the nature and degree of impairment or disability. However, as suggested by the WHO, there is not a simple linear relationship between disease, impairment, disability or handicap. The same level of disability in two different individuals can result in markedly different levels of handicap, depending on the demands upon, and supports available to, that individual. Handicap needs to be assessed as a phenomenon in its own right. As Haffey and Johnston (1990) have pointed out, as a consequence of a failure to consider handicap, many rehabilitation professionals do not fully understand how TBI individuals are actually disadvantaged in their social context. This results in many well-intentioned rehabilitation efforts having a minimal long-term impact.

Judgements relating to all three concepts of impairment, disability, and handicap depend on deviations from norms. Normal may relate to a statistical concept of "average", with current performance measured against these standards. More acceptable in neuropsychological practice is the comparison with what was "normal" for the individual premorbidly. This is achieved by obtaining an estimate of premorbid ability and measuring current performance against this prediction. Normative views regarding handicap are determined, either by reference to some "ideal", or to the individual's or society's perceptions as to the degree of disadvantage resulting from the injured person's disabilities and/or impairments. Assessment of handicap may vary according to the viewpoint from which the disadvantage is perceived, namely, that of the individual, those close to the individual or the community. As the WHO point out, such assessments are difficult to categorise in a reproducible way. Clearly, the establishment of appropriate criteria against which to judge performance in order to assess handicap presents a complex and difficult challenge. As a consequence, handicap has historically been very poorly measured.

Assessment of handicap
The handicap classification provided by the World Health Organization supplies a framework for studying disadvantage directly. The WHO (1980) classification of handicaps is a classification of circumstances in which the people with disabilities are likely to find themselves, and which, in relation to society's expectations, place that person at a disadvantage relative to peers. Six major survival roles are listed. They include:

- *Orientation*—the ability to "orient himself in regard to his surroundings, and to respond to these inputs" (p.38) This disadvantage is classified as an Orientation Handicap.
- *Physical Independence*—the ability to "maintain an effective independent existence in regard to the more immediate needs of his body, including feeding and personal hygiene" (p.38). This disadvantage is classified as a Physical Independence Handicap.

- *Mobility*—the ability to "move around effectively in his environment" (p.39). This disadvantage is classified as a Mobility Handicap.
- *Occupation*—the ability to "occupy time in a fashion customary to his sex, age, and culture, including following an occupation (such as tilling the soil, running a household, or bringing up children) or carrying out physical activities such as play and recreation" (p.39). This disadvantage is classified as Occupation Handicap.
- *Social*—the ability to "participate in and maintain social relationships with others" (p.39). This disadvantage results in a Social Integration Handicap.
- *Economic self-sufficiency*—the ability to "sustain socioeconomic activity and independence by virtue of labour or exploitation of material possessions, such as natural resources, livestock or crops" (p.39). This disadvantage results in an Economic Self-Sufficiency Handicap.

Studies of handicap following TBI

There have been no studies focusing on handicap, according to the WHO definition, following TBI. Studies examining outcome following TBI have tended to focus on a range of dimensions, some pertaining to impairment, some to disability and some to handicap. For example, Jacobs (1988) examined the domains of self-care, mobility, cognition, communication, social and adaptive living skills, behaviour and emotional problems, household business and housework, child care, community skills, education, seeking employment, and employment. Brown and Nell (1992) examined recovery in the areas of activities of daily living, employment, family relationships, physical functioning and psychological functioning. From the results of these and other studies, it is reasonable to infer that TBI may result in handicap on all of the WHO dimensions, but that long-term handicap in the domains of orientation, physical independence and mobility are relatively less common than handicap in the domains of occupation, social integration and economic self-sufficiency. However, there is clearly a need to study dimensions of handicap more directly and specifically.

The dimension of handicap which has been most comprehensively studied is that of occupational outcome, largely because it is relatively easy to measure (e.g. Brooks et al., 1987b; Crepeau & Scherzer, 1993; Dikmen et al., 1993; Ezrachi, Ben-Yishay, Kay, Diller, & Rattok, 1991; Ponsford et al., 1995b; Ruff et al., 1993). From the results of these studies it appears that occupational outcome is affected in 50 to 90% of cases. It varies as a function of many factors, including the age of the person injured, injury severity, degree of cognitive impairment, particularly in the areas of attention and executive function, self-awareness, disability in activities of daily living, and behavioural, environmental, and social factors (Crepeau & Scherzer, 1993; Ezrachi et al., 1991; Ponsford et al., 1995b).

Developing a measure of handicap

Whiteneck, Charlifue, Gerhart, Overholser, and Richardson (1992) recently developed the Craig Handicap Assessment and Reporting Technique (CHART) as a means of quantifying the extent of handicap in individuals with spinal cord injury in a community setting. Using the dimensions of handicap identified and described by WHO (1980), but excluding Orientation, items were constructed that identified the degree to which roles were fulfilled. The assessment consists of a series of questions, administered to the injured individual by way of an interview. Physical independence is assessed by the number of hours per day in which care is provided on a paid, unpaid, regular or occasional basis. If the individual takes primary responsibility for instructing or directing caregivers, the hours of care are given a lesser weighting, reflecting the lessened degree of handicap. Mobility is measured by the number of hours per day out of bed, the number of hours per week out of the house, accessibility to the home, nights spent away from home, and independence in managing transportation.

Within the domain of occupation, number of hours spent working, at school, homemaking, maintaining the home, doing volunteer work, pursuing recreation, and other self-improvement activities are recorded. An estimate of the relative value placed by the general population on alternative methods of fulfilling social roles is used to assign weights to the CHART items. In the occupational domain, work, school, homemaking, and home maintenance are given twice the weighting of volunteer work, recreation, and other self-improvement activities. Activities not generally valued by society as productive, such as watching television or sleeping, are not included. Social integration is measured by way of questions pertaining to household composition, romantic involvement, number of relatives, associates or friends with whom contact is maintained, and frequency of initiating conversations with strangers or acquaintances. Economic self-sufficiency is measured by the total household family income from all sources not used for medical care, compared with US governmental poverty scales. Each dimension has a maximum possible score of 100 points, so that the maximum total CHART score is 500 points.

Whiteneck et al. (1992) have established the validity and reliability of the CHART for use with spinal cord injured individuals. The inter-rater reliability between injured raters and a family member or other proxy was good on all dimensions except social integration. On this dimension, the degree of agreement appeared to be a function of how well the proxy knew the subject. With some small modifications, the CHART would appear to be a potentially useful tool for measuring handicap following TBI. Whiteneck and his colleagues are currently conducting a study of the validity of the CHART for use with TBI individuals. One potential difficulty may be in establishing the most reliable source of the information. As with the assessment of disability, the information would probably be most accurately obtained by way of a joint interview with the TBI individual and a family member or attendant carer. The Orientation dimension could be developed for use with TBI individuals.

The Community Integration Questionnaire (CIQ) is an outcome measure of community integration designed to assess role performance in the areas of home/family, social and productive activities in people with acquired brain injuries (Willer, Linn, & Allen, 1993; Willer, Ottenbacher, & Coad, 1994). Willer and his colleagues prefer the term community integration to the potentially pejorative term of handicap, but items relate to the WHO handicap categories of occupation, social and economic self-sufficiency. The questionnaire comprises 15 items administered in an interview format. The scale was designed for the purposes of programme evaluation. Its use within the rehabilitation facility may assist the team to centre their efforts on handicap-related goals. However, the scale does not allow for assessment of premorbid role performance, and does not elicit the detailed information required for planning individualised community integration programmes.

In an attempt to improve the focus of the rehabilitation team on handicap in determining goals for rehabilitation, Davis et al. (1992), from the Rivermead Rehabilitation Centre in Oxford, developed a life roles questionnaire. This has since been redeveloped, and is termed the Life Goals Questionnaire (Fig. 3.1). As opposed to the CHART, which is based on societal norms, this questionnaire is designed to measure handicap from the perspective of the injured individual. It requires the injured person to rate the personal importance of residential and domestic arrangements, ability to manage personal care, leisure, hobbies and interests, work (paid or unpaid), relationship with a partner, family life (e.g. as a parent), contacts with friends, neighbours and acquaintances, religion and financial status. There is a need for further work on the development of such scales, which might also be completed by relatives.

In assessing handicap, rehabilitation team members need to be sensitive to the cultural, societal and peer norms that prevail for the injured individual. The common demographic features of the TBI

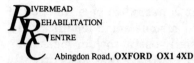

IVERMEAD
EHABILITATION
ENTRE
Abingdon Road, **OXFORD OX1 4XD**

Life Goals Questionnaire

Various aspects of life are given below. I would like you to tell me how important each is to you.
Please rate the importance of each from:

0 = of no importance
1 = of some importance
DATE:_____
2 = of great importance
3 = of extreme importance
COMMENT

My residential and domestic arrangements are:	0 1 2 3	
My ability to manage my personal care is:	0 1 2 3	
My leisure, hobbies and interests are:	0 1 2 3	
My work (paid or unpaid) is:	0 1 2 3	
My relationship with my partner is:	0 1 2 3	
My family life is:	0 1 2 3	
My contacts with friends, neighbours & acquaintances are:	0 1 2 3	
My religion is:	0 1 2 3	
My financial status is:	0 1 2 3	

FIG. 3.1. Rivermead Life Goals Questionnaire. (Reprinted with permission of Rivermead Rehabilitation Centre, Oxford, UK.)

population may mean that these norms are very different from those of the rehabilitation staff. As with disability and impairment, handicap is likely to change over time as a function of recovery, personal development, availability of supports and other environmental factors. The nature of long-term handicap may not be apparent for a significant period after injury. Therefore, assessment of handicap needs to be available over an indefinite time frame.

CASE REPORT—PETER

Peter was a 34-year-old man who had sustained a severe TBI, with coma lasting ten days and PTA of six weeks. He had completed nine years of schooling, and an apprenticeship as an upholsterer. When injured, Peter was single and working in his father's upholstery business. Peter was assessed for medicolegal purposes, in order to determine his care needs, seven years post-injury. By this time he had failed in his attempts to return to work, had married and had a 12-month-old child. Neither he nor his wife were working.

Neuropsychological assessment

On the National Adult Reading Test Peter obtained a predicted premorbid IQ score of 95, consistent with his average educational and occupational background. The following age-scaled scores were obtained on the WAIS-R:

Information	8	Picture completion	9
Digit span	6	Picture arrangement	11
Arithmetic	7	Block design	8
Comprehension	7	Digit symbol	4
Similarities	6		
Prorated verbal IQ scores = 78		Prorated performance IQ score = 87	
Prorated full scale IQ score = 79			

On the Verbal scale, scores were consistently below Peter's predicted level of intelligence. This may have partly reflected premorbid factors, as Peter indicated that his practical skills had always been better than his verbal skills. However, a number of qualitative features suggested the presence of impairments related to the TBI. Many items on the WAIS-R Comprehension and Similarities subtests elicited concrete responses. He was also quite verbose and tangential. A word-finding deficit was apparent. The Controlled Word Association test was performed at the level of the 10th percentile (F-8; A-6; S-6). Peter was very slow to take in information, often requiring questions to be repeated. Basic arithmetic skills were intact. However, with more complex arithmetic problems he typically responded on the basis of one aspect of the problem. He didn't check his answers or recognise errors.

Performance subtests from the WAIS-R revealed similar problems, although some scores were at or close to predicted levels. Slowness was evident, particularly on the Digit Symbol subtest. Problem-solving difficulties were demonstrated on the more difficult items from the Block Design and Picture Arrangement subtests. Overall, Peter was prone to distraction, and frequently made irrelevant comments, especially as he fatigued or lost interest in persevering with tasks. These features suggested underlying impairments of attentional and executive functions.

On the Austin Maze Peter was required to learn a pathway across an electronic stylus maze. He made 20 errors on the first trial, with subsequent error scores of 15, 17, 19, 33, 38, 15, 10, 21, 21, before the test was discontinued. Peter's performance was characterised by rule-breaking and perseverative errors. He demonstrated a dissociation between knowing and doing, with such spontaneous comments as, "I know this is green [correct], but I'll press this one [incorrect]". The Trail-Making Test was performed very slowly, Part A taking 104 seconds (below the 10th percentile) and Part B 293 seconds (below the 10th percentile) to complete. On Part B, Peter also had difficulty in switching flexibly between numbers and letters, making four errors.

Peter's learning and memory abilities were severely impaired, as reflected in his WMS Memory Quotient of 67. It was clear that attentional problems contributed to his memory difficulty, as he missed a significant amount of detail on initial presentation. There was also a failure to organise material and apply strategies to enhance learning. This resulted in a flattened learning curve on the Rey Auditory–Verbal Learning Test:

Trial	1	2	3	4	5	B	A	Recognition
Words recalled	5	7	8	9	9	4	6	11

Following a delay, Peter rapidly forgot material he had previously acquired. For instance on the Rey Complex Figure he obtained a score of 13 following a 3 minute delay (below the 10th percentile), but after an hour his score had dropped to eight, and after a week he had no recall of the Figure at all.

It was concluded that Peter exhibited impairments of attention, speed of information processing, memory, abstract thinking, planning, problem-solving, and self-monitoring.

Functional assessment

Direct observation, supplemented with subjective reports from Peter and his wife, revealed the following profile of everyday abilities and disabilities. Peter was able to independently shower, dress, and groom himself. However, these activities took one and a quarter hours to complete each morning, due to slowness and obsessive attention to his personal appearance, with rigid adherence to a lengthy routine of face and hair care. Peter required his wife's input to select clothing appropriate to the weather and the day's activities.

Peter had a very simple daily routine, which he followed with prompting from his wife. He experienced confusion if there were sudden changes in the routine.

Domestically, he was capable of preparing himself uncooked snacks (e.g. fruit), breakfast (e.g. cereal) and drinks (e.g. coffee). He was unable to prepare a light cooked meal (e.g. toasted sandwiches) or prepare food or drink for his son. Problems with cooking were illustrated by his efforts to use the microwave oven. His wife had once left him a frozen meal with detailed cooking instructions, which Peter followed. However, he found the food was still partly frozen when he took it out of the oven. He could not work out the extra cooking time and, afraid of burning the meal, he ate it frozen.

Under supervision, Peter could perform tasks such as hanging out washing, vacuuming, and feeding pets. He painstakingly washed the dishes each morning and evening, taking up to an hour, but left the rest of the kitchen in a mess. He was dependent on his wife for overall household organisation, for prompting as to when to perform activities, and how to adapt them in response to a change in routine. He had extreme difficulty making even trivial decisions, such as which table mats to use when setting the table. The cognitive problems apparent on neuropsychological assessment, such as slowness, poor planning and rigidity, clearly formed the basis of his domestic difficulties.

Peter's involvement in community activities was limited. He had to be driven or walk to destinations. He could find his way around familiar routes close to home, but was unable to use public transport or navigate unfamiliar areas. Peter assisted his wife in physical aspects of the weekly shopping, such as pushing the supermarket trolley. He was unable to make reasoned decisions as to what to buy, as price was the only factor he took into account. He did not contribute to financial decision-making or budgeting. He never carried more than a few dollars in coins, as he forgot where he put it or what he spent it on.

Peter had no recreational pursuits, whereas he had previously had many sporting interests and enjoyed socialising. This was partly due to a lack of financial resources, but also to his difficulty initiating and organising activity, as well as a lack of confidence socially. Peter had no friends, and social contacts were largely confined to family members. He had difficulty following conversation and frequently misinterpreted communications. He could not think of things to say and often, without realising it, repeated himself. As already noted, Peter had also failed in his attempts to return to work.

Qualitative features of Peter's difficulties in everyday life were consistent with the findings of neuropsychological assessment. However, his disability and handicap could not be predicted from the knowledge of that impairment alone, since individual factors, such as his lifestyle, social expectations and family support structures had influenced the expression and impact of his impairments. This case demonstrates the usefulness of combining neuropsychological and functional assessments to develop an integrated understanding of the cognitive problems associated with TBI. Intervention to address some of Peter's problems will be discussed in Chapter 4.

CASE REPORT—DEBORAH

Deborah was a 32-year-old woman who had sustained a severe TBI in a motor vehicle accident 10 years earlier, with a PTA duration of 8 weeks. Prior to her injury she was in her fourth year of a law degree, studying part-time and working part-time as a public servant. She described herself premorbidly as very bright, with many interests, including student politics and gourmet cooking.

Following her injury, Deborah had attended a rehabilitation programme for one year. She then attempted to return to work, but was gradually downgraded to a clerical position because of cognitive and behavioural difficulties. Eventually she was retired from the public service. Two years post-injury she returned to full-time study, but due to failure in many subjects, she withdrew after three months. Deborah then married and had two children, now aged six and four. She separated from her husband during her second pregnancy. Deborah subsequently returned to study, and successfully completed one and a half full-time years of her law degree in three years.

She sought neuropsychological assessment 10 years after injury because of her growing awareness of cognitive difficulties and her need for assistance. She presented with a range of subjective complaints, identifying her main problem as a lack of organising ability, a tendency to be easily distracted, to panic with unexpected demands and to procrastinate. When questioned about her previous studies, Deborah said her marks were significantly lower than those achieved prior to injury. She identified her main problem as abstracting and generalising concepts from one legal case to another. She also failed to complete work on time, was late for lectures and fatigued easily, so she could not devote sufficient time to private study.

Neuropsychological assessment
On the National Adult Reading Test Deborah obtained a predicted Verbal IQ score of 120. On the WAIS-R she obtained the following subtest scores:

Digit span	12	Picture arrangement	16
Vocabulary	19	Block design	15
Similarities	15	Digit symbol	9

Subtest scores were felt to be within expected limits, except for the Digit Symbol subtest score, which was reduced relative to other scores, indicating a reduction in psychomotor speed. On Verbal subtests, Deborah's responses were quick and concise, although she evidenced occasional word-finding difficulties. On the Controlled Word Association Test she scored at the 80–85th percentile (F-17, A-12, S-20). On the Rey Auditory–Verbal Learning Test, Deborah achieved a perfect recall of 15 words by the third trial, and recalled 12 words following an intervening list. On the Rey Complex Figure she performed well, scoring 36 for the copy and 25 (65th percentile) for recall following a 30-minute delay. Part A of the Trail-Making Test was completed in 27 seconds (50th percentile), and Part B in 51 seconds (75th–90th percentile), with no errors. Sixteen trials of the Austin Maze were administered, with the following error scores: 14, 10, 7, 3, 2, 3, 2, 4, 2, 1, 2, 1, 1, 1, 0, 0. Whilst this performance falls within normal limits, it was observed that she had difficulty eliminating the last few errors. Apart from this and the Digit Symbol score, there was little evidence from Deborah's neuropsychological test scores of the presence of cognitive impairment.

However, Deborah reported that her earlier therapy programme had included practice on tasks modelled on many of the neuropsychological tests administered. It was felt that her familiarity with some of the test material may have rendered it insensitive to the presence of executive impairments. Moreover, the absence of distractions and lack of competing demands in the test situation was not mirrored in her everyday life. It was felt that the test results overestimated Deborah's actual capabilities of fulfilling the demands of her lifestyle, although the Austin Maze performance did suggest the presence of executive dysfunction. Functional assessment was performed to investigate more directly her subjective complaints.

Functional assessment

Deborah was able to describe a range of situations in everyday life where she encountered difficulties. For brevity, only the main aspects of household organisation will be described. The therapy programme instituted to address Deborah's problems will discussed in the next chapter.

Deborah lived with her children and her sister, who had moved in to assist in running the household. Deborah had responsibility for her children, half of the domestic chores, and was working part-time in a law office as an article clerk. Her elder child attended school and the younger child a child-care centre. Her typical weekday would commence with her waking late and subsequently rushing to complete the morning's activities. The oldest child was responsible for dressing himself and his sister, but usually Deborah would not have clean clothes organised for them, so they often had to wear dirty clothes. Deborah's own clothing was similarly disorganised. She procrastinated over what to wear, often trying on a number of outfits and invariably had to iron several items of clothing. The children made their own breakfast. Deborah usually did not have time to eat. Preparation of the children's lunches was also problematic, as necessary ingredients, such as bread, were often lacking. In the rush to leave the house each morning, items such as lunch or important documents were often left behind.

Thoughts of things she had to do during that day apparently occurred to her at times, but she only inconsistently noted them down on scraps of paper. These pieces of paper, as well as accounts, forms, school notices, legal briefs, etc. were placed, unorganised, in a section of her briefcase. Periodically during the day Deborah searched through this wad of paper, looking for details of something she only vaguely remembered she had to do. This process would typically lead to her discovering, say, an urgent bill, which would then distract her from her initial goal. Both vital and trivial tasks (ranging from payment of overdue accounts to purchase of a new toothbrush) tended to accumulate or were forgotten.

Deborah returned home with the children in the late afternoon. Activities to be completed included attention to school-related issues, such as homework, preparation of the evening meal, housework, such as washing and tidying up, bathing the children and preparation of legal material for the following day. Deborah had no set routine, and tended to focus on the most pressing issue at any moment. The house remained untidy, dinner was served late, and she relied heavily on convenience foods such as canned baked beans. Deborah was also very reliant on her sister to rescue her when things got out of hand. She was usually exhausted by the end of the day, but invariably stayed up late working on legal cases, which exacerbated her tiredness. Deborah could see that her problems stemmed from an inability to plan, prioritise and organise her daily activities, but ironically these same problems prevented her from finding her own solutions. Her sister confirmed that her difficulties reflected marked changes relative to her pre-injury level of function.

This case illustrates the fact that, in some cases, neuropsychological tests may not clearly reveal executive dysfunction. Close examination of the nature of everyday difficulties reported by Deborah showed a consistent pattern of executive dysfunction in daily life which lent strong support to the subtle qualitative features seen on testing.

CONCLUSIONS

The assessment of cognitive and behavioural changes following TBI poses an exceedingly complex challenge. No single method or approach to assessment will meet the rehabilitation team's need for objective, reliable, comprehensive, practical and individualised information on which to base interventions. Impairment assessment provides valuable information as to the person's strengths and the problems underlying the individual's difficulties, in a relatively objective, reliable and replicable form. It provides little information, however, as to how the person is functioning in daily life, and the extent to which the fulfilment of previous roles and responsibilities has been affected. This is the role of assessment of disability and handicap. However, the more the focus moves towards the individual in the context of everyday life, as it must in the case of TBI, the more one loses objectivity, reliability and replicability. There has, however, been relatively little research on the development and application of measures of disability and handicap for individuals who have sustained TBI. Such research directions, whilst posing many methodological challenges, are going to be essential to the development of more effective means of dealing with the complex cognitive difficulties confronting those who have sustained traumatic brain injury.

CHAPTER FOUR

Managing cognitive problems following TBI

Sue Sloan and Jennie Ponsford

INTRODUCTION

The cognitive changes which result from traumatic brain injury commonly cause ongoing disability and handicap for the person who is injured, and may create a significant burden for relatives. They also affect the individual's capacity to benefit from other aspects of the rehabilitation process. As outlined in Chapters 1 and 3, the nature and extent of these problems varies according to the site and severity of injury, as well as factors relating to the individual prior to injury, and the environment. Those deficits seen most frequently include impairments of attention, speed of thinking, memory, and executive functions, the latter incorporating the ability to plan and organise, think in abstract terms, initiate, think flexibly, and control and monitor thought processes and behaviour. The nature and complexity of the cognitive impairments associated with TBI renders them particularly difficult to assess. Issues pertaining to the assessment of cognitive difficulties have been discussed in the previous chapter. Such difficulties are outweighed only by the challenges presented in treating these problems. Following the principles of the REAL approach, this chapter aims to establish some guidelines for the design, implementation and evaluation of interventions for cognitive deficits resulting from TBI.

It has been well established that cognitive deficits show at least some degree of spontaneous recovery in the months and years following TBI. As Miller (1994) has argued, an understanding of this recovery process and factors which influence it should form the basis of intervention. Theories of recovery of function and available research evidence have been discussed in Chapter 1. It is clear that the domain of recovery of function is exceedingly complex. Recovery may well be mediated by a number of different mechanisms, although at his stage there is a lack of definitive evidence supporting any single mechanism. This is at least partly due to limitations, both in current knowledge of neuro-physiological processes, and in technology for exploring brain-behaviour relationships. Further developments should open up possibilities for further experimentation which will enhance our understanding of recovery processes. As Miller (1994) has concluded, according to the evidence available at this point in time, it appears that the bounds of physiological restitution, or pre-existing structural potential for substitution, should be reached within weeks after injury. Beyond this period, behavioural compensation or functional adaptation offers a more satisfactory explanation of recovery. This has the potential to be facilitated by rehabilitative interventions.

A number of factors, relating to the injured person, the nature of the injury and the post-injury environment, have been shown to influence the recovery process. Of particular relevance to the development of interventions for cognitive problems is the potential influence of environmental factors on recovery of function. Miller (1994) has pointed out that there is evidence from both animal and human studies that outcome can be influenced by manipulations after the injury (Basso, Capitani, & Vignolo, 1979; Eclancher, Schmitt, & Karli, 1975; Glisky & Schacter, 1987; Goldman & Mendelson, 1977; Will, Rosenzweig, & Bennett, 1976; all cited in Miller, 1994). There is some evidence to indicate that early intervention may be more effective than late intervention (Black, Markowitz, & Cianci, 1975; Cope & Hall, 1982; Rappaport, Herrero-Backe, Rappaport, & Winterfield, 1989; Spettell et al., 1991). However, this is an extremely complex issue, particularly in the case of TBI. Some recent studies have found that an important determinant of the ability to benefit from cognitive interventions is self-awareness (Ezrachi et al., 1991; Kovacs, Fasotti, Eling, & Brouwer, 1993). Increasing self-awareness over time after injury may mean that there is a better response to intervention at a later stage. Certainly there is evidence that TBI individuals are able to benefit from rehabilitation several years after injury (Burke, Wesolowski, & Guth, 1988; Mills, Nesbeda, Katz, & Alexander, 1992; Tuel et al., 1992).

APPROACHES TO COGNITIVE REHABILITATION

Wood (1990) describes cognitive rehabilitation as "an assortment of procedures to improve or restore a diverse collection of abilities and skills" (p.3). This "assortment of procedures" may be classified into four main categories: restorative, compensatory, environmental, and behavioural. The first approach, reflecting the rationale of theories of restoration of function, attempts to restore the specific impairments that may underlie a range of everyday problems. The second approach, based on theories of behavioural compensation or functional adaptation, targets the problem at the level of the disability, attempting to teach the brain-injured individual strategies and skills to reduce the impact of the impairment as it is manifested in everyday settings. The third approach involves manipulation of the environment or task in order to maximise performance of daily tasks. The second and third approaches are closely related, both being linked to the functional adaptation theory of recovery. They will therefore be considered together within this chapter. The final approach involves the use of feedback and reinforcement to maximise the speed, extent and level of learning or adaptation on the part of the injured person.

Restoration of cognitive impairment by retraining

This form of therapy focuses on the neuropsychological impairment. It aims to modify the structure or capacity of specific cognitive functions that have been affected by injury (Cicerone & Tupper, 1990). The procedure is to isolate impairments, using detailed psychometric or neuropsychological assessments. The brain-injured individual is then provided with repeated and highly structured practice on psychometric, computerised or pen-and-paper tasks believed to exercise the area of deficit. Parameters, such as complexity, quantity, speed of presentation, or the amount of cueing given, are gradually altered, depending on the goal of therapy. Such tasks often bear little resemblance to tasks encountered in real life settings, but it is argued that they exercise the cognitive processes required to perform functional activities. Proponents of this approach argue that it is more efficient to focus on the causes of difficulties, rather than the symptoms (Mateer, Sohlberg, & Youngman, 1990). The aim of this type of therapy is to restore the impaired function.

There have been many research studies conducted with TBI subjects which fall under this rubric. These include the work of Ben Yishay, Piasetsky, and Rattok (1987), Diller et al. (1974), Gray, Robertson, Pentland, and Anderson (1992), Malec, Jones, Rao, and Stubbs (1984), Niemann, Ruff, and Baser (1990), Ponsford and Kinsella (1988),

Robertson, Gray, and McKenzie (1988), Ruff et al. (1989), Sohlberg and Mateer (1987) and Wood and Fussey (1987). Most of them have focused on the remediation of deficits of attention. These studies have been reviewed in detail elsewhere (Ponsford, 1990). Findings have been mixed. Some have unfortunately had methodological problems, placing limitations on the conclusions which may be drawn from the findings. Relatively few studies have controlled adequately for spontaneous recovery, effects of practice and concurrent therapy, or have assessed the degree to which training generalises to aspects of everyday life, and whether gains are maintained over time. The two studies which did meet all these criteria, particularly in terms of measuring generalisation of effects to everyday life, namely those of Ponsford and Kinsella (1988) and Wood and Fussey (1987), were not able to demonstrate significant gains.

The importance of controlling for the effects of concurrent therapies is underscored by the findings of Ruff et al. (1989), who examined gains (albeit only on neuropsychological measures) in two groups of TBI subjects. The first group received intensive neuropsychological training in the areas of attention, spatial integration, memory and problem-solving, as well as supportive psychotherapy. The second received the same amount of supportive psychotherapy together with unstructured therapy. Both groups made significant gains, but the gains in the group receiving intensive neuropsychological training were not significantly greater than those in the other group.

If restorative approaches are to achieve their purported aim of reducing the cognitive impairments which underlie difficulties in everyday life, it is important to establish a clear relationship between the cognitive deficit, the training tasks used, and the dependent measures of the effectiveness of training, particularly those relating to everyday function. The study of Ponsford and Kinsella (1988) is one of the few to have attempted this. They conducted a preliminary study examining the nature of the attentional impairment in a group of severe TBI subjects, and established a group of neuropsychological measures which reflected this deficit. They then developed a rating scale of attentional behaviour as an "everyday" measure of attentional function, and established a significant relationship between rating scores on this scale and performance on the neuropsychological measures of attention and speed of information processing. Both the neuropsychological tests and the rating scale, as well as a video of attentional behaviour whilst performing a clerical task in the occupational therapy department, were used as dependent measures of the effectiveness of a training programme. This focused on deficits in speed of information processing.

A single-case multiple baseline across subjects design was used to evaluate the effectiveness of the training programme, carried out with ten severe TBI subjects, with demonstrated attentional deficits, an average of 14 weeks after injury. Following a 3-week baseline phase, subjects received half-hour daily training sessions over a period of 3 weeks on a range of computer-mediated attentional tasks. In the next 3 weeks this practice continued, but systematic feedback and reinforcement was added to maximise performance. The final 3-week phase involved a return to baseline procedures. Results indicated that the subjects generally showed a gradual improvement across all phases of the study, suggesting that spontaneous recovery was taking place. However, there was no evidence of a consistently increased rate of improvement in response to either of the interventions on any of the measures. There were, however, three cases in which there was a significant response to feedback and reinforcement, when this was added to computer training. Unfortunately it was not possible to differentiate these cases from others on the basis of age, educational background, injury severity or time since injury.

The failure of this study to demonstrate a significant impact of retraining for attentional deficits is consistent with the findings of Malec et al. (1984) and Wood and Fussey (1987), who failed to demonstrate significant responses to computer-mediated attention training programmes. Other studies, such as those of Sohlberg and Mateer (1987) and Gray and Robertson (1989) did show more positive results, but their studies had methodological limitations. Niemann et al. (1990) were able to demonstrate some treatment effects on one set of neuropsychological measures, but these did not generalise to another set of neuropsychological measures, and no attempt was made to examine everyday attentional performance. Gray et al. (1992) also found that a group of brain-injured subjects who received microcomputer-based attentional training improved more than a control group on a variety of untrained neuropsychological measures of attention. Interestingly, the differences between the groups were stronger at six-month follow-up than at completion of training. It was suggested that this effect may have been due to increased proficiency in the use of strategies. However, no studies have, as yet, demonstrated conclusively that this form of training has had an impact on the everyday lives of the TBI subjects being trained, whether the intervention has been conducted whilst spontaneous recovery is taking place, or afterwards.

There is even less evidence that repeated drills on memory tasks, such as list-learning tasks, has any impact on performance on untrained memory tasks or everyday memory performance (Mateer & Sohlberg, 1988; Schacter, Rich, & Stampp, 1985). More recent descriptive studies by Sohlberg, White, Evans, and Mateer (1992a,b) in which "prospective memory" was trained by repeatedly asking the patient to perform tasks at specified future times, have revealed mixed results. Whilst there was an increase in the span of prospective memory within the experimental paradigm, evidence of generalisation to naturalistic settings was unclear. The subjects were also receiving other forms of therapy concurrently.

It must be acknowledged that it is not easy to conclusively demonstrate the efficacy of any form of therapy. It is always possible to argue that more intensive or lengthy training may have brought greater gains. This approach to therapy is certainly appealing for a number of reasons. Non-functional activities such as these may be less threatening to some TBI individuals, and therefore serve as a medium for establishing a relationship and level of trust with the injured person. Some will be more motivated to work on a computer than to engage in other aspects of therapy. This may, in turn, enhance motivation and self-esteem, which may lead to other improvements. The tasks allow therapists to monitor the person's responses relatively objectively and systematically, and provide helpful feedback. The level of control the therapist can exert over the task and the environment is generally greater than in functional activity, allowing for controlled experimentation with strategies. Finally, this type of therapy is less demanding on the therapist both in terms of time and creative energy, and is therefore less costly. This is a significant factor in many rehabilitation settings, and may be the reason why this approach is so common.

Some researchers, such as Mateer et al. (1990), Weber (1990) and Molloy (1994) have argued that training on tasks such as these provides an opportunity to enhance the injured person's awareness of specific areas of difficulty, and to develop strategies to enhance performance. For example, on a computer task of visual detection, a strategy of slowing down visual search, and systematically scanning the computer screen may be taught. Performance may improve with practice at implementing the strategy. This may well be the reason why some studies have demonstrated gains on training tasks. However, we would argue that such improvements in performance on specific tasks actually reflect behavioural compensation, rather than restoration of the underlying impairment of cognitive function which the task is purported to measure.

By virtue of their adaptive difficulties, many people who have sustained TBI will have a very limited capacity to generalise strategies from such abstract tasks to the real world. It would seem to be more productive and cost-effective in the long term to apply such strategy training directly to the everyday tasks which need to be performed by the injured person. There may be a place for impairment-oriented restorative therapy for some individuals in the early stages of the rehabilitation process, but we believe that this is unlikely to result in a significant reduction in the injured person's disability and handicap. Whilst it may be less costly and more appealing in the short term, there may be little impact on the injured individual's lifestyle over the long term. It is natural for clinicians to want to restore lost functions. However, as will be clear from the previous chapter, our theoretical understanding of many of the impairments underlying cognitive difficulties remains very limited, providing no sound basis for the design of restorative treatment programmes.

Functional adaptation to cognitive difficulties

The cognitive retraining approaches described in the previous section have been developed on the assumption that "recovery" is defined in terms of restoration of the impaired function. As an alternative, Schacter and Glisky (1986), O'Connor and Cermak (1987), and many others have suggested that recovery may be defined in terms of the alleviation of the disability and handicap resulting from the impairment. As noted by Laurence and Stein (1978), this requires that recovery of function be assessed in terms of the goals attained, rather than the means used to attain those goals. The evidence available from research on recovery of function, outlined in Chapter 1, suggests there is limited potential for restoration of function within the damaged system, and that longer term recovery may occur by a process of adaptation. This, together with our knowledge of the TBI individual's common weaknesses in the domain of executive or adaptive function, would suggest that at this point in time rehabilitation should focus on the alleviation of disability or handicap resulting from cognitive dysfunction. Functional adaptation may be achieved in two ways—via behavioural compensation or environmental manipulation.

Behavioural compensation

According to the behavioural compensation approach, which targets disability directly, the emphasis is shifted from the weaknesses of the injured person to strengths. These are used to assist the individual to develop and learn strategies or skills in order to perform necessary daily tasks or components of tasks more successfully. At the most cognitively demanding level are attempts to train the injured person to use self-instructional or self-monitoring strategies in a variety of situations, for example, training a sequence of steps to be followed in different problem-solving situations. At a more basic level, the strategies are applied directly to specific daily living tasks which present problems for the injured person. An example of this would be the use of a checklist to ensure a necessary sequence of steps is followed for completion of a task. As the skills and techniques taught are largely task- and environment-specific, generalisation of gains to untrained tasks or even different environments should not be expected to occur. It has been demonstrated in numerous studies that brain-injured individuals are capable of learning compensatory strategies to overcome a broad range of cognitive difficulties. Of particular relevance to TBI are those in the domains of memory and executive function.

A variety of compensatory strategies have been used in the treatment of memory problems. The most commonly studied strategies have involved the use of visual imagery mnemonics to compensate for verbal memory deficits (Binder & Schreiber, 1980; Cermak, 1975; Crovitz, 1979; Gasparrini & Satz, 1979; Jones, 1974; Lewinsohn, Danaher, & Kikel, 1977; Patten, 1972; Ryan & Ruff, 1988; Stern & Stern, 1989; Thoene & Glisky, 1995; Wilson, 1987a) or verbal mediation strategies, such as the PQRST technique, to improve comprehension and recall of written or lecture material (Glasgow, Zeiss, Barrera, & Lewinsohn, 1977). Many of these studies have demonstrated successful use of the strategies when applied in experimental settings. A recent well-controlled study by Berg, Koning-Haanstra, and Deelman (1991) evaluated the use of a range of memory strategies applied to specific difficulties experienced by brain-injured individuals. They were able to demonstrate more positive effects on memory test performance than those resulting from repeated practice on memory tasks or no treatment. On the other hand, Benedict, Brandt, and Bergey (1993) found no significant effects of guided practice in the use of semantic elaboration for recall of word lists, conducted over 13 weeks in a severely amnesic woman.

It would appear that severity of cognitive impairment may be a factor influencing the success of such interventions. However, none of the studies has provided substantial evidence of successful application of cognitive strategies to reduce memory difficulties in everyday life. As Schacter and Glisky (1986) have pointed out, complex strategies based on imagery require elaborate processing and thus a great deal of cognitive effort, potentially rendering them impractical for day-to-day use. It would appear that many TBI individuals do not have the cognitive capacity to apply such strategies without the structure and prompting provided by the therapist or experimenter (Lawson & Rice, 1989).

An alternative means of compensating for memory problems is the use of external memory aids or cueing devices, such as diaries, timers, alarms and electronic memory aids. The use of such aids falls into the category of behavioural compensation only where it involves the active participation of the injured person. Those cueing devices which are externally programmed fall under the rubric of environmental manipulation. A recent development in this category is the NeuroPage, developed by Hersh and Treadgold (1994). This is an externally programmed paging system, which allows for reminders and cues to appear on a standard pager carried by the injured person.

Several studies, reviewed by Schacter and Glisky (1986), suggest that memory aids may be useful for some amnesic individuals. Wilson (1991) found that a significant proportion of memory-impaired individuals followed up 5–10 years after rehabilitation were using memory aids successfully. Zencius, Wesolowski, and Burke (1990) found that memory notebook logging was a more effective means of increasing recall in TBI subjects with severe memory problems than written or verbal rehearsal, or acronym formation. However, there may be difficulties in learning how to use memory aids (Wilson, 1984), or the injured person may not use or apply them effectively in daily life (Phillips, Ponsford, Saling, Sloan, Benjamin, & Currie, 1991; Sloan, Benjamin, & Hawkins, 1989; Sohlberg & Mateer, 1989). The results of research conducted to date suggest that external aids may be used effectively, provided they are consistent with methods used by the individual prior to injury, the individual is motivated to use them, they are relatively easy to use, and are taught and applied directly to specific daily memory difficulties experienced by the injured person (Burke, Danick, Bemis, & Durgin, 1994; Phillips et al., 1991; Sohlberg & Mateer, 1989; Zencius, Wesolowski, Krankowski, & Burke, 1991).

In the domain of executive function, studies may also be grouped into those which have attempted to train self-instructional strategies to be applied in a range of situations, and those which have trained strategies specific to a given task or situation. Those which fall under the rubric of the former include the work of Cicerone and Wood (1987), Cicerone and Giacino (1992, cited in Sohlberg, Mateer, & Stuss, 1993) Lawson and Rice (1989), von Cramon, Matthes-von Cramon, and Mai (1991) and von Cramon and Matthes-von Cramon (1994). Cicerone and Wood (1987) reported the treatment, four years post-injury, of a TBI client with impaired planning ability and poor self-control using a self-instructional procedure. This required him to verbalise a plan of behaviour before and during execution of a training task, a modified version of the Tower of London. Overt vocalisation was gradually faded. Generalisation training in applying planning and problem-solving strategies in real-life situations was conducted over 12 one-hour weekly sessions after completion of the self-instructional training. There was marked improvement in performance on the Tower of London task, administered four months after training. More significantly, there was evidence of transfer of gains to planning behaviour on some other neuropsychological measures. There were significant increases in self-control ratings made by independent therapists during the period of generalisation training, but not during the initial phase of training in self-instruction on the Tower of London task. The authors concluded that self-instructional training was likely to be most successful if applied directly to real-life situations. Cicerone and Giacino (1992, cited in Sohlberg et al., 1993) had similar findings with a further six subjects, and, in another single case, trained a formal error monitoring procedure.

Lawson and Rice (1989) described a case of a boy with significant memory difficulties affecting his school performance. He did not benefit greatly from training in a range of compensatory strategies until he was taught a specific series of steps to follow in selecting and implementing an appropriate strategy. This training resulted in improved memory test performances, and greater initiation and use of memory strategies over a six-month follow-up period. However, the training did not have a significant influence on aspects of academic performance, such as progress in reading skills.

In the only well-controlled group study of this nature, von Cramon et al. (1991) trained a group of brain-injured subjects with problem-solving difficulties in different aspects of problem-solving behaviour, including recognition and formulation of problems, generating alternative solutions, considering their pros and cons, selecting a solution, and recognising and correcting errors. A matched control group underwent memory training. The problem-solving group showed significant gains on neuropsychological measures of planning, and in everyday problem-solving behaviours rated by therapy staff. There was, however, no follow-up regarding the impact of the training on problem-solving behaviour beyond the rehabilitation setting.

In a more recent case report, von Cramon and Matthes-von Cramon (1994) were able to demonstrate a significant impact on the work performance of a medical doctor who was exhibiting executive problems nine years post-injury. Intensive training was conducted over a 12-month period. Problem-solving strategies were applied directly to his work-related difficulties using self-instructional techniques, initially with external guidance from the therapist, which was gradually withdrawn.

Kovacs et al. (1993) reported on a study where they attempted to train TBI subjects with slow information processing to implement strategies to circumvent the effects of time pressure. They found an increase in the use of such strategies in the trained group, but no concurrent improvement in actual task performance relative to that shown by controls. They concluded that the subject's ability to use such strategies effectively depended on the level of awareness of deficits.

Burke, Zencius, Wesolowski, and Doubleday (1991) described four case studies, in which checklists were used successfully to train injured individuals to follow through with a sequence of tasks in work settings. In all cases, the routine was performed without the assistance of the checklist within 12 days. Sohlberg, Sprunk, and Metzelaar (1988) described the use of an external cueing system to improve the verbal initiation and response acknowledgement behaviour of a severely injured male with marked initiation problems. In a group therapy setting, he was given regular cues, written on a card, to monitor first, his initiation of conversation, and second, his acknowledgement of others talking. There was a significant increase in the target behaviours during intervention. Performance declined when intervention was withdrawn. No attempt was made, however, to ensure maintenance or generalisation of gains.

Environmental manipulation

According to the model of environmental manipulation, the tasks themselves, or factors in the environment may be modified in order to maximise performance. For example, in the case of an injured person in the workplace, duties may be altered so as to minimise demands on memory or initiative, the worker may be placed in a quieter environment to avoid distraction, and other workers may modify their patterns of interaction with the injured person, so as to minimise interpersonal conflict. In the home, relatives, or even a computer, may provide necessary prompting or structure in order to maximise the injured person's ability to perform activities of daily living. Such adaptations are likely to be necessary in cases where the injured person has severe cognitive deficits, lacks self-awareness, motivation and the capacity to adapt. This is frequently the case following severe TBI. In spite of this, little emphasis has been given to this approach in the cognitive rehabilitation literature.

A case described by Kirsch, Levine, Fallon-Krueger, and Jaros (1987) has illustrated the successful application of a computer-mediated cueing system to improve the performance of a severely amnesic woman on a cookie-baking task. Bergman (1991) designed a customised text writer in order to accommodate the cognitive deficits and use the residual skills of a highly intelligent woman who had sustained severe TBI and was unable to write or use a standard word-processor. It had simplified commands and format, and provided on-screen cues and instructions, thereby minimising demands on her. She was able to master the text writer within three training sessions. Follow-up indicated that she used it at least several times daily for a variety of activities in the ensuing months. The text-writer thus greatly enhanced her self-sufficiency and emotional adjustment (Bergman & Kemmerer, 1991). However, there have been relatively few such attempts to systematically design and objectively evaluate the impact of environmental modifications.

In general, the research evaluating the impact of compensatory or environmental manipulation approaches to the alleviation of cognitive difficulties has had many of the same limitations as research on restorative approaches. Training has frequently been given on artificial tasks in settings which bear limited resemblance to those encountered by the injured person in everyday life. There have been relatively few studies which have comprehensively assessed the ability of the individual to use the strategies to overcome everyday difficulties and hence evaluated the impact of the intervention in alleviating the injured person's disability and handicap.

Behavioural approaches to cognitive difficulties

Behavioural techniques have been successfully applied to a range of cognitive problems associated with traumatic brain injury. They have been used to overcome problems in the domains of memory (Dolan & Norton, 1977; Wilson, 1984, 1987a), speech (Horton, 1979), attention (Wood, 1986; Wilson & Robertson, 1992), speed of response (Deacon & Campbell, 1991) and activities of daily living (Giles & Clark-Wilson, 1988; Godfrey & Knight, 1988). Behavioural techniques will be covered in detail in Chapter 6 and therefore will be discussed in less detail in this chapter. However, there is no doubt that they have much to offer in assisting TBI individuals to overcome problems resulting from cognitive deficits. There are generally fewer difficulties in evaluating the effectiveness of behavioural interventions, due to the fact that the behaviours to be trained are being measured directly and concurrently with treatment. It is still very important, however, to measure generalisation and maintenance of gains. This has not been done in some studies conducted to date.

Behavioural management strategies may be applied directly to behavioural difficulties. For example Wood (1986) used a token economy to increase attentive behaviour during therapy sessions, reporting significant gains in one subject, but minimal gains in a second subject. Wilson and Robertson (1992) used a behavioural shaping strategy, combined with inoculation against distraction, to reduce the frequency of attentional slips during reading in a TBI male, 9–13 months post-injury. Deacon and Campbell (1991) found that feedback and the imposition of time windows resulted in a significant decrease in reaction time.

Alternatively, behavioural techniques have been used as a means of training adaptive skills or compensatory strategies. For example, Giles and Clark-Wilson (1988) successfully used verbal prompts, which were gradually faded, to train very severe TBI individuals on washing and dressing tasks. Godfrey and Knight (1988) used verbal prompting and social reinforcement to train a TBI person in skills, such as medication management and use of public transport, to attain successful community placement.

Conclusions from the research to date

A number of points emerge from the substantial amount of research which has been conducted in the area of cognitive rehabilitation to date. From the findings of Ruff et al. (1989), Rattok et al. (1992), and Berg et al. (1991) it appears that any intervention or combination of interventions may have a positive effect on cognitive function, as measured either neuropsychologically or in the eyes of the treated individual. Whether these interventions actually alleviate the individuals' disability or handicap remains unclear. Those with less severe deficits are more likely to benefit from all types of intervention, particularly those involving self-generated strategies, but also including restorative training approaches (Berg et al., 1991; Fryer & Haffey, 1987; Zencius et al., 1990).

It is clear that no single approach to intervention is suitable for all TBI individuals. The most suitable approach will depend on the nature and extent of cognitive and behavioural impairment, particularly skills in the domains of memory, self-monitoring, and awareness of deficits. For those functioning at very low levels in these and other respects, environmental manipulation and behavioural approaches appear to be most effective in reducing disability and handicap. TBI individuals who have some degree of motivation and self-awareness, as well as a capacity to regulate and monitor their behaviour, may benefit from training in self-instructional or self-regulatory strategies to overcome areas of weakness (Crosson et al., 1989). The findings of Cicerone and Wood (1987) suggest that any strategies taught are most likely to be of lasting benefit if they are relevant to and applied directly in real-world settings. The criterion by which all interventions should be measured is the impact on everyday functioning. Sadly, to date, generalisation has usually been mentioned as an afterthought or qualification in a couple of sentences at the end of the paper.

There is now evidence from a number of studies indicating that substantial and lasting gains may be made by focusing directly on functional skills (e.g. Burke et al., 1988; Fryer & Haffey, 1987; Mills et al., 1992). These studies have demonstrated that such gains can be made at any time after injury and despite the presence of ongoing cognitive impairments. The approach to intervention needs to be flexible. Frequently, several different techniques will be used in a given individual to deal with different problems encountered.

Some researchers and clinicians working in TBI rehabilitation take the view that compensatory strategies should only be used after all recovery is known to have taken place. However, we would argue that facilitation of behavioural adaptation to the disabilities caused by the injury should commence early in the rehabilitation process. Methods used will need to be altered as the injured person recovers. This is not a negative approach. It is a realistic approach which is likely to maximise the outcome for the injured individual.

THE *REAL* APPROACH TO DEALING WITH COGNITIVE DIFFICULTIES

All the principles of Rehabilitation for Everyday Adaptive Living (REAL) are applicable in the design and implementation of interventions for cognitive difficulties associated with TBI.

Focus on the individual's disability and handicap
The REAL approach is focused on the TBI individual's unique constellation of problems and the ways these are manifested in everyday settings. To promote adaptive learning for everyday living, intervention should target the disability and handicap, rather than the underlying cognitive impairment. The focus of therapy needs to be on functional behaviours and skills evident in personal, domestic, community, and social activities, and on minimising the injured person's handicap in the longer term. This will not only maximise the impact of therapy, but also increase the probability that the injured person will see the relevance of therapy.

Identify and train adaptive behaviours using the individual's strengths
The REAL approach focuses on assisting the person to adapt to everyday living by modifying tasks, environments, or the strategies used to perform tasks. In this approach the identification of strengths is just as important as that of weaknesses. Analysis of tasks the person is able to perform will provide the therapist with clues about intact abilities, which can be used to develop workable strategies and modifications. Therapy becomes a positive experience that focuses not only on disabilities but also on abilities.

Actively involve the TBI individual and the family
It is vital that the individual and family members contribute to the setting of concrete goals that target problems evident in everyday contexts. Interventions need to be planned in the light of the individual's premorbid capabilities, as well as the real-life demands they and their families currently face. Training and practice in real life settings, and involving family members wherever relevant, is vital to ensure that skills will be applied in the contexts where they are most required.

Assess and utilise the most effective method of learning for the individual
Depending on previous abilities and methods of learning, and the specific nature and severity of cognitive impairments, TBI individuals will have widely varying capabilities as far as learning is concerned. For those with very limited memory skills, no self-awareness and poor behavioural regulation, learning abilities may be very limited. In such cases, the focus may need to be on environmental or task modification to reduce the demands on the injured person. Behavioural approaches may also be used successfully where learning abilities are very limited. At a slightly higher level, task-specific learning applied in everyday contexts is frequently possible. Strategies need to be concrete and any aids used simple and obvious. Some ongoing support and monitoring from a caregiver may be required. Generalisation from one setting to another will not occur automatically, and will need to be built into the therapy process. For those individuals functioning at a higher level, it may be possible to direct training at the injured person's self-awareness and capacity for self-monitoring and regulation. The individual may be trained to anticipate and recognise problems as they occur in a range of everyday environments, and equipped with strategies that can be applied with some degree of flexibility as specific demands change. Again generalisation should not be assumed. However, if enough examples of real life application are trained, then gains should be seen in a range of normal settings.

Take a team approach
The complexities of the cognitive deficits associated with TBI are best understood and managed via an interdisciplinary team approach. In addition to using their discipline-specific skills, each member of the treating team is encouraged to share responsibility for the broad spectrum of cognitive, behavioural, communicative and physical problems that contribute to disability and handicap. Assessment and management involving all team members maximises the understanding of the individual's strengths and weaknesses as they are manifested in

a range of settings and activities, and enhances learning and skill generalisation from one environmental context to another.

Evaluate the impact of interventions

Every effort should be made to assess objectively the impact of the intervention, both in alleviating the specific functional difficulty experienced by the injured person, and in reducing the individual's level of handicap. It is also important to examine whether the effects are maintained over time. In most cases this may be accomplished using single case designs, as outlined by Wilson (1987b). It is necessary to have some objective measure of the behaviour in question, obtained in the manner suggested in the previous chapter (e.g. frequency counts of instances of forgetting, made by a caregiver). Baseline measures need to be taken prior to intervention. The measure must continue to be taken throughout the period of intervention and during a follow-up period. It is also useful to ask the injured person and caregivers for their views regarding the problem and the impact of the intervention. This may be done using a standardised questionnaire, such as that developed by Sunderland et al. (1983), or questions developed specifically for the purpose. Again, such questions or ratings need to be made after a follow-up period. Neuropsychological measures are not the best measures of the effectiveness of this form of intervention.

CLINICAL APPLICATION OF REHABILITATION FOR EVERYDAY ADAPTIVE LIVING (REAL)

This section will outline how the REAL approach can be used by therapists planning intervention programmes for cognitive deficits following TBI. There are three main components to be considered when planning therapeutic input. These are goal setting, selecting therapy tasks, and implementing therapy. The latter incorporates provision of therapeutic input that will maximise learning, and selection and implementation of strategies or modifications which are appropriate to the injured person's strengths and weaknesses.

Goal-setting

As goal-setting underpins the treatment process, considerable time needs to be spent formulating goals. This may prove to be a stressful process. It is often difficult to engage the family and TBI individual in realistic goal-setting. The following section will address pertinent issues and provide guidelines for setting goals. For the purposes of the following discussion, a goal is defined as a desired outcome assigned within a time frame. Long-term goals are statements of broad outcomes that encompass expectations of the individual's future roles and responsibilities. These are formulated, taking into consideration a range of factors, including the TBI individual's goals, family goals, premorbid factors, injury-related variables, such as time since injury, and findings of clinical assessments. The time frame for achieving long-term goals is usually extended, and may be defined in relatively loose terms, for example, to return to work in six to nine months. Ideally, long-term goals are set first.

Typically, to achieve long-term goals, a diverse range of component issues and problems will need to be addressed. Medium-term goals tend to focus on the changes required to solve those component problems subsumed by the long-term goal. For instance, to return to work, the individual may need to develop specific job-related skills, attain a means of transport and adapt to the effects of a memory difficulty. Time frames of weeks to months may be assigned to attain these goals. Short-term goals represent a further breakdown of the steps required to achieve the medium and, in turn, the long-term goals. They focus on very specific outcomes that can be observed and measured behaviourally (e.g. learning to perform a sequence of tasks involved in cutting and planing timber, or learning to use a diary).

In order to arrive at goals that are meaningful to the individual and family, and shared by all members of the treating team, all parties need to be actively involved in the goal-setting process. Some goals may be specific to particular team members, whilst others will be shared across disciplines. For instance, in attaining independence in transport, it may be necessary to tackle a range of a problems, such as reduced mobility, socially inappropriate behaviour and poor planning. Communication strategies developed with the speech pathologist may be practised in the course of shopping activities with the occupational therapist. It is important as a team to prioritise goals. Goals also need to reviewed on a regular basis and revised as targets are achieved. The TBI individual should be included in all discussions whenever possible. A case management structure is helpful to ensure that someone takes responsibility for co-ordinating team planning, securing the input of the TBI individual, mediating between potentially conflicting points of view and making sure all those involved are kept informed on an ongoing basis.

Involving the TBI individual in goal-setting can be a difficult task. Goal-setting demands such cognitive processes as abstract thinking, judgement, idea generation and awareness of strengths and weaknesses, any of which may be impaired following TBI. When asked to state their goals, TBI individuals may proffer vague statements of their wishes, that fail to reflect an understanding of underlying impairments resulting from the injury. Often such statements centre on aspects of lifestyle that are of importance for the person. An inpatient immobilised in bed might say he wants to go home, or a severely cognitively impaired individual may say he wants to go back to his previous job or to drive a car. Such goals may not coincide with those of members of the treating team or the family, and may easily be dismissed as being unrealistic. In the resulting void, therapists may be inclined to impose their own goals and assume that the individual would concur if they had insight.

However, therapists' goals may be perceived as meaningless by the individual, and as a result there may be little active participation in therapy. The therapist needs to be prepared to provide an appropriate level of support to facilitate the development of realistic goals by the injured individual. To set goals successfully it is important that therapists adopt the perspective of handicap and use the language of the TBI individual. With the injured person's input, the therapist can use broad statements of "wishes" as a starting point to derive specific goals. The component steps and prerequisite skills required to achieve goals can be teased out. These become subgoals. In this way an unrealistic and vague wish becomes a series of smaller, concrete and achievable goals, shared by the individual and therapist. The manner in which the subgoals contribute to the overall goal needs to be documented explicitly and the individual may need to be referred to this document frequently.

CASE EXAMPLE

Therapist: "What is the main goal [aim, target, thing] you want to achieve in the next few months?"
Injured person: "I want to go back to work as a motor mechanic."
Therapist: "What is stopping you from going to work at the moment?"
Injured person: "They [hospital staff] told me that I cannot lift anything heavy and I forget things. Because of that they say I wouldn't be able to do my job, so they're not letting me go back."
Therapist: "How do you think you would go at work right now?"
Injured person: "No problems."
Therapist: "What aspects of your work would be no problem?"
Injured person: "I've been going over my service manuals and can still remember all the car parts and how they are pulled apart, repaired and put back together."
Therapist: "So the information seems familiar when you reread your manuals, but have you tried to do any mechanical work to test yourself out?"

Injured person: "No, apart from a little job when I helped my brother fix his radiator."

Therapist: "Do you think that practising the things you need to do at work would be an important step before going back to your old job?"

Injured person: "Yes."

Therapist: "Could we agree then that the goal in the next month is to start a programme of work experience, so you can try out your motor mechanic skills?"

Injured person: "Yes."

Therapist: "Let's start by listing all the different tasks you have to do at work. We can use this as a guide to setting more specific goals during the work experience programme..."

Implementing therapy

Selection of therapy tasks

Provided the assessment and goal-setting processes have been followed in the manner suggested, selection of treatment activities should be fairly straightforward. Therapy tasks are chosen from those everyday activities (see pp. 84–86) which the injured person cannot currently perform. Priorities will be set according to the person's overall level of function, and current and projected demands in the individual's daily life. Wherever possible, activities should be performed within the context of the normal daily environment and routine, also incorporating activities the individual is able to perform. In order to maximise motivation, activities should be related to the injured person's goals for independence in a clear and concrete manner.

Therapeutic input

Therapeutic input may be provided by therapists, family members, or others involved in relevant aspects of the injured person's lifestyle (e.g. fellow workers, friends). It should be given in such a manner as to maximise learning and the attainment of goals. As discussed earlier, the approach taken to therapy will depend on the level of functioning of the injured person.

Ways of facilitating the learning process

- Harness motivation by selecting tasks which are seen as relevant by the injured person. It may be prudent to allow supported risk-taking in order to enhance this aspect, and develop more realistic self-awareness.

- Break tasks down into steps or components, focusing on one at a time, and gradually linking them together into a routine. Begin with maximal assistance using cues or aids and gradually withdraw these.
- Provide frequent feedback. Feedback should be provided immediately, and in a concrete and uncritical manner. Negative feedback should be preceded by a comment on a positive aspect of performance, and presented in conjunction with suggestions as to how performance may be improved. Wherever possible, it is important to create opportunities for the injured person to receive feedback from peers, fellow workers or family members, as this is likely to be more meaningful.
- Give repeated practice until the skill or strategy is mastered within one context, then provide further practice in a range of other relevant settings.
- Educate the TBI individual and relevant others regarding the nature of changes and specific strengths and weaknesses. Educational input needs to be tailored to the individual's general intelligence, knowledge of TBI, level of cognitive function, degree of insight and emotional status. Written material or tapes may be used. Groups involving other TBI individuals also represent a useful means of enhancing understanding of problems and ways to circumvent them.

Involvement of close others

Families provide a vital role in managing functional cognitive problems, and will continue to do so long after therapy input has ceased. It is important, therefore, that management strategies are devised in consultation with the family or other caregivers, ideally in the home or other relevant context. Family members may be involved in therapy sessions where strategies are modelled and discussed, either in vivo or using videotapes.

An assessment of the overall demands on the family is important, so that a realistic level of involvement can be encouraged. For example, the TBI individual may be lacking in initiative in ADL. Within the hospital it may be possible to introduce a structure to maximise independence to the level where the person requires four specific verbal prompts to get up, shower and dress. At home, however, the therapist may find that the TBI individual is being fully supervised and physically assisted to perform the same activity. Whilst this may be acceptable for the family in the short term, it is potentially burdensome in the longer-term, and the family may find it difficult to withdraw this level of support.

It is important to try and help the family establish routines that are able to be sustained, and which maximise the independence of the injured person. However, in suggesting alternative approaches it is essential not to denigrate the family's efforts or forcefully present one's own opinion. Mutual exchange of information, and gently pointing out the likely consequences of the family's actions, may assist in bringing about consistency between hospital and home. This approach demands humility and flexibility from therapists, who must be willing to subsume their own goals to those of the individual and the family. Ultimately the therapist needs to accept the views of the TBI individual and the family, and search for some common ground on which they can be engaged. Some families will reject help altogether and they should not be punished for this. Therapists should attempt to part on terms that leave the door open to the family should their situation change and they later wish to receive assistance.

Structuring tasks and introducing strategies

Task modifications and strategies designed to compensate for everyday difficulties arising from cognitive impairment cannot be prescribed in the manner of a recipe. The choice, and effectiveness, of strategies will depend not only on the difficulties observed in everyday life, but also on the individual's strengths and weaknesses, the specific demands of the task in question, and environmental variables. An individualised approach that accounts for these factors is recommended.

The process of structuring tasks and introducing strategies commences with an analysis of both the task and the injured person's performance on it. Modifications and strategies need to be introduced in a systematic manner and their effectiveness for the individual evaluated. Modifications can be made at a number of different levels, depending largely on the severity of the injured person's cognitive problems. First, easier versions of the same activity can be selected. Some tasks may be avoided altogether. Second, the tasks themselves can be adapted to alter (up- or downgrade) specific cognitive demands. Third, environmental variables can be changed. Fourth, the input from external sources can be varied in terms of the amount or type of assistance provided. Finally, the methods and cognitive strategies used by the injured person can be altered, drawing on relatively intact abilities. For those individuals with relatively severe problems, choices may be restricted to task and environmental modifications, and externally generated prompts. A wider choice of strategy is available for those individuals functioning at a higher level. Overall, the aim of the therapist will be to establish the minimum level of input/adaptation required, to support maximal, sustained independence. Behavioural techniques may be used to assist in training strategies or shaping task modifications. Group discussion may also facilitate the development and acquisition of strategies.

The following section contains some suggested modifications or strategies for dealing with some of the more common cognitive problems associated with TBI. Further examples of the application of the REAL approach to overcoming the impact of cognitive difficulties on the performance of a range of roles are contained in Chapter 7. For ease of organisation, the information in the following section is set out under the headings of attention, memory, executive dysfunction, initiative and insight. However, in this context they are used to categorise functional cognitive behaviours arising from impairments of specific functions, rather than diagnostic labels.

Attentional problems and fatigue

- Build rest-breaks into the activity (e.g. 5 minutes rest for each 15 minutes).

- Schedule more complex tasks at the time of day when fatigue levels are lowest and there are fewest competing demands.

- Change activities frequently to maintain interest.

- Modify the environment to reduce distractions (e.g. work in a quiet room, facing a wall, reduce interruptions and background noise, clear workspace).

- Modify the task to reduce the amount of information to be processed, or the speed at which it is presented.

- Provide verbal prompts to encourage the person to refocus on the task and train others to do so.

- Provide verbal or written prompts that assist the person to move from one component of the task to the next in a logical fashion. By removing unstructured periods there is less opportunity for the person to become distracted.

- Allow for repetition of material to be remembered, such as instructions. In work or study environments a dictaphone may be useful to record and replay important material.

- Allow a realistic time frame for completion of tasks to reduce time pressure and associated stress.

- Train the injured person to ask questions to slow down the delivery of spoken material and clarify points, or introduce other self-talk strategies to maintain the focus of attention (e.g. repeating what has to be done to avoid distraction).

- Train the injured person and others to identify the signs of fatigue and take appropriate action. Stress management, relaxation or meditation techniques may be helpful.

- Structure a graduated return to activities and demands.

Memory and learning difficulties

- If the TBI person is unable to participate actively in applying strategies, use close others to provide necessary prompting or reminding, externally programmed aids, or modify the environment to reduce demands on memory.

- Downgrade the memory demands of the task to a manageable level (e.g. reduce the amount of material to be remembered, reduce the periods of delay between presentation of information and recall, simplify material to be remembered and present information in a logical and structured manner).

- Provide opportunities for repetition of information/frequent practice of tasks.

- Reduce environmental distractions.

- Provide verbal reminders or written prompts and train others to do so.

- Encourage the person to develop a set routine, within which adaptive habits can be trained.

- Assess strategies and techniques used to assist memory before the injury and those employed spontaneously since. These may be broadly divided into internal and external memory aids. Internal aids include mnemonics, such as visual imagery and the PQRST technique. External memory aids include use of a diary, calendar, lists, notes, putting things in special places, as well as a range of programmable electronic or computerised aids.

- Select strategy or strategies based on an analysis of the task and the injured person's performance including their overall level of cognitive function (e.g. many internal mnemonic strategies are very demanding cognitively), premorbid strategies, environmental supports and motivation and interest.

- Go over methods of applying the strategy and review anticipated problems (e.g. how will you remember to use the strategy?; what will you write in the diary?). Develop and implement solutions to these problems.

- Provide opportunities to practice relevant tasks during which the person is trained when and how to use memory strategies.

- Involve family members in the implementation of strategies, and have them monitor their use in the home and community. The therapist will also need to observe the use of the strategy in real-world settings.

Executive problems (incorporating impaired planning and organisation, problem-solving and self-monitoring):

- Choose less complex versions of the relevant activity (e.g. select easy recipes).

- Break task into components and present them one at a time.

- Simplify tasks by condensing or eliminating non-vital steps. Once a basic level of skill is obtained these steps can be reintroduced.

- Provide clear, simple instructions that impart a structure for performance of the task.

- Ensure consistency of approach between therapists and family members.

- Utilise all relevant resources in the individual's environment (e.g. public transport times and routes may be more easily accessed through telephone information services than from maps and timetables).

- Include familiar activities, triggers, strategies, etc. and draw on premorbid skills. Provide opportunities for practice in familiar environments.

- Provide external cues that enable the TBI individual to recognise and complete each step of the activity. This may be in the form of written checklists (the individual or the therapist may tick off completed steps), verbal prompts (these range from general prompts such as "what comes next?" to specific prompts such as "turn on the oven"), or environmental signals (e.g. setting the oven timer to prompt steps in cooking).

- Behavioural methods outlined in Chapter 6 (such as shaping, chaining) can be used to train the person to perform a routine series of steps in response to a designated trigger.

- "Internal" compensatory strategies can be used for specific situations (e.g. using self-talk to prompt oneself to "slow down" when searching for items in the supermarket).

- "Internal" strategies can also be used more flexibly in a range of situations where the person is able to anticipate problems or adequately self-monitor performance. Such strategies primarily utilise self-talk to cue adaptive behaviours. For example "plan what to say" may be an effective cue prior to making telephone calls, attending meetings and social events. A protocol for activating adaptive behaviours can be taught (i.e. routine steps to follow that facilitate "planning what to say").

Lack of initiative

- Educate the individual and family as to the nature of the problem, so they understand lack of initiative is not laziness.

- Break down the task into components. Use prompting and reinforcement to shape desired behaviour, chaining steps together, then fading prompts (see Chapter 6).

- Use verbal, written or external prompts. Checklists may be used to check off components of tasks as they are completed. An alarm clock, wrist watch, computer or electronic diary may be programmed to alert the individual to perform specific activities.

- Increase the salience of the task for the individual (e.g. give the person ultimate responsibility).

- Allow the individual to experience the normal consequences of failure to perform the task. Follow up with feedback and discussion.

- To maximise motivation, make sure tasks are relevant and involve the TBI person in goal-setting and decision-making.

Poor insight/self-awareness

- Delay confronting the person directly with their cognitive problems, and work on disabilities the injured person can recognise (e.g. physical disabilities).

- Convey information about problems in a way that is meaningful, focusing on everyday life activities.

- Allow supported risk-taking within meaningful environments.

- Educate family, friends and fellow workers or students, and seek their assistance in giving feedback, providing supervision, etc.

- Have the TBI individual monitor and record the incidence of specific behaviours when performing activities.

- Audio- or videotape task performance. In playing back the tape the individual may be asked in a general way to report on "what you notice about the way you performed the activity". Alternatively, self-evaluation may be enhanced by providing some structure to guide observations such as a checklist of behaviour(s) to be self-rated.

- Keep a log book of therapy, domestic and/or community activities in which TBI individuals can record daily experiences in their own words. The injured person may be prompted to include both success and failure in their performance of daily activity. Discussion and questioning aimed at highlighting strengths and weaknesses can be undertaken by the therapist.

- Give feedback immediately, and precede negative comments with positive ones.

CASE REPORT—GEORGE

George worked as the manager of a video wholesaling business. His job involved researching latest video releases, selecting purchases based on anticipated client demand, ordering, checking off deliveries and arranging distribution to retail outlets. He received and made between 30 and 40 telephone calls per day, and had three people working for him in the business, which he co-owned. Following a TBI six months earlier, George returned to work and reported a number of problems. He said he had difficulty recalling all relevant details of information or instructions, provided over the telephone or in face to face interactions. He attempted to compensate by writing everything down, but because of attentional problems he was limited in his ability to take notes at the same time as he held a conversation. He said he tried to make notes at the end of an interaction, but found he was often distracted by subsequent demands. These problems resulted in frequent failure to follow through with instructions and complete the things he was expected or had agreed to. Overall, he was anxious about his memory failures and their implications for his vocational future.

Observation of George's work environment and performance in response to specific everyday demands was undertaken by the occupational therapist. A baseline measure was taken. The behaviour selected was "doing the things I said I would do". Over a three-day period George recorded the number of successes and failures that occurred in this category of behaviour. On each of these days he was also asked to select and record in detail one example of difficulty. This information formed the basis of discussions with George, in which the nature of his difficulties, and the conditions under which they occurred, was analysed. Possible strategies to minimise the effects of memory problems were discussed with George, beginning with the identification of previously used aids and techniques. Together, external memory aids were chosen and a routine of recording and checking information was devised.

A desk diary was to be used for planner entries such as appointments, placement of orders and dates of delivery. Additionally, journal entries were made in a notebook with a separate page for each day, and cross referenced with the diary. Journal entries included notes on the content of meetings, conversations and telephone calls. An "action plan sheet" detailed a list of tasks to be carried out that day. The action planner was yellow and was displayed prominently on his desk. It was prepared at the start of each day and included actions relating to things he said he would do, as well as items transferred from his diary and notebook. The action plan was updated throughout the day. George was encouraged to establish priorities, act immediately where appropriate, record the results of his actions, and tick off each item as it was attended to. An answering machine was purchased. This could be switched on if he required time to follow up and finish off details pertaining to one telephone call, before he took a subsequent call. Notes of telephone calls were made in his journal and any follow-up was recorded on the action planner. If telephone calls were particularly long or detailed they would be audiotaped. A dictaphone was also purchased to allow George to tape important meetings and conversations. The tapes were used as a back-up to the pen and paper techniques.

George received concurrent intervention for the anxiety he was experiencing in the work situation, specifically that associated with taking phone calls. This was caused by his cognitive difficulties, but ultimately exacerbated them. He was trained in some self-talk strategies to prevent him from panicking whilst on the phone, and given relaxation training to assist his general anxiety levels. Such methods are discussed in detail in Chapter 8.

Reassessment on the baseline measures, regarding George's ability to "do as he said he would" indicated substantial improvement in response to the intervention. However, the additional effort required of George in order to cope with his job resulted in significant compromise of his social and recreational activities. Thus, although he is successfully managing his memory problems, George has required ongoing support to deal with the impact of the head injury on his lifestyle.

CASE REPORT—BRADLEY

Bradley was a semiskilled labourer of low average premorbid intelligence, who had sustained a severe TBI two months earlier. He did not have much contact with his family. Cognitive problems of attention, memory and executive functions were evident on neuropsychological assessment, and it was anticipated they may have a significant impact on his lifestyle. He had no awareness of them. He was living alone and his only goal was to return to work. He was unwilling to practice domestic, community, or vocational tasks in the hospital setting. The occupational therapist's short-term goals were to fully assess the impact of his cognitive deficits on daily tasks, to increase his awareness and understanding of his problems, and to introduce compensatory strategies. Many of the tasks he was asked to perform in the hospital were simulations of real-life demands, but Bradley was unable to abstract the reasons for this approach. He reported that he was independent in domestic and community tasks he had undertaken, and would not agree to a home visit. He refused psychological counselling. Bradley was becoming increasingly disillusioned with therapy and had a very poor attendance record. Due to severe orthopaedic injuries involving his left leg it was not anticipated that he would return to work for at least six months, and he required intensive medical treatment and physiotherapy in the interim.

In order to maintain his commitment to the rehabilitation process, and ensure he received treatment for his leg injuries, a team meeting between Bradley and the therapists involved was arranged by the case manager. The team agreed to adopt Bradley's goals and modify or suspend their own. Goals that were physically oriented and focused on work requirements, such as standing tolerance and endurance, were documented in simple and concrete terms— for example, "to increase the length of time Bradley can stand before needing to rest from 30 to 45 minutes". A time frame of four weeks was set before a review meeting would be held. In the meantime Bradley agreed to attend four times per week for physiotherapy and medical appointments. Occupational and speech therapy sessions were discontinued.

Prior to the next review meeting Bradley initiated an appointment with the case manager. He expressed an interest in doing further training to increase his skills in preparation for return to the workforce. He wanted to discuss this in the forthcoming meeting, and requested the assistance of the team in identifying appropriate courses and arranging funding. At the review meeting the physiotherapist reported that Bradley had attended regularly and had made significant progress. His standing tolerance was now 60 minutes. The physiotherapist suggested that two sessions per day working on standing tolerance would be beneficial. He agreed that he would resume occupational therapy, with the focus of the programme being on researching available courses, and improving standing tolerance in functional activity. The occupational therapist arranged that standing practice would be conducted at home in the context of his daily routine. Selected activities, which he had largely performed sitting, were now to be performed standing. He actively participated in the choice of activities and the structuring of the programme.

The occupational therapist was able to assess his ability to organise and carry through a number of daily tasks. Bradley began to report some difficulties he was experiencing. It became clear that Bradley was not shopping or cooking for himself on a regular basis. He reported that he ate cornflakes whenever he got hungry. He had lost a substantial amount of weight. Bradley acknowledged that he would like to eat better, but said he often ran out of money, forgot or couldn't find the time to go shopping. In the course of this discussion, Bradley said that he was tending to spend his fortnightly worker's compensation cheque within the first week, leaving himself very little for the second week. He had accumulated a number of debts, and had to borrow money from friends. His friends were becoming annoyed about this and asking for the money back. This prompted Bradley to seek assistance from the occupational therapist. They worked together to develop some solutions.

The occupational therapist had Bradley keep a record of how he was spending his money over a two-week period. It was apparent that he spent most of it on various social activities, before he had paid bills or bought food. She assisted Bradley to work out a budget for his fortnightly income, setting aside amounts for food and bills, which were to be paid before any money was spent on social activities. They also set aside an amount to be banked to pay off old debts. Arrangements were made for Bradley to join a credit union, which would pay his bills, provided Bradley banked a regular weekly amount. Bradley was also encouraged to purchase a diary, which was used to plan the week's activities in detail, setting down times for banking, paying bills, shopping, and performing other necessary tasks. A great deal of time was spent working on ways to ensure Bradley would refer to this diary, and eventually they arrived at a system whereby the alarm on his wrist watch was programmed to go off at specified times to remind him to refer to the diary.

They also put notes in various places in his flat. They developed a standard shopping list for him to use for his weekly shopping. The occupational therapist also worked with Bradley on some basic cooking skills, providing him with simple, step-by-step recipes for a small range of meals which he had chosen. She monitored his use of the recipes on a regular basis. She also had him keep continuing records as to how his money was spent over several months, until she felt sure that the routines established were working. In the course of this intervention, Bradley's diary was used to help him plan the necessary phone calls and arrangements to enrol in a forklift-driving course, which he carried through successfully.

CASE REPORT—PETER

The background details regarding Peter's injury and results of assessment are outlined in a case study in Chapter 3. Management of Peter's cognitive problems was undertaken within the context of their impact on his lifestyle. Intervention consisted of home visits by an occupational therapist over a 12-month period, initially twice a week and reducing to once a month. Peter was monitored for a further 12 months. Some examples of the intervention are detailed below.

The introduction of a computerised diary, programmed by his wife, was central to Peter's improved ability to compensate for cognitive problems. The diary functioned as both a planner and a journal. Peter was able to access a plan of the day's activities, both routine and non-routine. Prompts as to how to perform a specific task, what to take with him when he went out, etc. were also spelled out. A plan was printed out each day so it could be carried with him. Peter was also able to make journal entries of his day's activities. Intensive training was given to both Peter and his wife on how to use the computer and the diary programme. For Peter, verbal instructions were supplemented with written cues.

Peter and his wife identified social isolation as a major problem, because it contributed to his anxiety and depression. A recreation and social skills programme was devised. This was complemented by counselling for psychological problems. Over a three-month period a range of activities were introduced, to a level where Peter was involved on five half days. Activities included social outings with a local Headway group, painting, guitar, and Tai Chi. An occupational therapist assessed the cognitive demands of each activity and advised on appropriate compensatory strategies. Wherever possible they were linked to the diary. An attendant care worker was employed to accompany Peter to recreational or social activities, and to provide assistance to develop Peter's skills and level of independence. For instance, he rehearsed greetings and topics of conversation with Peter, provided cues in social settings (e.g. as to people's names) and assisted in resolving any misunderstandings that arose.

Assessment had revealed that, within the home, Peter was not fully independent in any routine of personal or domestic activity (see Chapter 3). Discussions with Peter and his wife revealed that they would prefer him to spend more time on fewer activities and complete them, rather than leave a number of activities unfinished. Five activities were selected by the couple. Training focused initially on cleaning the kitchen. Peter was already washing the dishes independently, but the activity was broadened to include putting away food items, wiping the benches and, finally, putting away dishes. Analysis of the demands of this activity, combined with observations of Peter in the kitchen, led to a step-by-step plan of an effective routine for cleaning the kitchen. Each component of the activity was introduced gradually. Written prompts (including activity checklists and labels on cupboard doors) were supplemented with verbal cues from his wife. These later cues were gradually withdrawn. Peter's wife endeavoured to make less mess in the kitchen when she cooked, in order to reduce the overall load on Peter. Prompts as to when to perform this activity were included in his diary.

With repetition, Peter was able to reach full independence in this activity over a one month period. These methods were later used to teach Peter when and how to cook bacon and eggs, to sterilise baby bottles, feed his dog and to tidy up the bathroom after use. Over a 12-month period, Peter developed greater independence in managing his daily routine, performing routine personal and domestic activities more efficiently and with less supervision, based on formal assessment on ADL and IADL measures. He also increased his social network and recreational interests. Anxiety and depression reduced considerably. Peter reported significantly greater satisfaction with his lifestyle. Although severe cognitive difficulties remained, he had systems in place which, if followed routinely, allowed him to compensate to some extent. This case illustrates that, by focusing on developing strengths, and by utilising available supports, those with severe injuries can develop some degree of independence and satisfaction in their daily lives.

CASE REPORT—DEBORAH

The background regarding Deborah's injury, the problems she described, and the results of assessments are outlined in a case report in Chapter 3. Intervention for Deborah's difficulties with household organisation consisted of eight sessions of occupational therapy conducted in her home over a four-month period. The intervention focused primarily on developing and implementing strategies and daily routines that assisted her to compensate for her poor executive abilities.

Deborah had difficulty waking up on time. It was discovered that Deborah had a radio/clock alarm, but she had not worked out how to set it. This was rectified and her evening routine included setting the alarm. In order to deal with the problem of not having clothes ready to wear, an ironing/drycleaning service was located. This picked up and delivered clothing to the home. It ensured that Deborah's own clothing was selected and prepared each week. Five outfits were also chosen for each child to wear. A washing basket was placed in the bathroom and the children were trained to place their dirty clothes in the basket when they undressed for their bath. At the end of the week these clothes were washed, folded, and put away where the children would find them.

Deborah was also extremely disorganised in her approach to cooking. Discussion between Deborah, her sister and the occupational therapist resulted in the identification of eight meals. These called for ingredients which could be purchased during the weekly shopping trip and cooked by Deborah in less than 15 minutes. The recipes were written out in clear steps and placed in a folder. Following discussions involving Deborah's oldest child, a list of food items to be purchased for school lunches was also generated. It was agreed that 20 sandwiches would be made on Sunday and frozen for use during the week.

In view of Deborah's absent-mindedness as far as shopping was concerned, a master shopping list was devised, using headings meaningful to Deborah, such as "fruit and vegetables", "breakfasts", "school lunches", etc. Copies were made, and each week Deborah was asked to highlight those items she required for the meals she intended to cook and for the children's lunches. Deborah's sister added her requirements to the list and completed the shopping.

In an attempt to assist with Deborah's organisation of appointments, accounts, notices, etc. previous and current methods of organising paperwork used by Deborah were discussed. It was decided that a diary would be the central organising tool, supplemented with additional strategies. An account book was purchased, into which Deborah wrote details of all new accounts, the date they were due and when they were paid. The accounts were placed in a pocket in the book. A weekly time for banking, bill-paying, etc. was set aside. Any action required outside this routine time was recorded in her diary. A noticeboard was purchased, onto which all school notices and forms, etc. were pinned. Important dates were transferred into her diary.

Deborah was asked to plan her daily activities by way of an "action plan sheet". Deborah was trained to check her diary each evening and write out the things she had to do the following day. She rehearsed how she would incorporate these activities into her normal routine. In order to establish this as a habit, her sister was initially asked to facilitate this process. Deborah recognised that she usually panicked when required to adapt her plans to cope with new demands. It was stressed that new items should be dealt with or recorded immediately on either her action planner or in her diary. To assist in this task, a series of questions was developed to be used in conjunction with a self-talk strategy to control anxiety. The questions included "is this urgent or can it wait?", "how long will this take to do?", "what will it involve?", and "should I do it now or add it to the list?" Deborah found that, by answering these questions systematically, she was able to more effectively decide on an appropriate action.

To address the problem of leaving items behind in the morning, a checklist of routine items was placed by the door. "Post-it" notes stuck to the front door were used as reminders for non-routine articles.

Effectiveness of these organisational methods was assessed via subjective reports by Deborah and her sister, as well as direct observation by the occupational therapist. Objective ratings of functional performance were made wherever possible, for example, by monitoring the time at which she left the house in the morning, what the family ate for dinner and at what time. Substantial improvements were evident in each of these areas, and these had been sustained at follow-up three months later.

CONCLUSIONS

There are a number of different approaches which may be taken in the remediation of cognitive dysfunction. These fall broadly into the categories of restorative therapies, behavioural compensation or environmental manipulation, and behavioural approaches. A review of the literature indicates that there is more evidence supporting the efficacy of compensatory or behavioural approaches to remediation, in alleviating the everyday difficulties experienced by TBI individuals as a consequence of cognitive impairments, than there is in support of restorative therapies. However, the optimal approach will depend on the severity and nature of the cognitive deficits. Whatever approach is selected, it is important that therapy is focused on real-life difficulties, and that family members or others close to the injured person are involved wherever possible. It is also vital that attempts are made to evaluate objectively the impact of the intervention on the everyday life of the injured person and the family.

CHAPTER FIVE

Assessing and managing changes in communication and interpersonal skills following TBI

Pamela Snow and Jennie Ponsford

INTRODUCTION

Communication is a rich and subtle form of higher order human behaviour. As such it not only commands a central role in the individual's ability to negotiate the business of everyday life, but also requires the successful interaction of a range of cognitive, linguistic and behavioural skills. Many of these skills may be impaired as a consequence of TBI, resulting in a complex range of communication difficulties. These include word-finding problems, excessive talkativeness, difficulty staying on topic, poor turn-taking skills, difficulties thinking of questions or comments to promote and sustain a conversation, problems following conversation in groups or noisy settings, tactlessness, difficulties understanding abstract language, such as metaphor, sarcasm and analogy, and repetitiveness (Braun, Lussier, Baribeau, & Ethier, 1989; Hagen, 1984; Hartley & Levin, 1990; Holland, 1982b; Malkmus, 1989; McDonald & van Sommers, 1993; Prigatano, Roueche, & Fordyce, 1985; Snow, Lambier, Parsons, Mooney, Couch, & Russell, 1987). Other difficulties include problems recalling details of past and present conversations, reduced sensitivity to nonverbal or situational cues, inappropriate use of gesture, facial expression and/or proximity to the other speaker, difficulty modifying tone of voice in relation to the context, and difficulty structuring discourse so that information is supplied logically and sequentially.

CASE EXAMPLES

Tracey was a 26-year-old woman who worked as a receptionist/typist prior to her injury. Her conversation was characterised by a tendency to jump from one topic to another, without warning, and without providing the other speaker with adequate background information. Tracey was uncharacteristically blunt in her dealings with others, causing offence to family and friends. She also spoke too quickly, compromising her speech intelligibility, and developed a repertoire of off-putting facial expressions, including eye-rolling and eye-brow raising. These seemed to occur when she had difficulty thinking of something to say. Tracey was aware that her speech was not always intelligible in conversation, because others frequently asked her to repeat or clarify what she had said. She was surprised, however, when she saw video footage depicting her excessive facial expressions, and was initially reluctant to consider a need for greater care in how she phrased comments to others.

Paul was 31 when he sustained a severe brain injury. Problems evident on assessment, and reported by family members included verbosity, and a tendency to provide almost excruciating detail about even minor matters. This was associated with insensitivity to turn-taking cues, and a preoccupation with topics of immediate relevance and interest to himself. Paul's girlfriend was quite distressed by what she saw as his insensitivity to her needs. Paul was also inclined to invade the personal space of the other speaker, and to generally assume an overly familiar manner with others. In discussion about these behaviours, Paul insisted that they reflected his gregariousness, and were no different from his pre-injury characteristics. This was strongly denied by family and friends.

Kerry was 22 at the time of her injury, and was working full time in the hospitality industry, whilst studying part time towards a business degree. She displayed excessive and inappropriate smiling. This was not only off-putting to others, but at times was incongruous with the emotions associated with the topic under discussion. Kerry also had difficulty monitoring her speaking volume when she became excited or animated in conversation. She was aware that her excessive volume was a disadvantage to her in her work setting.

These case examples illustrate just some of the communication disturbances commonly seen following TBI. These have been increasingly recognised as significant factors in determining failure to resume former life-roles, and poor psychosocial adaptation following injury (e.g. Marsh & Knight, 1991a,b; Brooks et al., 1987b). This realisation brings with it the need for a systematic understanding of the components of interpersonal functioning affected by TBI, and acknowledgment of the need to manage these within the rehabilitation context and on return to the community. Interpersonal skills encompass not only verbal and non-verbal abilities, but also social perception, social learning, and the ability to modify behaviour in response to subtle features of the context in which an interaction is occurring. The nature of difficulties in these areas will be outlined in this chapter, and a multifaceted approach to communication assessment and rehabilitation proposed.

A FRAMEWORK FOR ASSESSING PRAGMATICS IN THE TBI INDIVIDUAL

In Chapter 3, the importance of the distinction between impairment, disability, and handicap was stressed. This applies as much to the assessment of communication, as it does to the assessment of cognitive abilities. As McGrath and Davis (1992) have noted, some impairments and disabilities highlighted by structured testing may not result in handicap for the individual concerned. Similarly, the individual's handicaps may not become apparent in assessment conditions which are sensitive only to impairment and disability. Assessment of language skills via selected subtests of various aphasia batteries allows specific communication impairments (such as reduced auditory processing, or word-finding difficulties) to be isolated and measured. The use of pragmatic profiles to evaluate conversational samples enables pragmatic disabilities to be determined. Assessment of handicap, however, is best achieved via careful discussion with, and feedback from the injured person and close others. This is particularly so as time elapses after injury, and opportunities exist for changes to be experienced at first hand. Each of these approaches will be discussed below.

The study of communication following TBI is plagued with unclear terminology, references being made to pragmatics, conversational skills, social skills, cognitive–communicative changes, and/or discourse errors. Pragmatics was defined by Davis and Wilcox as "...the study of the relationships between language behaviour and the contexts in which it is used" (1985, p.1). Throughout this chapter, the term pragmatics will be used to refer to both conversational and interpersonal skills. Indeed, the inherently social nature of conversation calls into question any attempts to separate it from interpersonal functioning. This needs to be emphasised in relation to both assessment and management of pragmatic difficulties in the TBI individual.

In Chapter 3, it was stressed that no formal evaluation should commence until the injured person has emerged from post-traumatic amnesia (PTA). Management of the communication changes associated with PTA is discussed in Chapter 2. Prior to assessment, all relevant biographical, educational, and medical information needs to be collected and carefully considered. The speech pathologist, psychologist, social worker, and other team members will need to liaise closely in this process, so that test results can be interpreted in the light of the unique characteristics of the individual concerned. Because factors such as time since injury, the development of insight, and the process of spontaneous recovery will all impinge on communication, it is vital that assessment and intervention be seen as inextricably related, on-going processes. The "battery approach" to assessment should be avoided in favour of exploring all available sources of information—quantitative and qualitative.

Information derived from neuropsychological assessment forms an important background against which performance on speech pathology evaluation can be considered. Communication is not a unitary concept. The role of supporting cognitive processes such as attention, planning and organisation, self-monitoring, and ability to think in the abstract all need to be considered in relation to pragmatic abilities. The person who displays significant difficulties with attention and concentration on neuropsychological assessment is likely to have difficulties following conversation, particularly in noisy environments. Similarly, the individual with planning and·organisational difficulties may not be able to consistently structure verbal output so that ideas are presented in a logical, sequential manner for the listener. Self-monitoring difficulties may manifest as repetitiveness, or difficulty staying on topic. Reduced ability to think in the abstract can have debilitating effects on the individual's ability to understand humour, metaphor, sarcasm, and other forms of figurative language. As will be stressed throughout this chapter, however, assessment of communication only in terms of impairment and disability may fail to illuminate these problems. More informal approaches need to be employed, in order to ascertain the level of handicap experienced by the individual, as a result of difficulties highlighted by both neuropsychological and speech pathology testing.

ASSESSMENT OF COMMUNICATION IMPAIRMENT: LANGUAGE TESTING

Some workers in this field have proposed a causal link between cognitive dysfunction and pragmatic disturbances after traumatic brain injury (e.g. Hagen, 1984). Whilst this is certainly a valid viewpoint, it is important that language problems are not overlooked in the enthusiasm for examining verbal skills within the broader framework of cognitive dysfunction (Sarno, Buonaguro, & Levita 1986, 1987; Wiig, Alexander, & Secord, 1988). In view of the enormous heterogeneity across TBI individuals, both in terms of premorbid factors (such as personal adjustment and level of education), and aspects of the brain injury itself (e.g. severity of primary and secondary brain damage), all aspects of communication should be carefully and systematically evaluated. These range from basic language processes, such as comprehension and word-finding skills, through to all aspects of pragmatic competence in a variety of real-world contexts.

A number of studies have identified word-finding difficulties as the most common form of linguistic impairment seen following traumatic brain injury (e.g. Levin, Grossman, & Kelly, 1976; Levin, Grossman, Sarwar, & Meyers, 1981; Thomsen, 1975). Other difficulties have included verbal paraphasia (Thomsen, 1975) and reduced verbal fluency skills (Levin et al., 1976; Lohman, Ziggas, & Pierce, 1989). Levin et al. (1981) found that impaired comprehension of oral language accompanied expressive difficulties in patients with generalised language impairments. Recently, Yorkston, Zeches, Farrier, and Uomoto (1993) examined the concept of "lexical pitch" in relation to demographic factors following TBI. Lexical pitch refers to word choice and word access in relation to the audience being addressed. These workers found that TBI compromises lexical pitch in more highly educated TBI individuals. They suggested that difficulties with lexical access are likely to contribute to pragmatic disturbances in TBI individuals who had a wide vocabulary premorbidly.

Traditionally, speech pathology assessment of the TBI individual has begun with the administration of a battery of tests designed to evaluate a number of isolated linguistic skills. The inherent structure in this type of testing serves to obscure, rather than highlight pragmatic difficulties, because language is assessed not as a tool of interaction, but as a collection of discrete skills, such as naming or repetition. Indeed, many of the items in these tests require the individual to perform tasks rarely (if ever) performed in the real world, whilst failing to assess the verbal skills the individual is almost certain to require outside the hospital setting. Judgements based solely on performance on such tasks are likely to result in inappropriately optimistic estimates of the individual's pragmatic competence, and thus provision of inadequate services. Whilst sensitive to linguistic disturbances, structured language testing, alone, has significant limitations as a means of delineating treatment priorities.

In addition to the excessive structure and ceiling effects of aphasia tests, test performances may be affected by a wide range of individual variables. Consequently, scores should not be viewed in isolation from the person's social and educational background. Test responses need to be supplemented with clinical observations regarding the individual's behaviour during testing. Important features to note include restlessness, fatigue, delays before responding, self-monitoring (with or without attempts at self-correction), perseveration, and ability to utilise cues. This information is valuable when designing an intervention programme. It can also be used in discussions with family members, and other staff, in order to maximise the success of the injured person's interactions.

The selective use of language assessment tasks, in conjunction with other forms of assessment, can, nevertheless, enable the clinician to gain an understanding of the specific impairments underlying pragmatic disturbances. In order to be able to participate successfully in conversation, the individual needs to be able to process sentence-length utterances delivered at normal speed, whilst ignoring other incoming, but irrelevant stimuli. At the same time, the individual is formulating a response and selecting appropriate vocabulary and grammatical structures with which to express this. It is important that these components of normal communication be explained to the injured individual and family members, so that communication difficulties are not misconstrued as rudeness or laziness on the part of the injured person. Above all, an understanding of impairments underlying pragmatic problems will facilitate the design of intervention strategies, as this type of assessment delineates not only linguistic difficulties, but also specific strengths.

It is unfortunate that there are few well designed measures which are sensitive to the communication problems seen in the TBI population. For this reason, clinicians need to employ a flexible, individualised approach to assessment, essentially using the measures available as screening techniques for gross difficulties. Clinicians must bear in mind that satisfactory performance on discrete measures does not guarantee that the injured person will be able to deal with the demands of similar tasks in the real world. This means finding out what language demands (spoken and written) will be made of the injured person, and determining the extent to which these can be met. For example, an apprentice fitter and turner may be able to successfully deal with a range of traditional reading comprehension tasks but still be unable to cope with the reading demands of his study materials. The speech pathologist, in conjunction with other team members, needs to carefully present tasks of immediate relevance to the individual in question. This not only enhances the ecological validity of assessment, it should improve the individual's motivation, and assist staff to determine which cognitive and/or linguistic factors need to be addressed in therapy. Thus whilst there is a role for some language testing, the old adage that "absence of evidence is not evidence of absence" reminds us of the limitations of any type of clinic-based testing.

Table 5.1 outlines certain commonly used measures for assessing the language skills of the TBI individual. The majority of these are borrowed from aphasia batteries designed for use with stroke patients. This is not an exhaustive list of available tests.

The Test of Language Competence—Expanded, Level II (Wiig & Secord, 1989) provides the clinician with additional information about the injured person's ability to use problem-solving skills to manipulate linguistic elements, such as ambiguity, and ability to understand figurative language. The four subtests cover areas not accounted for by the tests listed in Table 5.1. Indeed, it is performance on tests such as these which may distinguish some higher-level brain-injured individuals from non-injured counterparts. This information can provide valuable clues as to which features of conversation tax the individual's cognitive and linguistic skills. Families and friends may need to be advised to simplify their own language, avoiding overuse of shades of meaning (e.g. sarcasm, metaphor, analogy), which may obscure the literal meaning.

TABLE 5.1
Structured language tests and their role in the assessment of the TBI individual

Test	Use
Boston Diagnostic Aphasia Examination (Goodglass & Kaplan, 1972)	Assessment of auditory and reading comprehension at a range of levels
Neurosensory Centre Comprehensive Examination for Aphasia (Spreen & Benton, 1969)	Token test for auditory comprehension of non-redundant material. Word fluency subtest for assessment of rule-governed idea generation
Boston Naming Test (Kaplan, Goodglass, Weintraub, & Segal, 1983)	Assessment of confrontation naming skills
Wiig-Semel Test of Linguistic Concepts (Wiig & Semel, 1976)	Auditory comprehension of short, logicogrammatical items
Luria–Christensen Neuropsychological Investigation (Christensen, 1984)	Section N for assessment of abstract language skills

ASSESSING COMMUNICATIVE DISABILITY:
PRAGMATIC ASSESSMENT

Until the early 1980s, communication problems following TBI were examined within the framework of traditional aphasia classifications, which had evolved from the study of stroke and missile wound populations (e.g. Groher, 1977; Heilman, Safran, & Geschwind, 1971; Levin et al., 1976). There has been, since that time, a growing awareness that the verbal impairments displayed by TBI individuals are not readily accounted for by the term "aphasia". Assessment of isolated parameters of language form, such as naming, auditory comprehension, repetition, reading, and writing, are not necessarily sensitive to difficulties interacting with others in "real world" settings. These assessment tasks have been gradually replaced by measures thought to be more sensitive to the use of language in a range of real-life situations. As Hartley (1990) observed, so-called "functional" assessments not only enhance the ecological validity of speech pathology assessment, but also comprise tasks with greater face validity for the injured person than those derived from aphasia batteries.

In assessing interpersonal or pragmatic competence, every aspect of social behaviour needs to be examined systematically, beginning with social perception. There are, however, no validated tests of social perception skills. Burke (1988) suggested having the injured person view or listen to video- or audiotaped interactions between adolescents or adults, evoking a range of emotions (e.g. happy, sad, angry, anxious), and having them comment on different aspects of the interaction. Cartoons or photographs depicting a range of facial expressions may also be used. According to Burke, potential sources of inaccurate social perception include failure to listen to the interpersonal partner, failure to look at the partner, paying inadequate attention to facial expression and body language, failure to integrate what has been said or heard, failure to understand the meaning of what has been said or heard, or a tendency to look or listen for cues which are not relevant. Some assessment needs to be made of the extent to which the injured individual considers different response options, and their potential consequences, before deciding on a response. A number of other measures to assist in this assessment have been recommended by Burke. These include the Social Skill Survey (Goldstein, 1976), a Self-Control Rating Scale, adapted from Kendal and Wilcox (1979), and his own Social Skills Assessment (Burke, 1988).

The notion of "functional assessment" is not new to speech pathologists in adult rehabilitation settings. For example, the Functional Communication Profile (Sarno, 1969) and the

Communicative Abilities in Daily Living (CADL) (Holland, 1980) have both taken their place alongside formal aphasia batteries in the assessment of the adult aphasic patient. Like the simulated tests of cognitive functions described in Chapter 3, these measures address, in part, the need to consider performance within an everyday context. However, by virtue of their structure, and their inability to capture the subtleties of real-life communication, they entail significant risks of over or underestimating the TBI person's ability to utilise language as a tool of social interaction in a variety of everyday contexts. For this reason, several attempts have been made to formulate specific measures of pragmatic ability. Some have been designed for use with dysphasic stroke patients (e.g. Penn, 1985; Yorkston & Beukelman, 1980), whilst others have been less prescriptive about the target population (e.g. Damico, 1985; Prutting & Kirchner, 1987). It must be stressed that these measures should complement, rather than replace assessment of language skills, as will be discussed further below.

One of the most well known approaches to the assessment of discourse is the Pragmatic Protocol (Prutting & Kirchner, 1983). This profile consists of 30 items, spanning verbal, paralinguistic and non-verbal aspects of communication, scored as appropriate/ inappropriate (or "no opportunity to observe"), based on a 15-minute sample of the subject's interaction with a familiar conversational partner. The authors opted for this type of assessment rather than frequency counts, on the basis that appropriateness needs to be considered in relation to important contextual factors (e.g. the physical setting, the relationship between speakers, and the purpose of the interaction). Appropriate behaviours are those which either facilitate the communicative process or exert a neutral influence. Inappropriate behaviours are those judged to detract from the communicative exchange and incur a penalty to the individual.

Prutting and Kirchner's Pragmatic Profile has been well received by workers in the TBI field (e.g. Ehrlich & Sipes, 1985; Hartley & Griffith, 1989; Milton & Wertz, 1986; Sohlberg & Mateer, 1990). It has been the subject of some research with this population (e.g. Ehrlich & Sipes, 1985; Milton, Prutting, & Binder, 1984). Milton et al. compared the performance of five TBI subjects with five matched controls on the Pragmatic Profile and the CADL. The experimental subjects also underwent examination on the Western Aphasia Battery (Kertesz, 1982), on the basis of which none was deemed to be aphasic. Whilst the TBI subjects performed above the cut-off for normal functional communication on the CADL, nearly a quarter of their behaviours (averaged across the sample) were judged inappropriate on the Pragmatic Profile. Every TBI subject exhibited some inappropriate behaviours. The Pragmatic Protocol identified specific strengths and weaknesses in such areas as topic selection and maintenance, turn-taking, quantity and conciseness. However, a significant disadvantage of the Pragmatic Profile is the fact that it relies on subjective judgements as to the appropriateness or otherwise of a particular utterance, without reference to the individual's sociolinguistic background.

Damico (1985) emphasised the need to consider verbal behaviour in as broad a context as possible, allowing for, rather than attempting to control, variations in speaker intent, physical setting, verbal context and social context. He designed a tool he termed "Clinical Discourse Analysis" (CDA), which is based on Grice's "Co-operative Principle" (Grice, 1975. pp.45–6). This consists of four overlapping maxims, and is summarised in Table 5.2.

The CDA requires that language samples are collected in "relatively open communication settings" (Damico, 1985, p.170) and are then transcribed for utterance-by-utterance analysis. "Problem" utterances are grouped into one of four categories, relating directly to Grice's four maxims. These categories are outlined in Table 5.3.

The scores derived from the CDA are as follows: total utterances, total discourse errors, total utterances with errors, and percentage utterances with errors. Advantages of the CDA include the fact that it is based on a frequency count of observable behaviours, rather than an individual's opinion about the appropriateness or otherwise of a particular utterance or non-verbal behaviour. Further, the distribution of an individual's errors across the 17 parameters can be used for the delineation of treatment priorities. The CDA can be used to objectively measure change over time, however it was designed to evaluate interactive discourse, and is thus unsuitable for discourse genres other than conversation (such as narrative and procedural discourse).

TABLE 5.2
Grice's (1975) "Co-operative Principle"

Quantity	Make your contribution as informative as is required Do not make your contribution more informative than required
Quality	Do not say what you believe to be false Do not say that for which you lack adequate evidence
Relation	Be relevant
Manner	Avoid obscurity of expression Avoid ambiguity Be brief (avoid unnecessary prolixity) Be orderly

TABLE 5.3
Damico's CDA (Damico, 1985, p.175).
(Reproduced with the permission of the publishers, Thinking Publications, USA.)

Quantity category
  Failure to provide significant information to listeners
  Use of non-specific vocabulary
  Informational redundancy
  Need for repetition
Quality category
  Message inaccuracy
Relation category
  Poor topic maintenance
  Inappropriate response
  Failure to ask relevant questions
  Situational inappropriateness
  Inappropriate speech style
Manner category
  Linguistic non-fluency
  Revision
  Delays before responding
  Failure to structure discourse
  Turn-taking difficulty
  Gaze inefficiency
  Inappropriate intonational contour

Like Grice, Damico emphasised that his categories are not necessarily mutually exclusive. He did, however, define each category and provided examples of utterance types which would be included in each. Damico argued that obtaining information about the individual's performance in each of the above areas allows a clearer delineation of behaviours to be targeted in therapy. Rather than the appropriate/inappropriate dichotomy proposed by Prutting and Kirchner, Damico's system requires the clinician to note (and sum) the incidence of discourse errors in each utterance, so that an overall percentage of utterances containing discourse errors may be calculated.

The CDA has been the basis of a number of studies examining discourse in TBI subjects, including both children (Jordan & Murdoch, 1990) and adults (Benjamin, Debinski, Fletcher, Hedger, Mealings, & Stewart-Scott, 1989; Snow et al., 1987; Snow, Douglas, & Ponsford, 1995). A number of important methodological issues have arisen from these studies. Not the least of these is the observation made by Jordan and Murdoch that this scale "... to some degree, examines normal discourse behaviours that become abnormal by nature of their frequency" (p.77). This is a problem inasmuch as very little is known about the discourse characteristics of non-injured subgroups within the population. The major clinical disadvantage of the CDA is the fact that a long-hand transcription must be performed on the discourse sample, and in most settings this is simply not practical.

Videotaping is an essential component of pragmatic assessment, regardless of the tool selected to analyse the conversational sample. Videotaping ensures that verbal and non-verbal aspects of communication are recorded, and are available for evaluation by the clinician and the TBI individual. This medium also ensures that accurate baseline measures are made. These are valuable for determining treatment priorities, and for assessing progress over time. TBI individuals and their families are often heartened and reassured about progress when they view videotape segments from earlier stages in the rehabilitation programme.

Limitations of pragmatic assessment

Although pragmatic profiles go well beyond the assessment of linguistic impairment covered by aphasia batteries, they are not without their own important limitations, and it is essential that clinicians are aware of these. First, when pragmatic assessment is carried out in a clinical setting, it has essentially been stripped of any relevance to important social roles the injured person aspires to resume, such as employee, student, or spouse. Further, only limited forms of reinforcement can be provided in a clinical setting, where the interaction is more of a semi-structured interview than a conversation. In the real world, reinforcement comes in many guises, overt and covert. These include attention, agreement, shared speaking time, and mutual enjoyment of the topic under discussion. In this sense, pragmatic assessment is probably guilty of many of the same "relevance crimes" as is structured language assessment.

Pragmatic assessment cannot reveal important strengths and weaknesses in the individual's ability to respond to subtle contextual features, where this assessment occurs in a setting cleansed of these. Interpersonal exchanges can have a range of purposes (e.g. socialisation, relaying of information), and vary according to the degree of formality required by the relative status of the speakers, and the environmental setting (e.g. background noise, visual distractions). These features supply a wealth of information about the inconsistencies likely to exist in the individual's performance on different occasions, and in different settings.

There is a paucity of information about the normal pragmatic behaviours of various subgroups within the population, as a function of cultural, ethnic, educational, and occupational factors. This is a particularly important issue, in view of the common premorbid characteristics of those who sustain TBI. Although it is generally agreed that certain discourse styles are associated with different sociolinguistic characteristics (e.g. Hudson, 1980; Stubbs, 1983), there is currently no systematic means whereby speech pathologists can allow for this in the process of pragmatic assessment. This underscores the importance of gathering information from the individual and relatives regarding premorbid communication style, as will be discussed in detail in the next section.

Assessment of conversation typically occurs in a quiet office setting, placing minimal cognitive demands on the injured person. Cognitive processes such as information processing skills, concentration, idea generation, planning and organisation of verbal output, and self-monitoring ability all come into play during normal conversation. Whilst assessing the TBI individual in a quiet setting may enhance the reliability of conversational sampling over time, it does little to tax the cognitive and linguistic processes which will be called into play in the real world. Speech pathologists need to spend more time directly observing the injured person in real-world contexts, rather than eliminating contextual features, or attempting to replicate these in the clinic setting. If this is not done, significant discrepancies may exist between clinical and real-world performance, and overly optimistic impressions may be formed about pragmatic abilities.

There are a number of threats to validity and reliability in applying rating scales to the assessment of pragmatic abilities. These have been discussed by Kearns (1990). They include reactivity (the tendency for observers or subjects to behave differently when they know they are being observed), observer drift (a gradual alteration in the way in which an observational code is applied over time), and observer expectancy and feedback (scoring bias associated with the scorer's expectation of change). Kearns cautioned that "... a group of observers that is trained to use an observational code may evolve into subgroups of observers that apply the code differently making comparisons across observers difficult or impossible" (1990, p.81). Further, as Bellack (1983) has observed, most interpersonal behaviours occur in continua, rather than in a normal/abnormal dichotomy. Bellack cited as examples of this, speaking volume, turn duration, and eye-contact. It is important, therefore, that clinical decisions are not made on the basis of discourse assessment tools alone. Taken in isolation, these may create false positives because of sociolinguistic factors, or false negatives because of their limited contextual sensitivity.

It is to be hoped that in the future, attempts will be made to examine the validity of techniques such as Direct Magnitude Estimation (DME) as a means of carrying out pragmatic assessment. DME was described by Campbell and Dollaghan (1992) as a technique for "... obtaining subjective judgements from listeners about various dimensions of a speaker's spontaneously produced language" (p.43). Using this technique, judges might be selected for their demographic similarities to the person from whom the language sample was elicited, and asked to comment upon a predetermined parameter, such as appropriateness or informativeness. This not only eliminates the need for long-hand transcriptions, but also potentially enhances the ecological validity of assessment, by virtue of its reference to normal sociolinguistic variations in the community.

ASSESSMENT OF COMMUNICATIVE HANDICAP

Although the assessment of pragmatic skills, using established measurement tools, is an important component of the speech pathology evaluation of the TBI individual, there is a need to look to other sources to obtain a clear understanding of how the injured person will function in a range of personally relevant settings. The speech pathologist needs to spend time learning about the various personal, social, recreational, educational, and/or vocational contexts in which the injured person will need to relate to others. This requires detailed discussions with the injured person and family members, and a recognition that communication requirements will change as a function of time, and increased participation in activities outside the hospital setting.

In addition to obtaining a detailed history, Hartley (1990) recommended that an "environmental needs assessment" (described by Beukelman, Yorkston, & Lossing, 1984) be performed, so that both current and projected communication needs can be considered as a basis for treatment. The environmental needs assessment considers communication needs under the following main headings: living/family environment, general community environment, educational environment, and work environment. In providing a rationale for this type of assessment, Beukelman et al. claimed that "Clinicians often do a better job of assessing the abilities in a traditional process model than they do in identifying specific communication needs. Failure to understand and account for these needs may result in training that fails to have a functional impact" (1984, pp.101–2). This type of approach enables clinicians to collect information about communicative strengths, and strategies the person employs to maximise success in different situations.

Questionnaires and checklists have been used to elicit the perceptions of brain-injured people and their close others in areas ranging from everyday living skills (Levin et al., 1987b) to psychosocial adaptation (Brooks et al., 1987a; Prigatano, 1986), attentional behaviour (Ponsford & Kinsella, 1991), cognitive functioning (Allen & Ruff, 1990), memory (Sloan et al., 1989) and social interaction (Elsass & Kinsella, 1987). Checklists with established inter-rater reliability and validity, such as the Neurobehavioural Rating Scale (Levin et al., 1987b) can be of assistance in the initial assessment phase, where problem areas are being identified. However, they do not usually provide sufficiently detailed or comprehensive information on which to base therapy.

Where questionnaires or checklists are employed, the question as to who should make the rating, and in what context, also requires consideration. TBI individuals and their families may have had insufficient opportunities to experience some of the potential changes wrought by the injury, or may have difficulties accepting and reporting on these. Notwithstanding this, Elsass and Kinsella made an important point when they observed that there needs to be "... a questioning of the general assumption that people with head injury are incapable of accurate perceptions and must necessarily be excluded from self-report changes in interpersonal relationships" (1987, p.76). It is also important to remember that the brain injury itself is not necessarily the only factor contributing to the individual's profile of communicative strengths and weaknesses. As Crosson (1987) has noted, other factors relevant to this include emotional reactions to injury and premorbid personality adjustment. The use of questionnaires such as that described above, together with close liaison between speech pathologist, psychologist, and social worker is important, therefore, in order to ensure that factors other than the brain injury are not overlooked in the course of assessment.

Although there are no tools which systematically account for premorbid personal and demographic aspects of communicative style, questionnaires, such as that designed by Swindell, Pashek, and Holland (1982), allow detailed investigation of the ways in which the injured person used verbal skills to negotiate a range of common communication tasks prior to injury. This questionnaire employs a five-point rating scale, on which relatives are asked to make judgements about the injured person's personal style and communicative style. Personal style includes parameters such as humour, problem solving, and flexibility. Communicative style covers such features as use of gesture during conversation, use of reading and writing in day-to-day life (e.g. reading newspapers, using a diary) and listening/turn-taking skills. Snow et al. (1995) have recently piloted a questionnaire version of Damico's CDA with TBI individuals and a close other. Preliminary results suggest that this form of assessment may be sensitive to changes not detected by conventional administration of the CDA alone. There is clearly a great deal of scope for developing measures of communicative handicap with this population.

In assessing the extent to which an individual is handicapped by communication difficulties, it is important that the role of motor speech disturbance is not overlooked. Dysarthria frequently results not only in compromised speech intelligibility, but also reduced speech rate, and inadequate volume. These features will compromise the individual's level of independence in social interaction, particularly with unfamiliar listeners, or in situations where there is even only moderate background noise. The presence of impaired speech intelligibility may cause others to assume that the injured person is intoxicated, or intellectually "subnormal", thus restricting the range of social, recreational, educational, and vocational options available. Even where this does not occur, the presence of dysarthria requires greater patience and perseverance on the part of the listener, and in many situations these are not forthcoming. It is important, therefore, that the assessment process considers the role of motor speech disorders in further handicapping the individual, so that appropriate strategies may be devised to overcome these. Such strategies include providing the injured person with a small card with a written explanation of the speech disturbance, which can be shown to unfamiliar listeners. This is particularly relevant where the dysarthria is so severe that strangers may be reluctant to persevere with the interaction. Family members can be advised to minimise background noise, such as television and radio, and should be encouraged to give the injured person their undivided attention on at least some occasions during the day. It is not always possible to cease other activities to interact with a dysarthric speaker, however it may be possible to make some uninterrupted time available, so that the injured person's communicative attempts are not constantly thwarted.

Finally, in considering communicative handicap, it is important to consider the role of language within the broad range of activities in which the individual may wish to participate, following return to the community. Return to study is particularly reliant on a range of language-related skills. These include reading comprehension, note-taking, ability to express ideas clearly and logically, ability to summarise written and verbal arguments, and the ability to understand shades of meaning. Whilst some of these skills can be assessed via clinic-based measures, many need to be monitored in the actual context of return to study. As outlined in Chapters 7 and 10, team members will need to liaise closely with teaching staff, in order to determine individual strengths and weaknesses in using language in this way. Therapists can then provide the individual with specific strategies, and practice on tasks which the person finds difficult.

USING THE PRINCIPLES OF THE *REAL* APPROACH TO MANAGE PRAGMATIC DISTURBANCES

General considerations in managing pragmatic disturbances

Just as assessment is approached as a problem-solving process, which incorporates information from a number of sources, so intervention demands constant attention to a range of complex factors. Both individual and group interventions should be considered for the management of communication difficulties, and these should be provided in a complementary manner. It is generally appropriate to commence with individual treatment, so that rapport can be established with the injured person, and time can be spent discussing particular difficulties and needs. The focus of both types of treatment needs to be on addressing communication problems within their real-world contexts.

In determining the type of intervention to be provided, it is vital that consideration be given to such factors as the injured person's age, gender, educational and occupational background, social and cultural experiences, severity of injury, time since onset, level of self-awareness, motivation for therapy, personal goals where communication is concerned, and the support available from family and friends. Any one of these variables may exert a powerful influence on decisions, such as whether to proceed with treatment, what focus treatment should have, and where the intervention should actually be provided.

In order for brain-injured people to participate meaningfully in communication therapy, they must be active participants in all stages, from discussion of assessment results, to delineation of goals, and selection of tasks and activities. Careful attempts should be made to determine the injured person's perspective about ways in which communication has or has not changed since the injury. This is an issue which needs to be handled with sensitivity, as it forms the basis of the rapport which will be required with the individual throughout treatment. Programmes that are divorced from the injured person's interests and preferences promote passive participation at best, and boredom or resentment at worst.

It is often helpful, at the commencement of therapy, to outline the components of normal communication, such as listening, turn-taking, observing politeness "rules" in relation to situational context, and noting the other speaker's non-verbal cues. These behaviours are gradually acquired through the process of social learning during childhood and adolescence, and are commonly compromised after brain injury. In our experience, many TBI individuals benefit from informal discussion about these facets of communication, as it helps them to analyse their own communicative strengths and weaknesses. This information can then be incorporated into therapy tasks.

Therapists need to have a flexible approach not only in targeting particular behaviours for treatment, but in amending the treatment programme in response to changes which occur in other aspects of the individual's rehabilitation. Some brain-injured people, for example, are very focused on physical goals, such as walking, in the earlier stages of their rehabilitation, and can see little relevance in improving communication skills (particularly where these are adequate for current day-to-day purposes). With the passage of time, however, these individuals frequently realise that subtle changes in communication affect them in the important social roles or relationships which they are attempting to resume. At this time, they may become receptive to (or actively seek) assistance with communication. For this reason, it is unwise to urge or cajole brain-injured people to accept therapy for which they are not ready. A negative experience in the early stages may result in reluctance to participate in intervention later on.

Communication is an inherently interactive process. However, being able to communicate "adequately" in a clinic setting with a therapist does not equip the injured person to make the myriad of subtle adjustments necessary in the real world. Such adjustments need to occur in response to changes in the environment, the relationship between speakers, and the purpose of the interaction. Clearly, therefore, treatment which takes place only in the clinic setting, using contrived tasks, and with only one interactant, will be insufficient to prepare the injured person for communicative success in the real world.

A variety of approaches have been taken to improving pragmatic skills. In those TBI individuals who have little awareness of their problems, limited capacity to benefit from feedback, or poor motivation for therapy, behavioural approaches are most appropriate. These are outlined in detail in Chapter 6. Giles, Fussey, and Burgess (1988) described one such case study, involving a 27-year-old male with severe TBI who presented with an inappropriate, attention seeking, circumlocutory style of conversation. In daily, half-hour sessions, he was repeatedly prompted, using the phrase "short answers", to use clear, concise statements, in three types of interactional tasks. Successful performance was rewarded with social attention, and praise and chocolate. Failure led to time out on the spot (TOOTS). Statistical analysis revealed a significant response to the intervention, which continued after treatment ceased.

The role of individual therapy in alleviating pragmatic disturbances

The therapist and TBI individual need to construct a list of personally relevant communication tasks, and practise these, both in and outside the hospital setting. Incorporating information from all levels of assessment, it is possible to provide role plays to practise specific verbal skills (such as job interview techniques, asking for information in shops), with both familiar and unfamiliar interactants. The level of complexity of such activities can be varied by altering the degree of co-operation provided by the other speaker, and by conducting sessions in noisy, distracting settings. Relevant components of structured programmes may be adapted for use with the injured person. Such programmes include Wiig's (1982) "Let's Talk" materials, and the conversational strategies outlined by Schwartz and McKinley (1984).

Where possible, sessions should be videotaped, so that the therapist and TBI individual can evaluate performance in terms of strengths and weaknesses. This feedback is then incorporated into the next attempt. When the injured person and the therapist feel that sufficient practice has been carried out, such tasks can then be performed in real-life settings, relevant to the person concerned. It is helpful to carefully plan the purpose and content of an interaction, so that feedback can be tailored to the original goals. Although one-to-one treatment has a role in providing specific practice of certain communication skills, efforts should be made to simulate as closely as possible, the demands of real-life communication. This will have greater salience for the injured person than contrived tasks, and will thus enhance motivation and learning. Addressing communication in relation to the roles the person wishes to resume means that generalisation is not a postscript to intervention, rather it is the focus from the outset. This approach also overcomes the TBI individual's often justified protest that therapy tasks bear little resemblance to situations they face in the real world. Therapists should seek to improve the person's motivation by presenting tasks which have good face validity for the individual concerned. This is particularly important for individuals who lack insight into their pragmatic difficulties. In such cases, carrying out treatment in personally salient settings is of even greater importance.

Whilst it is always important that feedback (verbal, graphic, videotape) be provided to the injured person and family by the therapist, it is also essential to create opportunities for the injured person and family members to give feedback to therapy staff. This can be done informally, via regular discussions and semi-structured interviews. TBI individuals need to be taught ways of evaluating their own performance, for example using rating scales and checklists devised with the therapist's assistance. Staff need to promote an atmosphere of shared responsibility for problem-solving where communication difficulties are concerned. It must be remembered that family members may spend vast amounts of time with the injured person, and are thereby well-placed to comment about communication skills in a range of settings. They are frequently resourceful and innovative in suggesting approaches to overcoming difficulties which the clinician has not considered. Discussions with the injured person and family members often reveals something of how realistic particular approaches are, in relation to the other constraints they face. Finally, consulting with all parties in this way promotes a sense of shared ownership for the outcomes of intervention, and provides a milieu in which decisions regarding the injured person's future can be made with some ease and trust.

Therapy tasks need to be broken down into logical elements and structured sequentially for the individual. For example, a person who wishes to obtain information about gymnasium programmes close to home may need assistance not only in accessing a list of telephone numbers from the directory, but also in planning the content and structure of the call. The therapist needs to help the injured person make written notes of the questions to be asked, how best to phrase these, and what relevant information to provide to the person who answers the call. Opportunities should be provided for tasks to be repeated, under identical and then later, different conditions. Feedback needs to provide clear and immediate information about why success did or did not occur, so that it has a modifying effect on the person's next attempt. Efforts should always be made to find some aspect of the attempt which can be praised, so that positive self-esteem is promoted at all times.

Notwithstanding this, in structuring intervention, a balance needs to be struck between the likelihood of success and the need for the individual to experience failure. Completely protecting the injured person from communicative situations in which failure may occur does not promote learning, and the attainment of greater independence. It is important, therefore, to allow the injured person to experience the logical consequences of pragmatic errors, in real-life situations. Such consequences may range from confusion on the part of the listener, where a question has been poorly organised, to offence being caused by an inappropriately familiar manner with a stranger. Reactions such as these can provide potent learning experiences. It is most important, however, that such situations are sensitively discussed afterwards, so that the injured person is confident to approach similar situations in the future. Therapists also need to bear in mind that the individual's performance may fluctuate as a function of fatigue and motivation, and this should not be mistakenly labelled as laziness or unco-operativeness.

Traditionally, restoration and compensation have been seen as opposing forces in the rehabilitation of cognitive and communicative disorders following acquired brain damage, with the latter being seen as something of a compromise when the former has failed (e.g. Milton & Wertz, 1986; Ylvisaker & Holland, 1985). As discussed in the previous chapter, repeated practice on isolated cognitive tasks does not automatically result in improved communication skills in real-world contexts. Throughout the rehabilitation process, the individual and those in the environment will need to find ways of minimising the impact of on-going communication difficulties in day-to-day life. This is the process of adapting to disability and minimising handicap. Some of these processes will be commenced quite naturally by the individual and family members. Others require concerted efforts at problem-solving, and a willingness to try a number of options before reaching an acceptable compromise.

Compensatory or adaptive techniques range from the use of amplification systems for the person with inadequate volume to the use of agreed cues for the individual who is talking excessively. Some TBI individuals benefit from the use of key phrases to bear in mind while conversing with others, such as "keep it short", for the person who loses the listener's interest by providing excessive detail. Initially this might be written on a card, and kept in the person's view during practise tasks. Later, this can be replaced with a more subtle visual reminder, such as an elastic band around the person's wrist. This is not obtrusive, but may be sufficient to remind the person to keep the amount of detail provided in check. The person with impaired speech intelligibility might be taught to engage the listener's attention before speaking, and to use short phrases to compensate for inadequate respiratory support for speech. Family members can be encouraged to use consistent cues to promote the injured person's interpersonal skills in settings outside the hospital. This may simply mean saying "I think you've already said that" to the person with memory difficulties, or using a hand signal to indicate inappropriate speaking volume. The adaptation process is likely to be a very lengthy one. Furthermore, the communication problems and needs of the injured individual will probably change over time. Therefore, as with all forms of therapy, access to assistance in adapting to communication problems needs to be available on a continuing basis.

CASE REPORT—TRACEY

Tracey, the 26-year-old woman introduced earlier in this chapter, needed to refine her telephone skills in order to commence a work trial in the position she had held prior to her injury. Her skills were compromised not only by reduced speech intelligibility, but also her tendency to omit important introductory comments and information required by the listener. Therapy tasks were concerned with planning telephone calls, which were audiotaped for analysis and discussion by Tracey and the therapist.

In the planning stage, Tracey was encouraged to write down the questions or information she needed to convey, before making the calls (which were genuine, not role-played). In this way, Tracey could not only plan the content, but she could also organise an appropriate sequence of ideas, and discuss ways of phrasing her message so as not to confuse or offend the listener.

Analysis of the taped conversations included comments on the appropriateness of her speech style and clarity, as well as the overall success of the interaction in terms of the original purpose of the call. Tracey's confidence and overall communicative effectiveness were strengthened prior to her commencement of a formal work trial. Her speech pathologist spent time with her in the workplace, giving similar feedback. This process revealed particular difficulties which were not apparent in the clinical setting, i.e. the fact that Tracey performed relatively well if dealing with one call at a time, but became anxious if required to ask one caller to hold whilst completing a call. Therapy was then concerned with strategies to deal with this pressure, such as writing down and using various politely worded phrases, taking written notes of the speaker's enquiries, so as to avoid confusion between calls, and explaining to the caller that a number of lines were busy simultaneously.

Ongoing therapy was concerned with developing strategies for problems as they arose in Tracey's work setting, and then breaking these down into logical steps. In this wayTracey was able to deal with increasing demands at work, and gained greater self-confidence as a result of this. This enabled her to be less defensive about difficulties when they arose, and she began to generate similar strategies for other communication tasks.

Tracey and her therapist monitored progress over time by evaluating her performance in relation to the goals agreed upon at the commencement of her work trial. Tracey was encouraged to monitor her own progress by using behaviour checklists. Discrepancies between her ratings and those of the therapist could then be used as a basis for determining new goals in therapy.

The role of groups in alleviating pragmatic disturbances

Group treatment, whether aimed specifically at conversational skills, or at other aspects of social behaviour, provides many opportunities to address pragmatic difficulties. Group treatment can allow the injured person to practise skills learned in individual sessions, to give and receive feedback and support from peers, and improve insight about communicative strengths and weaknesses. A number of studies have examined the role of groups in addressing impaired social skills in the TBI population (e.g. Braunling-McMorrow, Lloyd, & Fralish, 1986; Brotherton, Thomas, Wisotek, & Milan, 1988; Ehrlich & Sipes, 1985; Gajar, Schloss, Schloss, & Thompson, 1984; Lewis, Nelson, Nelson, & Reusink, 1988). This research has generally yielded promising results for the efficacy of this type of intervention, provided that therapists are prepared for change to be gradual. These studies point to the need to target only one or two behaviours at a time, and emphasise the importance of consistency of feedback across situations if changes are to be sustained over time. Residual cognitive and linguistic strengths have also been noted as important factors in determining the extent to which an individual is likely to benefit from this type of intervention.

In general, group treatment should be seen as an adjunct, rather than a substitute for individual therapy. The latter maintains the focus on individual goal setting, and allows practice of specific skills the injured person is finding difficult in the group, such as, anger control, initiation, following topic changes, inhibiting inappropriate responses, or difficulty asking questions which promote the flow of conversation. Individual sessions also allow some monitoring of the extent to which skills learnt in the group are being applied in the individual's everyday life. If this is a problem, as it frequently is, it may be useful to involve a close relative as a co-therapist, and conduct therapy in relevant, real-life settings. Such individual therapy may also be necessary for those who do not have the cognitive skills to cope with a group interaction or those with specific, and quite severe skill deficits.

For those who have some capacity to benefit from modelling and feedback, group interventions focusing on specific skill areas through role play, and the use of videotape and interpersonal feedback have been shown to be effective (Brotherton et al., 1988; Helffenstein & Weschler, 1982; Hopewell, Burke, Weslowski, & Zawlocki, 1990). Prior to starting a group, it is important to carefully assess the problem areas, and therapy goals of each individual, to ensure that these will be specifically addressed and incorporated into the goals of the group, rather than presenting a "package". The behaviours to be tackled in a group may include any, or all of aspects of social perception, impulsivity, non-verbal communication, conversational skills, anger control, and assertiveness. There may be specific training on how to apply these skills in a range of situations. Group interactions need to be highly structured, with constant repetition and review of goals (individual and group), and the means by which these are to be achieved.

It is generally advisable to run groups as a series, i.e. with defined beginning and end points, so that certain pragmatic skills can be targeted and prioritised, depending on the needs of the individuals to be included. In this way, participants can be informed of the goals of the group—general and specific, and can be invited to participate in evaluation at its conclusion. Such evaluation may take the form of informal discussion, or short, simple questionnaires or rating scales. It should be made clear at the outset that responsibility for the success of the group is a shared one. Issues such as punctuality need to be discussed, as do matters such as who will be responsible for setting up, and tidying the room, and who will ensure that refreshments are provided. Generally speaking these are not matters which need to be the sole responsibility of staff. If necessary, it may be helpful for group members to agree on "rules" for how the group should be run, for example, ensuring that everyone has an opportunity to contribute and making appropriate allowances for people with special limitations, such as motor speech disturbances. It is important that groups are kept small, and are comprised of individuals with some degree of compatability in terms of age, social and educational background, and general interest levels, in order to promote group cohesion. Group treatment needs to be made available not only during the rehabilitation phase, but also to injured people who have returned to the community, and are gaining direct experience of the consequences of impaired interpersonal functioning.

Following an introductory session, basic skills, such as listening, using eye contact, or observing personal space boundaries, can be introduced one at a time, and segmented into component behaviours. The skills selected will depend on the specific difficulties, and individual therapy goals of the participants. Explanations should be provided as to why each skill is important in social interactions. This process has been described in some detail by Goldstein, Sprafkin, Gershaw, and Klein (1980), who outlined the components of modelling, role playing, performance feedback, and transfer of training. Modelling by group leaders may be followed by practice in pairs, and then between the leaders and members of the group, with coaching and feedback from other group members. As with individual therapy, it is important that therapists adopt a flexible approach to goal-setting and the selection of tasks. Over time, certain problems may emerge as particularly relevant for a number of members. Group leaders need to be prepared to pursue these in greater depth, avoiding a prescriptive approach to the material to be covered. A number of members may, for example, have experienced difficulties with information processing in cognitively demanding situations. Specific strategies for dealing with this problem can then be discussed and practised, and group members can evaluate the success or otherwise of different approaches.

It is important that negative or corrective feedback is preceded by feedback which focuses on the positive aspects of the individual's performance. Feedback needs to be immediate and given in concrete, but not condescending terms, with repeated demonstration. This may be facilitated by the use of videotaping. It is important to practise each behaviour until certain agreed upon criteria have been achieved. It may be useful to have group leaders model inappropriate ways of interacting, such as talking without looking at each other, so that group members can gain a better understanding of the impact of inappropriate social behaviours on others. Wherever possible, role-play situations should be made relevant to group members. To this end, it may be possible to re-enact situations members themselves have experienced and found difficult. Catch phrases can be taught to prompt certain behaviours, for example "stop and think", "keep cool", or "look at him/her". Cue cards may be helpful in this respect. Relaxation training may also need to be provided wherever anxiety is contributing to difficulties interacting with others.

Participants may be given homework exercises to enable them to practise what they have learned in the group, in a variety of real-life situations. They should be encouraged to keep records of their practice, and these should be carefully reviewed. Families should be informed as to the skills being practised, and encouraged to give feedback to the injured person as well. Some sessions should be conducted in community settings, as applying new skills in other contexts is the most important, yet most difficult goal to achieve.

Retraining interpersonal skills is usually a very lengthy process, and is unlikely to be achieved successfully in a few sessions. Given the central role that effective communication skills play in the resumption of valued life roles, it is important to take a long term view of the therapy process. All staff and family members need to be aware of treatment goals, and provide consistent feedback to the injured person. Further detail on social skills training is provided by Burke (1988), Hopewell et al. (1990), and Boake (1991).

All intervention, whether individual or group, needs to be subject to on-going evaluation in terms of its relevance to specific skills the individual requires, and the extent to which these are being developed. Whilst reassessment on structured testing at regular intervals is an important aspect of monitoring change, these tests frequently have ceiling and practice effects when used with TBI individuals. Evaluation of the efficacy of therapy, therefore, must have behavioural change as its focus. Just as intervention should be carried out in settings which are relevant to the injured person, the extent to which the person has achieved and sustained behavioural change needs to be assessed in everyday contexts. This can be done via behavioural checklists, questionnaires, and interviews with the injured person and family members. Single-case, multiple-baseline designs may be used to assess the impact of therapy on specific skills. These processes allow for continuous modifications to be incorporated into the treatment programme, in response to improvements made by the individual, and/ or changes in the environment. They also provide a useful basis for discussion with family members and funding bodies about future therapy.

CASE REPORT—KERRY

When assessed at six months post-injury, Kerry (the 22-year-old woman introduced earlier in this chapter) was found to have a number of significant neuropsychological impairments. These included impulsivity, poor planning and organisation, a tendency to fatigue on tasks requiring sustained attention (resulting in an increased rate of errors, many of which she did not detect), and a slightly elevated affect. Strengths included her ability to benefit from structure, and her willingness to accept feedback. Speech pathology testing showed confrontation naming to be within normal limits, however Kerry's verbal fluency scores were significantly depressed in relation to her age and years of education. Qualitative features of her verbal fluency performance included slowness, and a tendency to repeat items she had already supplied. Kerry had difficulty with the ambiguities sub-test of the Test of Language Competence (Wiig & Secord, 1989). Auditory processing was not impaired at a sentence and short paragraph level, however Kerry complained of difficulty following conversation when in restaurants with friends. Assessment of pragmatic skills using Damico's CDA revealed difficulties in the quantity, relation, and manner categories. These included excessive detail, use of non-specific vocabulary, situational inappropriateness (smiling out of context and excessive volume when excited), revision behaviour, and failure to structure discourse. The speech pathologist also found Kerry to be somewhat unconcerned about the changes wrought by her injury, however she was found to be co-operative, and eager to participate in therapy aimed at return to work.

Therapy commenced with a discussion with Kerry about the assessment findings, viewing of videotaped segments of her conversation, and feedback from family members about ways in which Kerry's communication skills had altered post-injury. As she had recently commenced a part-time work-trial, Kerry felt that her problems with inappropriate smiling and excessive volume could disadvantage her, thus she saw these as the priorities for therapy.

In discussion with her psychologist and speech pathologist, it emerged that Kerry's inappropriate smiling was partly related to performance anxiety. This was addressed via a number of methods, including relaxation techniques and role plays. Role plays were carried out in both individual and group sessions, and were videotaped so that Kerry could evaluate her performance, and change could be monitored over time. Situations similar to those likely to arise in her work setting were simulated, and acted out using both familiar and unfamiliar interactants. As Kerry's confidence in her verbal skills increased, inappropriate smiling became a less frequent feature in her interactions with others.

Excessive volume was found to be a problem when Kerry became particularly animated in conversation with others. Again, videotaped role plays were a useful way of enhancing her awareness of this, and over time she was able to report on factors likely to cause an increase in her volume. These included being in settings where authority figures were not immediately present, being rushed, or recounting humorous events. During role play activities in individual therapy, a "Voice Lite" was used to give Kerry immediate visual feedback about her volume, and the desired threshold was lowered over time. In less structured settings, such as groups, Kerry found key phrases such as "keep it down" useful reminders. Initially she had this written on a cue card in front of her. Later, however, she learned to repeat this to herself during such interactions. In fact, Kerry spontaneously developed a number of key phrases to help overcome problems she encountered at later stages in her work trial. For example, she had difficulty making enquiries on the telephone, but found the phrase "stop and think" a useful reminder to make written notes prior to lifting the receiver. Kerry was fortunate to have a supportive family, and was willing to receive direct feedback from them about these problems. This enhanced her use of strategies at home and in social settings.

Over the following six months, however, the other problems highlighted by the CDA began to interfere with Kerry's ability to resume and sustain friendships in her former social circle. The focus of therapy then shifted to her tendency to supply excessive detail and difficulties structuring discourse in a logical way. In individual therapy, Kerry and her therapist discussed the differences between concise and verbose communication, and practised videotaped tasks requiring clear, short answers. Kerry was taught to watch for non-verbal signs of restlessness on the part of the other speaker, and to avoid the embarrassment of repeating herself, was taught to use the phrase "I'm not sure whether I've told you this..." before continuing. This provided the listener with a comfortable way of averting an unnecessary repetition of things already said. In group sessions, other members were encouraged to tell Kerry when they found her conversation difficult to follow, or when she was repeating herself. Initially, Kerry was surprised at how frequently this occurred, and she was highly motivated to improve. She was encouraged to aim to supply less information in a clear concise way, rather than large amounts of poorly organised ideas. This sometimes meant spending more time listening than talking, a strategy which Kerry learned to employ where she felt unable to generate ideas and/or organise her thoughts sufficiently quickly to keep up with the interaction.

CONCLUSIONS

The role of communication in resuming valued roles in the community cannot be overemphasised. All members of the rehabilitation team need to understand pragmatic disturbances, and the effect these can have on the individual in a range of everyday settings. Assessment needs to incorporate information about premorbid lifestyle with both quantitative and qualitative aspects of performance on a range of communication tasks. The limitations of structured language testing must be stressed in this regard. Opportunities need to be made for TBI individuals to receive treatment both individually and in groups. The ability to talk well and the ability to communicate effectively are not synonymous, and this distinction often assumes greater significance as the individual moves away from rehabilitation, back into the real world. It is vital, therefore, that services are available in the community to assist the TBI individual to overcome pragmatic disturbances, and thus participate in as wide a range of activities as possible.

CHAPTER SIX

Assessment and management of behaviour problems associated with TBI

Jennie Ponsford

INTRODUCTION

One of the greatest sources of stress for those living and working with people who have sustained TBI is dealing with changes in behaviour. Whilst it must be acknowledged that those with TBI are all individuals, and may have displayed antisocial behaviour prior to injury, many outcome studies have shown that significant changes in behaviour and personality are common following TBI. The behavioural changes most frequently documented have been outlined in Chapter 1. They include the development of impulsivity, a low frustration tolerance, verbally threatening or physically aggressive behaviour, disinhibited, inappropriate or irresponsible social behaviour, self-centredness leading to attention-seeking and/or manipulative behaviour, changes in emotional expression, and, at the other end of the spectrum, reduced drive, initiative, and motivation, often accompanied by extreme slowness (Brooks et al., 1987a; Lezak, 1987; Ponsford et al., 1995a).

Such changes occur alone or in combination, and in widely varying degrees. In many instances they are also accompanied by a lack of insight on the part of the injured person, who may therefore fail to acknowledge or understand the differences others perceive. This can result in an unwillingness or inability to modify the difficult behaviour. Poor self-monitoring can mean that even when TBI individuals acknowledge the nature of behavioural difficulties and show a desire to do something to change the situation, they continue nevertheless to behave in the same manner.

There are also complex secondary reactions that emerge in response to the specific problems caused by the injury. For example, a hospitalised TBI individual may behave so inappropriately as to be avoided by staff, family and friends, thereby receiving much less attention. This may lead to the development of maladaptive attention-seeking behaviours, such as constantly screaming out, in order to gain attention. If left to continue without intervention, these behaviours may, in themselves, become part of the person's established behavioural repertoire.

These behaviour problems, when severe, can potentially result in danger to the person who has sustained TBI and others, causing great stress to rehabilitation staff and families. As a result, the TBI individual may receive less rehabilitation than required. They are also the greatest barriers to return to normal social function. Interventions to change behaviour should only be applied for these reasons. *It is not acceptable to attempt to modify a person's behaviour just because it causes inconvenience to staff or is slightly unusual.* If used for the right reasons, the application of appropriate behaviour management techniques can be an important part of the rehabilitation process following TBI. The development and use of such techniques with severely behaviourally-disturbed TBI individuals owes much to the work of Peter Eames and Rodger Wood (Eames & Wood, 1985; Wood, 1984, 1987), upon whose work this chapter draws. The emphasis of this chapter will be on dealing with behaviour problems which arise during the course of rehabilitation. There will be further discussion of techniques for dealing with behaviour problems in the community in Chapter 9.

EDUCATION AND INVOLVEMENT OF STAFF
AND FAMILY

In applying behaviour management techniques, it is most important that staff, family and friends understand the basis of the problems in question and the reasons for intervention. In particular, there must be an understanding that many behavioural changes are a direct result of the brain injury itself, and that the injured individual may not have the capacity to recognise such changes, or to spontaneously modify behaviour. This should be the first step in the behaviour management process. It is also important that staff understand the distinction between the person they are working with and that person's behaviour. Whilst a particular behaviour may be undesirable or offensive, it is not acceptable to generalise from this to make negative judgements about the whole person. Staff need to understand the individual's strengths, as well as weaknesses, and believe that there is some capacity to replace problem behaviours with more adaptive ones.

In the rehabilitation setting, behaviour management techniques must be applied consistently by the entire rehabilitation team if they are to be effective. This means working together from the beginning in attempting to understand the reasons for the injured person's behaviour, devising a plan for addressing the problem, consistently and co-operatively implementing the plan, checking its progress, making necessary adjustments, and assessing its effectiveness. Such involvement, which should also extend to the family and any others having frequent contact with the injured individual, will maximise the commitment of all team members and the family to the implementation of any procedures agreed upon.

It is also particularly important for all members of the rehabilitation team to have a clear understanding of principles of behaviour management. Where this is not the case the team co-ordinator should see that the assistance of an appropriately qualified psychologist is sought to provide staff with the necessary training. The application of principles such as those outlined below in daily interactions with TBI individuals can in many instances circumvent the development of serious behaviour problems and hence the need for formal behaviour modification programmes.

ASSESSMENT OF BEHAVIOUR PROBLEMS

Objective recording

Careful assessment must precede any attempt to deal with a behaviour problem. The first step should be to obtain an accurate and objective picture of the behaviour in question by observation and careful recording. In order to achieve a clear definition of the behaviour which is causing a problem, staff need to record behaviour in observable terms which require no interpretation. For example, "David hit another patient with his fist", rather than "David had an aggressive outburst"; or "Peter touched the breasts of a female therapy aide", rather than "Peter exhibited inappropriate sexual behaviour" This ensures agreement as to the behaviour being documented, avoiding interpretation of terms, such as "aggressive" or "disinhibited".

Once such agreement has been reached, all instances of that behaviour should be recorded over a specified period, such as a day or a week, depending on the frequency with which the behaviour occurs, or by "time-sampling" (Wood, 1987). Time-sampling involves observation and recording of behaviour for two periods of an hour each day for 6 days, the times being varied, so that over the 6 days behaviour is sampled across a 12-hour period. Recordings should be accompanied by information as to the time, the setting, the circumstances leading to the behaviour, and what followed. The circumstances should be viewed in the broad, as well as the immediate context. For example, the injured person may have been upset by some other event prior to the incident, such as the failure of a relative to visit, or a disappointing result at a driving assessment. In recording the consequences of the behaviour, it is important to consider the following:

- Whether the person received a pleasant sensory experience or obtained relief from an unpleasant sensory experience as a result of the behaviour.
- How people responded to the behaviour.
- Whether the person avoided doing something as a result of the behaviour.
- Whether the person obtained access to an activity or object after the behaviour.
- What seemed to improve the behaviour, or make it stop? What made it worse?

Recording of the frequency with which the behaviour being modified is exhibited must continue throughout the management phase and for a period after the intervention has ceased.

Consideration of causative factors
There should be careful consideration of factors which may be contributing to the behaviour problem. As Eames (1988) has pointed out, a brain-injured individual's behaviour is the result of a complex interplay of causative factors.

Brain injury
First, there are factors relating to the nature of the brain injury. Whilst it is impossible to obtain an exact picture of the extent of damage to the brain following TBI, the results of CT and MRI studies, neurological examination, and neuropsychological assessment can give some indication as to the nature and severity of injury, and the extent to which different functional systems having some bearing on behaviour may have been affected. For example, brainstem dysfunction may result in reduced alertness and consequent confusion. Injury to limbic structures may affect emotional expression and lead to unprovoked outbursts of anger. Frontal lobe damage is known to cause a general reduction in the

regulation and control of behaviour, leading to a low frustration tolerance, increased irritability and aggression, disinhibition and other antisocial behaviour. Responses tend to be disproportionate to the precipitating circumstances.

Person
Second, there are factors relating to the person who has sustained the brain injury. According to Eames (1988, p.3), "the family, developmental, medical, psychiatric, and personal histories of the patient all contribute vulnerabilities and predispositions that are likely to be relevant to both the form and the content of any behaviour disorder". It is important to obtain a very careful and detailed picture of these aspects of the TBI person's background. In particular, an attempt should be made to obtain a profile of the premorbid personality, previous modes of emotional expression, and whether there has been any previous psychiatric disturbance, either in the brain-injured individual or the family.

Context
Finally, it is important to consider the context within which the disturbed behaviour is occurring. From the point of view of the person who has sustained TBI, the experience of being cared for in a setting such as a hospital ward or a rehabilitation unit will almost certainly be unfamiliar and may be extremely threatening. When one has previously had control over one's life, it can be very difficult to accept help or take direction from others. The fact that the majority of those injured are male and the majority of those assisting in their recovery are female may add to this problem, as may the fact that TBI occurs so frequently in adolescence and early adulthood. In the longer term, it may be necessary to adapt to physical or cognitive limitations, greater dependency on others, a different living situation, a new daily routine or lack thereof, as well as the loss of the social network which existed prior to the injury. Such experiences undoubtedly contribute to the development of confusion, frustration, anger, depression, and lack of motivation.

PHARMACOLOGICAL TREATMENT OF BEHAVIOUR PROBLEMS

The vast majority of behaviour problems can and should be managed behaviourally or environmentally. In most instances, pharmacological treatment of behaviour problems should be used with TBI patients only after behavioural and environmental approaches have been tried and failed, because of the possibility of its diminishing impact on cognitive function and deleterious effects on recovery.

In many instances, the primary action of a pharmacological agent on one system has associated secondary effects on other systems, so that it is difficult to target a particular problem without influencing other aspects of the patient's functioning. Many TBI individuals experience problems with fatigue, arousal, attention, memory and initiation. Sedation and/or impairment of memory are common side-effects of medications used to control aggressive behaviour, such as major tranquillisers and benzodiazepines (Swonger & Constantine, 1983). Administration of these medications can exacerbate such problems, sometimes increasing confusion and prolonging agitation, and clouding cognitive recovery. A recent case report by Sandel, Olive, and Rader (1993) suggested that the administration of neuroleptics, in this case chlorpromazine, may actually induce a delusional state in brain-injured patients, as well as impair cognitive function. Antianxiety drugs can result in disinhibition of behaviour (Gardos, 1980). Other common side-effects of drugs used to treat behaviour problems can include a range of motor disturbances and changes in blood pressure. There is evidence that some major tranquillisers are epileptogenic (Cope, 1987). Some animal studies have also suggested that they may slow recovery of brain function (Feeney, Gonzalez, & Law, 1982). As Cope (1987, p.3) has pointed out, "the final clinical effect of any neuroactive drug in TBI therefore will depend on a complex mixture of the neuropathology and various primary and secondary drug actions".

Pharmacological intervention is particularly inappropriate for TBI people who are still in PTA, because their agitation is largely caused by confusion, which may be prolonged by the administration of medications. It may need to be considered, as an adjunct to other approaches, at a later stage, where recovery appears to be plateauing, where behavioural or environmental approaches have not been sufficiently successful, and where the behaviour problem, in most instances aggression, is compromising return to the community or long-term placement. The responsibility for prescribing medication should lie with a specialist in rehabilitation medicine or psychiatrist experienced in the management of TBI. As there have been few controlled trials examining the efficacy of certain drugs in the treatment of TBI individuals, there are few diagnostic and treatment guidelines available. Thus great care needs to be exercised by the medical practitioner administering pharmacological treatment, both in commencing treatment and weaning the TBI person off the medication. It is also very important to assess objectively the impact of the medication on the behaviour in question, using similar methods to those used for evaluating behavioural interventions.

Careful selection of medication is very important. An appropriate anticonvulsant may be the drug of first choice in cases where aggression is thought to be epileptogenic, resulting from temporal lobe damage. According to Wood (1984, p.196), this "is characterised by a sudden, spontaneous outburst of probably violent aggression which is unprovoked, poorly controlled and usually short-lived". Such outbursts are also usually followed by emotional distress and remorse, and are out of character with behaviour seen between outbursts. Carbamazepine is the anticonvulsant which has been shown to have fewest effects on cognitive function (Duncan, Trimble, & Shovon, 1989; Thompson & Trimble, 1983). It is therefore the anticonvulsant most frequently used with TBI individuals.

Beta-adrenergic blocking medications, such as propranolol, have been the most widely studied and used pharmacological agents in the treatment of chronic aggression secondary to organic brain disorders, including TBI. Propranolol reportedly does not significantly alter cognitive function (Yudofsky, Williams, & Groman, 1981), and has been shown to reduce the intensity, but not the frequency of agitated behaviour in TBI subjects, when used in doses of 60 to 420 mg (Brooke, Patterson, Quested, Cardenas, & Farrel-Roberts, 1992). Yudofsky, Silver, and Hales (1990) recommend maintenance on the highest dose for eight weeks, prior to determining that the injured person is not responding to the medication. There are, however, some significant contra-indications to its use. These include the presence of asthma, severe cardiopulmonary disease, severe diabetes and significant vascular disease (Yudofsky et al., 1990).

In cases where the behavioural disturbance is related to a pre-existing psychiatric condition the need for medication may be more pressing and appropriate. TBI can lead to the development of psychiatric disturbances in the form of manic-depressive psychosis or schizophrenia. Lezak (1987) reported a relatively high incidence of hallucinatory or delusional ideation and paranoia. Such disturbances also require prompt pharmacological intervention. The use of antidepressants may be necessary where there is development of severe depression that does not respond to psychological therapy alone.

ENVIRONMENTAL APPROACHES

In many instances, a careful analysis of the context in which the problem behaviour is occurring can provide information which allows the behaviour to be tackled by changing the injured person's environment in some way. For example, it may be that agitation is precipitated by noise, the presence of too many people, therapy which is placing too many demands, or simply fatigue. Confusion may be aggravated by moving the injured individual around the hospital. It is frequently possible to reduce a problem significantly by removing precipitating environmental factors, which should become evident during the baseline period. When assessing possible reasons for the development of behaviour problems it is also important to consider how comfortable and pleasant the environment is, how stimulating it is, and whether there is adequate privacy. Cultural issues may need to be taken into account. Additionally, there are issues particularly important in adolescence, such as body image, peer group influence and independence, which may be contributing to the difficulties.

BEHAVIOURAL APPROACHES

If environmental changes alone are insufficient to reduce the problem, the recommended approach follows a behavioural philosophy. Behaviour therapy focuses primarily on observable behaviour, regardless of the underlying cause. It involves the application of experimentally established learning principles to change maladaptive behaviour. Social behaviour is shaped by environmental factors or responses. That is, an individual may be more or less likely to behave in a certain way in the future, depending on the response to that behaviour received in the past. TBI can result in a reduced ability to use feedback to judge the social appropriateness of behaviour. It may be necessary to introduce appropriate contingencies so that more adaptive behaviour can be relearned. Hence, behaviour modification procedures are designed either to increase the probability of desirable behaviours, or to decrease the probability of undesirable behaviours, by altering responses or consequences of that behaviour.

As outlined by Wood (1984), reinforcement is the usual means of increasing a given behaviour. *Positive reinforcement* is the presentation of some desirable consequence so that a person will be more likely to behave in a certain way again. *Negative reinforcement* involves the removal of something undesirable with the same goal. Methods used to decrease the probability of a given behaviour being exhibited again include *negative punishment* or *response cost*, where something desirable is removed, or *positive punishment*, where some undesirable consequence follows a behaviour.

Such consequences must be *meaningful* (that is, truly desirable/undesirable to the person). They must follow the behaviour *immediately*, and should be given in an *obvious* way, so there is a clear association between the behaviour and its consequences. They should also be given *frequently* and *consistently* over an extended period, in order to consolidate the response. If the behaviour is not followed consistently by the chosen reinforcer, the problematic behaviour may reappear.

There are a number of different approaches to behaviour modification. The choice as to which is most appropriate will depend on a number of factors, including the nature and severity of the problem, the TBI individual's level of cognitive function and the environment in which the intervention is to be carried out. It is generally preferable to use positive reinforcement wherever possible.

Use of positive reinforcement

Probably the most powerful form of positive reinforcement is *social reinforcement*—praise, encouragement, or simply giving the person attention. If applied consistently and appropriately, social reinforcement can be sufficient to shape and sustain desirable behaviour. In the majority of cases it is also the easiest to apply.

Sometimes more material forms of positive reinforcement are required in addition to praise and attention. *Material reinforcement* may consist of special foods or drinks, sweets, cigarettes, money, other privileges, such as outings, telephone calls, watching television, or whatever is important to the person whose behaviour is being modified.

Token economy

Within a rehabilitation unit, a *token economy* may be used as a medium of exchange for these material rewards. Such systems should always be administered and supervised by a psychologist. Within a token economy, plastic tokens are used as a means of administering rewards as positive reinforcement for desirable behaviour. A token economy system can provide a useful structure which ensures that staff will respond to the TBI person's behaviour in a systematic way. Once the behaviour or behaviours which are to be promoted have been identified, ideally with the aid of the injured individual, a variety of "back-up" reinforcers must be selected, also with the aid of the injured person. These will be obtained in exchange for tokens. A set of rules must be established outlining the means and the frequency whereby tokens will be earned, and how and when they can be exchanged for the secondary or "back-up" reinforcers.

Tokens may be given as soon as the target behaviour occurs. Alternatively, they may be given at specified intervals, when the aim is to maintain a target behaviour, such as attention to task, over time.

Initially, tokens may need to be given at short intervals of, for example, 15 minutes. These intervals can be extended as the TBI person's capacity to sustain the desirable behaviour improves. Where there is very severe cognitive impairment, it is important to make the interval between receipt of the token and its exchange for material reinforcement as short as possible. In some cases it may be necessary to give the material reward in the first instance. It is vital that tokens be given with social reinforcement in the form of praise.

As recordings indicate a decrease/increase in the frequency of the target behaviour, the number of tokens required to earn the back-up reinforcement can be increased, along with the intervals at which tokens are given. Eventually, the tokens should be replaced by social reinforcement alone, as a means of weaning the injured individual off the programme, and achieving generalisation of gains. So that it is maximally effective, the process of weaning the TBI person off such a programme should be taken very gradually and applied in a variety of settings, including those which are less structured and controlled, and in which the injured individual is most frequently going to spend time in the future.

Some TBI individuals find a token economy demeaning. In such instances the use of a points system may be more useful in harnessing their co-operation. However, it is vital that points earned be awarded and recorded in as immediate and obvious a way as the tokens, and be accompanied by praise and encouragement. Points earned may be recorded on a wall chart or in a diary carried by the person. Whatever means of recording is selected, it must be immediately accessible at all times when points are being awarded.

Time-out

Time-out can be particularly useful in the management of attention-seeking, aggressive, or otherwise disruptive behaviour. It involves the removal of social reinforcement or attention. It can be applied in various ways, depending on the extent of the problem. Wood (1984) outlines various forms of time-out. The method to be tried in the first instance is known as *time-out-on-the-spot* or "TOOTS'. This involves simply ignoring the undesirable behaviour, if necessary by averting one's gaze or walking away for a few seconds, without saying anything, then continuing the interaction as if nothing had happened.

If this approach is unsuccessful, either because it is too difficult for staff to apply, or the behaviour is too disruptive, *situational time-out* may need to be applied. This involves physically removing the person from the situation, either putting them outside the door or in another room for a few minutes. Again, this should be done without interaction.

If situational time-out fails or if there is violent physical aggression, removal of the TBI person to a *time-out room* is necessary. This should be done with a minimum of fuss, involving as few staff as possible, and making no eye contact or verbal exchange with the individual. Obviously those in wheelchairs are simply wheeled to the time-out room. TBI individuals should be left in the time-out room for a designated period of no more than five minutes, during which they should be observed. If they have calmed down at the end of the five-minute period, they should be allowed out of the time-out room, again without reference to the incident. If the TBI individual remains agitated, the procedure may need to be repeated.

Careful thought needs to be given to the placement and fitting out of a time-out room. It must be readily accessible from all areas where the individual spends time. There should be no potentially harmful fittings or light switches. It may be a good idea to line the floors and walls with vinyl mattresses, but there should be no other furnishing which might make the room attractive. It should have a hole in the door to enable constant surveillance of the person inside. The door should not be able to be opened from the inside, preferably opening inwards and having no handle inside the door. Although a time-out room is likely to be needed in a minority of cases, it must be available for use at all times. It should never be used as a storage room. Ideally the need for use of a time-out room may be obviated by staff following behavioural principles in their daily interactions with TBI individuals.

Response cost

Alderman and Ward (1991) advocate the use of response cost as a more effective technique in those TBI people who have very severe memory deficits and executive problems as a consequence of severe frontal lobe injury. According to Alderman and Ward, such individuals sometimes have difficulty in responding to behaviour programmes based on positive reinforcement or time-out. Response cost is believed to be more effective because the consequences are immediate, thereby minimising the limitations imposed by memory problems. Attention is focused on the aberrant behaviour in an exaggerated way, with the introduction of verbal mediation, thereby facilitating the normally limited capacity to use feedback from the environment to modify behaviour. The TBI person plays an active role in the process, which may allow for utilisation of relatively intact procedural learning skills.

Alderman and Ward (1991) used a response cost approach in treating a 36-year-old female, AB, who constantly repeated stereotyped verbal phrases. The treatment was conducted in one-hour sessions, five days per week. Following a baseline period spent engaging in a range of therapy tasks, AB was given fifty pence, which could be exchanged for a chocolate bar at the end of each 15-minute trial. However, she lost money if she repeated herself. Each time AB repeated herself, the therapist asked her to state what she had just done and hand over one penny. Written instructions were also kept on the table to remind her of the requirements of the programme. The "cost" of the chocolate was calculated so as to maximise the likelihood of success. It was gradually increased as AB gained control over her verbal behaviour. Alderman and Ward found that the effectiveness of the programme was enhanced by the addition of what Wood (1987) refers to as "cognitive overlearning". AB was required to repeat the aim of treatment over and over, each time the aberrant behaviour was exhibited. Significant treatment effects were evident in all phases of the intervention, and these were maintained in both structured and unstructured settings over a three-month follow-up period.

Treatment of avoidance behaviours by satiation

Alderman (1991) has noted that the use of positive reinforcement and time-out are also generally ineffective in the treatment of avoidance behaviours. In such cases the TBI individual may learn that by engaging in certain behaviours, it is possible to escape from rehabilitation activities. Alderman (1991) described a case, SJ, in which avoidance behaviour, in the form of excessive shouting, was successfully diminished by satiation through negative practice. Satiation is, according to Alderman (1991, p.78), "repeated, continuous presentation of a reinforcer until it becomes neutral or develops aversive qualities". Baseline data indicated that SJ's shouting tended to occur when he was engaging in tasks demanding a high degree of physical activity, and that by shouting he could avoid these activities.

Treatment was conducted in two 30-minute sessions each day. Four techniques were used during the training period. First, SJ was required to listen via headphones to a tape of himself shouting repeatedly. Next he was encouraged, whilst listening to the tape, to sit using a posture which resulted in long periods of spontaneous shouting. Third, he was encouraged to shout for 2- to 3-minute periods, interspersed by a 1-minute rest period. During the last few training sessions, he was asked to perform functional tasks of which he was capable, but which he found frustrating, leading to further shouting. He was encouraged to continue this shouting for another 2 to 3 minutes after he had stopped, as in the earlier sessions. There was a significant downward trend in the frequency and level of shouting during conductive education sessions whilst the behavioural intervention was being instituted, a trend which was reversed following the withdrawal of this intervention.

Satiation training was later extended to all individual therapy sessions. Whenever SJ shouted he was allowed to continue until he stopped, at which point a staff member encouraged him to continue for a further 2 to 3 minutes. SJ was also required to listen to the tape of himself shouting for 15 minutes before his washing and dressing programme. This resulted in further decreases in shouting, measured by the hour in all settings, until it ceased after 18 weeks. After 5 weeks on the second programme, SJ was able to be reintroduced to group activities, and could participate more actively in conductive education sessions, resulting in significant gains, physically and functionally.

Alderman concluded that the repeated shouting imposed on SJ led, not only to the weakening of its value as a reinforcer, but also to its acquiring aversive qualities. Whilst such treatment approaches may appear to be time-consuming, their long-term impact on the quality of life of the injured individual may render the time invested both worthwhile and cost-efficient.

Positive punishment

In our experience it has never been necessary to use positive punishment as a method of behaviour management, and it is considered to be undesirable. However, Wood (1984) advocates the use of ammonia vapour, in a small bottle, which is passed under the TBI person's nose immediately after they have exhibited an aberrant behaviour, such as head-banging, spitting or sexual exposure, that has not responded to any other approach.

PRACTICAL GUIDELINES FOR IMPLEMENTING
BEHAVIOUR MODIFICATION PROGRAMMES

- Involve all those who have contact with the TBI person in each aspect of planning and implementation of the programme.

- Ask how the modification of the behaviour/s in question will be of benefit to the person who has sustained TBI.

- Define the behaviour/s which are to be the focus of intervention in readily observable terms. These will be referred to as target behaviour/s.

- Before commencing any intervention, take baseline measures of the frequency of the target behaviour/s, covering all time periods and settings in which the person exhibiting the behaviour spends time. Record possible triggering factors or reinforcing consequences. These measures need to be taken throughout the period of the intervention and afterwards.

- Try to involve the person exhibiting the behaviour in planning the programme, and wherever possible obtain written agreement to its principles. This may not be realistic in cases of very severe TBI and/or particularly aggressive or antisocial behaviour.

- At least initially, one behaviour problem should be tackled at a time, and goals should be easy to achieve. Otherwise the programme may fail because the TBI person may not clearly understand which behaviours elicit reinforcement or negative consequences. Once one behaviour has responded, another target behaviour may be introduced. Try to maximise the probability of success at all stages of the programme.

- All details of the programme should be written down clearly and distributed to all involved, including the TBI person's family and friends.

- Consistency in implementing the guidelines agreed upon is vital. Staff and relatives must adhere closely to these guidelines. A person should never be deprived of reinforcement for any behaviour other than that which is the target of the programme.

- Be prepared for the fact that the incidence of the undesirable behaviour may increase at first, after the programme has been introduced. Prepare team members and family for this possibility.

- At no time should consequences be applied in a punitive fashion. Responses to behaviour should be made quietly and without debate.

- It is particularly important for everyone involved to remember to give those whose behaviour is being modified lots of attention and praise whenever they are behaving in desirable fashion. This is one of the most difficult things for staff and others to remember. Not uncommonly, after a positive initial response to the programme, the target behaviour re-emerges. Careful examination of staff and family interactions with the person whose behaviour is being modified frequently shows that they have become less careful about responding positively to desirable behaviour.

Achieving generalisation of gains

- In order to be maximally effective, behaviour programmes need to be implemented over an extended period of time.

- Once success has been achieved with a given reinforcement schedule, the frequency of reinforcement can be reduced, the "cost" of back-up reinforcers increased, and material reinforcement replaced by social reinforcement.

- Over time, try to extend the programme to as many settings as possible in which the TBI person spends time or is likely to in the future. This will maximise the probability of successful generalisation of gains. Involvement of family and friends in this is important.

- Once the intervention has ceased, continue monitoring the frequency of the target behaviour on an intermittent basis, in order to determine whether gains made are being maintained.

PROBLEMS AND LIMITATIONS OF BEHAVIOURAL APPROACHES

There are times when changes in behaviour cannot be achieved using behavioural approaches. In those TBI individuals who are particularly lacking in drive and motivation, it can be difficult to identify reinforcers, or even negative consequences which have any impact on their behaviour. For such people it may be that sitting in a chair doing nothing is the only effective reward. In such cases the opportunity of doing this for a specified period may be made contingent upon completion of a given activity. Those with dissociative disorders with hysterical symptomatology usually fail to respond to reinforcement or punishment (Wood, 1984). Behaviour problems which were an entrenched part of a TBI person's behavioural repertoire prior to injury are also likely to be very resistant to change. It should never be the goal of rehabilitation to make a person anything other than they were before the injury.

At times it can be difficult to harness the support and co-operation of particular staff or family members involved with the TBI individual. This may lead to inconsistency in the implementation of guidelines, or even active sabotage of the programme. Such problems must be avoided. Staff who are not able to reach agreement with the rest of the team as to an appropriate behavioural strategy should preferably stop treating the person whose behaviour is being modified. Clearly this is not possible in the case of families, and a careful judgement needs to be made as to whether it is worth proceeding with a programme under circumstances where it is not supported by the family. Unless the behaviour being modified is restricted to therapy sessions when family are not present, it is usually not worth proceeding with a formal behaviour modification programme.

Finally, it must be stressed that behaviour therapy is not a cure for impairment resulting from brain injury. Rather it serves to optimise behaviour to enable more active participation in a rehabilitation programme or community-based activities, thereby reducing the handicap resulting from impairment.

APPLICATIONS OF ENVIRONMENTAL AND BEHAVIOURAL APPROACHES TO PROBLEMS COMMONLY ENCOUNTERED IN A GENERAL REHABILITATION UNIT

Whilst there are brain injury rehabilitation units which are set up primarily to implement behaviour management approaches, in the majority of rehabilitation centres this is not the case. Staff have to deal with injuries of widely varying severity and presenting a broad range of problems. A number of approaches may be taken in order to achieve goals. This can make it difficult to ensure consistent implementation of formal behaviour modification programmes when these are necessary. However, many problems can be successfully tackled in general rehabilitation units using the principles which have been outlined. Some general guidelines for dealing with specific problems are described below. If these are followed consistently by both rehabilitation staff and families or friends, the need for formal behaviour modification programmes may be circumvented.

Suggested guidelines for dealing with some behaviour problems encountered following TBI

Verbal aggression/irritability

- The most important thing to remember when dealing with aggression of any kind is that it is usually occurring as a result of the brain injury. TBI individuals cannot always help it and therefore do not deserve to be blamed. *Try not to take such anger personally.*

- Try to educate all those having contact with the injured person to react to aggressive behaviour in a consistent fashion.

- It is important to ignore angry outbursts, making no direct response. Never react to any form of aggression by shouting, arguing, hitting back, or becoming upset in front of the injured individual. This will only serve to increase the level of agitation and/or reinforce the behaviour. If it is possible, remove the TBI person from the situation that provoked the anger or leave the situation yourself, as long as this does not place the injured individual or others at any risk. In doing so, make no comment. Return after a couple of minutes, and if the TBI person has calmed down, continue the activity. *Respond positively to appropriate behaviour*. If abuse continues, postpone the procedures or the interaction, although care must be taken that this does not lead to avoidance behaviour.

- Try to identify the kinds of things that cause the TBI person to become agitated and avoid these. Some precipitating factors may include fatigue, noise, overstimulation, pain, therapy that is too demanding or frustrating, incompatibility with other patients or staff, feeling put down, or feeling neglected. It may also be possible to learn the signals of impending agitation and take steps to calm or reassure the agitated individual, to divert attention, to alter the activity or to remove the individual from the situation.

- After calming down, the TBI person is sometimes very apologetic. Use this as an opportunity to suggest better ways of dealing with the situation next time, and make it clear that you are willing to help. *Don't be critical and don't hold grudges*.

- It is very easy for staff or family to become irritable or angry with a TBI individual for being irritable with them. As a result, physical and emotional distance between them is increased. An unfortunate pattern can develop, whereby the TBI person's acting out is met with seclusion, restraints, or medication. All of this tends to exaggerate feelings of panic, disorientation, frustration, and loneliness, eventually leading to further isolation, restriction, and rejection of the person. It is very easy to take personally what is essentially random acting out behaviour on the part of a TBI individual, and to become fearful. This can develop into covert or overt attempts to retaliate. Good staff and family support and communication are essential to avoid such situations. It is very important that staff and family be able to talk about such feelings.

Physical aggression

- Wherever possible, staff or others should try to identify the presence of agitation before it escalates to physical violence. An attempt should be made to defuse the situation—to gently "talk the person down" in a calm and reassuring fashion. Acknowledge the person's feelings and never confront in any way, or try to reason with the agitated individual. Use isolation or distraction where appropriate. Try to remove any disruptive stimulus or individual. Avoid "cornering" the agitated person.

- If physical violence occurs, time-out procedures should be followed (see earlier section for details). Two or three staff should always be available to accompany the TBI person to the time-out room. They should be trained in the appropriate methods of coping with physical violence, such as those outlined by Bowie (1989), and in methods of escorting the aggressor to the time-out room which invite compliance, rather than conflict. If necessary a "team" of suitably trained staff may need to be on call.

- Avoid eye contact and verbal exchange.

- All instances of physical aggression should be documented. The team co-ordinator and treating psychologist should be notified as soon as possible.

- The TBI person will sometimes feel distressed and/or guilty following such an outburst. It is important to provide an opportunity for the TBI person to talk about the incident afterwards if they want to, and explore alternative ways of dealing with the problem.

- All staff involved in the incident should meet with the rest of the treating team to discuss the incident as soon as possible. They need to discuss why it might have happened, how it might be prevented next time, and how staff involved are feeling about the incident. A plan for ongoing management of the problem should be agreed upon.

- Almost invariably, staff who are the focus of an aggressive outburst feel very upset afterwards, and may be fearful of further interaction with the TBI person who has been aggressive. They may not feel comfortable about discussing their feelings with the whole team, but the team co-ordinator has a responsibility to see that they are given an opportunity to talk through their feelings, with the psychologist, social worker or other suitable team member.

- It is important that no member of staff is left alone with a TBI person who has become aggressive.

- All staff need to be aware of the procedures for management of aggression, which should be clearly documented and practised regularly.

Socially inappropriate behaviour

- Lack of behavioural control as a consequence of injury to the frontal lobes following TBI can, in addition to irritability and aggression, lead to swearing, sexual disinhibition, or other socially inappropriate behaviours. It must be understood that many TBI people are, by virtue of their disability and/or confinement, sexually frustrated. However, because of reduced behavioural control this may be expressed inappropriately. When this occurs the first time, it is best to tell the person quietly that this is not appropriate and proceed with whatever you were doing. Subsequently, ignore the behaviour completely. Any form of reaction, either laughing or becoming embarrassed or angry, may only serve to encourage such behaviour. Try not to take swearing or sexual advances personally.

- Respond to socially appropriate behaviour with attention and praise.

- At the same time, it is important to acknowledge the sexual needs of TBI people and, wherever possible, to provide outlets for these. This issue is discussed in detail in Chapter 8.

Self-centredness

- Those who have sustained frontal lobe injury as a consequence of TBI are prone to be self-centred. This can lead to demanding, attention-seeking and manipulative behaviour. Jealousy, failure to see others' points of view, or insensitivity to the needs and feelings of others are also common in such cases. Self-centredness is the source of many relationship problems following TBI. There may be a tendency to develop ways of attracting attention from others by joking or clowning around, constant demands for toileting, food or other forms of assistance, swearing, making inappropriate sexual advances, shouting, becoming physically aggressive, engaging in self-abusive behaviour, or absconding.

- Whilst it is obviously important to first assess whether the TBI individual is in genuine need of help, staff, families, and others need to be sensitive to the development of such behaviour and, whenever it occurs, to ignore it. By reacting, either positively or negatively, one is reinforcing the behaviour by giving the TBI person what they want most, namely attention.

- At the same time it is important to reinforce or reward appropriate and considerate behaviour with praise and attention. If this happens consistently, the injured person will learn that behaving appropriately and considerately brings the reward they want.

- Try to avoid being manipulated in other ways. Staff and family should set firm rules together, for example regarding regular toileting or smoke breaks, and stick to them. Threatening or bargaining with a TBI person on an *ad hoc* basis is not a good idea.

- It is also important that staff and families do not allow the TBI individual to come to expect all demands to be met. On the other hand it is not realistic to expect the injured person to respect the rights of staff and family, who have to do some demanding of their own. Those who have sustained TBI can become very dependent on those caring for them. Such relationships may be difficult to sustain, so total dependency on one person is not to be encouraged.

Emotional lability

- Emotional lability may continue for some time, causing the TBI individual to laugh or cry too much at inappropriate times. It is important to realise that although the response may be overtly dramatic, the underlying emotion may not be all that strong. It is best to ignore the behaviour when it occurs, and model calm behaviour yourself.

APPLICATIONS OF BEHAVIOURAL TECHNIQUES TO ACHIEVE THERAPEUTIC GOALS

Shaping and *chaining* may be particularly useful means of attaining goals in the areas of physical mobility, activities of daily living, work skills, communication, and social skills. Shaping involves the provision of positive reinforcement of either a social or a material nature for successive approximations of a desired behaviour. Chaining involves breaking down the behaviour into a sequence of steps or units which build upon one another. Each step is reinforced until it has been successfully learned, before incorporating the next step. As Wilson (1987b) has illustrated, these methods may be applied in training physical skills needing to be relearned, such as the ability to initiate and carry out a transfer. Chaining procedures may also be used to train specific work skills or a sequence of activities of daily living, such as getting up in the morning, showering and dressing.

MANAGEMENT OF BEHAVIOUR PROBLEMS IN COMMUNITY SETTINGS

The management of behaviour problems in community settings presents a new set of challenges. Common presenting problems include poor anger control, lack of initiative in performing a range of tasks, from basic self-care to more complex social or work activities, and socially inappropriate or demanding behaviour. Many of the principles described above can be applied to such problems in the home or work setting. The first and most important step in assessing and managing behaviour problems in the community is to harness the support of those who have most contact with the TBI person when the undesirable behaviour is exhibited, or the skill to be learned is performed. In most instances this will be a family member, but where behaviour is a problem in social situations or at work, the assistance of friends and employer or fellow employees will need to be sought. In some cases that person will have been putting up with the behaviour for a considerable period of time and may have developed idiosyncratic ways of dealing with it. These may include cajoling, attempting to reason with or arguing with the TBI person. It is particularly important not to be critical at this point, and risk creating resentment. Try to be positive about the contribution that person has been making to the care of the TBI individual, at the same time gently pointing out that there may be more effective ways of dealing with the problem.

The assistance of these people will be required in all phases of the intervention. TBI individuals who have good insight and motivation for change, and sufficient cognitive capabilities, may be actively involved in taking baseline recordings of the behaviour. However, in many cases this will need to be done by someone else. Clear guidelines as to the nature of the recording required must be given. As in the hospital or rehabilitation setting, there needs to be careful documentation of precipitating circumstances and consequences. If at all possible, the psychologist should spend some time in the community setting in order to gain a comprehensive picture of the milieu in which the behaviour is occurring.

Both the TBI individual and family member or friend should be actively involved in discussing alternative responses to the problem and in planning the intervention, which may involve any of the environmental or behavioural methods outlined above. Every detail of the programme needs to be clearly written down and shown to all those who are likely to be responding to the behaviour. Recording of the behaviour must continue throughout the period of the intervention and afterwards.

For those TBI individuals with sufficient cognitive abilities, including some insight and motivation, a range of "cognitive–behavioural" techniques, such as anger management training, may by useful in dealing with behaviour problems. These will be discussed further in Chapter 8.

CASE REPORT—TIM

Tim was a 29-year-old treefeller, married with two young children, when he sustained an extremely severe head injury in a logging accident. He remained comatose for several weeks, and was subsequently transferred to a rehabilitation unit. Gradual progress was made and, after two months, Tim was eating and drinking well, transferring and walking a few steps with assistance. He was communicating verbally without prompting. However, a few weeks later, Tim became increasingly agitated and unco-operative, with frequent outbursts of both physical and verbal aggression, which included shouting, hitting staff and throwing his food tray across the room. Such behaviour was occurring many times a day, to the point where staff found it difficult to attend to his basic needs. Rehabilitation therapy was gradually ceased. The use of tranquillisers and sedatives resulted in Tim becoming drowsy, and his general level of physical dependency increased. He could no longer walk. There was, however, no decrease in the behaviour problems. Attempts to take him home for visits resulted in aggressive outbursts, directed at both his wife and children. He began to suffer frequent epileptic seizures, thought to be related to the medication.

Fifteen months after his injury the rehabilitation unit began to make arrangements for Tim's transfer to a large psychiatric institution. His family became very distressed at this prospect, as the institution was a long distance from his home, and regular visiting would be impossible. They sought interstate referral to Bethesda Hospital for further assessment and management.

Assessment indicated that Tim had extremely severe and widespread impairment of cognitive function. His level of alertness was reduced and he was very slow in his responses. He was disoriented in time and place, giving his age as 16. He stated that he was married with one child. Whilst he showed recollection of distant past memories, he showed retrograde amnesia for a period of some years. He exhibited no capacity to learn or retain anything new. He appeared to comprehend questions only inconsistently, answering with a yes/no or another one- or two-word response, often a stereotyped phrase. He tended to confabulate. He could not read the names written on his birthday cards. Most of the time he sat and watched television, never initiating any verbal interaction, apart from shouting. Physically, Tim had a left hemiparesis, affecting the arm more than the leg, trunkal ataxia and general weakness. He was incontinent. Tim needed maximal assistance to transfer, bathe, and dress, and was supervised when eating.

From observation and questioning of the staff on the ward where Tim had previously been treated, it became apparent that Tim's shouting and hitting behaviour occurred particularly when he was being handled physically, especially when having his clothes removed for bathing and toileting. He also tended to throw his food across the room when he was being given assistance to eat. He had had no therapy for 12 months because of his aggressive behaviour. The staff were clearly fearful of him and avoided contact, except to carry out duties of care. They had been told that Tim had, prior to his injury, had a short fuse, and had, on occasion, struck his wife. They considered that his behaviour was consistent with his premorbid personality, and appeared to feel he had some control over it. His wife had also become quite fearful of him.

Following his admission to the head injury unit at Bethesda Hospital, Tim was taken off the medications he was taking and carbamazepine was prescribed. This successfully controlled his epilepsy. He was placed in a single room. His behaviour was observed over a two-week period, during which the usual nursing routines were performed and therapists attempted to assess him. Shouting occurred, on average, eight times daily. Hitting out occurred, on average, twice daily. It became clear that Tim tended to become agitated and shout or hit out mainly in the presence of noise and a lot of activity around him, but also when he was being handled physically, when he was being put under pressure to do things quickly, when he was engaged in verbal interaction, or when he was tired. It was also apparent that he liked to gain the attention of staff, and that shouting was used as a means of this. He tended to become agitated when his wife and mother were visiting, which they tended to do at the same time.

At a meeting of all those staff involved in Tim's care, the following management guidelines were agreed upon:

- It is important to remember that Tim is very confused, and cannot remember ongoing events, so he does not fully understand where he is and what is happening. His agitation and aggression are a direct result of his brain injury. He cannot help responding in the way he does. Therefore he does not deserve to be blamed for it.
- Tim's surroundings are to be kept as quiet as possible, with the door to his room closed.
- Preferably only one person is to be with him at a time, and certainly only one person talking to him at once. Overstimulation will make him agitated.
- Approach Tim gently and to explain to him what you are going to do before you do it (e.g. take off his clothes before a bath). Demonstrate or use gesture to help him understand.
- Speak to Tim slowly and wait for him to answer. His thinking is extremely slow and he becomes agitated when he is rushed. Demonstrate or use gesture to help him understand. Similarly, he needs to be given time to perform physical tasks at his own pace.
- Try to spend some "quality" time with Tim, which does not involve care or therapy tasks, and which does not place physical or cognitive demands on him.
- If Tim shouts, ignore it. If he hits out, say nothing, leave the room immediately, closing the door. After two minutes, return as if nothing has happened and continue whatever you were doing. Leave the room again in the same way if the behaviour is repeated.
- It is very important to give Tim attention and praise if he is quiet, co-operative, or interacting without shouting or hitting.
- It is vital that these guidelines be followed consistently.

These guidelines were given to all ward and therapy staff, and they were carefully explained to Tim's wife and mother.

In response to this management, Tim's behaviour problems settled down over a matter of weeks, although he continued to become agitated when his wife and mother visited. It was suggested that they should visit separately, as it was felt that he was having too many conversational demands placed on him. During the third month of his admission there was only one instance of shouting and hitting out. He was also more alert. He was much easier to handle on the ward. He could feed himself using normal cutlery and a non-slip mat, provided only one course was presented at a time and he was left alone. He continued to require assistance in all other activities of daily living. He had brief daily sessions of physiotherapy, occupational therapy and speech therapy, conducted in his room on a one-to-one basis. Physiotherapy focused on hand activities, and practising walking in a frame with assistance. He tolerated daily practice of this without outbursts. However, therapy gains were very slow, due to his poor memory and limited capacity to regulate his behaviour. He appeared to enjoy social contact and played simple games for 15–30 minutes, responding to a calm, friendly approach. He began to spend time in the day room, when it was quiet.

Four months after his admission, Tim was transferred back to the rehabilitation unit whence he came, in order to be close to his family. He was accompanied by the charge nurse from the head injury unit, who spent time with the staff and others, educating them as to appropriate management of Tim's behaviour. Eight months later, he was reportedly still there, attending the hospital's day centre on a daily basis for ongoing therapy. He had been out on leave with his family, without problems arising. Whilst it was clear that Tim was likely to require institutional care for the foreseeable future, the potential for his placement in a pleasant environment was enhanced by this intervention, which consisted largely of environmental manipulation, combined with some behavioural principles and alteration of his medications.

CASE REPORT—CHRIS

Chris was a 20-year-old wool baler, living at home in a country town with his parents, sister and mentally retarded brother, when he sustained a very severe TBI in a motor vehicle accident. Coma lasted three weeks. Two months after the injury he was transferred to a rehabilitation centre, conscious, but unable to communicate verbally. He had swallowing and saliva control problems, an unsteady gait and paralysed right arm. He was also reportedly very aggressive, and urinated and masturbated in public. Two weeks later he was transferred to the local psychiatric centre, because nursing staff could not handle his behaviour. He remained there for six months, receiving some therapy. His behaviour was brought under control to some degree, but he developed some bad habits, such as flicking a cigarette lighter in people's faces. He remained sexually and socially disinhibited.

Chris's family was extremely supportive and felt the environment of the psychiatric centre was not good for Chris. So they insisted on taking him home. However, Chris's family was completely unable to cope with his behaviour, particularly with the added burden of caring for their mentally-retarded son, whom Chris taunted constantly. Fourteen months after his injury he was referred to Bethesda Hospital for a period of family relief and assessment as to his potential for rehabilitation. He had regained power in his right arm, and was quite independent physically. However, he still exhibited severe receptive and expressive communication difficulties, his speech being quite perseverative. Chris also had a very short attention span and a very poor learning and memory capacity. He showed severe planning and self-monitoring problems. His behaviour resembled that of a child. He lacked normal social inhibitions and said "G'day mate!" to everyone he saw. He sought attention from people constantly, and when he did not get a response he would engage in inappropriate behaviour, such as putting his arm around a person he did not know or threatening a punch. He had a low frustration tolerance, and became agitated and aggressive, shouting and threatening to punch them, particularly when he was bored, or when others were aggressive towards him. He became bored easily, requiring frequent changes in activity. He had an obsession with money, spending it freely on food for himself or buying things for others. Chris adored children, and often approached them and gave them sweets or drinks, to the consternation of their parents. If money was left lying around he would take it. He also had an obsession with keys.

The team decided that Chris's aggressive or threatening behaviours, namely shouting, flicking a cigarette lighter, threatening punches and, at times, actually hitting people or damaging property, were the greatest barriers to his capacity to participate in rehabilitation, and function within his family and the community. A programme was therefore designed to encourage non-aggressive behaviour. Baseline measurements, carried out daily for a week, indicated that episodes of physical aggression, where Chris hit people or damaged property, occurred four times in a week, in all cases when Chris had been denied something he wanted, such as the right to leave the ward to go and buy something, or when others reacted aggressively to his threatening behaviour. Shouting or threatening behaviour occurred, on average, six times daily. These behaviours were exhibited in order to gain attention from staff who were otherwise occupied, when Chris was bored and restless, particularly late in the day.

A programme of time-out, combined with positive reinforcement for periods of non-aggressive behaviour, delivered via a token economy, was instituted. For all acts of physical aggression, Chris was removed to the time-out room for a period of five minutes. Staff, family, and friends were instructed to completely ignore shouting or threatening of punches, or flicking of a cigarette lighter, and to continue with what they were doing, paying no attention to Chris. They were also requested to reinforce non-aggressive, pleasant and helpful behaviour from Chris with attention, smiles, and praise. A token economy was instituted, whereby Chris was to be given one token every 15 minutes, with praise, if there had been no actual or threatened physical or verbal aggression in that period of time. If he did exhibit any of these behaviours during the previous 15 minutes, no token was given. Each token could be cashed in for five cents from the charge nurse on his ward at four designated times in the day. This was his pocket money. Staff, family, and friends were asked not to lend or give Chris any other money. A programme of activities was also set up to keep him occupied for much of the day. He spent a lot of time in the occupational therapy department.

These measures resulted in a marked improvement in Chris's behaviour. After three weeks there were no further instances of physical aggression, requiring removal to the time-out room. The shouting and threatening behaviour occurred more frequently in the first few days, on the second day twelve times. In subsequent weeks it gradually dissipated, until by the sixth week it occurred only four times, and by the eighth week only twice. After two weeks, Chris was given tokens every half hour only, and after six weeks at two-hour intervals. After four weeks another target behaviour was added to the programme, namely putting his arm around people. Staff, family and friends were instructed to ignore such behaviour and Chris received no token for the period during which it was exhibited. The frequency of this behaviour also dissipated gradually.

Chris spent a lot of time in the occupational therapy department "helping out". He developed a strong attachment to a male occupational therapist, on whom he began to model his behaviour, and from whom he would accept some direction regarding what was and was not socially acceptable behaviour. After three months in the rehabilitation centre, Chris's behaviour within that setting was quite acceptable. He was slowly weaned off the token economy. This was replaced with social reinforcement. There was, however, no change in his level of cognitive function. He enjoyed physical activities within his capabilities, such as bouncing and throwing a ball and badminton, games such as Uno and bingo, and simple writing activities. He also enjoyed helping put things away, washing up or other simple cleaning tasks. However, due to his short attention span, poor memory and limited capacity to regulate his behaviour, he benefited little from formal therapy.

A decision was made to continue Chris's rehabilitation in his home town. It was considered important to maintain a similar daily routine. A young man who lived in Chris's home town was appointed as an attendant carer, to work with Chris for 30 hours per week. Both he and Chris's parents and sister spent time at the hospital being trained as to how to manage Chris's behaviour and most productively occupy him. He returned home four months after his admission, and the following letter, written by his attendant 19 months later, attests to the success of his reintegration into the local community:

"I have been working with Chris for the past 19 months and in that time there has been a slow but noticeable improvement in most areas. Chris's speech has improved considerably and I find that the people who we see on a day-to-day basis can on most occasions understand Chris's speech, whereas earlier on people would look to me to help out. He is difficult to understand mainly when he is tired. Chris's attention span has improved and he is now able to stick at tasks much longer, for example he will play monopoly until other players are worn out. Recently he mowed a pensioner's lawn, which took two hours, and he did not stop until the lawn was completed. He also maintains his attention well in group activities and will join in until exhausted.

Chris's social behaviour has improved markedly and he seems to understand social requirements much more than earlier on. His awareness in this area has been assisted greatly by our regular attendance at the local Community Youth Support Scheme (CYSS). Although it has not been without problems, the attendants and project officers have shown patience and have been a great help in the modifying of Chris's behaviour. Chris also enjoys the interaction with the group of young people and looks forward to "going and seeing his mates". Occasions of aggressiveness, tantrums, and swearing are now extremely rare and the CYSS peer group have been largely responsible for this.

In regard to money, Chris receives a weekly amount and we try to regulate his spending so that his money will last the full week. I found early on that it was extremely difficult to stick to a programme, therefore I formulated activities that seemed to be most appropriate on a daily basis. Our activities include basic schoolwork, reading, writing, and arithmetic, also working out change, educational games, cooking a balanced meal, doing odd jobs, shopping, maintaining a vegetable garden, and fishing. We also attend the local CYSS approximately four half days per week which gives us a far greater scope for mental and physical stimulation. Activities at the CYSS include woodwork, leatherwork, oil painting, gardening, group sporting activities, such as cricket, basketball, football, table tennis, group discussion. Chris also participates in a handyman service which the CYSS runs for pensioners—this includes lawn-mowing, wood chopping, and gardening. I became a member of the management committee of the CYSS to help continue what I see as a very beneficial support to Chris and young unemployed people.

Overall Chris is a much more aware and happier person than he was 19 months ago and I feel that with continued support his improvement will continue."

CASE REPORT—WAYNE

Wayne was a 19-year-old factory worker, when he sustained an extremely severe closed head injury. Coma lasted two to three weeks and PTA three months. He underwent a long period of inpatient rehabilitation at Bethesda Hospital. Nine months after his injury he was considered ready for weekend leave with his family. As he was confined to a wheelchair, a ramp was installed at his family home to enable him to gain access to the house independently. Assessment by the occupational therapist initially indicated that Wayne was capable of safely negotiating the ramp. However, the family subsequently reported that he was having difficulty with the task in the absence of the occupational therapist, and had fallen out of his wheelchair on a number of occasions. Further therapeutic intervention was required. It was apparent that

Wayne's inability to perform the task, of which he was physically capable, stemmed from his cognitive difficulties, specifically impulsivity, poor self-monitoring, a poor memory for instructions, slow information processing, and lack of initiative to ask for help. The task had to be restructured to reduce the impact of these problems on task performance.

Initially, the task was practised several times daily in the rehabilitation centre. The programme was explained to his family, who were asked to wheel Wayne up and down the ramp at home until further progress had been made. The physical presence of the therapist appeared to be necessary to ensure that Wayne focused on the task. It was broken down into three simple steps:

- Put footbrakes up.
- Hand on rail.
- Look ahead while going down.

Initially maximal involvement of the therapist was required for successful performance of the task. She had to give hands-on cues, putting her hand on his shoulder, to help him monitor his impulsivity on commencement of the task. Verbal cueing was given by the therapist at each step and Wayne was asked to repeat the verbal cue before carrying it out. When each step was completed successfully, Wayne was given positive feedback in the form of praise. Once each step was successfully performed in this manner, on ten consecutive occasions, the hands-on cue was withdrawn, and praise given if he waited for the first verbal cue. When he had done so successfully ten times, the first prompt was withdrawn, and praise given only if he successfully verbalised the cue himself, and put the footbrakes up without prompting. If he failed to do so, the cue was supplied without further comment. Once this was achieved ten times consecutively, the second prompt was withdrawn and so on, until he had negotiated the ramp, verbalising and following through with each step ten times without any verbal cueing. A chart was maintained by the therapist to record progress, and this was shown to Wayne at the end of each practice session.

Once this was achieved, the ramp was used at other times during the day to move around the hospital. Initially this was done under the supervision of an orderly, who was trained to carry out the programme, giving praise only when all three steps had been verbalised and completed. Distractions were introduced, such as a therapist holding a conversation with Wayne whilst he was negotiating the ramp. At this point the occupational therapist began taking Wayne home twice during the week to practice negotiating the ramp. Initially this was done under her supervision, but without any physical or verbal cueing. Praise was given on completion of the task. Her presence was then withdrawn, and replaced with that of a family member, praise still being given if he succeeded in negotiating the ramp. After four visits, this was achieved.

His success was maintained following the withdrawal of the presence of the family member, and then the praise. It continued on weekends, when he was home with his family. The entire process took about six weeks. This programme demonstrates the successful use of shaping and chaining to train a skill, with praise as the main form of positive reinforcement.

CONCLUSIONS

Appropriate intervention for behaviour problems represents an important means of maximising the TBI individual's capacity to benefit from rehabilitation and reintegrate into the community. A careful and objective assessment will provide clues as to the most appropriate form of intervention, whether this involves altering environmental factors, structuring the interactions of others with the TBI person, and/or implementing a formal behaviour modification programme. It is vital that all those spending time with the individual be actively involved in behavioural interventions. In order to maximise generalisation of gains, the strategies need to be applied in a broad range of settings of relevance to the injured person, with a very gradual weaning process. Except in the presence of frank psychiatric disorders, pharmacological management should only be considered as a last resort, and careful attention needs to be paid to the potential impact of medications on cognitive function.

CHAPTER SEVEN

Returning to the community after TBI

Jennie Ponsford

INTRODUCTION

Of all points in the rehabilitation process following TBI, none is more critical than that at which the individual who has sustained TBI begins to return to the community, attempting to pick up the threads of a previous lifestyle, or to construct a new life which brings some satisfaction. As a myriad of problems and issues become pertinent at this stage, this is a time when the need for rehabilitation support is paramount. Indeed it is arguable that, in many cases, at least some of the time devoted to therapy in the hospital setting in the acute phases of recovery could be more profitably spent at this later stage. For it is frequently not until this point that the TBI individual, the family, and the therapy staff can truly assess and face up to the real limitations and lifestyle changes which will confront the injured person.

There is a danger at this point of return to the community that services may become fragmented. This happens for two reasons. First, as Jacobs, Blatnick, and Sandhorst (1990) and Willer and Corrigan (1994) have pointed out, traditional rehabilitation service delivery models tend not to allow for community-based services over an extended period of time. Second, because health care services emphasise acute care, funding limitations frequently become pertinent at this stage. It is extremely important to make every effort to maintain as integrated a system of service delivery as possible after return to the community.

The extent and manner in which this occurs will be dictated by services available and funding issues. In this respect the "Whatever It Takes" model for community-based services, described by Willer and Corrigan (1994), seems appropriate. This model, which incorporates many of the same principles as the REAL approach, does not rely on any specific funding sources. Rather, it proposes that a broad range of community resources and natural supports be used to assist those who have sustained TBI to attain self-determined goals, maximising their control over and the quality of their lives.

There is a need for recognition of the fact that such resources will, for many, be required for a lifetime. Some means of seeking and co-ordinating funding and/or services is possibly the most essential (but commonly lacking) component of such a model. As Vander Schaaf (1990, p.40) has pointed out, "to create effective, community-based care alternatives for this population, national advocacy groups, caregivers, families, and concerned citizenry must piece together federal, state, county, municipal and private funds." Case management services are being established in some countries to meet this need. However, many TBI individuals still move from one service to another as different crises occur. Moreover, there is no doubt that a large proportion of those who sustain TBI have no access to any support or assistance beyond the hospital setting. Rehabilitation service delivery models need to be modified to allow for lifelong support by reducing acute care costs, minimising time spent in hospital settings, and developing more accessible, low-cost options at the community level.

For those who do have access to funding, there have, since the early 1980s, been quite a number of day treatment and community residential or transitional living programmes established. These focus on return to all aspects of community living. As Fryer and Haffey (1987) have pointed out, the emphasis in these programmes has gradually changed from a primary focus on cognitive skills training towards a broader focus on barriers to return to a range of roles in the community. There have been relatively few outcome studies examining the efficacy of such community re-entry programmes. Those studies which have been conducted have been plagued with methodological problems, including heterogeneity in aetiology of brain injury, variations in severity measures, failure to employ control groups and difficulties in arriving at suitable outcome measures.

Amongst recent studies which have used outcome measures based upon objective measures of independence and productivity in the community, the most notable are those of Burke et al. (1988), Cope, Cole, Hall, and Barkan (1991a,b), Johnston (1991), Johnston and Lewis (1991), Mills et al. (1992), and Harrick, Krefting, Johnston, Carlson, and

Minnes (1994). These have demonstrated significant gains in independence levels and productivity, over and above those which would be expected on the basis of spontaneous recovery. Gains were maintained over significant periods of time after discharge. However, none of the studies included a valid comparison group. Furthermore, on the basis of these studies it is difficult to establish which specific approaches to intervention in these settings were most effective.

Due to the complexity of dealing with groups of TBI individuals who have such heterogeneous abilities and goals, it is really very difficult to conduct large studies of this nature. There is, however, a significant need for more detailed single case studies comparing the efficacy of different approaches. In the absence of such research evidence, the guidelines presented in this chapter have been based largely on clinical experience. It is acknowledged that these recommendations represent the ideal and that, in many instances, "Whatever It Takes" will be needed to attain maximal independence and fulfilment in terms of living situation, employment, recreation and driving, in the most cost-effective manner possible.

LIVING SKILLS AND ACCOMMODATION

Whilst a great deal of energy is likely to have been devoted to the development of independence in a range of activities of daily living during the inpatient and outpatient hospital-based rehabilitation phase, it is frequently not until the TBI person has to apply these skills on a daily basis in the community that some problems become apparent. As noted in earlier chapters, the TBI individual with executive or adaptive problems may have difficulty in applying skills practised and mastered under structured therapist supervision once that structure is removed. Many will have difficulty adapting to the varying demands of different situations. Lack of initiative, impulsivity, attentional and memory difficulties can also affect the reliability with which a TBI person can carry out skills which have been learned in rehabilitation. Therefore it is essential that performance in carrying out a range of living skills be monitored carefully in whatever community setting is being returned to, so that necessary supports and/or strategies can be implemented.

There are several ways in which this can be accomplished. For those already living in the community, such services may be provided by therapists working with the injured person, family members, and others at the community level, using methods outlined in Chapter 4. Indeed, this is the most desirable approach, because this is the real setting in which the injured person will be living in the future, and there is no need for carry over from another setting. In order to circumvent funding problems for community-based therapy, this form of intervention needs to begin as early as possible in the rehabilitation process.

Transitional living programmes

Whilst it is arguably preferable to provide all assistance in real settings, this is not always feasible. For some injured individuals who are aiming to live independently in the community but do not already have accommodation, and for some who will return to live with their families, but are not yet able to do so, another means of assessing and retraining living skills may be through a transitional living programme, otherwise known as a community re-entry programme.

Aims of a transitional living programme

The aim of a transitional living programme is to provide TBI individuals with the experience of living in a shared house or a flat in a residential community, if this is the kind of setting to which they wish to return. The person who has sustained TBI needs to be willing and motivated to participate in the programme, and to work towards its goals.

Whilst participants in such a programme are potentially responsible for all the tasks required of a person living in this setting, an appropriately trained staff member is available to observe and assess performance in all areas, including personal care, household planning and budgeting, shopping, cooking, home care, laundry, gardening and maintenance, banking, paying bills, use of public transport, and the general ability to carry through with a range of such tasks as needed on a daily basis. Other areas which may be addressed include the capacity to get on with others in a household situation, and the pursuit of social and recreational interests within the local community. Many will also be involved in work-related activities or study, and have to learn to fit all these other responsibilities into the daily routine.

Probably the most important goal of a transitional living programme is to facilitate the development of awareness of limitations, as well as strengths, in the TBI person. Realistic self-appraisal has been identified by a number of groups as one of the most important factors associated with a successful return to community living (Ezrachi et al., 1991; Prigatano & Altman, 1990). It is vital, therefore, that the TBI individual is involved in the assessment process, is made aware of strengths and problem areas, and is actively and willingly involved in developing a plan to overcome difficulties. Staff should play a supportive role which is *interactional*, rather than *interventional*.

Overcoming problem areas

A number of approaches may be taken to overcoming difficulties. These have been described in detail in Chapter 4. As outlined in that chapter, it is important to conduct a detailed analysis as to the reasons why certain tasks are not being performed adequately. This should provide a basis for the intervention. Depending on the nature of the problem, it may be appropriate to practise the task under supervision, providing feedback regarding aspects of performance. Tasks may be broken down into steps, with maximal prompting given initially, and gradual fading of this until the TBI individual is able to follow the sequence independently. It might be necessary to modify the task or the environment in some way, to make successful performance possible. Ultimately, it may become apparent that the TBI individual requires ongoing supervision in certain areas, and this will need to be incorporated into plans for the future living situation.

Interpersonal skills may be enhanced by interactions with other household members, who can provide useful feedback. This can have a greater impact than feedback from therapists. It is inevitable that some conflicts arise in group living situations. This provides an opportunity to develop and practise group problem-solving skills, as well as methods of controlling anger. These skills may be facilitated through regular "house meetings", where household members discuss housekeeping issues, plan meals, shopping, or social activities, or attempt to resolve conflicts that have arisen. Such meetings may need to be facilitated by a staff member. Other pertinent issues are likely to relate to acceptance of, and adjustment to, the changes imposed by the injury. These might also be tackled within a group setting. However, in most instances there is a need for individual psychological support and assistance for brain-injured household members in developing methods of dealing with interpersonal and adjustment difficulties. Such methods will be discussed in detail in Chapter 8. It is important to explore every avenue to make this support available.

One of the most difficult tasks for many people who have sustained TBI is using spare time, particularly on weekends. It is commonly reported that they spend much of the day sitting in front of the television. TBI individuals need to be assisted in developing skills that will enable activities to be planned and carried out as independently as possible. This can be done with a friend or attendant, rather than by organising structured activities for them.

Moving from the transitional living centre into permanent accommodation

Those who aim to live alone may progress from a shared house to a trial in a flat or apartment, where they have total responsibility for all tasks. Supervision can be systematically withdrawn as independence increases, although some ongoing supervision may need to be planned for. The final and most important step in the process is the planning and implementation of the move to a permanent place of living in the community. For those finding new accommodation, this will involve planning how much can be paid in rent, bond, etc., searching for a suitable place, negotiating with agents or fellow tenants, planning the purchase of necessary items of furniture, and organising the move. For most TBI individuals, this represents an enormous task, which cannot be achieved without assistance.

Some TBI individuals may wish to move back into previous accommodation, either alone, with friends or with family. Whilst this involves less planning, it can present other problems. In particular, fellow tenants or family may have expectations based on the performance or personality of the TBI person before the injury, which can no longer be met. There are likely to be significant role changes in the household. For example, a son who was previously independent emotionally, socially and financially, may find himself dependent on ageing parents for supervision in getting around in the community and managing his money. Or a husband who has been the breadwinner and played an active role in parenting may rely on his wife to fulfil all these responsibilities. A great deal of mutual adjustment is necessary.

The TBI individual may need to accept supervision in certain areas. Family or fellow tenants can be trained to provide necessary prompting, structure and feedback to maximise the TBI person's ability to function, and to respond to certain behaviours in a consistent and constructive fashion. It may be difficult for both the injured person and others to accept such supervision. Therefore, regular contact by a therapist or support worker to provide ongoing monitoring and support is essential.

As already noted, the efficacy of transitional living programmes has yet to be established. However, a review of the first 24 severe TBI residents at the Bethesda Hospital Transitional Living Centre (TLC) demonstrated statistically significant gains in all aspects of domestic (e.g. meal preparation, laundry) and community (e.g. shopping, financial management) activities of daily living following a mean period of 100 days spent at the centre (range = 22–271 days). There had also been significant gains in independence in leisure activities. Prior to injury, 50% of this sample had lived in their own house or flat, 37% in a rented house or flat, 4% in a boarding house and the remainder in other types of accommodation. On discharge from the TLC, 41% returned to their own house or flat, 33% to a rented house or flat and 4% to a hostel or special accommodation house. Whilst 83% of the sample had lived independently in their accommodation prior to injury, 58% were independent on discharge from the TLC, 16% required some supervision and 25% required assistance with daily living activities on discharge (Olver, 1991).

For some TBI individuals, return to independent living is not a realistic goal. Ideally, however, they should have the opportunity to live in the community, rather than in an institution. Some of those who are dependent on assistance and/or supervision for most activities of daily living are able to live with their families. This may be desirable, provided both parties are happy with the arrangement. However, it is usually unwise to allow the care to be provided solely by the family on an ongoing basis, even if they seem willing and able to do so. Over time, this may become an enormous burden, creating a great deal of stress for all parties. In many instances the caregivers are elderly parents who have difficulty in meeting the physical and emotional demands of caring for a dependent son or daughter. They become very anxious as to what will happen when they are no longer able to continue. In others, the burden falls on a spouse, who may already carry the responsibility of caring for children and/or earning the family income. Above all, the TBI person, who was previously an independent member of the household, or may have lived away from the family home, is unlikely to feel happy about being so dependent on care and supervision from parents or spouse.

Attendant care
The use of attendant care presents the most desirable solution to this problem, if funding is available. Even if no private funding is available, there may be publicly funded disability support schemes which provide for attendant care. Every possible avenue needs to be explored in this respect. Alternatively, it may be possible to use volunteers or even friends in this capacity.

Roles of an attendant carer
Attendant carers can assist a TBI person who wishes to live alone in a house or apartment in the community, or those living with family or friends. Attendant carers may be employed in either a full- or part-time capacity, performing a broad range of functions. In some instances it will be necessary to have more than one attendant carer. Depending on the capabilities of the TBI individual, attendant carers may assist in, or supervise the performance of, a range of activities of daily living, such as showering, toiletting and dressing, meal preparation, shopping and banking.

Attendant carers can be trained to implement specific therapeutic exercises aimed at assisting or maintaining physical or cognitive recovery, or assist the TBI person in pursuing home-based activities of interest. They may provide transport and/or accompany the injured person to ongoing centre-based therapy activities, or assist in involvement in community-based activities of a social, recreational or work-related nature. Above all, an attendant carer may become an important friend to the TBI individual, actively assisting them to reestablish previous activities or social contacts, or establish new ones.

Selection and training of attendants

Careful selection and training of attendant carers is essential. Occupational background is less important than personal qualities. A good attendant carer is one who comes to the job with an open mind about what to expect of the TBI individual, and what can be achieved. Desirable qualities include patience, tolerance, flexibility, initiative and creativity. A proven ability to stick with a job is important, as frequent changes in attendant carer can be very difficult for the TBI person to cope with. Above all, an attendant must be compatible with the TBI individual and the family, who should be involved in the selection process. Questions as to the age, gender and cultural background of the attendant carer/s to be selected need to be negotiated with the TBI individual, and an attempt should be made to match their interests.

Once the selection has been made, the attendant carer/s need to spend time with the therapy team. It is important to convey a clear understanding of the strengths and weaknesses of the injured person, physically, cognitively, and behaviourally. Where relevant, there should be training in appropriate methods of assisting with physical mobility, activities of daily living, and/or communication. A good understanding of the principles of managing problem behaviours also needs to be conveyed. In many instances attendant carers can provide an excellent model for family and friends to follow, since they are less emotionally involved and have no previously established patterns of interacting with the injured person. Therapists can also assist the attendant carer in planning and implementing suitable activities of a therapeutic, recreational or social nature.

After an attendant care programme has been set in place, frequent contact should be made with the attendant, the injured individual and the family, to ensure that arrangements are working, and to assist in addressing any problems. Over time, there will be a need for reassessment of the programme, and assistance in developing new exercises or activities. Inevitably, there will also be changes in attendant carers, and the careful selection, training, and support process must be repeated each time this occurs. Those who have sustained TBI and their families tend to find changes in attendant carers extremely stressful and disruptive, and the process of readjustment is usually slow. Support needs to be provided throughout this period.

Long-term supervised accommodation

For a small number of very severely injured and dependent TBI people, or those without family support, the only available option is care in a supervised setting. Unfortunately, for some this means a geriatric nursing home, where there are rarely suitable social or recreational activities provided. Clearly, placement in such settings is completely undesirable and should be avoided. Ideally, long-term accommodation should cater specifically to the needs of TBI individuals. Adequate privacy needs to be provided, individuals having their own room. Provision of a structured programme involving suitable activities of a social or recreational nature is also essential. Encouragement should be given to pursue interests or work activities in the local community.

As the findings of Thomsen (1984) have indicated, many severe TBI individuals continue to show recovery over many years. It is therefore important that their capabilities and needs are reviewed on a regular basis, and opportunities provided to move to a less supervised living situation if this seems feasible.

Another accommodation option for those dependent on care and supervision is a shared home in the community, with necessary assistance from attendant carers. This is an option being developed increasingly by community groups, case managers, TBI individuals and their families. It should be explored wherever possible.

CASE REPORT—DIANNE*

Dianne was a 27-year-old woman who had sustained a very severe injury, with seven months of coma, nine years earlier. Following her emergence from coma she had undergone a period of inpatient rehabilitation for 12 months. She lived with her father and stepmother for a while, but this did not work out, so she went to live in a hostel catering specifically for young people who had sustained TBI. She had her own room and bathroom there, received regular therapy to enhance her mobility and greatly enjoyed the social and recreational activities which were arranged on a daily basis. However, as she

* This case was kindly made available by the staff of the Bethesda Hospital Transitional Living Centre.

had lived independently prior to her injury she maintained a strong desire to buy and live in her own unit. With this aim she was referred to the Bethesda Hospital Transitional Living Centre.

Dianne walked independently with a single point stick, but was slow, had some balance difficulties and tired easily. She was unable to manage public transport due to these limitations and used a motorised scooter for long distances. She had problems with attention and speed of thinking, memory, planning, and self-monitoring, and her thinking was somewhat inflexible. In communication she tended to be egocentric in conversation, having difficulty taking turns, but was otherwise independent. She had difficulty making enquiries on the telephone. She was, however, extremely sociable. Dianne was also aware of her disabilities and their impact on her everyday function. Her ability to solve problems fluctuated and she was frequently tearful and anxious about the future.

Initial assessment indicated that, although independent in most aspects of personal care, Dianne required supervision in taking her medication and preparing, timing and cooking meals. She was independent in light cleaning and laundry, but was physically incapable of heavy cleaning. Unable to use public transport, Dianne independently accessed taxis, for which she paid half-fare. In crossing roads she was cautious, but slow and unreliable in scanning. Although independent in simple shopping, Dianne required assistance to plan what to buy, how much to spend and how to organise herself to shop. She did not ask questions or use signs to find items, and tended to be easily distracted and somewhat impulsive in buying. She had difficulty in managing her finances both on a day-to-day level, in terms of monitoring what she could, and had spent money on, and with financial planning. She also had difficulty in organising her daily or weekly routine, coping with novel events or making long term plans.

Dianne spent a total of 12 months, first in the house and then in a flat at the Transitional Living Centre. She was assisted in buying, furnishing, and moving into a unit, and networking supports and resources in her local community. The emphasis was on teaching her strategies to compensate for her disabilities, in order to be as independent as possible. Particular emphasis was placed on setting up and training her to follow structured daily and weekly routines in her unit and in the community. The use of a diary as a planner, and checklists also helped Dianne to organise her day and week. In areas where she could not function independently, supervision and/or assistance was provided by attendant carers. Two attendant care workers were recruited, trained, and commenced work with Dianne before she moved into her unit. These attendants supported her in her routines and checked her reliability in areas such as money management and keeping appointments, as she was prone to make occasional errors. They also provided assistance in accessing social and recreational activities as well as psychological support.

Dianne became independent in taking medication, and was able to prepare simple meals. She tended to cook large amounts with the supervision/assistance of an attendant carer, divide it into meals, and freeze it. Although she had learned to cook a small repertoire of recipes independently, she would generally heat a meal and use frozen vegetables. Dianne continued to require assistance with heavy household duties, and home maintenance had to be performed by someone else. Dianne improved her ability to make enquiries in person or by phone by developing a routine of writing down the question beforehand and recording the answer on paper.

Although requiring assistance from her attendant in writing a weekly shopping list, Dianne could shop independently. She would go to the shops on her scooter, manage a trolley independently and carry her shopping home on her scooter. She learned to use a shopping checklist and a whiteboard to plan her shopping. With feedback, she learned to be less impulsive in her shopping. With the supervision of an attendant carer, Dianne managed her money on a daily, and weekly basis by recording expenditure in a book and keeping receipts. This routine reduced the risk of impulsive buying. Dianne continued to use her familiar bank branch and ask the tellers, whom she knew, to withdraw the money for her. She learned to count and place her money in her bag before leaving the bank. She organised a second account in which she regularly deposited money to pay bills.

As she became more confident in mastering her routines, Dianne was less prone to be anxious, tearful, and depressed. She participated in a support group with the other residents throughout and after her stay, and was able to share her worries about moving out into the community. She also had individual counselling, which equipped her with some strategies to cope with her anxiety. Her sessions with the psychologist continued after she had moved into her unit, as she continued to be depressed at times. Having always been very sociable, Dianne made many friends amongst other residents at the Transitional Living Centre and this contact was maintained after they left the centre. Dianne became involved in a riding group for the disabled and commenced sewing classes at her local YMCA.

After Dianne was established in her unit, the Transitional Living Centre took on a case-co-ordinating role, providing ongoing support and practical assistance when needed, as Dianne had little support from her family. Her funds continued to be held in trust by the court.

Dianne's unit was burgled two months after she moved into it, and she required a lot of practical and emotional assistance at this time. Shortly afterwards one of her attendants resigned, and the centre assisted Dianne in the selection and training of the new attendant. Dianne continued to have difficulty in planning activities for her spare time, particularly on weekends, when she became lonely. The new attendant's time with her was restructured to include a visit or activity on Saturday and Sunday. Dianne was supported in asserting herself with her attendants to address any problems which arose, particularly in terms of clarifying their role. At follow-up six months after leaving the centre, Dianne had maintained her level of independence and was coping reasonably well. There was no doubt, however, that she would require ongoing support in order to deal with many new problems as they arose.

RETURN TO EMPLOYMENT

Although outcome statistics vary significantly according to methodology and the severity of injuries studied, most studies indicate that less than half of those who sustain severe TBI are successful in returning to employment in the longer term (Brooks et al., 1987b; Crepeau & Scherzer, 1993; Dikmen et al., 1993; Ezrachi et al., 1991; Jacobs, 1988; Ponsford et al., 1995b; Ruff et al., 1993). However, in view of the established relationship between work involvement and the gratification of basic needs for physical and emotional well-being, as well as family, social, economic, and vocational needs, this is a goal which is of central importance to most of those who have sustained TBI (Melamed, Groswasser, & Stern, 1992). Moreover, given the youth of so many TBI individuals who remain unemployed and dependent upon public assistance, "the potential loss in earnings, expense to society, and negative impacts on quality of life to the individual and his or her family members are tremendous" (Abrams, Barker, Haffey, & Nelson, 1993, p.59).

Factors influencing return to employment

A number of factors have been shown to be significantly correlated with employment outcome. These include the injured individual's age, those over the age of 40 years being less likely to return to work, previous employment status, severity of injury, degree of resultant cognitive impairment and disability in performing activities of daily living, self-awareness and the presence of multiple trauma (Crepeau & Scherzer, 1993; Ezrachi et al., 1991; Moore, Stambrook, Peters, Cardoses, & Kassum, 1990; Ponsford et al., 1995b). However, each of these factors predicts less than a third of the variance between groups, and frequently much less, so that it is difficult to make accurate predictions for individual cases, even where multivariate statistics are used (Ponsford et al., 1995b; Vogenthaler et al., 1989).

Ponsford et al. (1995b) and Haffey and Abrams (1991) noted a range of other factors which influenced individual employment outcomes in severe TBI subjects. Positive factors included employer support and the presence of determination and adaptability on the part of the injured individual. Negative influences on the likelihood of the injured person being employed in the longer term were the lack of employer support, the presence of psychiatric illness, substance abuse or other adjustment problems, behavioural and interpersonal difficulties resulting from the injury, and availability of other means of financial support, such as support from a spouse or compensation income.

Models of vocational rehabilitation

In recent years there has been a great deal of discussion in the literature regarding the most appropriate means of maximising or enhancing the ability of those who have sustained TBI to return to work. As Jacobs (1989) has noted, traditional vocational assessment and rehabilitation approaches involving generic assessment procedures are generally less effective than those which focus on assessing and retraining the injured person within the real work environment.

In 1986, Wehman and his colleagues (Wehman et al., 1988, 1990) began to develop and evaluate the application of the Supported Employment Model for TBI individuals. This model, which was originally developed for those with developmental disabilities, allows for intensive on-site job skills training and support. It has been shown to be successful (with a 71% job retention rate), and cost-effective, for a significant proportion of individuals, who have not responded to more traditional methods of rehabilitation, and who would not be considered able to work without on-site support. This model will be described in more detail below.

More recently Haffey and Abrams (1991) and Abrams et al. (1993) have argued that such intensive on-site support and follow-up may not be necessary in all cases. Their "Work Re-entry Program" model emphasises careful assessment, job development and job analysis processes to match client capabilities with job requirements, but provides less follow-up support on-the-job. It has, nevertheless, shown a 68% placement rate and a 75% employment stability rate. The clients involved in the evaluation of this programme appear, however, to have had less severe injuries overall (median coma = 7 days for the sample reported) than those in Wehman et al.'s (1990) Supported Employment sample (mean coma = 53 days). It is probable that those with more severe injuries and consequent cognitive and behavioural disabilities would require more intensive on-site support on a continuing basis.

The optimal approach for a given individual will depend, therefore, on a broad range of variables. These include those relating to the injury, such as the nature and severity of physical, cognitive, and behavioural sequelae, particularly the degree of self-awareness; the injured person's premorbid ability levels, personality, adjustment and attitudes; and the nature of the work options available, whether these be through the previous place of employment or from other sources, as well as co-operation from the employer and others supporting the injured person.

Above, all, however, the methods used to return the TBI individual to employment will depend on the resources available in terms of private funding and/or publicly-funded vocational rehabilitation services. It is nevertheless important that those advocating for the injured person try to ensure that large amounts of money are not wasted on expensive vocational assessments which are not of direct benefit to the TBI individual. The procedures suggested below are intended as a guide to maximise successful employment outcomes, but will need to be adapted according to the resources available.

Suggested guidelines for return to employment

The question as to when vocational rehabilitation should begin in order to be maximally effective is not one which is easily answered. The timing of return to employment is likely to be determined by a myriad of variables, including the nature and severity of disabilities, the kind of work available, and the level of insight and co-operation of the injured person, family and employer. It is important, however, to begin planning for the TBI individual's vocational future early in the rehabilitation process.

Returning to a previous employer

It has been established that return to work in some capacity with a previous employer is more likely to be successful than attempting to find work with a new employer (Johnson, 1987). Therefore, in all cases where this seems a possibility, it is important to establish a good relationship with the injured person's employer early in the rehabilitation process. Beginning soon after admission, regular contact should be made to provide an explanation as to the nature of the injuries sustained, the likely time frame of the rehabilitation process, and the progress made to date. In this way employers can feel involved in the rehabilitation process, in which they may later become key participants. It is important to establish the employer's willingness to accommodate limitations of the TBI individual, either by modifying the job requirements or finding alternative duties, as well as acceptance of the need for a graduated return to work. Where this is not the case, careful thought must be given to whether it is worth pursuing that employment option, as this is not likely to be conducive to a successful outcome.

Seeking new employment options
Where return to a previous place of employment is not a realistic option, the task of the rehabilitation team is more difficult. One of the most important challenges for those working in vocational rehabilitation is to establish relationships with a broad range of employers to develop a pool of potential job placement opportunities. These will need to be carefully matched with the ability levels, previous work experience and interests of the injured worker, as well as the potential for acquiring new skills.

Work assessment
Whether the TBI individual is aiming to return to a job held prior to injury or another position selected as potentially suitable, a detailed analysis of the requirements of the job will need to be carried out, together with an assessment of the capacity of the injured worker to perform each of these requirements. Neuropsychological assessment and diagnostic vocational testing may be of some assistance in delineating the TBI individual's strengths and weaknesses. However, assessment can be most accurately conducted in the real work setting. Following the philosophy of the REAL approach, outlined in Chapters 1 and 4, it is desirable to introduce real work tasks as early as possible in the rehabilitation process. This is not only the most efficient means of assessing and retraining skills, but is also likely to facilitate the development of the TBI individual's awareness of limitations and enable more realistic planning.

In some cases it may not be in the interests of the person who has sustained TBI, or the employer, for this to occur initially in the actual work setting. It is important that some measure of success is attained on initial return to the workplace. The presence of severe behavioural or cognitive problems may result in the development of a negative attitude on the part of the employer, and an overwhelming sense of failure and humiliation on the part of the TBI individual. It may be more appropriate to simulate work requirements in the rehabilitation setting, to use role-play, or to provide unpaid "work experience" in a different setting, as long as the injured person understands the relevance of this.

Under these conditions a therapist can assess not only specific work skills, but also the ability of the TBI individual to follow, remember and carry through with instructions, sustain attention to work tasks over time, check for and correct errors, and work at an optimal pace. The injured worker's punctuality may also be assessed, as well as reliability, initiative, and ability to get on with others in the workplace. Difficulties in any of these areas can be addressed gradually, without pressure from the employer. It may be possible to train the TBI individual to perform components of a job in sequence and at an optimal pace under controlled conditions. Speed and accuracy can also be developed over an extended period. The therapist should try to identify whether problem areas are most likely to be overcome by retraining, compensatory techniques, manipulation of the work environment, or altering the job requirements. It is important to focus only on those skills which are involved in the job which the worker will be performing.

Returning to the workplace

The move to the actual work setting requires careful planning. Many issues may need to be addressed beforehand. These could include the organisation of transport, physical access to the worksite, and financial arrangements regarding work subsidies or ongoing disability benefits. If at all possible, a person should be designated to assist in the return-to-work process. If this is deemed necessary, such assistance should, ideally, include the provision of supervision or assistance at the worksite.

This is the central component of the Supported Employment model developed by Wehman et al. (1988, 1990). It enables the person who has sustained TBI to return to the workplace without all the necessary skills to perform the job. According to this concept, a therapist, or "job coach", is available at the worksite to assist in learning tasks, developing means of compensating for difficulties, dealing with interpersonal or other behavioural problems, and any other problems which may arise in the course of the transition into the workplace. This person also maintains regular contact with the employer, acting as an advocate, and facilitating communication between the injured worker and the employer.

In a recent paper, Wehman et al. (1993) investigated factors identifying those TBI individuals who were most difficult to place successfully in employment using a Supported Employment approach. Those rated most difficult to place tended to be younger, possess physical limitations, such as visual and fine motor impairments, and display significant deficits in work-related skills. Such deficits included the inability to move from one task to another without prompting, presence of unusual or inappropriate behaviours, repeated requests for assistance or direction, consistent inability to recall visual information, and inability to respond appropriately to non-verbal cues, observe safety requirements and use compensatory strategies. Concern over potential loss of disability benefits was another influential factor. These findings suggest that all of these areas should be carefully assessed when return to the workplace is being planned.

Preparation

It is important that the employer and fellow employees be given a clear understanding of the strengths and weaknesses of the injured worker, and how these are likely to affect performance in the workplace. Most injured workers initially need to return to work on a part-time basis. Provided the job allows for this, duties may be altered or simplified, according to the worker's capabilities. Wherever possible, time should be spent with the TBI individual assessing how they are managing, providing feedback, and devising ways of overcoming difficulties. If it is not possible for a trained person to spend time with the worker performing the job, then it is important to assign a person at the workplace, such as a fellow worker, or site supervisor, to monitor the worker's performance in terms of productivity, accuracy, behaviour, and any other relevant areas.

Modifying the work environment, skill retraining and the development of compensatory strategies

Additional time may be required for retraining of particular skills. As Parente, Stapleton, and Wheatley (1991) have pointed out, it is useful to assess the ways in which the worker is best able to learn. For example, it has been shown that some amnesic people have relatively preserved procedural learning skills and may benefit more from "hands-on" experience than verbal instruction. Schachter, Glisky, and McGlynn (1990) have provided an excellent demonstration of this emphasis on preserved skills in training an amnesic woman to perform a complex data processing job. She was motivated and aware of her memory difficulty, and showed relatively preserved motor learning skills, as well as normal priming effects. A method of "vanishing cues" was developed to teach her a vocabulary of computer-related terms, how to write simple programmes and perform disk storage and retrieval operations. The same technique was used to train her in the specific data entry sequence required in her job. Also of relevance to skill retraining is the finding of Wilson, Baddeley, Evans, and Shiel (1994) that the provision of maximal cueing to prevent amnesic subjects from making errors during the learning process (errorless learning), is a more effective training method than one where amnesic subjects are allowed to guess the correct response along the way, thereby making errors (errorful learning).

As an alternative, compensatory strategies may be developed to enable the worker to perform work tasks independently. These might include the provision of a checklist, or a sequence of cues of a written or pictorial nature to be followed in performing a task. As outlined in Chapter 4, Burke et al. (1991) demonstrated the use of a checklist to be an effective means of training TBI individuals with executive problems to follow a sequence of steps involved in performing a work task. Those with memory difficulties may be assisted by the use of a notebook, diary, watch alarm, or electronic appointment minder. A dictaphone can be used to record conversations in meetings, on the telephone, or in lectures, to enable these to be reviewed later. Computer programmes designed to check spelling and grammar are useful for detecting errors in word processing.

The work environment may be modified to minimise the impact of difficulties. As Parente et al. (1991) suggest, items or geographic locations can be clearly labelled or colour coded. Earplugs may be provided to minimise background noise, or the worker provided with a quieter or less congested area in which to work. Fellow workers can be given guidelines as to how to minimise and respond to inappropriate behaviour on the part of the TBI individual. Work duties themselves may also be altered to place fewer demands on memory, work speed, planning or initiative.

Review meetings

Regular meetings need to be held between the TBI individual, the employer, and the therapist or job coach to review progress, discuss any problems which are arising, and, if appropriate, to upgrade work hours or duties. This also provides employers with an opportunity to give feedback to the injured employee regarding job performance which may not otherwise be communicated. All too frequently an injured worker is dismissed without clear reasons being given, and therefore does not benefit from the experience. The therapist or job coach can subsequently clarify the feedback with the injured worker, who may not have fully understood it.

Exploring alternative employment options

Over time it will become clear whether the injured worker is likely to be capable of meeting the demands of the position, albeit with some assistance or modifications, or whether an alternative job has to be found. If this is not possible with the current employer, such a position will need to be sought elsewhere. This may necessitate training and assistance in job application and interview skills. There might be a need for some skill retraining, and arrangements made for such retraining to be funded and undertaken. The extent to which this is feasible will depend on the ability levels of the TBI individual. Obviously, for a significant proportion, employment is not going to be a realistic option.

All of these forms of assistance should also be available to TBI individuals who were not working prior to injury, but who are now wishing to seek employment. These people face a far greater challenge than those who were employed prior to injury, because they have no previous experience or behaviour patterns to form a basis for a vocational future, and often have a limited capacity to acquire new skills. There may be a need for prevocational skills training, as well as exposure to a number of different work environments through work experience, prior to selecting a vocational direction. If an acceptable position can be found, a similar process to that already described could be followed. However, the likelihood of success will be determined by the injured person's level of cognitive, behavioural and emotional functioning.

Sheltered employment

In most instances, sheltered employment is unlikely to present a viable option. Sheltered workshops tend to be geared to the needs of those with congenital intellectual disabilities. TBI people do not generally view themselves as disabled and frequently do not wish to be associated with other disabled groups. Furthermore, such settings usually require the worker to sustain attention to a repetitive task over a long period, and most of those who have sustained very severe TBI are not capable of this. Behaviour problems can also present a significant barrier to successful integration into a sheltered employment setting.

Adjustment issues in the workplace

One of the most difficult hurdles for an injured worker who has previously held a position of some responsibility is accepting a less responsible or more menial position. This can be a very lengthy and traumatic process, often requiring psychological support and counselling. Indeed according to Wehman and Kreutzer (1994), those from professional backgrounds are less likely to succeed in supported employment programmes due to difficulties of this nature.

The period of return to work is almost invariably one of considerable stress. The injured worker may, for the first time, be forced to face up to changes in ability level and personality, and become aware that others are responding differently. At the same time, attempts are usually also being made to establish an appropriate residential situation, and to reestablish personal and social relationships. These other stresses, when added to those already present in the workplace, may result in substance abuse and/or further compromise the worker's performance.

Assessment of the individual's ability to cope with such stresses should be carried out prior to return to work, and problems circumvented wherever possible. It is also important, however, to provide ongoing assistance to the injured worker in addressing problems as they arise, as well as continuing psychological support. Resources for such assistance should ideally be sought in the injured person's local community. If support groups are available, participation in a discussion group may facilitate sharing of difficult situations which arise and discussion of coping strategies.

Follow-up support

Follow-up support is essential to the maintenance of successful return to employment. As Kreutzer and Morton (1988) have pointed out, TBI individuals frequently have less difficulty in finding employment than in maintaining it. Sale, West, Sherron, and Wehman (1991) attempted to identify the reasons underlying 38 consecutive separations from employment in a Supported Employment programme for people with TBI. Most of the separations occurred during the first six months of employment. Over three-quarters of them occurred for more than one reason. In about half the cases, however, the reasons reflected problems in interpersonal relationships, including misinterpretation of social cues, conflicts with fellow workers and supervisors, and inappropriate verbalisation to fellow workers, supervisors or customers. Alternatively, there were problems in the employment setting, such as a change in supervisor, a change in work duties, perceived lack of upward mobility, and poor match between worker preference/ability and job characteristics. In more than a third of the cases mental health problems, substance abuse or criminal activity were also contributing factors. Other reasons for separation included poor attendance, low motivation, and transportation problems.

It is extremely important to maintain regular contact with the injured individual and the employer in order to deal with such problems before they result in termination of employment. Where inappropriate interpersonal behaviour is an issue, clear and constructive feedback should be given to the TBI person by the job coach, co-workers, and/or the employer. Some educational input will usually be required to ensure that fellow workers understand the basis of the problem, and respond consistently and constructively. It may even be necessary to set up a behavioural programme.

In general it is best to avoid the necessity for change in the work routine, and this should be made clear to the injured person and the employer or site supervisor from the outset. It is unwise to allow TBI individuals who have executive or adaptive problems to return to positions which are likely to have variable routines and changing demands, or where the injured worker has an expectation of promotion. If changes are to occur, careful monitoring is particularly important. A scenario which is not uncommon is that of an injured employee who is coping well with a given work routine seeking or being offered a job upgrade or a change in duties. Neither the injured individual nor the employer can anticipate the difficulties likely to be experienced in adapting to such changes. Similarly, problems may occur if there is a change in supervisor. The employer needs to be encouraged to seek advice or support prior to making any such change.

When working with individuals who have sustained TBI, it is also important to accept that for some there are likely to be frequent job changes. This is particularly so when injured workers experience interpersonal difficulties and/or have an unrealistic view of their abilities. Whilst such changes are not desirable, it may still be possible to maintain the injured worker in employment for much of the time, provided the right supports are available to assist in times of difficulty. This is surely more desirable than long-term unemployment, which brings many additional stresses for the TBI individual and the family. Thus, support services of this nature need to be available to the injured worker indefinitely.

Some would argue that the provision of these services on an ongoing basis is not cost-effective. However, an analysis of the costs of a Supported Work Programme for TBI individuals in Virginia, USA by West, Wehman, Kregel, Kreutzer, Sherron, and Zasler (1991), spanning almost three years, indicated that these compared favourably with the cost of many TBI rehabilitation programmes. Moreover, West and his colleagues projected that the TBI clients' earnings would exceed programme costs after approximately 58 weeks of Supported Employment services. It was also estimated that, at current levels of income tax and Social Security payments, client contributions from Supported Employment would provide a net gain to taxpayers after approximately two and a half years. These estimates did not include savings from alternative programmes, contributions from family members who were also able to return to work, and other benefits from employment. A more recent analysis of costs for the same programme (Wehman, Kregel, West, & Cifu, 1994) revealed a 9% increase in mean annual expenditure. This was attributed to increased hourly "fee-for-service" rates and expansion of preplacement assessment and job development services. A relatively higher proportion of time was being spent in job site advocacy, encouraging involvement of supervisors and fellow workers in promoting employment retention. It was also noted that there was enormous variability in the amount and type of services required to promote long-term employment success.

One of the most important lessons to be learned by those providing support services to TBI individuals is that at least some of these services will be required indefinitely. In short, there is no "cure" for the problems arising from severe traumatic brain injury. Indeed, it is the expectation of such a cure, and the anticipation that assistance will be time-limited, that is undoubtedly the source of a great deal of frustration for many of those who have sustained TBI, and the people supporting them.

CASE REPORT—ALISON

Alison was a 29-year-old unmarried librarian when she was injured in a motor car accident. She sustained a severe TBI and multiple fractures. She was unconscious for several hours and had a period of PTA lasting 10 days. At the time of her injury Alison had been working as a librarian in a university library for about two years. She had previously completed an Arts Degree and a Graduate Diploma in Librarian Studies. She lived in her own apartment.

After discharge from hospital Alison had a period of outpatient rehabilitation lasting six months. She initially stayed with her mother, but later returned to her own apartment, managing independently. Early contact was made with her employer to explain the nature of her injury and provide some time frame for probable return to work. A detailed job description was obtained. Her job entailed managing a section of the library and supervising ten staff. She was responsible for maintaining workflow in accordance with fund allocations, staff deployment and prioritisation, staff development, reporting and liaison with other section heads, and contributing to planning and policy development within the division.

As a result of her head injury, Alison was experiencing a number of cognitive difficulties. These included problems in sustaining attention when reading, reduced attention to detail, reduced speed of information processing, affecting her ability to follow conversation in group situations, verbal learning and memory difficulties, word-finding problems, and a tendency to be somewhat verbose and tangential in conversation. She also had difficulty in controlling her emotions, tending to become easily upset and tearful. All of these problems had the potential to interfere with her ability to perform her job. Her strengths were her high level of insight into her difficulties and her motivation to overcome them.

Initially, occupational and speech therapy within the hospital focused on Alison's attentional, comprehension and memory skills in written work, because her job involved dealing with a lot of paperwork and reading lengthy reference material. With the assistance of the therapists, she developed strategies to check her paperwork. In order to assist her comprehension and memory of material she had read, she was taught to use the PQRST strategy of scanning the article, asking key questions, rereading carefully and extracting the answers. Some time was also spent in developing Alison's skills in using a diary to organise her time, as well as remember things. In order to develop her awareness of her conversational difficulties she engaged in role-play situations which were videotaped, reviewed, and repeated. She also participated in a conversational skills group, receiving feedback from others regarding her verbal skills.

As her confidence increased, an arrangement was made for Alison to assist in the hospital's library for two half-days per week. During this period some therapy was also devoted to developing Alison's confidence in travelling on public transport, because she was not yet driving and would need to use public transport to get to work. The paperwork for organising a work trial funded by the state accident insurance body, the Transport Accident Commission, was also set in motion.

A graded return to work commenced seven months after her injury. This was arranged at a meeting involving Alison, a vocational therapist from the hospital, her immediate superior at the library, and a case manager from the Transport Accident Commission, which would fund the work trial. At this time Alison was still experiencing the same cognitive difficulties, although these were, by this stage, relatively mild. She was also still prone to fatigue. At the initial meeting Alison and the therapist outlined the difficulties they felt she might encounter, and her work programme was designed accordingly. Her work hours were upgraded at fortnightly intervals, beginning with four half days, over a 10-week period, by the end of which she would be working full-time. In the first month, Alison would do only the paperwork aspects of the job and not attend meetings, teach or deal with staff problems, as she anticipated these being the most stressful. These other duties would be performed by the second-in-charge, who had taken over her job in her absence.

Alison was highly anxious about returning to work, but became calmer after the first couple of days went reasonably smoothly. She was very tired initially. Her performance was monitored by her immediate superior, with whom she had always had a good relationship and felt she could trust. Initially she met with her superior daily to review her performance. Weekly meetings were held between Alison, her superior and the vocational therapist, before upgrading the programme. The vocational therapist initially telephoned both Alison and her superior every few days to ensure things were going smoothly. As she upgraded her duties she arranged meetings with staff for the mornings and did her paperwork in the afternoons, since fatigue was an ongoing problem.

Although generally managing her job satisfactorily and successfully completing her work trial, Alison did experience a number of problems. She had regular consultations with her psychologist and speech pathologist over a period of 18 months, in order to help her deal with various practical and emotional difficulties she encountered in returning to work. She had previously been a highly organised person. She found she was less so, and had occasional memory lapses. She needed to write many more details in her diary and record these immediately. She was encouraged to take a pen and paper to meetings in order to make notes and record important points in her diary afterwards. Fatigue was an ongoing problem, and she needed to take a day off when this built up. She used up her annual leave and sick leave in this way. She also had to restrict her social and recreational activities. She managed to continue working full-time. Although her coping abilities gradually increased, fatigue has continued to be a significant problem.

Alison's supervisor was generally satisfied with her performance, but there were several problem areas which she drew to Alison's attention. They largely concerned her interpersonal skills. When speaking in meetings, Alison was, at times, quite verbose, repeating the same points over and over. She had difficulty sticking to the topic she was addressing, tending to go off on tangents. These difficulties were also apparent when she answered queries or gave lectures. Alison found dealing with other staff extremely stressful, particularly in meetings. When others disagreed with her suggestions she immediately took their comments personally and became very upset and tearful. This was a source of considerable embarrassment to her. Having previously set very high standards for herself in terms of work and behaviour, Alison had always had a high level of self-control. Since the accident she had lost confidence in herself, and frequently felt anxious and nervous.

Alison's supervisor was advised as to the most constructive ways of pointing out and assisting her to deal with these problems, with emphasis on the need to couple negative feedback with positive feedback. Alison also addressed her difficulties directly with her psychologist and speech pathologist. They worked on enhancing her awareness of, and vigilance for verbal and non-verbal cues to indicate that she needed to stop talking or be more concise. She developed a strategy of preparing for meetings very carefully, asking herself a fixed set of questions as to the main issues for discussion, what she would like to say, who would be there, what points they were likely to raise, and what were the time constraints. She jotted down the answers to these. She took along these notes to the meetings and regularly referred to them to avoid going off track. Even when a meeting was called at short notice she would take a few minutes to jot down some points. In reflecting on her thoughts in these situations, Alison noted that when she became aware that others were getting bored, she tended to panic and make negative comments to herself, such as, "I'm a hopeless communicator". She developed more positive self-talk strategies to put such thoughts out of her mind and focus on her key thoughts. Prior to meetings she also tried to anticipate possible responses to what she said and plan how she would deal with these. She developed self-talk strategies to help her calm down if she began to feel upset. For example, she would stall for time by saying, "That's an interesting point. I'll have to think about that", or "Maybe we need to take some time to think about these things and discuss them at a later time". Alison also worked with her speech pathologist to develop a system for preparing lectures and responding to queries as concisely as possible.

Alison experienced difficulty handling and disciplining staff who worked under her. She was aware that certain staff were not completing work satisfactorily and not following certain necessary procedures. However, she found it very difficult to assert herself with them and they tended to manipulate her. She worked on her anxiety and assertiveness skills with her psychologist and sought some assistance as to the best way of dealing with these issues from her supervisor. Individual work on Alison's interpersonal difficulties, her anxiety, and self-esteem also extended to her social interactions. She attended a group held at the hospital in the evenings on a weekly basis, the aim of which was to provide support in dealing with issues confronting those who had recently returned to the community.

Although she learned to cope reasonably well in her job, Alison faced further problems when she changed to a similar position in another branch of the library 18 months later. She did not have the same degree of rapport with her new superior and felt this woman was undermining her. She had great difficulty in generalising the strategies she had learned in her previous position to deal with the problems she was facing. Her lack of assertiveness and strong emotional reactions again presented her with significant problems. She required intensive assistance along the same lines as that given previously in order to assist her to cope. Although she has unsuccessfully applied for several other positions in the library, Alison remains in the same job. Although she is now coping better, she is likely to require assistance from time to time for the foreseeable future.

RETURNING TO TERTIARY STUDY

A model similar to that outlined for return to employment is applicable to those returning to school or to a tertiary educational environment. Common difficulties manifested in the educational setting include deficits of attention, concentration and speed of thinking, fatigue, poor planning and organisational abilities, communication problems, and impaired self-awareness. Personality changes, such as impulsivity, aggression and difficulty in getting along with others may affect the injured student's social network. As a consequence of both sets of problems, students who do not receive ongoing support and assistance may suffer repeated failure, develop low self-esteem, become socially isolated and lose direction (Hall & DePompei, 1986; Ylvisaker, Hartwick, & Stevens, 1991).

A detailed discussion of pertinent issues, with guidelines for returning children and adolescents to school, is set out in Chapter 10.

For TBI students returning to, or embarking upon tertiary study, the process is even more difficult for a number of reasons. The demands being made on the student are likely to be greater than at school. The student will be required to concentrate on lectures for periods of at least an hour at a time. Far less structure is provided, the student being required to show considerable initiative and organisational ability to fulfil the requirements of the course. Assessments may only be conducted at lengthy intervals, so that it may be difficult to gauge how the student is coping. There also tends to be less room for flexibility in the curriculum.

There has been little evaluative research conducted regarding the most effective ways of maximising the success of return to tertiary study, although a number of authors have presented case reports to support recommended principles (e.g. Cook, 1991). The guidelines suggested here are consistent with the recommendations of Cook (1991), Hall and DePompei (1986) and Ylvisaker et al. (1991), but are based largely on the author's experience.

It is important early on to recruit the assistance of a disability liaison officer, if such a position exists in the educational institution, and/or at least one teacher or lecturer from the course, making them aware of the likely problems to be faced and discussing the feasibility of a graduated return to study. Aspects of coursework studied previously may be reviewed within the rehabilitation setting, under the supervision of therapists, who can assist the student in developing strategies to cope with potential difficulties. For example, strategies might be devised for recording the content of lectures, such as methods of identifying key themes or words, or the use of audiotaping. It may also be useful to work on written expression, proof reading and summarising skills. Short courses may be undertaken in preparation for return to the former course of study, allowing the student to gain some awareness of problems likely to encountered and practise compensatory strategies.

On return to study, the student may, in the first instance, attempt only one or two subjects. Close supervision will need to be requested of the lecturer, and possibly arrangements made for special tutoring. Ongoing follow-up support is essential. Peer group support may be provided through a study skills group, in which a group of TBI students discuss their difficulties and share ideas as to how to overcome these. Such a group can be a good forum in which to present students with coping strategies, including the use of a diary and action-planner, and methods of organising study time, note-taking, reviewing the content of lectures, essay-writing, coping with fatigue and so on, as well as providing moral support. A "study buddy" may also be recruited to assist in providing accurate lecture material and help with revision for exams.

No matter how much assistance is given to the student, most will feel quite alone within the educational environment, as other students and lecturers are likely to have difficulty in comprehending their problems. It is advisable, therefore, to establish some form of ongoing support on-campus, ideally through a student counselling service. They will probably need to be educated regarding the consequences of TBI.

It is not uncommon for TBI students who lack awareness of their difficulties to insist on returning to study when it seems clear to others that they will not cope. The experience of failure may be necessary in order to engender a more realistic self-appraisal by the student. However, this can also be a time of enormous stress, and it is vital that students be supported throughout this period, and assisted in the pursuit of alternatives to study if they do fail. Moreover, as the findings of Ponsford, Olver, and Curran (1994) have demonstrated, some students may, with assistance, manage to complete their studies, but have difficulty in obtaining employment afterwards. Ongoing contact needs to be maintained in order to provide necessary support in finding employment, or establishing a meaningful lifestyle.

CASE REPORT—ERIC

Eric was a 24-year-old student when he was hit by a car. He sustained a severe TBI, with one day of coma and a PTA lasting seven days. Prior to his injury, Eric, who was Vietnamese, was completing the final year of a degree in Electrical Engineering. He had been in Australia, sponsored by a scholarship, for three and a half years. Eric was sharing a flat with another Vietnamese student. His family was living in Vietnam. His mother visited for a couple of weeks after his injury. Eric was described as being intelligent and conscientious in his studies prior to the injury.

Neuropsychological assessment indicated that Eric was of above average intelligence. His English was good. He had reduced speed of information processing, difficulty sustaining attention due to fatigue, moderately severe difficulties in learning and retaining both verbal and non-verbal material, reduced planning and problem-solving abilities, poor self-monitoring, and word-finding difficulties in English. Eric showed some awareness of these problems at the time of the assessment, but did not realise their implications for his return to study. He showed no problems physically, or with personal, domestic or community ADL, although he tended to attempt too much and become very fatigued. He was intolerant of noise, and found it difficult to cope on return to his flat because his flatmate always had friends around until late at night. He spent a period at the Transitional Living Centre, before moving into a flat by himself.

Early contact was made with the university, initially with the liaison officer for overseas students, and then with Eric's lecturers. Because of his scholarship, he would need to return to the course in some capacity within three months, or suspend his enrolment and return to Vietnam. Some familiar coursework was obtained for him to work on in therapy. Eric was unable to concentrate for more than 30 minutes at a time, becoming overwhelmed and fatigued, and developing headaches and dizziness after this. He was given systematic feedback and reinforcement in order to increase his attention span. Eric was very keen to complete his course. He could not see the implications of the problems he was experiencing in therapy for his return to study. Against the advice of the therapists, he re-enrolled in two subjects and started attending some lectures. However, he rapidly became overwhelmed by the material presented in lectures and began to realise that he could not cope. Eric became highly anxious at his stage.

A meeting was arranged between therapists from the hospital, the liaison officer, and the course co-ordinator. It was decided that Eric would attempt one subject, which had the least lecture content. Additional tutoring in that subject was arranged for four hours per week. He also attended the rehabilitation centre twice a week. In addition to carrying out a fitness programme to increase his endurance, Eric attended a study skills group, where he worked on strategies for note-taking and summarising notes, and structuring study time. With the help of his speech pathologist he worked out a system of taperecording lectures and reviewing the tape later. He also had sessions with the psychologist to develop self-talk and relaxation strategies to reduce his anxiety when he became overwhelmed. Eric was also feeling very socially isolated, because he had tended to avoid social situations due to his information processing difficulties. He was encouraged to begin contacting some friends and to go out on weekends, when he felt less tired. He was very self-conscious regarding his slowness in keeping up with conversations. He attended a conversational skills group to boost his abilities and confidence.

Eric successfully completed the subject and returned to Vietnam for a holiday. He still had three subjects to complete, and it was decided to spread these across the year, rather than attempt them in one semester. Some tutoring was maintained in order to provide back-up support, and Eric was contacted by his speech pathologist on a regular basis. He required some further input to help him structure his time to meet the demands of the additional subjects. He also attended an evening discussion group to assist him in dealing with some ongoing social difficulties. He had fallen in love with a girl at the rehabilitation centre, but she was not returning his affection, causing him additional stress. As the year progressed his confidence and coping abilities gradually increased, however. He successfully completed his studies and returned to Vietnam, where he is now working for the government.

AVOCATIONAL INTERESTS

Whether or not return to work or study is possible, recreational interests assume a very important role in the life of a person who has sustained TBI. In spite of this, rehabilitation efforts focusing on this aspect of the TBI individual's lifestyle tend to assume secondary importance. Perhaps reflecting this, there has been little emphasis on return to leisure pursuits in the rehabilitation literature. Results from a follow-up study by Ponsford et al. (1995a) indicated that only about 10% of the group of 175 moderate to severely injured subjects were able to independently engage in all previous activities and interests 2 years after injury. A further 15.5% of subjects were involved in previous activities and interests with some assistance. Nearly half (49%) said they independently participated in alternative activities and interests; 21% of the subjects required some assistance to pursue alternative interests. These results indicate that TBI has a very significant impact on avocational interests. They underscore the importance of the assessment and development of the TBI individual's ability to pursue previous or alternative recreational activities.

As Jacobs (1989) has pointed out, many factors may contribute to difficulties in pursuing recreational interests following TBI. These include the presence of physical disabilities, problems with transportation, limited finance, impairment of cognition, behaviour and social skills, lack of initiative or self-confidence, poor family or social support, or simply a lack of networking. As with all other aspects of return to community living, the extent to which these hurdles can be overcome will be largely determined by the presence of funding support and/or community-based resources for the development of leisure pursuits in young people with disabilities. However, an awareness of the importance of recreation in the earlier stages of the rehabilitation will lay a valuable foundation for some success in this domain.

Assessment and rehabilitation of recreational abilities

Individual and group recreational and social activities are frequently organised within rehabilitation programmes in order to provide participants with an opportunity to develop certain skills, or relax and socialise. However, these activities do not necessarily bear a close resemblance to those pursued by the TBI individual prior to injury, and may not be available after discharge from rehabilitation. It is important that regular individual therapy time be devoted to the assessment and development of the injured person's capacity to pursue activities of relevance and interest to themselves. As with other aspects of the TBI individual's lifestyle, a comprehensive assessment of previous recreational and social interests should be made at the time of admission to the rehabilitation programme, and an analysis made of the skills required to participate in such interests. Wherever possible the individual who has sustained TBI should be encouraged and given therapeutic assistance to continue pursuing these interests during the rehabilitation phase.

As it becomes clearer what level of mobility, communication, and cognitive function is likely to be reached, an assessment can be made as to which activities may be continued, albeit with some modifications, special equipment or assistance, and rehabilitation goals set accordingly. For the many who are not able to return to previous avocational activities, a comprehensive assessment of their interests and ability to pursue alternatives will be required. Whilst this role may be performed primarily by a recreational therapist or occupational therapist, all team members need to share in the process of formulating and working towards the achievement of such goals. For example, specific assessment and therapeutic input is likely to be required from the physiotherapist when return to sporting activities is being contemplated, and from the speech pathologist when reading or communication skills are involved.

Where a number of TBI individuals have a similar interest, a group may be formed to pursue that interest during the rehabilitation phase, in order to provide an opportunity for skills to be practised. However, wherever possible, the TBI individual needs to be encouraged to pursue avocational activities in the local community, rather than being dependent on the rehabilitation centre. In order to achieve this, the rehabilitation team should apply a similar model of intervention to that applied to return to work or school.

Developing activities at the community level

A great deal of energy will need to be devoted to searching for relevant resources. These should be contacted and educated as to specific needs or limitations of the TBI person. Time needs to be spent with the injured individual engaging in the activity in the community and assisting in overcoming any problems encountered. An attendant may be appointed to provide necessary assistance. Above all, ongoing follow-up is essential. Whilst many TBI individuals may be discharged from a rehabilitation programme with a comprehensive set of activities, over time these tend to dissipate for a variety of reasons. The TBI person may not have the initiative or organisational ability to pursue alternatives without assistance. Indeed, in the Los Angeles Head Injury Survey, Jacobs (1988) found this was the case for 54% of TBI individuals. Many turn to their families or caregivers for such support in the longer term, but this is not ideal because it adds to their burden and reduces opportunities for both parties to have recreational time on their own.

For those who are unable to participate in regular community activities, an appropriate day activities programme may be sought. Ideally, such a programme should cater specifically to the needs of young people with acquired brain injury. TBI individuals are not likely to be successfully accommodated in programmes designed for the elderly disabled or those with congenital disabilities. Young people who have sustained TBI tend not to identify themselves as disabled, frequently do not look disabled and may resent being with other disabled people. They retain the motivations and interests which they held prior to injury. A day programme should enable them to pursue these interests. It needs to provide an appropriate degree of structure, but be sufficiently flexible to allow those who have behaviour problems and limited concentration to participate.

A variety of activities should be available, ranging from productive work tasks to creative activities. One of the greatest needs met by such a programme is for social interaction, and some participants may wish only to sit and smoke, drink coffee, and listen to music. An opportunity should be provided to do this. If a suitable programme can be found, issues of transportation and meeting the cost of the programme still need to be dealt with. As programmes such as these are few and far between, it is more probable that a range of suitable generic activities will need to be sought. If funding is available, an attendant could facilitate the TBI individual's involvement. Again, ongoing follow-up is vital in order to sustain such a programme of activities.

DRIVER ASSESSMENT AND REHABILITATION

For many young people who have sustained TBI, return to driving represents a major goal. The inability to drive may compound low self-esteem and the injured person's sense of dependency and isolation. However, because of the inherent risks involved in driving, careful assessment is essential. This is frequently difficult to enforce, as in many countries the drivers' licence remains technically valid unless steps are taken to cancel it. The assessment of driving capability is extremely difficult, due to the number, complexity, and frequently abstract nature of the skills involved. Many of these skills may be impaired following TBI, including motor control and co-ordination, visual perception, speed of information processing, various aspects of attention, memory, behavioural control, planning, judgement, and decision-making. Increased fatiguability may also present a problem.

However, as van Zomeren, Brouwer, and Minderhoud (1987) have cogently pointed out in an excellent review of the subject, the precise manner in which these deficits interfere with the injured individual's actual driving performance is very difficult to predict. The presence of a given cognitive deficit may not necessarily result in unsafe driving. Factors unrelated to the injury, such as the injured person's previous driving experience and habits have also been shown to play a significant role.

Until relatively recently, the decision as to whether an injured person could return to driving was made by medical practitioners, based on the probability of epilepsy, the patient's neurological status and speculation as to the nature and manner in which the injured person's cognitive deficits would affect driving capability. However the findings of Fox, Bashford, and Caust (1992), have suggested that medical assessment alone is not a reliable means of judging driver competence. Neuropsychological assessment has also been used as a predictive tool. Although findings in this respect have been mixed, the predictive validity of neuropsychological tests in relation to actual driving performance remains questionable (Brooke, Quested, Patterson, & Valois, 1992; Fox et al., 1992; van Zomeren et al., 1987; van Zomeren, Brouwer, Rothengatter, & Snoek, 1988). A number of authors have even expressed doubts as to the usefulness of brake reaction time tests and driving simulators in assessing or training the ability to cope on the road (Hopewell & Price, 1985; van Zomeren et al., 1987). There is now a growing awareness of the need for multidisciplinary evaluation, incorporating on-road assessment and training by appropriately qualified instructors.

Recommended driver assessment procedures
In the case of severe TBI it is now generally recommended that assessment not be conducted until at least several months after injury, during which the injured individual should be advised not to drive. The first stage in a comprehensive driver evaluation is usually a motor–sensory assessment, encompassing vision, hearing, strength, sensation, range of movement, co-ordination, and endurance in arms and legs, neck and trunk, and mobility, with specific identification of whether and how any impairments impact on the injured person's ability to operate and drive a vehicle. Numerous mechanical adaptations are now available to assist in compensating for motor–sensory problems.

Aspects of cognitive function for consideration include the ability to sustain and divide attention, tracking more than one thing at a time, distractibility, speed of information processing, visual scanning and orientation, memory, impulsivity, planning, anticipation, judgement, and decision making, as well as behavioural responses under stress and emotional control. Whilst the results of a neuropsychological assessment may assist the driving assessor by pointing to the potential presence of certain difficulties, the actual impact of such impairments on driving performance needs to be assessed on the road. Reaction times may also be assessed using an off-road brake reaction tester, with the introduction of distractions. However it is important to note that slower reaction times do not always result in unsafe driving. This depends on the presence or otherwise of other cognitive deficits (van Zomeren et al., 1987). Off-road tests of road law and road craft should also be carried out.

Provided a baseline standard has been reached on the off-road assessment, the injured individual may proceed to an on-road assessment. Such assessments must be conducted in a dual-control car by an instructor who is trained in driving assessment, has a good understanding of the impact of brain injury on cognition and behaviour, as well as an understanding of the normal variation in driving habits and behaviour. The drives should be graded in terms of their demands, commencing in quiet residential streets and gradually being upgraded to more complex traffic situations which include busy shopping areas, main roads and inner city streets. An automatic car may be used for the first drive to reduce the demands on the injured person, and a manual car used in subsequent drives. Distractions and other demands may be introduced systematically to assess the injured driver's response to these.

According to the model of car driving put forward by Michon (1979, cited by van Zomeren et al., 1987), the task of driving involves three hierarchical levels: (1) the "Strategical level", which involves planning and decision-making regarding the route to be taken, the time of the journey, etc., before driving starts; (2) the "Tactical level", which involves behaviour and decisions in traffic, such as adapting speed to the area, considering when to overtake and switching on headlights to improve visibility; and (3) the "Operational level", which incorporates the actions and decisions involved in driving, such as perception of traffic situations, use of controls and mirrors and generally handling the car. On-road assessment needs to cover all of these aspects of driving. Given the frequency of executive dysfunction following TBI, it is particularly important to examine planning, anticipation, the ability to adapt to different situations on the road and avoid time pressure. Unfortunately there are no standardised techniques available to make such assessments. Indeed a significant limitation of most current on-road assessment procedures is the lack of standardised procedures, normative data which clearly differentiate safe from unsafe drivers, and follow-up data regarding actual driving performance. Whilst the move towards on-road assessment of driving capability has been a very important step forward, much further work is needed in this area before the process can be considered a valid one.

Driver rehabilitation

The question as to whether it is possible to retrain aspects of driving behaviour also remains open, although there is some positive evidence to this effect. Certainly there is considerable scope for overcoming motor–sensory limitations through adaptive modifications to the car. The injured person will need to be trained to use these modifications, and may also learn other compensatory strategies.

Sivak, Hill, Henson, Butler, Silber, and Olson (1984) and Sivak, Hill, and Olson (1984) have claimed success in decreasing perceptual impairments and improving driving performance by training on paper-and-pencil and computer-mediated video tasks. However these studies did not employ a control group, and the improvements seen may have reflected a practice effect. In a study which did incorporate a control group, Kewman, Seigerman, Kintner, Chu, Henson, and Reeder (1985) trained 13 brain-injured subjects in visuomotor tracking and divided attention skills using a small electric-powered vehicle. They were able to demonstrate a positive impact of this training on on-road driving performance relative to controls.

Comprehensive driver training programmes are now conducted in many rehabilitation centres. These generally incorporate sessions in the classroom, practice in handling and manouvering a car and on-road instruction. Hopewell and Price (1985) reported a return-to-driving rate of 53% following such a driver training programme, although no comparison was made with a matched, untrained sample. The importance of factors, such as the nature of cognitive deficits and previous driving experience, in determining the ability to benefit from such programmes remains unclear.

The probability of success of driver training or retraining is likely to be maximised if training is focused on the specific limitations of the injured individual. The emphasis of most training programmes described is generally placed on operational aspects of driving, such as handling and manouvering the car. Given the frequency of executive dysfunction following TBI, there is undoubtedly a need for development of training strategies focusing on strategic and tactical aspects of driving, such as those piloted by Kovacs (1995) with bicycle riders. In this study subjects were trained to anticipate problems and take necessary steps to avoid them. The success of this training depended on the level of self-awareness of the injured individual. The importance of self-awareness as a predictor of driving performance has not yet been adequately investigated. However, it may well be a highly significant determinant of the degree to which the injured person can adapt to limitations and learn to drive safely.

CONCLUSIONS

Considerable time and effort needs to be devoted to assisting TBI individuals to return to a living situation which maximises their independence, work, study, recreational and social interests, and driving. This is best achieved via a thorough assessment of premorbid status in these areas, identification of relevant strengths and weaknesses since the injury, and available supports. Therapeutic input may focus specifically on developing the skills needed to resume activities or develop a new lifestyle, task modification, or the provision of necessary environmental supports. Above all, it is vital to provide ongoing support and assistance over an extended time frame, in order to deal with the inevitable problems and changes which will occur in the lifestyles of TBI individuals and those around them. Given the traditional focus of rehabilitation in the acute phase of recovery, there are likely to be many difficulties in finding the means of meeting all these challenges. In most cases a broad range of community-based resources will need to be tapped, together with the assistance of the injured person's own network of supports.

CHAPTER EIGHT

Dealing with the impact of traumatic brain injury on psychological adjustment and relationships

Jennie Ponsford

INTRODUCTION

Psychological reactions to TBI are extremely complex and variable, being determined by a broad range of factors. These include the nature and severity of the injury, the manner in which it was sustained, and whether the injured person can recall the accident, as well as the age, developmental stage, and previous psychological and social adjustment of the injured person and family. Psychological consequences of mild TBI tend to differ somewhat from those associated with moderate or severe TBI. The impact of mild TBI will therefore be dealt with first. However, the major emphasis of this chapter will be on dealing with emotional and adjustment issues following moderate and severe TBI.

PSYCHOLOGICAL CONSEQUENCES OF MILD TBI

As outlined in Chapter 1, mild TBI can result in persisting symptoms, known collectively as the post-concussional syndrome. These include mental slowness, concentration and memory problems, as well as fatigue, irritability, headache, sensitivity to noise, bustle or light, dizziness, tinnitus, crying, anxiety, and depression. It has been proposed that at least some of these symptoms are a result of the stress of coping with a reduced information processing capacity, whilst attempting to perform previous roles as before (Gouvier, Cubic, Jones, Brantley, & Cutlip, 1992; van Zomeren & van den Burg, 1985). Gouvier et al. (1992) have demonstrated a significant association between the frequency, intensity and duration of post-concussional symptoms and daily stress levels. As Cicerone (1991) has pointed out, in the case of mild TBI there may be little relationship between objective assessments of cognitive impairments and the magnitude of complaints by those injured. The degree of subjective awareness of limitations is more closely related to subjective distress.

There have been no studies formally evaluating the impact of interventions for psychological problems following mild TBI. Gronwall (1986), Kay (1992), and Mateer (1992) have suggested that the early provision of information, support and assistance in making a graduated return to previous activities may alleviate the development of stress. There is a need for research evaluating the impact of such interventions.

Cicerone (1991) has provided a detailed exploration of psychological issues pertaining to mild TBI, and psychological approaches to dealing with ongoing adjustment difficulties. He emphasises the importance of modifying the injured individual's belief system regarding the severity of deficits, or the impact of these deficits on daily functioning. There is a need to normalise symptoms, by providing realistic explanation as to their basis. Those injured may be assisted in learning to regulate their lifestyle to avoid problems, recognise the early signs of stress and take steps to avoid it developing. Assistance may be given in developing methods of compensating for cognitive impairments (e.g. by reducing overall workload, introducing a diary). Somatic and emotional sensitivities may be alleviated by cognitive–behavioural techniques, which assist the injured person to develop a more realistic appraisal of their abilities, tolerate or shift the focus of attention off their symptoms, and re-establish a sense of mastery over the environment. In some cases, pre-existing adjustment issues may need to be addressed.

POST-TRAUMATIC STRESS DISORDER

A minority of TBI cases may develop Post-traumatic Stress Disorder (PTSD). This condition may occur when a person has experienced an event that is outside the range of usual human experience, such as a serious threat to one's life or physical integrity, or that of another person. It is characterised by re-experiences of the trauma (nightmares, flashbacks and/or intrusive recollections of the trauma); avoidance techniques (avoidance of situations that trigger recollections of the event, blocking feelings, feeling detached and estranged from others);

and excessive arousal (sleep difficulties, poor concentration and memory, hypervigilance, being easily startled) (Horne, 1994). As Horne (1994) has pointed out, a crucial issue in the development of this disorder appears to be the individual's own perception of what happened. In this sense there is usually some recollection of the events preceding the accident and the sense of impending disaster, if not a recollection of the accident itself and events afterwards. The development of PTSD is therefore generally confined to victims of mild TBI or those with no head injury, where such recollections may be possible.

For a detailed discussion of methods of treating PTSD the reader is referred to Miller (1993) and Thompson (1992). Graded exposure therapies may be used to assist those injured in gradually confronting the stimuli they would otherwise seek to avoid. They are encouraged to talk about the traumatic events, both within therapy and at home. The aim is to reduce post-traumatic reactions, such as flashbacks, intrusive memories and startle responses through habituation, and thereby bring about extinction of the conditioned aversive arousal response. Desensitization therapy may be carried out using imagination during relaxation exercises, or through graduated exposure to real-life situations.

When behavioural techniques prove ineffective, there may be some underlying personality dimension that needs to be addressed psychotherapeutically. According to Miller (1993), fear of abandonment and loss of control are two predominant psychodynamic issues, which may be complicated by family dynamics. Deitz (1992) provides a detailed discussion of psychotherapy for the brain-injured person with PTSD.

EMOTIONAL REACTIONS TO MODERATE AND SEVERE TBI

A large number of outcome studies have documented the significant psychosocial impact of moderate and severe TBI. For many, this results in a decline in vocational status, family or marital relationships, and social or leisure activities (Oddy, 1984a; Lezak, 1987). A number of authors, such as Tyerman and Humphrey (1984) have also documented the emotional or psychological consequences, which include reduced self-esteem, loneliness, and depression. The devastating nature of this psychosocial impact is linked strongly with the demographic characteristics of those who most commonly sustain TBI, and the unique pattern of cognitive, behavioural and emotional changes which tend to result from TBI.

Whilst TBI can occur in people of any gender, age, or socioeconomic class, it is most frequently sustained by adolescent and young adult males (Anderson & McLaurin, 1980; Health Department of Victoria, 1991; NHIF, 1984). They may still be still in the process of attaining emotional separation and independence from parental support, establishing an identity, and forming important social and intimate relationships. A relationship or marriage is likely to have been of relatively short duration, and any children are likely to be young. Most have not fully established a vocation. Some are still at school, or undergoing training or study towards a vocation. For those working, there has been limited time to establish skills and experience. As Cottle (1988) has pointed out, the attainment of these milestones is interrupted by the occurrence of TBI. By virtue of their circumstances, as well as physical, emotional and social disabilities, many TBI individuals have a reduced capacity to resolve age-relevant issues.

Reflecting on the work of Erickson, Fryer (1989, p.257) has noted that an inability to resolve adolescent issues can result in "lack of purpose, inability to find intimacy with others, and self-defeating behaviour (i.e. substance abuse)". All of these behaviours may also result directly from the brain injury. Rejection by peers and the inability to pursue vocational goals and recreational interests tends to result in frustration, low self-esteem and social isolation. A new peer group may be formed, but new friendships tend to be more superficial and less enduring (Oddy, 1984a). Elsass and Kinsella (1987) found that individuals with severe TBI had significantly fewer opportunities for social interaction and were more vulnerable to psychiatric disorders.

For those who prior to injury were in a long-term relationship or marriage, changes in personality and behaviour, such as irritability and aggression, self-centredness, and childishness place significant stress on the relationship, which may already be strained by financial hardship and other role changes (Panting & Merry, 1972; Rosenbaum & Najenson, 1976). There may also be changes in sexual drive and performance (Rosenbaum & Najenson, 1976). Relationships with children may deteriorate to the point where the person who has sustained TBI is competing with them for the attention of spouse or mother (Thomsen, 1984).

Some findings suggest that a significant proportion of TBI individuals also come from a lower socioeconomic group, have experienced an unsatisfactory education, unstable employment, conflict with authority, and problems with drug or alcohol abuse prior to injury (Rimel & Jane, 1984). Psychiatric disorder, family problems and previous head injury are also relatively common. Pre-existing maladaptive problems, or the effects of a prior head injury, may be exacerbated following TBI, having a further negative effect on emotional adjustment and psychosocial outcome (Gronwall, 1989; Kreutzer, Leininger, Sherron, & Groah, 1989; Sale et al., 1991).

The psychosocial and emotional consequences for the individual who has sustained moderate or severe TBI thus represent a complex interplay of changes in cognition, behaviour and personality resulting directly from the brain injury and reactive problems, including depression, low self-esteem, and lack of motivation and purpose. Reactive problems may be exacerbated by the inability to pursue developmentally important goals, or previous maladaptive problems. There has been relatively less documentation of the emotional and social consequences of TBI from the point of view of the person who has sustained it than from the point of view of the family. This is at least partly due to a perception that TBI individuals are less aware of their responses than others, less able to reliably report inner experiences or, by virtue of cognitive dysfunction, simply do not experience a significant emotional response to the injury. As Tyerman and Humphrey (1984) have quite rightly emphasised, whilst the impact of TBI on the family is also very significant, and arguably more easily documented, the emotional consequences of such devastating changes to a person's lifestyle for that individual deserve greater attention.

Paralleling this, and in spite of clear evidence of the existence of emotional and interpersonal problems, there has been insufficient emphasis on the development of management strategies to alleviate such difficulties, which represent an important dimension of quality of life (McSweeny, 1990). Whilst many hours of therapy may be devoted to the development of important life skills, relating to self-care, mobility, home management, employment or study, and recreation, many individuals who have sustained moderate or severe TBI receive no assistance in dealing with emotional or relationship problems throughout their rehabilitation. As a reflection of this, there have been very few experimental studies evaluating the effectiveness of interventions for such difficulties.

It is a commonly held view that psychological therapy is unlikely to be successful with TBI individuals. This may be true in some cases, particularly in the acute stages of recovery, or in those whose cognitive impairment is extremely severe. However, although there is a lack of scientific evidence, in our experience many TBI individuals can obtain some benefit from psychological therapy, particularly in the postacute phase of recovery, when they are in the process of returning to live in the community, to work or study, and to social and leisure activities. Support for this contention comes from the findings of Kinsella, Moran, Ford, and Ponsford (1988), which suggested that the availability of a close confiding relationship was significantly associated with a more positive emotional disposition in TBI individuals.

Psychological and interpersonal problems following moderate or severe TBI are frequently numerous and interrelated with one another and with changes in cognition, behaviour, and personality. The most common difficulties include poor self-awareness and self-esteem, depression, anxiety, impaired social or interpersonal skills, anger management problems, marital or relationship difficulties, and sexual problems (Lezak, 1987). Approaches to therapy for social or inter-personal skills have been described in Chapter 6. Methods of dealing with the other problem areas are discussed below. It must be stressed that all techniques recommended require further experimental validation.

SELF-AWARENESS AND SELF-ESTEEM FOLLOWING TBI

A number of authors have pointed to the significance of unrealistic self-appraisal as a source of problems in psychosocial adjustment and adaptation to the impact of moderate or severe TBI (Ezrachi et al., 1991; Prigatano & Fordyce, 1986). Reduced awareness of changes in cognition, behaviour and personality following TBI is thought in most cases to result directly from neurological impairment, specifically impairment of frontal lobe function, rather than from a psychological need to deny the impact of the trauma. However, as Langer and Padrone (1992) point out, it is important to be aware of the possibility that denial of deficits may, in some cases, have a psychogenic basis. Lack of insight commonly reduces motivation for rehabilitative therapy, results in unrealistic decisions regarding work or study, and conflict with family members, who may be seen by the injured individual as overly protective or negative.

Prigatano and Fordyce (1986, p.13) found that when TBI patients, relatives and rehabilitation staff in the rehabilitation setting rated the patient's ability to perform a variety of everyday behaviours, "the majority of patients seen in rehabilitation tend to rate themselves as generally more competent, compared with the ratings of family members and rehabilitation staff members." Prigatano and Fordyce found a positive correlation between differences in perceived competency by TBI patients and staff members and degree of neuropsychological impairment. There was a negative correlation with emotional distress, as assessed on the MMPI, in the TBI patients. The findings of Fahy, Irving, and Millac (1967), Thomsen (1984) and McKinlay and Brooks (1984) also support the view that there is a discrepancy between the problems reported by TBI individuals and their relatives. They found that such disagreement was most likely to occur over changes in behaviour and personality.

According to Ezrachi et al. (1991) and Prigatano and Fordyce (1986) the development of realistic self-appraisal is essential if the TBI individual is to return successfully to a productive lifestyle. Recent studies evaluating the effectiveness of specific cognitive interventions have also identified self-awareness as an essential ingredient to their success (Crosson et al., 1989; Kovacs et al., 1993; Lam, McMahon, Priddy, & Gehred-Schultz, 1988). It is therefore an important focus of the rehabilitation process.

Developing self-awareness

Information regarding the causes and nature of the changes resulting from the injury needs to be conveyed to the TBI individual by the rehabilitation team from the time of admission to rehabilitation. It is important that such information, and feedback regarding performance, be given in clear and simple terms, which can be understood by the TBI individual, repeated as often as necessary and written down. Attempts should be made to demonstrate changes on tasks and in settings that the TBI person engaged in or was familiar with prior to the injury and sees as meaningful. In this respect it is important not to shield injured individuals from failure by avoiding opportunities to engage in previous activities. It is better to allow them the experience and assist them in benefiting from it through supportive discussion.

Whilst all team members will be involved in this process, it may be appropriate to designate a member of the rehabilitation team, with whom there is good rapport, to see the TBI person on a regular basis and discuss progress in the programme, particular problems which are emerging, and goals which are seen as relevant. As noted in Chapter 4, such ongoing dialogue enables the team to understand the extent to which the injured individual comprehends and concurs with the goals therapists see as important and to incorporate that individual's goals wherever possible.

For a variety of reasons, however, the severely injured person will rarely be capable of fully comprehending the impact of the injury in the early stages of recovery, let alone accepting it and understanding its implications for the future. Individuals with severe TBI frequently become resentful and even hostile if constantly confronted with their failures. Therefore, therapists should take pains to highlight strengths and positive attributes. There is little to be gained, and a great deal to be lost, by reiterating information and continuing to emphasise problems which the TBI person aggressively refuses to acknowledge. This usually results only in refusal to co-operate with the programme and, in some cases, premature discharge. Unfortunately there is simply no way of convincing TBI individuals of the presence of problems which they cannot perceive. Thus, the manner and frequency with which feedback is given requires careful consideration at all times and must be discussed regularly by the team. Over time, but at a widely varying pace, there are likely to be changes in the injured person's capacity to receive feedback and begin to understand its implications for the future.

It is frequently not until TBI individuals have returned to the community and had more direct experience of changes in capabilities, as far as living skills, work, leisure activities, and social relationships are concerned, that they gain some awareness of change. At some point after the injury, perhaps not until more than a year later, some insight may begin to develop. It is at this stage that an opportunity should ideally be provided for psychological assistance in developing a realistic self-appraisal, whilst minimising the loss of self-esteem. Such therapy might aim to convey an understanding of the changes in cognition, behaviour and personality which have been brought about by the injury. These changes need to be discussed both from the perspective of the injured individual and from the perspective of family and others. Encouragement should be given to express emotional reactions to these changes. The therapist needs to reiterate objective information, which may be comprehended more easily at this stage than when it was presented earlier.

As a means of rebuilding self-esteem, it is extremely important to highlight positive changes and residual strengths, as well as weaknesses, and explore how these can be used to build a new life which has some meaning. The ultimate goal of such therapy is the attainment of some degree of acceptance, and an ability to like the "new" person who has survived the injury. For adolescents and young adults in particular, the therapist needs to make a careful assessment of pertinent developmental issues, and address the impact of the injury in this respect. For some, an important focus may be on body image and forming relationships with the opposite sex, whilst for others it may be moving out of home and achieving independence of parental support.

As with behavioural problems after TBI, emotional problems and impaired self-awareness which follow TBI may result directly from the injury itself, but may also be related to the injured person's current emotional state or to pre-existing problems of a psychological nature. It is necessary, therefore, to make a careful assessment of the TBI individual's previous and current psychological state and personality, and methods of coping with stress. As Langer and Padrone (1992) point out, approaches to managing psychogenic denial differ from those recommended for organically-based denial. Where denial has an emotional basis, psychological therapy will need to target the underlying problems and "strengthen the ego" before any attempt is made to come to terms with change.

As will be discussed in detail in Chapter 9, the TBI person's emotional state can also be influenced by the manner in which the family has coped with the injury. This, in turn, will be influenced by the family's established response to crises and the role of the injured individual in the family. It is vital that families be involved in this therapeutic process. Many families initially fail to recognise or acknowledge the presence of changes in their relative. When they do recognise such changes, family members and others may also find it very difficult to give the TBI individual realistic feedback regarding changes. They may require assistance in understanding the importance of feedback and how to give it in a supportive way. Issues regarding families' awareness of the impact of injury and ways of assisting them in dealing with this will be explored further in Chapter 9.

Group therapy to enhance self-awareness and self-esteem
In those individuals who have sufficient language and memory skills and behavioural control, individual therapy may be supplemented with group therapy, which provides an opportunity for peer group feedback and support. Group therapy can be a particularly useful means of addressing developmental issues. Prigatano and Fordyce (1986) have proposed a framework for group therapy following brain injury. They recommend that groups focusing on adjustment issues should consist of around six brain-injured individuals and two therapists who have background in neuropsychology and clinical psychology. These groups should be closed, to allow for continuity and the development of a sense of trust and belonging. In addition to achieving some awareness of the impact of the injury on each person's thinking, behaviour and emotional state, and resulting lifestyle changes, group therapy can assist in elucidating how problems are perceived by and affect others, and how they compare with those experienced by other TBI individuals. This experience potentially enhances insight and reduces the TBI person's sense of isolation.

Self-esteem may be boosted by exercises in which individuals identify positive attributes in themselves and in one another or talk of their accomplishments. Such exercises represent an important component of the head trauma programme at the Rusk Institute of Rehabilitation Medicine in New York, developed by Yehuda Ben-Yishay and his colleagues (Ben-Yishay, Lakin, Ross, Rattok, Cohen, & Diller, 1980). With the assistance of a therapist, all participants are required at various times to talk to the group about their life, the impact of the injury, their accomplishments and positive attributes, and those of another participant. Afterwards, feedback is given by all group members regarding content and style of presentation, but criticisms are carefully couched within positive feedback. Ben-Yishay and his colleagues believe that, by publicly stating the impact of one's injury and receiving positive feedback for this, TBI individuals eventually come to believe the truth of their statements, without loss of self-esteem.

Participation in such a group programme provides an opportunity to work on interpersonal skills. Inevitably some conflict develops in the course of these interactions. It is important in this respect to follow up group sessions with individual work focusing on issues arising in the group or individual strategies for dealing with conflict. Reviewing videotapes of the group in individual sessions may be helpful. Group leaders generally need to be very directive when working with TBI clients, assisting individuals who have difficulty initiating or conveying their thoughts clearly, clarifying what group members say and intervening when group members' comments are perceived as being overly hurtful, aggressive or otherwise inappropriate, as well as keeping the group "on track".

The frequency with which groups meet is likely to be determined by practical issues. However, there is little doubt that in order to be maximally effective, such groups should be held as frequently as possible, ideally on a daily basis or several times a week. This is not to say that groups held only once a week will not be successful, but participants will need to be functioning at a higher level in terms of memory and executive function.

Whilst Prigatano and Fordyce (1986) and Ben-Yishay et al. (1980) have reported success from their group-oriented interventions in many individual cases, there is a need for more objective research evaluating the effectiveness of this form of therapy. In particular, it is necessary to assess which aspects of the therapy process are most helpful, and which individuals with TBI are most likely to benefit. Such evaluation is extremely difficult, largely because of the lack of objective measurement tools, particularly in the domain of self-awareness. The impact of any gains in self-awareness and self-esteem on psychosocial adjustment should also be assessed.

In those who have sustained very severe TBI with amnesia, attentional problems and very limited behavioural control, attempts to develop realistic self-appraisal, either through individual or group therapy, are very unlikely to be successful. However, the insight of these individuals may be enhanced by feedback and experience over an extended period. Moreover, their emotional responses are worthy of respect and consideration, and opportunities should be given for ventilation of feelings on a regular basis. It is equally important to highlight successes and strengths in these individuals in order to maximise self-esteem.

Circles of support

The formation of a "Circle of Support" is another method of enhancing self-awareness and self-esteem following TBI. The usefulness of this concept to assist young TBI individuals in developing a support network has recently been elaborated by Willer, Allen, Anthony, and Cowlan (1993). According to Willer et al. (p.7), "A circle of support is a semi-structured approach to the establishment and operation of a small circle of friends who meet on a regular basis with an individual who has experienced brain injury and has disabilities". It is formed after the injured person has returned to the community, with the broad aim of assisting that individual to identify and attain personal goals. Health professionals are rarely involved, although a facilitator needs to take responsibility for keeping the group focused on its goal.

At monthly meetings, the injured person is given an opportunity to articulate his or her most important dreams or goals (e.g. to live independently, or get a job). Other group members then express their goals for the injured individual, also describing what that individual brings to their life and the person's most positive attributes. This reduces the sense of loneliness and fosters a more positive self-image. Goals are broken down into steps by the group, encouraging reflection on them by the injured person, who will frequently revise unrealistic goals. Others may offer suggestions to overcome barriers and assist the individual to reach solutions to problems. At times negative feedback may need to be given, but this is more easily accepted if the group has developed a sense of trust and mutual friendship.

Given the availability of a motivated and energetic facilitator (who should not be a family member), this process represents a more natural and enduring method of enhancing self-esteem in those who have sustained TBI, at the same time as increasing self-awareness and achieving some longed-for goals. These friends are more likely to remain a part of the injured person's life in the years to come. In many instances they are also more able to focus on the individual's strengths and less likely to be constrained in their capacity to dream with that person.

APPROACHES TO THERAPY FOR SPECIFIC EMOTIONAL OR INTERPERSONAL PROBLEMS

By virtue of their cognitive difficulties, many individuals who have sustained TBI have difficulty in benefiting from traditional psychotherapy, which is heavily reliant on verbal interaction, and a capacity to remember the content of that interaction from one session to the next. There is a lack of scientific evidence regarding the success or otherwise of any particular therapeutic approach. However, cognitive–behavioural techniques lend themselves to dealing with these difficulties quite well, both in terms of the nature of the problems most commonly presenting and the approach to therapy, which can be adapted to certain cognitive limitations. Those difficulties which most commonly interfere with the capacity to benefit from psychological therapy include problems with attention and memory, concrete thinking, poor organisational skills, limited behavioural regulation and lack of insight. Cognitive–behavioural approaches tend to be well-structured, focus on concrete behaviours or thoughts, allow for the use of written aids, and lend themselves to the involvement of a family member or other suitable person in the therapy process.

It is important at the outset to make a careful assessment of the kinds of limitations the TBI person is likely to have in such a therapy situation and to adapt the prescribed techniques as needed. Generally, it is necessary to keep sessions short and build in a great deal of repetition, writing all important points down in the person's diary or in a special "therapy diary". The therapist will usually need to be very directive.

With the agreement of the injured individual, it may be helpful to involve a supportive family member or close friend as a "co-therapist". This person may assist in carrying out homework exercises, where thoughts and behaviour are being monitored, and prompt adherence to guidelines agreed upon in therapy sessions. In a sense, the family member may act as the TBI individual's "frontal lobes", providing concrete feedback in situations which are familiar to the TBI person, and prompting more adaptive responses. It is, however, extremely important to convey a clear understanding of the aims and process of therapy to the relative who is acting as a co-therapist.

Involving a family member in this way potentially facilitates the development of good communication between TBI individual and family, and an understanding on the part of family members of the most appropriate ways of helping their injured relative. Family members may be able to provide valuable information regarding the TBI person's behavioural and emotional responses in a variety of situations, and the triggers and consequences of such responses. They are also likely to be able to help maintain the impact of the intervention in the future, and report on its effectiveness.

As pointed out by McKinlay and Hickox (1988), however, the therapist must be sensitive to family dynamics, which may prove to be counterproductive. For example, relatives may deny or have difficulty in accepting the presence of changes in behaviour, therefore being unable to make realistic assessments or give appropriate feedback to the TBI individual. Pre-existing tendencies towards overprotectiveness on the part of parents may result in some ambivalence and even active sabotage of interventions which are likely to result in a greater amount of time being spent by the TBI son or daughter away from the home. The use of a spouse as a co-therapist where there is marital disharmony, particularly involving issues of control or role conflict, may contribute to further disharmony. TBI adolescents may reject the involvement of a family member who is seen as taking control, and this needs to be respected.

DEALING WITH DEPRESSION

Depression is a relatively less common feature in the acute phase of recovery from severe TBI. This is thought to be largely due to confusion and lack of insight on the part of the injured individual, but it may also be related to the fact that relatively greater support from health professionals is available during this period. However, it is clear that depression does develop over time in a significant proportion of cases. It may persist over many years. Tyerman and Humphrey (1984) found that 60% of a group of 25 severe TBI subjects interviewed from 2 to 15 months after injury were clinically depressed, whilst Kinsella et al. (1988) found an incidence of depression in a severe TBI group interviewed within 2 years of injury of 33%. Both these groups were still undergoing rehabilitation, but Kinsella et al. suggested that the availability of a close confiding relationship contributed to the lower incidence of depression in their sample. Bond (1984) and Fordyce, Roueche, and Prigatano (1983) have noted an increasing incidence of depression with the development of more realistic self-awareness. Brooks et al. (1986) found that 57% of a group of relatives of severe TBI patients indicated that depression was a significant problem for the patient 5 years after injury.

These figures are not surprising, given the losses and changes in lifestyle which may follow TBI. Indeed grieving is to be expected under such circumstances, and is a normal part of the adjustment process. The provision of ongoing support through individual or group counselling may circumvent the development of more serious, symptomatic depression. However, this is not always the case. The chronic loss of motivation and self-esteem and the sense of hopelessness that accompanies severe depression will seriously interfere with attempts to rebuild a new lifestyle. Therefore it is important to be sensitive to the development of depression and see that the assistance of a psychologist or psychiatrist is offered.

Depression may manifest itself in many different ways, resulting in changes in mood, thinking patterns, behaviour and physical well-being. Any or all of the following symptoms may be apparent:

- *Changes in mood:* tearfulness, flat or blunted affect, aggressiveness or irritability.
- *Changes in thinking patterns:* sense of hopelessness, helplessness, worthlessness; negative or pessimistic attitude; frequent self-criticism; self-pity; suicidal thoughts; poor concentration and memory; worry over health; lack of motivation or interest in activities normally engaged in.
- *Behavioural changes:* reduced attention to physical appearance and hygiene; social withdrawal; relationship difficulties; suicidal behaviour; substance abuse.
- *Physical symptoms:* excessive sleeping, or sleep disturbance, with difficulty falling asleep, frequent waking, nightmares, and/or early morning waking; loss of appetite; weight loss or weight gain over a brief period; elevation of blood pressure; physical complaints.

Some of these symptoms are also seen as a direct result of the brain injury itself. In making an assessment, the clinician must be careful to discriminate between organically-based changes and those reflecting emotional disturbance, on the basis of a careful history and the results of neuropsychological assessment. The development or worsening of such symptoms at a time after injury suggests that they are associated with depression, although appropriate investigations may be necessary to rule out the development of medical complications (e.g. hydrocephalus).

As in dealing with all problems, an assessment should also be made of the injured individual's personality and emotional state prior to injury. In a very small proportion of cases it may emerge that the injury was the result of a suicide attempt. It is useful to obtain some objective picture of the manner and degree to which the depression is manifesting itself using an appropriate scale, providing the TBI person has the cognitive capability of completing such a scale. The Leeds Scale for Depression (Snaith, Bridge, & Hamilton, 1976) has been found to be useful with TBI subjects (Kinsella et al., 1988). Whilst concern has been expressed as to the reliability of TBI patients' self-report of their emotional state due to lack of self-awareness and other cognitive impairments, the findings of Kinsella et al. (1988) suggest that TBI individuals do have a reasonably accurate awareness of their emotions. Moreover, as Tyerman and Humphrey (1984, p.14) have pointed out, "It is the subjective impairment which represents distressing reality for these patients and dictates their psychological adjustment. Personality change following head injury cannot be understood nor appropriate interventions determined without taking account of the individual's own perceptions."

Psychological approaches to management should be taken in the first instance. However, it is vital that the clinician managing the problem have some experience in dealing with TBI individuals and understand their special limitations. Following a careful assessment of the TBI person's psychological state, the clinician should assess what coping strategies, whether adaptive or maladaptive, are currently being used, and what strategies were used before the injury. An attempt should be made to identify specific sources of stress which need to be addressed. For example, the injured individual may be experiencing failure at work or at school due to unrealistic demands. Alternatively, there may be relationship problems within the family or socially.

Depressed TBI individuals should be given an opportunity to express emotional responses to the losses that have been incurred. There is frequently a great deal of anger, which may be focused on the person they perceive as having been responsible for their injury or on health professionals. They must be given permission to express this anger and to grieve their losses. Family members, who may have felt very uncomfortable in discussing or sharing such emotional reactions with the injured relative, should also be encouraged to do so.

It is important, however, that the injured individual and the family be encouraged to move beyond their anger and grief and to put it in perspective. In many cases these emotions can become all-consuming, to the point of being destructive rather than constructive, and leading to a sense of being out of control. This is particularly so when the TBI person has difficulty with the control and regulation of thought processes and tends to get "stuck" on particular ideas.

Cognitive–behavioural techniques may be a useful means of helping those who have sustained TBI to regain a sense of control and perspective. A family member or close friend could be involved in the therapeutic process, provided the injured person is happy with this. Some suggested strategies include encouraging the depressed TBI individual, with the assistance of a relative, to monitor their moods, rate their intensity, and identify and document the thoughts that accompany negative emotions. The therapist may assist them to understand the link between these thoughts and their emotions and challenge these thoughts with more constructive ones. With the help of a relative, cue cards might be used to prompt more adaptive thinking. The injured person may be encouraged to see that brooding over the injustices of the situation or losses will not provide any answers or help them to feel better. Therapeutic assistance may be given to help the depressed individual to see the differences between the "old" person and the "new" person who has survived the injury in a more positive light, and to begin to measure themselves by what they have achieved since the injury, rather than what they achieved prior to the injury.

It is also useful to monitor activity levels, and explore ways of increasing the number of meaningful and enjoyable activities in which the person engages. Targets may be set for gradually increasing such involvement. In this respect the therapist may need to work with other members of the rehabilitation team in exploring realistic alternatives. Further detail regarding the use of cognitive–behavioural approaches to the management of depression may be obtained from a number of sources, including Beck, Rush, Shaw, and Emery (1979).

If the depressed person is suicidal, cannot be engaged in or fails to respond to psychological therapy, pharmacological management will need to be considered. Indeed, in severe cases medication may be needed to bring the injured individual to the point of being able to benefit from other forms of therapy. However, pharmacological interventions should always be managed by a physician who understands the likely impact of such medications on the TBI person's cognitive processes. For further discussion of drug treatment following TBI, see Chapter 6.

Suicide threats should always be taken seriously. Family members and members of the rehabilitation team are to be encouraged to contact a mental health professional for assistance. This person can make an assessment as to the potential risk and organise appropriate treatment. Those dealing with a person who has expressed suicidal intention must make it clear that the threat is being taken seriously, and that there is an understanding of the intensity of the injured individual's feelings. An attempt should be made to negotiate a contract whereby there is agreement to talk with someone before attempting any self-harm. If the risk is considered to be immediate and high, hospitalisation and the use of medication will almost invariably be required.

MANAGEMENT OF ANXIETY

As with depression, anxiety tends not to manifest itself in victims of severe TBI during the acute stages of recovery. However, whilst the incidence of anxiety reported in follow-up studies varies widely according to the severity of injuries under study, and the method whereby it is measured, it is clear that a significant proportion of those who sustain severe TBI experience anxiety at clinically significant levels. According to findings reported by Lezak (1987), anxiety is most common in the second 6 months after injury. Tyerman and Humphrey (1984) found that 44% of a group of 25 young people who had sustained severe TBI between 2 and 15 months earlier were rated on the basis of self-report as clinically anxious. Kinsella et al. (1988) found that 26% of a sample interviewed within two years of injury were clinically anxious, as assessed on the Leeds Scale for Anxiety (Snaith et al., 1976). Age was a significant predictor of anxiety in this sample, those who were older being more prone to anxiety.

Anxiety may manifest itself only after the TBI individual has begun to be involved with activities in the community. It may occur when the individual experiences difficulty in coping with a situation as a result of cognitive deficits, for example, in social settings, where the injured person may feel self-conscious or have difficulty keeping up with conversations, in the workplace, or when engaging in study activities. In this respect the anxiety response is a normal one, because the coping difficulties are usually real. However, it may be significantly out of proportion to the situation. If not brought under control it can become self-perpetuating, exacerbating the organically-based problems, and leading to avoidance of the stressful situation, and further loss of confidence.

As with depression, anxiety can manifest itself in a number of ways, affecting thinking patterns, feelings, bodily sensations and behaviour as follows:

- *Changes in thinking patterns:* anticipation of things going wrong, catastrophising, black and white thinking, e.g. "I am a total failure", making predictions not based on fact.
- *Feelings:* out of control, fearful, embarrassed, nervous, tentative, uncertain about making decisions, confused, self-doubting.
- *Bodily sensations:* physiological arousal, with increased heart rate, muscle tension, headache, nausea, shaking.
- *Behavioural changes:* withdrawal, inhibition, flustered behaviour, escape from or avoidance of situations.

In order to obtain a clear picture of the problem it may be useful to have the injured individual keep a diary, monitoring and recording the situations in which the anxiety occurs, any associated thoughts, feelings, bodily sensations and behaviour, and rating its severity. This places a realistic perspective on the problem, which in itself may help to alleviate some anxiety. A number of self-administered inventories are also available to assist in the assessment process. These include the Leeds Scale for Anxiety (Snaith et al., 1976) and the Spielberger

Self-Evaluation Questionnaire (Spielberger, Gorsuch, Lushene, Vagg, & Jacobs, 1983). Other methods of assessing anxiety are reviewed in Montgomery and Evans (1984).

The aim of anxiety management is to give the client control over the anxiety, rather than to abolish it completely. As in the case of the depressed client, it may be possible to make certain external modifications, for example, to a work or study regime, to reduce the demands on the injured individual. Assistance in timetabling daily activities could also serve to alleviate anxiety. The extent to which other forms of intervention are successful is likely to depend on the injured person's level of cognitive functioning, particularly the ability to learn, self-monitor and to carry through with intentions. As with other forms of psychological therapy there has been little research evaluating the impact of interventions for anxiety in TBI individuals.

Where social interactions are a source of anxiety, it may be helpful to provide training in specific skills, such as conversational or social skills, or assertiveness. It is important to convey to the anxious person a clear understanding of the ways in which anxiety occurs, how it can be perpetuated by thoughts and feelings, and the relationship of these with the autonomic nervous system.

Symptoms of anxiety may be alleviated in a number of ways. The first of these is muscle relaxation. This can relieve anxiety, either by providing a distraction from anxious thoughts or by decreasing bodily symptoms, such as muscle tension. As Lysaght and Bodenhamer (1990) have pointed out, the relaxation technique needs to be adapted to suit the individual, particularly in the light of specific cognitive or behavioural limitations. For those who fatigue easily and tend to fall asleep during relaxation sessions it may be necessary to make changes to positioning, lighting and timing of sessions. Relaxation instructions should be taped for practice at home. It is useful to develop both a longer and a shorter version, the latter being suitable for use in anxiety-provoking situations. Relaxation can usually be facilitated by deep breathing. Biofeedback may also be useful. Lysaght and Bodenhamer (1990) showed that biofeedback-assisted relaxation was successful in reducing anxiety in four severely head-injured subjects more than two years post-injury.

It may be possible to teach the injured person to pick up the early signs of anxiety, so that relaxation techniques can be applied before the anxiety takes over. This requires some self-monitoring capability, however. Practice should be provided in the application of relaxation in stressful situations. This can be done using mental imagery, role-play or real-life situations. Some TBI individuals have difficulty in benefiting from relaxation techniques, and particularly in using imagery, because they are unable to focus and maintain attention to a sufficient degree. As Lysaght and Bodenhamer suggest, careful guiding of relaxation procedures is important in such cases, with frequent cueing. For those completely unable to benefit from this approach, a useful alternative may be physical exercise. This can be particularly helpful for those who harbour a great deal of anger.

Distraction and cognitive restructuring may be used to attain control over the thoughts which accompany and perpetuate anxiety. It may be possible to teach the injured individual strategies for refocusing thoughts, either onto the immediate surroundings, listing things or reciting a poem, or redirection in terms of a physical activity. Records kept by the injured person may be used as a basis for challenging and disputing irrational thoughts, which are fuelling anxiety. Assistance may be given to interpret situations in alternative ways, and thereby develop more positive self-talk. Again, cue cards may be useful in implementing self-talk strategies.

Problems with avoidance can be dealt with by constructing an hierarchy of situations, from the least to the most distressing. These should be tackled in small and achievable steps. Work on avoidance needs to begin early in the intervention process. As in the case of other cognitive–behavioural strategies, the assistance of a relative or friend may be sought to help in the implementation of these strategies.

ANGER MANAGEMENT

Problems in controlling anger are commonly experienced by those who have sustained severe TBI. Such difficulties persist over many years after injury. They contribute to problems in establishing and/or sustaining employment, personal relationships, and social or leisure pursuits (Brooks et al., 1986, 1987a; Jacobs, 1988; Lezak, 1987; Thomsen, 1984). They also represent a significant source of stress to family members (Brooks et al. 1986, 1987a; Livingston & Brooks, 1988; Oddy et al., 1978b; Thomsen, 1984). Approaches to controlling anger, and dealing with other behaviour problems manifested in the earlier stages of recovery, or within the rehabilitation setting, have been outlined in detail in Chapter 6. As discussed in that chapter, these methods can be adapted for use in community settings. In those TBI individuals who remain very severely impaired from a cognitive point of view, with little or no self-awareness, memory or capacity for self-control, purely behavioural approaches, as detailed in Chapter 6, appear to be most suitable. Carers, family members, or whoever is most frequently present when the behaviour is exhibited, will need to be involved as co-therapists, however.

Those who have returned to the community, have some awareness of their problem and motivation for change may be able to participate more actively in the therapy process, monitoring their own behavioural responses and applying various coping skills, with the assistance of a family member. In such cases, a cognitive-behavioural approach to anger management, along the lines of that outlined by Novaco (1975) may be a useful alternative. A number of single case studies have suggested that such methods can be used successfully to reduce anger problems in people who have sustained TBI (Lira, Carne, & Masri, 1983; McKinlay & Hickox, 1988; Uomoto & Brockway, 1992). The following guidelines are based upon these reports, together with the author's experience.

Some suggested guidelines for improvement of anger control

Initially it is important to make an assessment of the nature of the anger problem, clarifying in precise terms how the anger is being manifested behaviourally (e.g. shouting, swearing, throwing objects, hitting others). It is helpful to discuss any methods which are currently being used by the injured individual and family members or others to resolve the anger. The responses of others may be contributing to the problem, and this should be pointed out tactfully. As Uomoto and Brockway (1992) point out, it is also useful at this stage to reach agreement as to what is an acceptable level of aggression in the household or elsewhere. This may represent the goal for treatment.

It is helpful to have the injured person and family member keep a record of angry outbursts, what led to them and what happened afterwards over a period of a week initially, but throughout the intervention period. This can be used as a baseline record, to identify the circumstances which provoke anger, and ways in which the responses of others can either fuel the anger or have a calming influence.

This record provides a basis for educating both the person who has sustained the injury and the family member as to how to avoid provoking anger. For example, it may be that angry outbursts tend to occur when there is a lot of noise and bustle, such as when the television is on and small children are around, or when particular issues are being discussed, when the TBI individual is having trouble keeping up with a conversation or is being criticised for making mistakes. Steps can be taken to modify the environment or other people's interactions with the injured individual to avoid causing frustration.

Following anger management guidelines suggested by Novaco (1975), in those individuals with sufficient self-monitoring capabilities, it may be possible to encourage awareness of thoughts, feelings and bodily sensations which signal an impending outburst of anger. These can be used as cues for the implementation of strategies to circumvent the outburst. Such strategies may include deep breathing or removing themselves from the situation, either to a designated space in the house or going for a walk. When the injured individual is not able to do this alone, the assistance of the family member may be sought, firstly to identify behaviours which signal impending anger. The family member can remove the trigger, for example by changing the subject or turning off the television, or prompting the TBI person to use whatever strategy has been agreed upon. This may be done using a verbal cue which has been agreed upon and rehearsed in therapy sessions. If necessary, family members may need to physically leave the situation themselves. Coping skills should be practised in progressively more anger-provoking situations using role-play techniques.

McKinlay and Hickox (1988) have summarised the steps involved in this anger management process with the acronym ANGER:

A: Anticipate the trigger situations.
N: Notice the signs of rising anger.
G: Go through your "temper routine" (which includes relaxation exercises, breathing exercises, and finding an alternative way of handling the situation).
E: Extract yourself from the situation, if all else fails.
R: Record how you coped: What lessons can you learn for next time?

Whilst the family member and the injured individual should attend most sessions together, it is useful to see each individually at times to discuss specific concerns or issues. Where the anger has been contributing significantly to social isolation, it is important, as the anger is brought under control, to increase involvement in enjoyable activities. Follow-up sessions after the strategies have been implemented successfully are also very important to ensure that their use is maintained. In this respect it is necessary to ask the parties involved to keep a record of angry outbursts for a week prior to attending a follow-up session.

MARITAL AND RELATIONSHIP PROBLEMS

The negative impact of TBI on marital relationships has been extensively documented (Lezak, 1978; Panting & Merry, 1972; Rosenbaum & Najenson, 1976; Thomsen, 1984; Tyerman, Young, & Booth, 1994). Whilst there are relatively few divorces in the early years after injury, there are many more in the longer term, especially in cases of extremely severe TBI (Tate et al., 1989; Thomsen, 1984). There is also substantial evidence of a decline in the quality of marital relationships. Spouses of TBI individuals, most commonly wives, show a high incidence of depressed mood, which is highly correlated with reduced sharing of responsibilities, such as parenting and financial management, a perception of child-like dependency of the injured spouse and other personality changes, such as irritability and childishness (Rosenbaum & Najenson, 1976). For the TBI partner there are also significant role changes with which to come to terms. Depending on roles prior to injury, reduced independence, with the loss of the capability of earning an income to support the family, managing the family finances, managing the household and engaging in parental activities can be a major source of stress and loss of self-esteem within the relationship (Willer, Allen, Liss, & Zicht, 1991). Almost inevitably, couples have to come to terms with some change following TBI, whether it be temporary or permanent.

Couples need support in dealing with these changes, not only individually, but also together. In the majority of cases, and for a variety of reasons, couples may not have been communicating honestly and clearly with each other. The injured person's spouse is likely to be afraid of hurting the TBI partner or provoking an angry outburst by discussing changes in personality and behaviour. The TBI individual may be feeling very insecure and uncertain in the relationship, having "lost control" in areas previously considered important. As Willer et al. (1991) have demonstrated, the issues of dependency and role change are likely to be a particularly significant source of stress and conflict for many couples. It is important, therefore, to facilitate communication between couples, helping them develop skills in levelling, listening and validating, as outlined by Montgomery and Evans (1983). Active guidance will be needed to assist in reaching solutions to problems. In particular, couples may benefit from assistance in mutually defining new roles and responsibilities within the relationship, not necessarily excluding the TBI partner from involvement in family decisions.

As with other psychological therapy, changes in cognition and behaviour, which are contributing to the relationship problems, are also likely to impose significant limitations on the TBI partner's ability to participate in such therapy. The therapist needs to have a good understanding of these limitations, so that unrealistic demands are not placed on the couple.

With the active co-operation of the non-injured spouse, however, and a great deal of repetition and structure, supplemented with simple and clear written notes, slow progress may not necessarily be impeded. The therapist may need to have additional sessions with the uninjured partner in order to achieve this. A co-therapist may be recruited to work with the TBI person individually. Where irritability is a significant problem, anger management techniques or other behavioural strategies, as outlined earlier, will need to be introduced.

One of the most important components of marital therapy in these circumstances is to facilitate the couple in giving each other positive feedback, rather than focusing always on negative changes. For a variety of reasons it is likely that they are not able to pursue social or recreational activities together, which may have been an important basis of shared pleasure in the relationship. The therapist can assist the couple in seeing the importance of sharing enjoyable time together and finding new ways of doing this. Where the injured partner is very dependent upon the spouse, it is also important, however, to schedule time for them to spend engaging in social or recreational activities separately. Not uncommonly, TBI individuals become jealous when their spouse wants to pursue outside activities. This results in increasing social isolation and bitterness on the part of the caregiving partner, with consequent stress on the relationship. The need for the caregiver to have free time must be discussed openly in therapy. The uninjured partner may need some individual training in assertiveness skills in order to deal with such issues.

Introduction of the couple to a support group involving other couples in which one partner has sustained TBI may also be mutually beneficial, as will referral for practical assistance in dealing with financial or legal problems, another significant source of stress.

Inevitably there will be some relationships which fail after TBI, either because of the extent of cognitive and behavioural change in the TBI partner, or because of an inability of either party to adapt to role changes within the relationship. Both the TBI individual and the uninjured partner will require a great deal of support in making such a decision, and dealing with the practical and emotional issues involved in separation. Inevitably, the spouse who has not sustained an injury will experience much guilt, and may be offered little support by the family of the TBI partner. For the injured individual, there may be a great deal of anger and bitterness, due to an inability to see the point of view of the partner. There are also likely to be many practical issues to be resolved, such as who will provide care or supervision for the TBI individual, and how access to children can be arranged. Financial settlement may be complicated by legal claims for compensation. These issues are explored further in the next chapter.

For those not in a long-term relationship at the time of injury, there are likely to be many difficulties in establishing relationships, as a consequence of changes in sexual behaviour and self-confidence, in addition to other personality changes affecting interpersonal relationships. These need to be addressed, both in the context of individual therapy and group therapy, focusing on the development of insight, self-esteem and interpersonal skills in the manner outlined in other sections of this chapter, and Chapter 5.

SEXUALITY FOLLOWING TBI

In spite of the importance of sexuality for all people, but particularly adolescents and young adults, sexual issues are rarely addressed adequately following TBI. TBI potentially disrupts many important aspects of sexuality, including social and relationship skills, self-esteem, and behavioural control, as well as libido and the physical capacity to perform sexually. In some instances these skills may not have been adequately developed or expressed prior to injury, thus adding to the complexity of the rehabilitation process.

Research on changes in sexuality associated with TBI

Studies of sexuality following TBI have focused on changes in sex drive and sexual behaviour. These appear to be relatively common. Lezak (1978) has reported that TBI may result in either a loss of sex drive or increased sexual desire. Oddy et al. (1978a) found that half of a group of 12 married TBI individuals reported increased sexual activity and half reported a decrease.

However, according to the results of a more recent and extensive study by Kreutzer and Zasler (1989), involving 21 married and unmarried TBI individuals, a majority (57%) reported a decrease in sex drive, whilst only 14% reported an increase and 28% indicated that there had been no change. Significant changes in sexual behaviour were also reported. In most instances these were of a negative nature. Fifty-seven percent of respondents indicated a diminished ability to maintain an erection. A third of the sample reported greater difficulty in achieving an orgasm. Sixty-two percent of subjects reported diminished frequency of sexual intercourse, whilst only one person indicated an increase in the frequency of intercourse.

Kreutzer and Zasler (1989) also examined affect, self-esteem and relationship characteristics in the same group of TBI subjects. Two-thirds (67%) of the sample reported a decline in self-confidence, 52% a decline in sex appeal, and 71% increased depression. Not one of the five TBI subjects who were single had a steady heterosexual relationship. A third of the married respondents indicated a decline in the marital relationship since the injury. Half of the sample said communication remained the same, whilst a third rated communication as worse. There was no statistically significant correlation between level of affective disturbance and scores on the sexual behaviour items in Kreutzer and Zasler's (1989) study, in which TBI individuals were reporting. On the other hand, Rosenbaum and Najenson (1976) did find a significant association between mood disturbance and sexual activity, as reported by the wives of brain-injured subjects.

Addressing sexual issues in the rehabilitation setting

In spite of the reported frequency of change in sexual behaviour following TBI, in many instances sexual issues are not even discussed in the course of rehabilitation. As Davis and Schneider (1990) have documented, rehabilitation staff tend to feel uncomfortable and ill-prepared in discussing sexual concerns with patients. This problem is exacerbated by the fact that the majority of staff are females and the majority of those injured are males. There is little privacy and opportunity for sexual expression within the hospital environment. The majority of TBI individuals do not have an ongoing sexual relationship and have little prospect of forming one in the foreseeable future. Expressions of sexual frustration are frequently interpreted by rehabilitation staff in a judgemental fashion.

As with other aspects of the rehabilitation programme, it is extremely important that the rehabilitation team reach some understanding and agreement as to their approach to issues of sexuality. This process will necessitate education in aspects of sexuality and how it may be affected by TBI, training in basic counselling, social and behavioural skills, and clarification of values, along the lines suggested by Blackerby (1990) and Medlar and Medlar (1990). There must be a commitment to the philosophy developed by the team, so that personal attitudes are not imposed upon TBI individuals and their families. Whilst it is important that certain individuals within the team develop specific expertise in dealing with sexual problems, it must be recognised that sexual issues may be raised with any team member. TBI individuals and their families may not see the need or wish to confront sexual problems during the rehabilitation phase. However, it is extremely important that a team member draws their attention to the possibility of changes in sexual behaviour early on, indicating a preparedness to discuss these issues if and when they arise in the future. Many will not raise concerns until permission is given to talk about such matters.

Assessment and therapy for sexual problems

Horn and Zasler (1990) and Zasler and Horn (1990) have presented a detailed account of the causes, nature and management of sexual problems associated with TBI. Organic causes include endocrine dysfunction, sensorimotor problems, cognitive and behavioural impairment, bowel and bladder dysfunction, changes in libido, and genital dysfunction. Emotional and relationship problems and stress may also affect sexual behaviour. It is important to make a comprehensive assessment covering all of these areas as a means of determining appropriate intervention.

Where sensorimotor problems or genital dysfunction are interfering with the capacity to perform sexual acts, advice may be needed regarding alternative positioning, the use of assistive devices, artificial lubricants and/or alternative means of obtaining sexual satisfaction. Hormonal imbalance may be treated successfully with hormone replacement therapy. The possible negative influence of medications must also be considered (Zasler & Horn, 1990). Where sexual problems are related to behavioural disinhibition as a result of frontotemporal injury, behavioural methods may be applied along the lines outlined in Chapter 6. Zasler and Horn (1990) have suggested the possible use of certain medications in inhibiting sexually inappropriate behaviour, although there have been no controlled studies to assess this. Zasler and Horn point out the importance of distinguishing hypersexuality, thought to be associated with limbic dysfunction, from disinhibition. Rehabilitation staff and families also need to recognise the difference between expressions of sexual frustration and sexual disinhibition or hypersexuality.

From the results reported by Kreutzer and Zasler (1989), it would appear that sex drive tends to decline more frequently than it increases following TBI. There are a number of potential causes of such a decrease, all of which need to be explored and addressed in an appropriate fashion. These include injury to specific limbic and cortical structures, side-effects of medication, including major tranquillisers, anxiety, depression and stress. The reduction in self-confidence and self-esteem and poor body image known to occur in many TBI individuals undoubtedly contribute to changes in libido after TBI.

There is some evidence to suggest that the partners of brain-injured individuals also experience a reduction in sex drive for a variety of reasons (Rosenbaum & Najenson, 1976). These include stress due to increased responsibilities, loss of attraction to the disabled partner, a perception of personality change in the TBI partner, with a consequent decline in the quality of the relationship, and depression. Where such non-organic factors are thought to be contributing to the problem, intervention will need to focus in these areas.

As a result of their physical, cognitive and/or behavioural disabilities, the unfortunate reality for many of those who have sustained TBI is that there may be few opportunities to experience a sexual relationship.

This leads to considerable frustration, particularly where masturbation is considered unacceptable or cannot be achieved due to physical disability. There may be a need to give permission to explore alternatives or to teach specific sexual skills. Referral to a sex therapist may assist in this process, as staff may not feel comfortable in this role. Depending on local laws and moral and ethical views, the use of a surrogate sexual partner or referral to a massage parlour to assist in the development of appropriate sexual skills may be considered in certain instances. Whilst the rights and privacy of the TBI individual must always be respected, it may in some instances also be necessary to involve the family in such decisions.

Birth control

Assessment and advice regarding appropriate methods of birth control and protection from sexually transmitted diseases are a very important component of sexual rehabilitation for all TBI individuals who are potentially sexually active. This is particularly so where there is an increase in sex drive, or where the TBI individual is prone to impulsive behaviour and lacks the capacity for self-regulation. Whilst the rights of the TBI individual must be respected, physical and cognitive limitations must be taken into account when determining a suitable form of contraception. Where unplanned pregnancy occurs there will be a need for counselling to assist the TBI person in deciding whether to terminate or proceed with the pregnancy, and referral made to appropriate support services.

CASE REPORT—JULIE

Julie was a 45-year-old senior primary school teacher, who was married with no children. She had sustained a severe TBI and multiple fractures involving her shoulder, elbow and pelvis in a car accident six months earlier. Although unconscious for only a few minutes, Julie had a period of PTA lasting three weeks. She had undergone a period of inpatient and outpatient rehabilitation. Neuropsychological assessment had indicated that she was of superior intelligence, with intact verbal and visuospatial skills. However, she had residual attentional difficulties, moderately reduced speed of information processing, and showed poor planning and self-monitoring on complex or novel tasks. Nevertheless, whilst attending her outpatient therapy programme Julie felt she was coping reasonably well. Shortly after discharge from this she became highly stressed and depressed and sought counselling.

Whilst able to manage her domestic routine she had found she became easily fatigued and relied on her husband for a lot more assistance, whereas she had previously been energetic, independent, and the dominant partner in the relationship. She felt much more emotional and found it difficult to cope with being reliant on her husband. She had also become very irritable, whereas she had been a patient person prior to the injury. She described being able to physically feel the anger rising in her stomach and felt unable to control it. Her previously active social life had had to be significantly curtailed because she got too tired. She had also given up many of the activities which she and her husband previously enjoyed, such as bushwalking. Her activities were limited by pain and restriction of movement in fracture sites and visual problems, as well as fatigue.

Julie had returned to work at her school for two half days per week. As she was unable to take a class she did some work in the library. She experienced significant coping difficulties, reporting memory problems, reduced speed of thinking, difficulty dealing with unfamiliar situations or working under pressure, and a tendency to fatigue. Having been a high-achieving, career-oriented person prior to her injury, who had taken on administrative responsibilities and been highly respected for her expertise, Julie found the experience of not coping highly stressful. She became very anxious. She was prone to outbursts of anger and tearfulness and had occasional panic attacks. She worried what her fellow teachers and the parents thought of her, sensing that they did not understand the nature of her difficulties.

Julie thus presented with symptoms of both anxiety and depression and very low self-esteem. When at school, and when faced with anything out of her normal routine at home, she became extremely tense and had difficulty concentrating on the task in front of her. She was frequently tearful. She repeatedly made negative comments about herself and her situation, and had a very pessimistic view of the future. She was sure that others viewed her as strange. She had lost confidence in her ability to cope with situations. The concentration and memory difficulties she reported were out of proportion to those apparent on neuropsychological assessment. She was tending to withdraw from social contact. Her relationship with her husband had deteriorated. She had also lost interest in sex. In spite of her fatigue she was having difficulty sleeping through the night and her appetite had decreased. Julie expressed considerable anger and guilt over the accident and felt it would have been better for herself and her husband if she had died.

In the initial sessions Julie was given an opportunity to vent her anger over the accident and its effects. Initially Julie was worried that she may have been responsible, and expressed guilt about the burden she had placed on her husband. However shortly afterwards she received a letter from a witness indicating that the accident had been due to irresponsibility on the part of another driver. She developed extreme anger towards this person. She spoke at length of her insecurities in her relationships with her husband and with the staff at the school, repeatedly making negative comments about herself.

Julie was introduced to the concept of self-talk and her attention was drawn to the influence her negative self-talk was having on her emotional state. As a homework exercise she monitored her emotional outbursts, recording the precipitating circumstances, what she was saying to herself at the time, and the nature and degree of her emotional response. These records were reviewed in therapy, with a view to challenging negative self-talk and replacing it with more constructive thoughts. A number of coping statements were developed for Julie to use in stressful situations. These were rehearsed through role-play. The therapist also pointed out how little her anger over the accident was achieving, other than making her feel bad. They developed some coping statements to replace these angry thoughts.

Julie was taught relaxation techniques, which she practised with the aid of a tape whilst resting each afternoon, and again when she was awake at night. She practised inducing a relaxed state by taking deep breaths. She used this, in addition to her coping statements, to assist her to calm down when she became anxious at school, or when she felt angry.

From the records she had kept it became apparent that Julie became most anxious, upset, or angry when she was tired. At times she was clearly attempting more than she could reasonably manage. She began to monitor her activity levels very carefully. Her time at school was kept to two half days until her stamina and familiarity with the work she was doing had increased. She slept each afternoon and spent some time exercising. She was encouraged to pursue social activities with friends, as these were important to her, but to do this only on weekends, when she could have extra rest.

Some therapy time was spent reviewing Julie's strengths and weaknesses. She made lists of these and was surprised at the number of strengths she could find in herself. She identified her motivation, determination, initiative, conscientiousness, intelligence, and self-awareness as strengths. Discussion focused on how she could use these strengths to rebuild a meaningful life for herself. Over time it was becoming clear that she was unlikely to be able to return to full-time work. However an opportunity presented itself at the school to develop a programme for gifted children. She was able to use her considerable experience to do this very successfully and on a part-time basis. She received positive feedback from the school administration and the parents for her initiatives, and subsequently admitted that she had found this work in some ways more challenging than her classroom teaching.

Some joint sessions were held with Julie's husband in order to address the relationship difficulties. They had not been communicating very clearly since she the injury. He had never been one to talk about things, and she had felt too insecure about the relationship to do so. The couple had been unable to have children due to her infertility. Although her husband had indicated that he was quite happy not to have children, Julie felt she had let him down. Now she felt of no use to him in other respects, being reliant on him for assistance, and unable to participate in activities they had found enjoyable. Therefore she thought it would have been better if she had died in the accident, so that he could start a new life and have a family. Julie was encouraged to express her feelings to her husband in therapy. She was surprised to hear him reiterate his genuine relief at not having children. He told her how reliant he had always been on her to take the lead in the relationship, indeed he felt he had been lazy. He felt it had been worthwhile for him to have to take greater responsibility, which was no more than many husbands take under normal circumstances. He was also able to tell Julie how much he valued her in spite of the changes since her injury.

He was, however, having difficulty coping with Julie's anger and mood swings, often taking her anger personally. Julie agreed that he should assist her in minimising or dealing with such outbursts. After keeping a record of precipitating circumstances and how the situation was dealt with, it became apparent that the outbursts occurred most commonly when Julie was tired or when she was she was feeling overwhelmed by something she had to do. Julie's husband undertook to assist her in regulating her activity levels to minimise her fatigue. When she was beginning to feel angry or upset she would take three deep breaths to try and relax and, if necessary, go for a walk. He was encouraged to avoid trying to reason or argue with her at these times. He would assist her to break down tasks into achievable steps when she was feeling overwhelmed. It was agreed that he must do this in an atmosphere of encouragement rather than criticism, to which he had been prone in the past. He indicated that he had not fully understood Julie's limitations until the therapy sessions. He was encouraged to give Julie positive feedback for her achievements as frequently as possible.

Some time was also spent discussing ways in which Julie and her husband could increase the amount of time spent in pleasurable activities together, activities which did not create stress for Julie. Rather than attempting bushwalking, they took shorter walks around the local neighbourhood on weekends. Julie was encouraged to organise one social activity each weekend, also allowing adequate time for rest. As her confidence increased she held a small dinner party to thank a few close friends. However, this was planned very carefully so as to minimise her stress. She asked one of her friends to bring dessert, and recruited her husband's help to set the table and wash up—tasks in which he would not previously have been involved. The success of the dinner boosted her self-confidence. The couple reported after these sessions that their sex life had improved, largely as a consequence of the general improvement in the relationship, and of Julie being more relaxed.

This intervention initially spanned nine months, but therapeutic contact continued over a period of three years. As Julie faced new challenges and crises she was prone to become depressed and angry at times. However, she generally responded well to the therapy. Three years after her injury Julie wrote the following message on a Christmas card:

"Thank you very much for helping me back on the planet. I feel I have a future now—perhaps not as financially rewarding and very different, but one that provides new challenges and rewards. I may even end up like that butchered flowering gum I was waxing lyrical about, and give and consequently get more from life. Thank you also for including my husband in assisting my emotional recovery. I believe it has strengthened our partnership."

CASE REPORT - MICHAEL

Michael was an 18-year-old apprentice fitter and turner when he was injured in a motor car accident. He was in coma for about one week and had a period of PTA lasting 25 days. His inpatient hospitalisation and rehabilitation lasted seven weeks and he continued outpatient therapy for a further six months. He made a good recovery physically but showed persisting cognitive difficulties. These included reduced speed of information processing, attentional problems, poor verbal learning and memory skills, difficulty initiating and generating conversation, inflexible thinking and planning difficulties. He quickly became independent in personal, domestic and community activities of daily living. Work experience, followed by a work trial, extended over a five-month period, by which stage he was coping with full-time work at his previous level. He had also returned to driving. However he lacked confidence socially, because of his difficulty in generating conversation. Towards the end of the period of his outpatient therapy he attended a conversational skills group, with the aim of facilitating his ability to generate conversation when in new situations, and to improve his self-confidence in social settings.

When reviewed four months after discharge from outpatient therapy, and a year post-injury, Michael reported experiencing a number of adjustment problems and was referred for psychological counselling. Although coping with full-time work, he was not enjoying his apprenticeship. He had continued to lack confidence socially, having greater difficulty getting along with workmates, and having problems initiating conversations in social situations, such as at parties. He found it difficult not drinking, as his social life had previously revolved around the local pub, and he did not feel comfortable sitting in the pub and not drinking alcohol. He noted that his friends had drifted away, and he was more socially isolated. At the time of his injury he had been in a relationship of two years' standing and his girlfriend had ended the relationship shortly after his discharge from hospital. This had increased his social isolation. As a consequence of all these problems he had become depressed.

Michael's difficulties were tackled on a number of levels. The most pressing problem appeared to be his conversational difficulties and consequent social anxiety. He was referred back to his speech pathologist, who worked with him intensively to practice generating conversation on a range of topics. Role-play and videotaped feedback was used to facilitate this. *In-vivo* practice occurred on weekends and was reviewed the following week. Michael's psychologist trained him in relaxation techniques, which he practised daily. She had him monitor his thinking in social situations. It became apparent that he was very self-conscious socially. He tended to avoid approaching people, especially women, and, when engaged in conversation he tended to panic, saying to himself "I can't think of what to say. They must think I'm so hopeless and boring". These thoughts were interfering with his ability to get on with the conversation. Michael and his psychologist worked together to generate some competing and more positive thoughts, such as, "I'm going to stay calm and take this one step at a time". They rehearsed these along with his conversational strategies.

Michael was invited to attend a support group for young people who had sustained TBI. This provided an opportunity to discuss the difficulties they had experienced since discharge from rehabilitation. Michael was very reassured by the fact that many of the others in the group had been experiencing similar problems, and this boosted his confidence. It also made it easier for him to accept the changes in himself, of which he had become so painfully aware. Some group sessions were spent focusing on each individual's strengths. Michael began to appreciate that he still had many residual abilities and was very fortunate, relative to others in the group, to be able to continue pursuing his vocational goal to become a fitter and turner. Group members shared their individual strategies for dealing with problems of a cognitive or interpersonal nature. He contributed enthusiastically to the discussion and received positive feedback, which further enhanced his self-esteem. It also provided an opportunity to rehearse the conversational skills he had learned in individual therapy.

Michael was encouraged to become involved in some local sporting activities, which he had previously enjoyed, but which he had given up after the injury, due to problems with fatigue. He began playing squash competitively. Although initially reluctant, he joined a local youth group. This provided a forum in which to meet people and practice his conversational skills. Michael required considerable support with this initially. Michael also pursued an interest in gliding. Although we were less happy about this because of the risks it entailed, it did increase his social outlets and provide a regular activity.

Michael was very inexperienced sexually. This added to his anxiety with regard to forming new relationships with women. Several sessions were spent assisting Michael to work through and clarify his feelings regarding sexual relationships.

Michael also reported increasing conflict with his mother and particularly his stepfather since the injury. He felt his mother had become too protective since the injury. This was possibly true, since Michael's father had been killed in a motor car accident seven years earlier. Having idolised his father, Michael had had difficulty in accepting his stepfather. Michael perceived his stepfather as having been excessively critical since the injury. They had many arguments and came to blows on several occasions. A number of sessions were spent working through Michael's grief and anger over the loss of his father, and discussing how he could avoid conflict with his stepfather. Eventually Michael decided to move out of home. He could not afford to set himself up in a flat so he boarded with a woman who lived in the same street. The family was referred for family therapy to explore all of these issues and Michael's relationship with both his mother and stepfather improved somewhat.

Michael has required counselling on an intermittent basis over a period of four years. He completed his apprenticeship and started a new job, but had some problems adapting to this. His social network remains very limited and he still lacks a close friend in whom to confide. He has shown a tendency to lack judgement in his choice of friends, to become overly intense about relationships and very upset when the friendship drifts apart. He has had a couple of relationships with girls much younger than he, each lasting a couple of months, but these have not been very successful. He continues to experience anxiety in unfamiliar situations and when placed under pressure. Michael recently presented with paranoid ideation and is currently receiving psychiatric assistance. Thus, in spite of an excellent recovery in terms of performance of activities of daily living, Michael's psychological adjustment is far from good. He is likely to require intermittent psychological support for many years to come.

CONCLUSIONS

The importance of addressing the myriad of psychological and adjustment problems faced by TBI individuals cannot be overemphasised. At an appropriate time after injury, all those who have sustained TBI should have access to counselling and/or group therapy to enhance the development of self-awareness, whilst maximising self-esteem and providing an opportunity to rebuild a new sense of self. Individual assessment and therapy should also be available on an ongoing basis to deal with the development of depression, anxiety, anger and other interpersonal problems, relationship difficulties and changes in sexuality. Approaches to therapy need to be adapted to the specific strengths and weaknesses of the injured person, cognitive–behavioural interventions being particularly useful. Involvement of a close other in such interventions may be helpful in some cases.

CHAPTER NINE

Working with families of traumatically brain-injured individuals

Jennie Ponsford

INTRODUCTION

TBI creates a significant burden for the families of those who are injured, as it is they who most frequently must provide long-term support, socialisation and assistance to the TBI individual. Indeed the impact of TBI for relatives can be as devastating as for the person who is injured. This has been comprehensively documented in numerous outcome studies conducted over the past two decades, including those of Brooks et al. (1986, 1987a), Douglas (1994), Jacobs (1988), Lamont (1993), McKinlay et al. (1981), Oddy et al. (1978a,b), Panting and Merry (1972), Parry (1985), Rosenbaum and Najenson (1976), Thomsen (1984) and Willer et al. (1991). It is therefore essential to extend rehabilitation efforts to the family, as well as to the TBI person. This chapter aims to outline common family reactions to the occurrence of TBI, their evolution over time, sources of stress at different stages in the recovery process, and long term changes in family behaviour. This will be followed by discussion of ways in which the burden of families may be minimised.

COMMON FAMILY RESPONSES TO TBI

The occurrence of TBI creates an immediate crisis for relatives, disrupting established relationships, roles, expectations, and goals within the family unit. Emotional reactions are likely to be heightened by the fact that the injury occurred suddenly and may have been potentially avoidable. Whilst family responses to TBI have not been subjected to rigorous research, there have been a number of models put forward to describe or conceptualise their reactions over time. These are helpful in providing a perspective from which rehabilitation staff may come to understand the experience of families.

Douglas (1990) has characterised family responses to TBI in five stages, outlined in Fig. 9.1. It is important to recognise that there are likely to be differences in the sequence and rate at which families pass

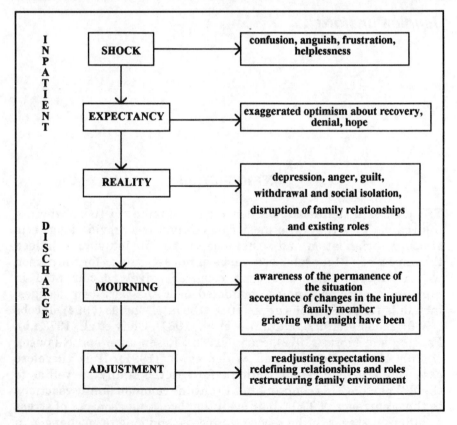

FIG. 9.1. Family responses to traumatic brain injury (Douglas, 1990). (Reprinted with permission of the author.)

through these phases, and not all families pass through all phases. Factors such as the pre-existing family structure, cohesion and coping skills, and resources available to the family, significantly influence family responses. According to Douglas (1990), shock and expectancy tend to characterise responses during the phase of inpatient hospital care. The stages of reality, mourning and adjustment are usually not encountered until the TBI individual has returned home.

Initially, families tend to experience a state of shock. The impact of seeing the injured relative fighting for life creates anguish, confusion, feelings of helplessness and frustration at having no control over the likely outcome. In many instances a very bleak outlook is given by doctors. All that is wished for is that the injured family member will survive.

Once the immediately life-threatening phase is passed there is frequently a sense of relief. As the TBI family member emerges from coma, and initially recovers relatively rapidly, there are likely to be feelings of expectancy, optimism and hope for full recovery. As Romano (1974) has described, there is a tendency to deny or ignore obvious changes in cognition and behaviour. Denial of the consequences of TBI may be strengthened by a number of factors. Early predictions that the patient might die, remain comatose or never walk and talk again may have proven to be incorrect, justifying a loss of faith in further medical predictions. It is, in reality, extremely difficult to prognosticate with any degree of accuracy regarding outcome. Families are frequently told that recovery may continue over a couple of years, and that the final outcome is uncertain. This tends to engender hope in relatives. Many of the problems are relatively intangible. It is much easier to focus on physical disability, which may show relatively rapid improvement, than cognitive and behavioural changes, which tend to be more persistent. There may be strong spiritual beliefs or a sense of faith that determination and hard work will overcome any problems. Alternatively, there may be an expectation that future advances in medical science will result in a cure for the damage incurred.

Denial is a very complex issue. It can be a source of considerable conflict in the relationship between family members and rehabilitation staff. As Novack (1993) has pointed out, however, denial may serve a beneficial purpose in the early stages of recovery, as families are trying to cope emotionally with the idea that life may never be the same again. Professionals working with families need to respect this. Attempts to confront denial frequently undermine the relationship between rehabilitation staff and family. Relatives may come to view staff as pessimistic, and lose faith in their commitment to making the best of the injured family member's future. Nevertheless, continuing denial makes planning for the TBI individual's future very difficult, and can create an enormous gulf amongst family members themselves, or between the family and the rehabilitation team.

Awareness of the reality of the impact of the injury frequently does not come until after the TBI individual has been discharged from hospital. Families are confronted more directly with the injured family member's coping difficulties and changes in personality and behaviour. Depression and anger may develop. Anger may be directed at themselves, another family member, rehabilitation staff, the driver of a vehicle involved in the accident, police or others, in an attempt to attribute blame for the accident or its consequences. In many instances there are legitimate grounds for such anger, when the party identified as having been responsible for the accident is found to have been behaving irresponsibly and/or under the influence of alcohol. There may be feelings of guilt or regret over whether something could have been done to prevent the injury. Experiencing negative feelings about the burden imposed by the injured family member, whose survival was so much wanted, may also cause guilt.

There is likely to be significant disruption of relationships and roles which existed in the family prior to injury. Middle-aged or elderly parents, who were making plans for retirement, or enjoying new-found freedom since adult children have left the family home, may be suddenly faced with caring for a newly dependent son or daughter at the expense of their own health and needs. There is likely to be concern as to what will happen to the injured child or adult when they can no longer provide the care that is needed. However, where both parents are still alive they are able to support each other and share the burden to some extent.

As Tyerman et al. (1994) have illustrated, spouses carry a somewhat different burden from that of parents. Where there are children, the spouse of an injured individual must take on the role of both parents, supporting the children as well as the newly injured husband or wife. Additionally, there are responsibilities for running the household, dealing with financial matters and earning an income for the family. The spouse who is injured may be childish, self-centred, and irritable, and therefore unable to offer the emotional support which formed an integral part of the relationship prior to injury.

Children of a TBI person may also have to take on new responsibilities. The uninjured parent is frequently absent, visiting at the hospital. When at home, the wife or husband of the injured family member is likely to be tired, irritable, and emotionally drained, with little energy to devote to dealing with issues of importance to the children. The children may experience, therefore, not only a loss of affection and support from the injured parent, but also from the one who is not injured. The mother or father who has sustained an injury may be irritable or aggressive towards the children and is no longer willing or able to share activities with them.

Faced with such changes, children may find it difficult or embarrassing to invite their friends into the home. As a consequence, children are likely to drift away from home and withdraw from their parents, particularly if they are adolescents. They may be reluctant to share their feelings with others. There may be a tendency to deny what is happening and avoid dealing with it. Younger children can develop behaviour problems in the face of such circumstances.

Unfortunately there has been relatively little documentation of the long-term impact of TBI on the children or siblings of those who sustain it. However, in her 10–15-year follow-up study of extremely severely injured TBI people and their families, Thomsen (1984, p.264) noted that, "The relationship between the patients and their children developed badly in all cases ...". Pessar, Coad, Linn, and Willer (1993) examined 24 families in which one parent was brain-injured. Children studied were born prior to the injury and were still living at home when interviewed. Reports of the uninjured parent indicated that most of the children experienced some degree of negative behavioural change after the parent's injury and, in ten families, significant and problematic changes occurred. Problems included a decline in the relationship with the injured parent, acting out behaviour, and emotional problems. Poorer outcomes were correlated with the gender of the injured parent— those having significant problems tending to have injured fathers, compromised parenting ability of the injured parent, compromised parenting performance by the uninjured parent, and the presence of depression in the uninjured parent.

Whatever the constellation of the family unit, there is evidence from a number of sources to suggest that it becomes increasingly isolated, as support from hospital and rehabilitation staff becomes no longer available. Friends and relatives, who initially rallied around, become less and less attentive. There is a growing awareness of the inadequacies of the TBI individual in coping with activities of a social, vocational, or recreational nature, so that increasing amounts of time are spent in the home. Caregivers may have to give up their own employment and leisure interests, providing care at the expense of their own health, needs and emotional well-being. As a consequence, the family unit gradually withdraws from social contact (Kozloff, 1987; Oddy, 1984a).

For many, there is eventually a growing awareness of the permanence of the situation and the need to become reconciled to lasting changes in the injured family member, the family's roles and relationships. Relatives experience grief over the loss of cherished qualities in the injured family member and unfulfilled potential. However, as Perlesz, Furlong, and McLachlan (1989) have pointed out, grieving is extremely difficult when it has to be done in the presence of the person who is being grieved for. There is a need not only to mourn the person who was prior to injury, but to adjust to the new person who has survived the injury. The fact that there may be little physical change in the injured individual may prevent or interfere with the grieving process, so that, "Patients and those close to them seem endlessly stuck between euphoric hope and resignation ... this burden of alternating hope and despair continues for many years" (Perlesz et al., 1989).

With the growing understanding of the new identity of the injured family member, there is, eventually, a need for permanent readjustment of expectations of the injured individual, a redefining of relationships and roles and restructuring of the family environment. The extent to which this can be effectively accomplished will depend on many factors, including the family's resources, coping styles and organisation, whether the family has been able to grieve effectively, the importance placed on qualities which have been lost, attitudes towards newly acquired behaviours, and "the flexibility of particular family beliefs" (Perlesz et al., 1989). Zarski, DePompei, and Zook (1988) have suggested that families which respond by focusing on and organising around the limitations of the TBI member are least likely to be able to deal with these changes and most likely to use denial as a major block to family reintegration.

From studies examining the impact of illness or disability on family adjustment, it is apparent that the families who adapt best are those who support one another, are able to express feelings and emotions openly, and able to be flexible in the face of change. They tend not to view the disability as harmful or challenging to family life, are able to discuss it openly, appreciate the affected family member's residual capabilities and allow them a continuing role in the household. These families also appreciate the need to remain involved in activities outside of the home. The presence of strong religious beliefs is also common (Martin, 1988; Power, 1985). From the work of Douglas (1994) it would appear that such patterns may also characterise well-adjusted families following TBI. Availability of practical assistance and support, such as attendant carer hours, was also a crucial factor in determining level of family coping in Douglas' (1994) study.

It appears that the responses of the family may have as significant an impact on the TBI individual's psychosocial adjustment as the specific disabilities resulting from the injury. Support for this contention comes from the finding of Leach, Frank, Bouman, and Farmer (1994), that effective use of problem-solving and behavioural coping strategies by the family in response to TBI was significantly related to lower levels of depression in the person who sustained the TBI. Hence the importance of focusing on the family system as part of the rehabilitation process.

METHODS OF COPING WITH TBI IN THE FAMILY

Douglas (1987) used the Family Environment Scale (Moos & Moos, 1981) to study the families of severe TBI individuals which remained together several years after injury. They found that the family environments were characterised by significantly higher levels of control than normal, suggesting that set rules and procedures were used to run family life to a greater extent than in normal families. These families were also less likely to make spontaneous decisions or change daily routines within the family. As Douglas (1987) pointed out, the family may have made such changes in order to meet the needs of the injured relative who, by virtue of problems with memory, executive function and behavioural control, is likely to function best within a stable and well-controlled setting. They also found a tendency for these families to be less open or expressive of feelings, and to communicate less about concerns and problems. This may represent an attempt to adapt to increased friction and strained relationships. Finally, there was evidence of less participation of such families in activities outside the family environment.

Willer et al. (1991) conducted a study of the problems and coping strategies reported by married couples in which one partner had sustained TBI a median period of 4 years earlier. Able-bodied husbands reported suppression of their feelings when reacting to mood swings as the most effective coping strategy. Other strategies included being careful not to attribute all family problems to the head injury, mutually defining new roles and responsibilities, support groups for their wives, and maintaining a sense of humour. Wives of injured husbands reported their most effective coping strategy as the development of a realistic but optimistic outlook. The development of assertiveness skills in relation to husband, health care providers, in-laws, and insurance representatives was also identified as important. Ranked third was the need to allow the injured husband to become independent, followed by the need to take time for one's self and for family outings. Participation in support groups was identified as another significant coping strategy.

Restructuring of the family environment may, in some cases, involve marital separation or a move of the injured family member to alternative accommodation. Finding a suitable long-term placement for a dependent spouse or adult child is likely to be a very difficult and stressful task. A majority of TBI individuals live with their parents in the long term (Jacobs, 1988). Whilst this largely reflects the fact that many are not married prior to injury, there is also evidence to suggest that parent-child relationships may be less vulnerable to the impact of TBI than marital relationships.

THE IMPACT OF TBI ON MARITAL AND PARENT–CHILD RELATIONSHIPS

Douglas (1987) found systematic differences in perception of family environment between families of severely head-injured husbands and those of adult children. In particular, families of husbands with severe TBI appeared to experience more conflict, were more socially isolated and generally less cohesive than families where the injured member was an adult child. A high level of continuing distress was apparent in the families where the husband was injured, whilst there was little apparent friction in the families of head-injured adult children. It must be noted, however, that by virtue of the fact that they were still living together two years after injury, these families may have represented a somewhat biased sample, presumably having made some adaptation to the situation.

Such findings support the view that spouses carry a greater long-term burden than parents. However, Brooks et al. (1987a) failed to find significantly greater burden in the spouses of TBI individuals relative to parents. They nevertheless acknowledged that the nature of the burden was likely to be different. Evidence in support of the stresses placed on marital relationships by TBI comes from the figures for divorce after TBI (Panting and Merry, 1972; Rosenbaum and Najenson, 1976; Tate et al., 1989; Thomsen, 1984). In Panting and Merry's (1972) follow-up study, conducted up to seven years after injury, three out of ten marriages in which a partner was injured had resulted in divorce, and another had resulted in separation. Thomsen (1984) found that of nine extremely severely injured patients married at the time of her first follow-up (two to five years post-injury), seven had divorced by the time of the 10–15-year follow-up. They all had children. The two who remained married had no children. In the years between the examinations six had married, but two had divorced again. In Tate et al.'s (1989) Australian follow-up study of severe TBI individuals up to six years post-injury, 63% of marriages had broken down in the group with moderate or severe levels of disability, whilst 42% of those with "good" outcomes had also divorced or separated.

Oddy (1978a) found less evidence of marital stress in their study carried out in a relatively less severely injured group of patients and within the first year after injury, although three out of seven spouses of very severely injured subjects reported feeling less affection for their partner at 12 months. Peters, Stambrook, Moore, and Esses (1990) found that spouses of severely head-injured husbands reported a greater amount of disagreement and difficulty reaching joint decisions than spouses of moderately or mildly injured husbands. They also reported fewer overt acts of physical and verbal affection expressed between themselves and their husbands, and had significantly lower overall "dyadic adjustment" scores than the other groups. It would appear that marital breakdown is most common following extremely severe injuries, where PTA exceeds one month, and that it tends to occur after a number of years. Presumably, during the early period after injury there is hope of recovery and an attempt is made by spouses to adjust to changes.

Rosenbaum and Najenson (1976) found that wives of head-injured soldiers were more lonely, isolated and depressed than the wives of paraplegic husbands, and more likely to have had to adopt roles formerly played by their husbands. The head-injured husbands were noted to be more self-centred and dependent than paraplegic husbands. Rosenbaum and Najenson found that the depression in the wives of brain-injured husbands correlated highly with reduced sharing of parental responsibilities and a perception of child-like dependency of the husband. Thomsen (1984, p.264) also reported that, "Spouses considered themselves to be the only grown-ups in the family".

It would appear from the findings of Tyerman et al. (1994) that, in addition to caring for the injured family member and dealing with changes in personality and behaviour, spouses must take on many additional responsibilities, and may no longer have their social, affectional and sexual needs met. The study by Willer et al. (1991) provided a rare opportunity for comparison of responses of wives and husbands to an injury in their spouse. Wives of TBI husbands identified the loss of emotional support, sharing and companionship as significant problems, after changes in personality, cognition and insight and reduced financial resources. On the other hand, the husbands of TBI wives expressed more concern over dependency, insecurity, overprotectiveness, and reluctance to leave the home on the part of the injured wife, in addition to mood swings.

Spouses may be less able to tolerate childish, demanding and irritable behaviour than parents, who are possibly relatively better equipped to resume their former caregiving role, and are often assisted and supported in this task by their spouse. Lezak (1978) noted that the spouses of TBI individuals find themselves in a social "limbo", being able neither to mourn their loss nor form new relationships. In addition, there may be little support from the extended family, who, by virtue of their lack of regular involvement, might show limited understanding of the changes in the TBI family member and the stress these have created for the immediate family.

Nevertheless, there is also considerable evidence of ongoing stress in families where parents are caring for a head-injured son or daughter. As Weddell, Oddy, and Jenkins (1980) have pointed out, many such parents are near or at retirement age and may have failing health. They tend to be greatly concerned about the eventual fate of their adult child. Oddy (1984a) and Jacobs (1988) noted the frequency with which one parent gave up a job in order to care for a head-injured son or daughter. There is also evidence of conflict between TBI individuals and siblings, as reported by their parents 12 months after injury (Oddy, 1984a). Kozloff (1987) noted that siblings eventually express jealousy and disapproval of the central role played by the TBI family member and withdraw their support.

SOURCES OF STRESS IN FAMILIES FOLLOWING TBI

It would appear that the major sources of burden to families of TBI individuals, whether they constitute a parental or a marital situation, are changes in emotional control, personality or behaviour, particularly irritability and aggression, and cognitive difficulties, such as slowness and memory problems (Brooks et al., 1986, 1987a; Hall, Karsmark, Stevens, Englander, O'Hare, & Wright, 1994; Jacobs, 1988; Kreutzer, Gervasio, & Camplair, 1994a; McKinlay et al., 1981; Oddy et al., 1978a,b; Oddy & Humphrey, 1980; Panting & Merry, 1972; Thomsen, 1984, Willer et al., 1991). McKinlay et al. (1981), Oddy et al. (1978a,b) and Hall et al. (1994) found that the stress created by these changes did not dissipate over time. Indeed Brooks et al. (1986) found a significant increase in subjective burden between one and five years.

Panting and Merry (1972) found that 60% of relatives required medication in the form of tranquillisers or sleeping tablets as a result of the stress created by having an injured person in the household. In an Australian study of 40 caregivers, Lamont (1993) found an incidence of psychiatric "caseness" on the General Health Questionnaire of 60%. In general, family distress does not show a statistically significant relationship with severity of injury, as measured by PTA duration. However, there are certainly strong trends suggesting that the families of those with long periods of PTA, exceeding four weeks, perceive significant changes in personality, behaviour and cognition, and experience a relatively high degree of subjective burden (Bond, 1975; Brooks et al., 1986, 1987a).

As Brooks et al. (1986, 1987a) have pointed out, factors other than severity become increasingly important as time progresses. Such factors might include the TBI person's premorbid personality. Another very significant source of variation must be the family's inherent capacity to cope with such changes, which is likely to be related to personalities and general stability within the family. Given the evidence that a relatively high proportion of TBI individuals have pre-existing maladaptive problems, it would not be surprising to find that some families have very limited resources for coping with such changes. Zarski et al. (1988) and Kozloff (1987) have drawn attention to the significant influence of family functioning in determining the family's adaptation to TBI. For many families, particularly those with pre-existing problems, TBI increases their vulnerability, making them weaker and more dysfunctional.

However, the picture is not always negative, or may not remain so. In his review of follow-up studies, Brooks (1984b) noted that some families appeared to cope surprisingly well, and may actually become stronger and more resilient in the face of the chronic challenges presented by TBI. Douglas (1994) found an increasing proportion of families who had stayed together had developed positive coping strategies more than five years after injury, and reported that the family had become closer as a result of the injury. It would appear from her findings that the readjustments necessary for more healthy family functioning after TBI do not tend to occur until between 5 and 10 years after injury. This points to the need to take a very long-term view in terms of availability of support and assistance. Finally, it must be noted that not all changes in personality following TBI are necessarily negative. For example, Fahy et al. (1967) found that two of 32 cases examined underwent positive changes in personality, becoming more even-tempered and compliant than they had been previously.

Another source of stress commonly reported by around 50% of the families of TBI individuals is poor communication with health professionals involved in treating the injured relative (Panting & Merry, 1972; Oddy et al., 1978b). This may reflect a lack of adequate communication by staff, a failure to understand or remember information given, or the presence of denial as a defence mechanism. It is probable that all of these explanations are true for a proportion of cases. This finding highlights the need for the rehabilitation team to give special attention to the manner and timing of information provision.

Many families experience great concern regarding availability of suitable accommodation and/or supervision for the TBI individual, should they be no longer able to provide the care that is needed. Financial and legal problems frequently add further to the burden of the families, who may have little understanding of such matters and few resources with which to obtain assistance. In the Los Angeles Head Injury Survey, long-term financial issues were a source of concern to most families (Jacobs, 1988). Moore, Stambrook, and Peters (1993) found that the presence of financial difficulties was frequently associated with family dysfunction. In the case of extremely severe injury there are likely to be issues regarding the TBI individual's ability to manage financial affairs, necessitating consideration of guardianship and organisation of interests. Such decisions are characteristically marked with emotion and conflict, reinforcing the loss of autonomy of the injured person, and further stressing family relationships.

HOW TO HELP FAMILIES

Given their crucial long-term role as caregivers, decision-makers, and providers of support to those who sustain TBI, families deserve to be involved, supported and assisted throughout the phases of acute care, rehabilitation and beyond. Indeed this is an essential component of the REAL approach to rehabilitation following TBI. Involvement with and assistance to families may take a number of forms. These include provision of information of a general and a specific nature regarding TBI and its impact on the injured family member, active involvement in goal-setting and the therapy process itself, particularly as it is being transferred into the home environment, supportive counselling and family therapy. The amount of intervention required may depend on the nature and extent of disability in the TBI individual, how the family was functioning prior to the injury, and how the "family system" is affected by the injury. As with many other aspects of TBI rehabilitation, there has been little research evaluating the impact of specific family interventions on the injured individual and the family. There is a significant need for systematic data on which to base family assistance. In the absence of such data, the approach recommended here has been based on the existing evidence from the literature, together with the author's experience.

Early intervention

As noted in Chapter 2, provision of information and support should begin in the intensive care unit. Families frequently report traumatic memories of how they were treated by medical or other hospital staff in this acute stage. Whether such memories are well-founded or reflect their confused state of mind at the time is unclear. However, in view of their fragile state, families are likely to be assisted by the presence of a support worker who understands their situation and has time to explain and interpret the sometimes overwhelming information provided by doctors. Neurosurgical staff face the difficult and stressful task of minimising the likelihood of mortality and morbidity in the injured person. They cannot be expected to look after families as well. Nevertheless, many neurosurgical staff would benefit from a greater understanding of the variability in long-term outcomes and family reactions to what they are told. This might help them to focus more on giving information regarding the patient's current condition and what is being done to help them, rather than unnecessarily or bluntly "preparing the family for the worst", which can be so traumatic as to have a lasting impact on family attitudes to health professionals.

When the TBI individual emerges from coma of significant duration, referral will, hopefully, be made for rehabilitation, either in another unit of the same hospital, or at another centre. Having just got to know and trust the staff in the neurosurgical unit, families are faced with a new environment, many unfamiliar faces, and a change in routine. It is very important that families are welcomed into the rehabilitation setting by a designated and appropriately-skilled member of the team, who may be a social worker or case manager. This person should attempt to establish rapport with the family and identify themselves as someone to whom the family can turn for information, assistance and support throughout the rehabilitation period. Such continuity of involvement is important.

The family should be given a tour of the ward and therapy areas and an explanation as to how the programme works. Staff who will be working with the injured person can be identified. These staff should also take time to introduce themselves and explain their role. A written booklet containing information about TBI and its consequences, and how the rehabilitation programme works can be particularly helpful. It is likely that by this stage close family members are feeling exhausted, having spent day and night at the bedside. There may also be pressure for them to return to work. It will be important to families to see their injured relative settled into the new environment, but once this has been achieved, they should be given permission to spend less time at the hospital, provided they feel comfortable with this.

Family assessment

A comprehensive assessment should be made of the family's constellation, the roles played by different members, including the one who has been injured, the nature of relationships and communication within the family. It is also important to consider other stresses on the family. Where staff with the appropriate family assessment skills are available, clinical interview may be supplemented by the use of a standardised assessment tool to examine objectively the family system and the responses of individuals to the injury. Such methods include self-report measures and observational techniques. No tools have been comprehensively validated for use with the TBI population. There is a need for further research in this area.

In reviewing the available tools for assisting clinicians, Bishop and Miller (1988) have recommended the Family Assessment Device (FAD) as a self-report measure which has been shown to have good psychometric properties, and has been used to study responses of family members across different disability groups, including those with cognitive disturbance. The FAD is a questionnaire designed to assess the six dimensions of the McMaster Model of Family Functioning and overall level of family functioning. The dimensions assessed include Problem Solving, Communication, Roles Dimension, Affective Responsiveness, Affective Involvement, Behaviour Control, and General Functioning.

Bragg, Klockars, and Berninger (1992) compared ratings on this scale by family members of a group of TBI adolescents with those of the families of a group of matched, non-TBI adolescents. They found that, whilst the injured adolescent and sibling tended to rate family functioning as being less healthy than did their parents, all family members perceived unhealthy family functioning in the domains of Roles Dimension, Affective Responsiveness, Affective Involvement, and General Functioning. Some family members also reported unhealthy functioning on the dimensions of Problem-Solving and Communication. These findings suggest that the scale is sensitive to changes occurring in families following TBI. A more recent study by Kreutzer, Gervasio, and Camplair (1994b) also revealed greater levels of unhealthy functioning relative to published norms in a group of caregivers of people with mild, moderate and severe TBI. Family communication problems were particularly prevalent.

Rosenthal and Young (1988) have proposed the use of an observational "Family Diagnostic Assessment", which involves observation of the family engaging in a designated task in relation to the TBI individual. Such tasks might involve assisting the TBI family member with dressing or transfers, or negotiating a list of deficit areas. This is designed to enable observation of the interactional patterns of the family in meeting the needs of the injured person, and identification of responses which may impede the rehabilitation process, such as overprotectiveness, anxiety and strong denial.

These assessments may provide a basis from which to decide whether supportive counselling or family therapy will be required. Those families who have show pre-existing maladaptive styles of problem-solving and communication, and poor cohesion and adaptability are less likely to adapt successfully to the impact of TBI (Perlesz et al., 1989). However, previously well-functioning families can also experience considerable difficulties in adaptation, and may benefit from active assistance.

In the course of the initial assessment period, families may want to discuss the circumstances of the accident and their feelings about this. The emotional reactions and needs of children and siblings should also be explored. It is important to establish what resources are available to the family, financially, in terms of support and assistance from extended family or friends, and whether they are able to have time off from employment. Arrangements may need to be made for home help, financial or legal assistance. The family's cultural background and beliefs and their value system must also be considered. It is important to ensure clear communication where English is not spoken, using an interpreter, and involving a social worker who understands their cultural background. This person can convey to the rehabilitation team an understanding of family reactions to the injury and attitudes to the rehabilitation process, as well as act as an advocate for the family. Wherever possible, written information should be translated into the family's native language.

Family members usually represent an invaluable source of information regarding the TBI individual's previous lifestyle, abilities, behaviour and personality. Such information is a vital aspect of the REAL approach, to enable the team to set realistic and appropriate goals. It is important to gain an understanding of the family's perception of the impact of the injury on the injured individual, physically, cognitively and behaviourally. Their expectations regarding the rehabilitation process, its goals and outcome, and their role in that process should also be explored. In many instances families may have quite different priorities and expectations from those of rehabilitation staff. Although these may seem inappropriate or unrealistic, they are likely to be maintained and conveyed to the TBI family member, even in the face of logical argument to the contrary by team members. The views of the family deserve respect and consideration from the rehabilitation team. Wherever possible an attempt should be made to negotiate goals which incorporate the aims and priorities of the family, as well as the TBI person. In some cases, the family's wishes and needs may not be congruent with, or in the best interests of the injured person. Where this is seen to be the case, active family participation in goal-setting and therapy is less desirable.

Provision of feedback and discussion of goals

In the early stages of rehabilitation the TBI individual may be exhibiting ongoing confusion, disorientation and agitation characteristic of post-traumatic amnesia (PTA). As outlined in Chapter 4, attempts to assess and treat the injured person at this stage are likely to result in a picture of global impairment and increasing agitation. Having had the expectation that rehabilitation was to commence in earnest, families may be disappointed at the lack of therapist involvement, and the lack of information available It is therefore important that staff explain the nature of PTA, and try to focus the family's attention on appropriate management of the TBI person during this phase of recovery, rather than attempting to assess or treat the injured individual.

Following emergence from PTA, a more detailed assessment by appropriate team members should be possible. The results of this assessment should be conveyed in a clear and simple fashion, and in a manner whereby it is most likely to be understood by the family, who will have differing capacities for absorbing such information. The method of communication needs to be adapted to the family. Some will cope with a meeting involving family, close friends and the rehabilitation team. Others will be overwhelmed by such an occasion and cope better with a smaller meeting with one or two key staff. Whatever the nature of the meeting, this should always be backed up with written notes in the family's native language. It may also be helpful to have a tape of the meeting made available to enable the family to review the meeting or for others to hear the team's feedback.

Whether the TBI family member should be present at family meetings is a matter for the family and the rehabilitation team to assess and discuss beforehand. It may prove to be too overwhelming, or embarrassing for the injured person, who might have a limited capacity to absorb such information. Family members may not feel comfortable about asking certain questions or discussing particular changes in the presence of the injured individual. It may be more appropriate to hold a separate meeting tailored to the capabilities of the TBI person. On the other hand, it can be very upsetting for TBI individuals to know that others are talking about them without their presence. In such instances it is wiser to include the injured family member.

It is important that team members introduce themselves and explain their role, even if they have already done so. Information should be conveyed clearly, avoiding the use of jargon. The views of the family (and the injured person, if present) regarding changes they see and progress being made should also be sought. Such a meeting can serve as a means of jointly determining appropriate goals and discussing how these are to be achieved. Family members may wish to raise other issues of concern to them.

These discussions need to be backed up with individual contact in order to assess the extent to which the family have understood or felt comfortable about discussing all relevant issues. The meetings frequently raise significant emotional responses which may need to be explored. Family meetings should be held on a regular basis, in order to review progress and set new goals. Discharge tends to create a great deal of anxiety for families, so it is particularly important to communicate frequently as this point approaches.

Family members are likely to ask what the eventual outcome will be. However, as many outcome studies have borne out, such predictions, even after the patient has emerged from coma and commenced active rehabilitation, are fraught with uncertainty (Ponsford et al., 1995b). Moreover, whilst families may repeatedly request information regarding the future, they are not usually ready to deal with the answers to their questions. For these reasons it is unwise to prognosticate in these early stages of recovery. Rather, clear and accurate information should be conveyed as to the nature of the injured person's injuries, what is being done to help, and the likely time frame over which treatment and improvement are likely to occur. As noted in Chapter 2, staff need to be prepared to repeat information many times, as families do not always take it in. Even when it is written down there is no guarantee that it has been understood. Douglas (1994) found lack of information to be one of the most common complaints of families interviewed between 2 and 10 years after injury. In many instances this may have been conveyed but not fully taken in. This underscores the importance of allowing for access to information over an indefinite period after injury.

Coping with denial

Not uncommonly, families will refuse to acknowledge the significance of the injuries, apparently failing to hear what medical and rehabilitation staff have told them. Their view of the TBI individual's capacity to recover and resume previous activities seems quite unrealistic. Such denial tends to be viewed very negatively by rehabilitation staff, and may result in continuing confrontation of the relatives with "the facts", as seen by therapy staff. This approach is, however, rarely beneficial. More often than not it results only in alienation of the family from the rehabilitation team, who may be viewed as condescending and negative. Once such a rift has developed it is difficult to mend. An open relationship between therapists and family is crucial to the success of the rehabilitation programme and every attempt should be made to preserve it. Whilst having little knowledge of head injury, they know a great deal about the injured individual and are likely to be actively involved in a caretaking, supervisory or supportive role in the long term.

In the majority of instances outcome cannot be predicted with any certainty, so that it is not possible to provide the family with facts about the future. Indeed the predictions of team members may prove to be little more accurate than those of the family. Under these circumstances it is wiser to acknowledge a difference of opinion than to label the problem "denial". For many families, denial develops as an adaptive mechanism, maintaining family stability whilst they are dealing with such sudden and devastating changes. These may be too painful to contemplate as being long-term in the early stages of the recovery process. However, with time, education and active involvement in the rehabilitation process, many families do become more realistic. When this occurs they are most likely to share their worries about the future with team members who have treated them with trust and respect.

When denial continues over a prolonged period it can become more problematic. It may affect the family's willingness to be involved in the rehabilitation programme, particularly in learning how to assist the injured family member with tasks that cannot be performed independently. It also becomes difficult for the team to make plans for the future. Prolonged denial suggests the need for structured family intervention. Confrontation is never likely to be an effective management strategy.

Involvement of families in the therapy process

In view of the fact that it is the family who are most likely to provide long-term care and/or support to the injured individual, it is vital that, under these circumstances, family members be actively involved in the therapy process at all stages. All too frequently relatives are seen as an irritating presence by rehabilitation staff, who want to get on with their job in peace. Clearly, there will be times when therapists need to work with the TBI individual alone, especially when the presence of others causes distraction or behaviour problems. However, participation of family members in relevant aspects of the rehabilitation programme will enhance their awareness of the TBI person's strengths and weaknesses, and their ability to assist in minimising the impact of the disabilities. It also presents an opportunity to model appropriate strategies of managing behavioural or emotional difficulties. Indeed, as outlined in the previous chapter, relatives may be invaluable as co-therapists in dealing with such problems. The exception to this is when family dynamics are such that this is not in the best interests of the injured person.

Planning for return to the community is easier when the family has had ongoing involvement in the programme. At this time there is likely to be a need for intensive co-operation, as families are prepared to take over the supportive role which has been performed by the rehabilitation staff, being trained to provide appropriate assistance, supervision and/or feedback. Staff should make themselves available for consultation and support after discharge from the programme. However, it is also important to link the family with appropriate resources in their local community, so as to minimise dependency on hospital-based services.

Family support groups

It is likely to be helpful to enable families to talk with one another during and after the rehabilitation phase, sharing information and emotional support. This is particularly beneficial because the general community tends to have little knowledge of TBI and its consequences, so that friends and other family members may not understand what they are going through. The issues addressed by family support groups will vary according to the setting, time since injury and nature of the relationship with the TBI family member. In the acute stages of recovery, families may be less ready to discuss their emotional reactions to the trauma, still focusing intensely on the needs of the injured family member. They may, however, benefit from educational input, both in structured form from members of the rehabilitation team or community agencies, or from other families who have already had the experience. Topics of interest may include mechanisms of TBI, management of coma and PTA, medical complications, such as epilepsy, the nature and management of disorders of mobility, communication, swallowing, cognition, behaviour and emotion, vocational issues, accessing community resources, and financial and legal issues. It is wise to tailor the content of educational sessions to the needs of the group. Supplementary notes are also helpful, as many issues may not be fully understood until much later. Such educational sessions may form a basis for broader discussion of issues relevant to individual group members, leading to a sharing of information and support.

Depending on the time since injury and their stage of adjustment, families may benefit from the opportunity of sharing their emotional reactions to the situation and discussing the impact of the injury on the family. It is important that one or two suitably trained rehabilitation professionals take a facilitative or guiding role in this process, in order to ensure that all families are encouraged to participate actively and that all relevant issues are covered. Some issues raised may need to be taken up individually. Such groups may help families to realise that their experiences and reactions are shared by others. This relieves their sense of isolation and provides family members with a feeling that they are accepted and understood.

The issues of importance to spouses of TBI individuals may be somewhat different from those of parents of injured adolescents or adults. They may feel uncomfortable about discussing relationship issues or their feelings about changes in behaviour and personality. It is therefore particularly useful to enable spouses to talk with one another, providing relief from the guilt which many experience regarding their negative feelings about the injured partner.

Many families form strong bonds through participation in family groups. Such relationships provide a useful resource for the future, when there is no longer active rehabilitation support. In this respect it is useful for support groups to be ongoing, so that families may return in times of need. If this is not possible within the rehabilitation setting, referral should be made to an accessible community-based group. Indeed it is after return to the community that family support groups may be most helpful, as there is likely to be less support from other sources, and family members may be more ready to benefit from them.

A recent study by Singer et al. (1994) compared the impact of two kinds of support groups for parents of children or young adults with severe brain injury. One group participated in a psychoeducational stress management programme that emphasised instruction in coping skills and group sharing of coping methods. The second group was an informational support group in which parents identified topics they wished to discuss and were encouraged to share their feelings. Parents in the stress management group showed significant reductions in depressive and anxiety symptoms, whereas the informational and support group did not. As the authors acknowledge, the conclusions from the study were limited by the small size of the groups and the varying aetiologies of brain injury represented. Moreover, the informational support group may have brought other benefits to its participants (e.g. increased knowledge or social support base). However, these preliminary findings suggest that training in adaptation and coping skills may be a particularly worthwhile focus of family support groups. There is a need for further studies of this nature.

Grieving and the readjustment process—supportive counselling and family therapy

Even those families who show relatively healthy functioning are greatly stressed by the occurrence of TBI. Provision of supportive counselling is a useful means of assisting them to adjust to the impact of the injury, both in terms of the emotional reactions of individual family members and the family system itself. Where there are pre-existing problems in the family, or where family reactions to the injury are considered to be maladaptive, formal family therapy is recommended.

Supportive counselling should provide an opportunity for family members to express and work through their emotional responses at different stages, including feelings of anxiety, helplessness, hope, denial, depression, guilt, anger, loss, and grief. The counsellor will need to be very flexible in this respect, as individuals within the family are likely to be experiencing differing responses at a given point in time. Many will not be ready to talk about their feelings until long after the injured relative has been discharged. Counselling also provides a forum in which to raise practical problems, particularly those occurring after discharge, and to discuss issues regarding management of the newly acquired disabilities of the TBI individual within the family.

Assistance may be required in restructuring the family system. As the family initially mobilises itself to deal with the crisis, this involves changes which are seen as temporary. Family members tend to put aside their own interests and needs in order to give maximum support to the injured relative. Such sacrifices cannot usually be sustained without a significant physical or emotional toll. At some point, longer term adaptations need to be made. However, it is usually not possible to consider long-term changes until the family has realised the permanency of the situation and grieved their losses. A great deal of work may first be required to assist the family in becoming realistic and grieving effectively. As Perlesz et al. (1989) have pointed out, grieving the losses resulting from TBI is complicated by the prolonged period of uncertainty regarding outcome. This tends to encourage unrealistic hope for recovery. It is also very difficult to "mourn in the presence of the one being mourned for". This is particularly so when the changes being mourned are relatively intangible alterations in personality, behaviour and cognition, rather than physical disability or disfigurement. The restructuring process may not begin, therefore, until many years after injury.

Many dimensions of the family system may be affected by TBI. In particular, there is likely to be a need for significant reorganisation of roles and relationships, as well as modes of communication, decision-making and problem-solving. The extent to which such changes can be made successfully will depend on the quality of functioning in these areas prior to the injury, and the family's level of cohesion and adaptability. Coping with role changes has been identified as a significant source of stress, particularly by spouses of those who have sustained TBI. The extent to which family members can successfully adopt new roles will depend on the flexibility of family beliefs, individuals' experience in adopting different roles and the extent to which resources can be utilised to provide information and support. For example, a wife who has never worked, been completely reliant on her husband for management of the family finances, and has difficulty asserting herself is going to find it much more difficult to take responsibility in these areas than one who has well-developed professional skills and previously played a more active role in decision-making and financial management. Similarly, fathers who have had previous involvement in child-rearing will adapt better to increased responsibilities in this area than those who for cultural or other reasons consider that to be a female domain.

Some families will achieve these adaptations without assistance. Others will do so with supportive assistance of various kinds. Family therapy aims to assist families who have not been able to grieve effectively and to resolve maladaptive patterns of communication and interaction which impede the adjustment of the injured individual and/or the family. A forum is provided in which family conflicts can be re-enacted and more adaptive strategies developed for resolving issues. Cultural influences and family belief systems can be explored. Families are encouraged to understand that the problems they are experiencing are often more related to the resources, coping styles and organisation of the family system, than to the limitations of the injured family member. An example given by Zarski et al. (1988) is that of the TBI relative who becomes emotionally dependent and demands constant attention. A spouse or parent may reinforce this behaviour to avoid further distress in the family. "The result is a dysfunctional circularity, whereby the overprotectiveness will foster further dependency and resentment and elicit additional overprotectiveness" (Zarski et al., 1988, p.32).

An attempt is therefore made to shift the focus from the brain injury and its negative consequences to the family system itself. Following from this, the family is encouraged to accept the new identity of the injured relative, without constantly making comparison with pre-injury qualities. The extent to which the family members "normalise" their altered situation and accept the TBI family member will partly determine whether a positive self-image can be adopted by the injured individual. As Perlesz et al. (1989) point out, the family itself also has to develop a new identity. Family therapy aims to assist families to focus on their strengths and come to recognise ways in which they have grown through the experience of TBI.

No controlled trials have been conducted to evaluate the impact of family therapy on the long-term adjustment of TBI individuals and their families, and there is an urgent need for such research to validate its use. However, the results of case studies seem promising (Perlesz et al., 1989). A significant problem in some cases is convincing families to accept the need for intervention. Unfortunately those who have had the most long-standing problems may be the most resistant in this respect. It is particularly important, however, that family therapy services be provided by clinicians who are skilled in this area. Ideally they should also have a good understanding of TBI and its consequences. If this is not the case, the referring agency has an obligation to see that such information is conveyed clearly. Because of the long timeframe over which these adaptations are made, it is also vital that access to both supportive counselling and family therapy services be available over an indefinite period after injury. For some families it may be 10 years before they are ready to benefit from such assistance.

ADVOCACY AND SUPPORT AGENCIES

The heterogeneity and complexity of problems which result from TBI places considerable demands on families, not only in terms of their interactions with the injured individual, but also in terms of the necessity to deal with many different professionals and agencies. Both they and the person who is injured are likely to be faced with choices regarding appropriate forms of treatment, who will deliver it and how long it should continue. In many instances there is a need for ongoing negotiation with insurance agencies in order to obtain funding. Later, decisions may be required regarding long-term care, guardianship and legal issues. By virtue of limitations in their background knowledge and capacity to comprehend information provided, the majority of families and TBI individuals are ill-equipped to make such decisions. Emotional distress adds further to their difficulties. In order to ensure that the TBI individual receives the best possible services it is important that assistance is offered to both the injured person and the family through explanation, interpretation, and advocacy. Where no family support exists, advocacy for the person who has sustained the injury becomes even more important.

This form of support is frequently offered during the rehabilitation phase, but after discharge the TBI individual and the family have few resources on which to draw. In this respect, agencies such as Headway in Britain, the National Head Injury Foundation (NHIF) in the USA, and the Head Injury Council of Australia (HICOA) in Australia, offer invaluable service, in terms of assisting brain-injured individuals and their families to negotiate their way through rehabilitation services and options for long-term accommodation and support, to become better informed, and to deal with financial, guardianship and legal issues. They also provide a support network in the form of regional support groups. However, perhaps the most important function of these organisations is that of drawing the attention of the public and the government to the unique and devastating consequences of TBI, and the services which are required to meet the needs of TBI individuals and their families. Rehabilitation professionals working with TBI have an obligation to contribute to such efforts.

LEGAL ISSUES

TBI individuals and their families confront a range of legal issues. These vary from one country to another, but generally include proceedings relating to motor vehicle or work-related injuries, issues of competency, financial management, guardianship, and the right to make decisions regarding treatment. In the early stages of recovery from TBI sustained in a motor vehicle accident, police may wish to interview the injured person regarding the circumstances of the accident. This can be distressing and bewildering for the TBI individual, who may still be confused and is likely to have no recollection of these events. Police should be encouraged to wait until there has been sufficient cognitive recovery to allow the injured person to cope with such an interview. It will also be important to make them aware of the cognitive limitations of the person who has sustained the injury, particularly the fact that recollection of the events surrounding the accident is never likely to be possible.

TBI individuals may find their inability to recall the accident and period afterwards quite distressing. Both they and their families may go to considerable lengths to find an explanation as to how it happened and who was responsible. There is frequently extreme anger towards the party deemed responsible, particularly where negligence and excessive alcohol are allegedly involved. This tends to be fuelled by the legal processes. Even where charges are laid and a conviction made, the punishment is rarely considered to be adequate relative to the losses incurred by the TBI person and family. In some instances there may be a continuing desire to retaliate. Counselling is frequently necessary in order to work through these feelings. It is important to encourage the TBI individual and the family to see that ongoing anger is likely to be more destructive to themselves than to the person perceived as causing the injury. There is a need to put the accident behind them and focus on the future.

Many countries still have an adversarial system in which compensation is awarded on the basis of proven responsibility for the injury, as well as degree of impairment. Legal proceedings usually continue over many years, often commencing at the point when the TBI individual and the family were beginning to adjust to the impact of the injury and look to the future. A multitude of assessments may be conducted, requiring the injured person and/or the family to reiterate the history and consequences of the injury many times. This can be very stressful. There may be pressure to prove the degree of disability, leading at times to exaggeration of problems and discouragement of return to previous activities, such as work, in order to maximise compensation. This can be extremely counterproductive, undoing rehabilitative attainments.

Some of the most disabling impairments resulting from TBI, particularly changes in cognition, personality and behaviour, will not be evident on physical examination or even standardised psychological assessment, and they may not be accurately reported by the TBI individual. Unless the examinations are carried out by practitioners who are skilled in the area of TBI, the degree of impairment and disability may be significantly underestimated. Clinicians are commonly required to estimate the degree of impairment of various functions in percentage terms, a practice of questionable efficacy. There is a need for development of methods specifically applicable to those who have sustained TBI and for use by suitably experienced practitioners.

Frequently the only parties to benefit from these processes are the lawyers. It is important that the rehabilitation facility encourage the family to use lawyers who have a good understanding of TBI, and who are willing to work with treating staff to maximise the interests of the TBI individual and the family. A no-fault system of compensation is desirable. This provides immediate funding for rehabilitation and other injury-related services, without the need to establish responsibility for the injury. Such a system, administered by the Transport Accident Commission, has been operating cost-effectively in the State of Victoria, Australia, since 1981.

The awarding of financial compensation may bring with it new stresses and responsibilities for the injured individual and the family. There may be bitterness over its inadequacy to compensate for losses. Advice will be needed regarding methods of preserving capital to provide for long-term needs. There is frequently concern regarding the TBI person's ability to manage even day-to-day finances or to make decisions regarding large sums of money. The assessment of these and other decision-making capabilities relating to the affairs of TBI individuals is extremely difficult, especially in cases where deficits are relatively subtle. There are few established guidelines. However, it is recommended that the process should involve not only neuropsychological assessment, but also assessment of daily functioning in these areas, in the manner suggested in Chapter 3.

The process of assessing competency is often complicated by lack of self-awareness on the part of the injured individual, leading to considerable conflict with family members and relevant authorities. In this respect it may be unwise for family members to take on the task of guardianship. Moreover, some families may be overprotective, and use this as a means of exerting control over the injured relative. Many TBI individuals are capable of managing all or part of their affairs, either alone or with assistance. Any restriction of rights should only be imposed after careful consideration.

It is not uncommon for TBI individuals who lack awareness of problems resulting from the injury to refuse treatment. In many instances their rights in this regard have to be respected. Indeed, there may be little to be gained in attempting to treat an individual who is actively resistant. However, where there is a perceived threat to the well-being of that individual or others, the family, a guardian or doctors may have to intervene on their behalf. Unfortunately, current procedures for the implementation of such intervention tend to be complicated, traumatic and counterproductive to the interests of the TBI individual. There is a need to address this issue, whilst protecting the interests of the person who has sustained the injury.

Finally, some TBI individuals have increased involvement with police and the legal system as a result of behaviour problems or substance abuse. It is important that they be given access to appropriate advocacy services and that the potential influence of the brain injury on behaviour be given consideration.

CASE REPORT—ABDUL

Abdul was 34 years old when he sustained an extremely severe TBI in a motor car accident. Coma lasted one month and PTA four and a half months. Abdul had emigrated to Australia from Turkey nine years earlier, and met and married his Turkish wife two years later. He was a professional soccer player and also worked in a factory. His wife was a welfare worker. They both spoke fluent English. The couple had two sons, the elder of whom was aged five at the time of his father's injury. He was a passenger in the car when the accident occurred. Although uninjured, he was trapped in the car for 40 minutes and experienced much distress at witnessing his injured, unconscious father, whom he idolised. The second child had been born only a few weeks prior to the accident.

Abdul's wife, Fatima, initially spent day and night at the bedside. As the couple had no family in Australia, she relied on assistance from friends to mind the children. She was first told that Abdul was unlikely to survive. After two days his condition had stabilised, but doctors indicated that he was likely to remain severely disabled, if not comatose. However, relieved that he had survived, and knowing that Abdul was a fit and determined person, Fatima felt very hopeful that he would recover. She was under a great deal of stress, trying to juggle the needs of her new baby and older son with hospital visits, but in the first few weeks friends were very helpful. The hospital social worker arranged for additional support from a Turkish welfare agency. She wanted to spend as much time with Abdul as possible, as she felt it was important that he was stimulated and that he was most likely to respond to her voice. After a month, Abdul began to respond, first by opening and tracking with his eyes, and later following some simple commands. However, he remained mute for some time, which made Fatima very anxious.

Six weeks after the injury, whilst still in this state, Abdul was transferred to Bethesda Hospital for rehabilitation. Before he was transferred she visited the hospital and was shown around by a social worker. She was also given a manual containing information about the programme and about TBI. She read this avidly, and also went to the medical library and sought out further information about TBI. As he was still in PTA, Abdul was initially managed only on the ward, receiving short sessions of physiotherapy, and having brief visits from the psychologist and other therapists. A small meeting was held to explain the nature of the injury and PTA, and to introduce the therapists. Abdul remained restless and agitated for the next two months. Although able to speak, his speech was very confused. Fatima became frustrated at the lack of progress and worried that he should be receiving more therapy.

Four and a half months after the injury, therapists determined that Abdul was no longer in PTA and conducted full assessments. Abdul was found to have severe and extensive cognitive impairments, affecting his expressive and receptive language abilities, with poor word-finding and paraphasias (as much in Turkish as in English), a short attention span, distractibility, slow information processing, very poor learning and memory skills, visuoconstructional difficulties, a tendency to perseverate, and extreme impulsivity, with a lack of ability to plan and self-monitor his behaviour or thought processes. He was also prone to laugh or cry uncontrollably at times. He showed virtually no awareness of his cognitive limitations, was extremely self-centred and had a low tolerance for frustration.

Physically, Abdul was also significantly disabled, being confined to a wheelchair and requiring assistance in all aspects of his care. This information was conveyed to Fatima. It was emphasised that the problems were severe, but that further recovery would be expected. Unfortunately progress was extremely slow. Reassessment conducted after a further three months, and then six months, of therapy indicated only small gains. Lack of initiative and impulsivity were presenting significant barriers to physical progress, and Abdul was still dependent in many aspects of self-care.

Fatima felt it would assist her husband's progress if she took him home. The rehabilitation team were worried as to how she would cope with Abdul as he was, but as this was very important to her they agreed. Abdul was discharged to attend daily outpatient therapy 11 months after his injury. At this stage Fatima was still hopeful of significant further gains, as she had been told that recovery usually continued for at least two years. However, things did not go as she had hoped. Abdul was very demanding at home, expecting his wife to attend to his every need. He constantly competed with the children for her attention, and argued with his son, for example over what television programme they would watch. He was completely unable to see how much stress she was under, trying to work full-time and care for two young children and for him. When he was frustrated he became very aggressive towards Fatima and his elder son. Fatima also reported that her husband had become very demanding sexually, which added to her stress.

A behavioural programme was instituted to try and increase Abdul's independence in the home. Fatima found it difficult to follow the guidelines consistently, due to the many competing demands on her attention and time. The couple were also seen together for counselling in an attempt to enhance Abdul's understanding of the impact of his behaviour, to develop anger management techniques, discuss their sexual problems and Fatima's concern over his intolerance of and lack of affection towards his elder son. Over an extended period some gains were made in terms of Abdul's independence in performing self-care activities, but he remained extremely egocentric and demanding. He would agree to attempt certain strategies in therapy, but was not able to carry them out consistently at home.

Fatima was also seen individually to provide her with a supportive outlet, a forum in which she could discuss concerns regarding the children and assist her to develop her assertiveness with Abdul. She was particularly self-conscious in dealing with the sexual problem, as this was an area in which she had always felt inadequate. She also attended a support group with several other spouses of severely injured husbands. She was still determined that the family would stay together and seemed desperate to try any intervention which might improve things. She explained that, as a Turkish wife, it would be unheard of for her to desert her husband. Abdul's elder son suffered ongoing emotional and behavioural problems after the injury. He was exceptionally intelligent, and this may have added to his difficulties. He was referred to a specialised children's counselling service. The younger son was less affected because he was still very young, and had not known his father prior to the injury.

Two years after the injury, Abdul had made only small gains and the same patterns of behaviour remained. The family was referred for family therapy, but Abdul refused to attend after the first two sessions. Fatima was beginning to express intense feelings of anger and resentment towards her husband.

She finally began to acknowledge the fact that her husband was unlikely to recover much further. She became extremely depressed, as she began to grieve for the husband she had lost. A Turkish attendant carer had been employed in an effort to relieve her burden, but Abdul still insisted that his wife perform many tasks for him, as he felt this was the duty of a Turkish wife. Having made little progress over the previous six months, he was referred for outpatient therapy at a day centre in his local community. His attendant was encouraged to involve him in a number of other activities, such as watching his soccer team.

Five years after the injury, Fatima finally decided she could no longer live with her husband due to his difficult behaviour. She had long since "separated" from him on an emotional level, but had, for a long time, struggled with her feelings of guilt. She eventually made this decision, not only because of the stress the changes in her husband had created for her, but more particularly because of its impact on the children. The children went to live with her.

A Turkish housekeeper was employed to cook and clean for Abdul, and an attendant carer was appointed for 30 hours per week to assist him in getting around in the community. Once alone, he did more for himself and showed a surprising ability to organise his day-to-day activities. He was, however, extremely angry with his wife, as he felt it was her duty to stay with him. He telephoned her constantly, usually with requests for money. He tended to spend his weekly income quickly because most days he took himself by taxi to a Turkish restaurant for lunch. He would have no money left to pay the bills. Out of guilt, Fatima would pay the bills. Abdul wanted to be a father to his children. Although worried about their welfare, Fatima allowed the two boys to go and stay with their father on weekends. Although continuing to have conflict with his elder son, Abdul developed a close bond with his younger son. Financial settlement of their separation and divorce were complicated by legal proceedings relating to the accident. Abdul eventually received a substantial settlement, some of which was allocated to pay expenses for the children, such as their education.

At the time of writing it is 11 years since the injury. Abdul's elder son has had significant adjustment problems, engaging in frequent antisocial behaviour. Although gifted, he has dropped out of school. He has only intermittent contact with his father. The younger son continues to visit Abdul every second weekend. Fatima is gradually rebuilding a life for herself, but still worries a great deal about Abdul. She has had a couple of relationships, of which Abdul angrily disapproves, but she has not remarried. Abdul returned to Turkey for six months in the hope of finding a new wife, but returned alone. He is constantly in conflict with the court which is holding his money in trust, as he wants more control over his money. Both Abdul and his wife have required counselling and assistance of various kinds on a number of occasions over the years since their separation and they are likely to continue to do so for many years to come.

CONCLUSIONS

There is substantial evidence that TBI has a significant impact on caregivers, and on the family as a whole. The long-term psychosocial adjustment of the person who is injured will to some extent be determined by the levels of adjustment and coping of the family unit. Follow-up studies also indicate that family members provide most ongoing support of a practical, social and emotional nature to the TBI individual. Therefore it is paramount that the family unit be as involved in the rehabilitation process as the injured person. This means frequent provision of clear information regarding TBI and its impact on the injured family member, active involvement in goal-setting and the therapy process itself, access to supportive counselling, and assistance in finding and dealing with service agencies and dealing with financial and legal issues. There is a need to recognise that the adjustment process for families is likely to be a very lengthy one. Access to family therapy services should be available to assist families who have difficulty in grieving, or adjusting roles and expectations of the injured individual. All forms of family support need to be available over the lifespan of the person with TBI.

CHAPTER TEN

Traumatic brain injury in children

Jennie Ponsford

INTRODUCTION

Whilst many of the issues and management strategies outlined in previous chapters also apply to children who sustain TBI, and certainly to adolescents, in a number of ways paediatric head injury differs from that in adults. There is, as a consequence, a need for research regarding sequelae of TBI, course of recovery, intervention strategies and long term needs in the paediatric population. It is also necessary to develop rehabilitation and support services focusing specifically on this group. The aim of this chapter is to explore issues and needs of unique or particular relevance to brain-injured children. Studies of paediatric populations cover varying age ranges, some up to the age of 18 years. However, the focus of this chapter will be on children up to the age of 15 years. Many of the issues pertinent to older adolescents have been explored in detail in Chapter 8.

CAUSES OF INJURY

The causes of TBI in children differ from those in adults. Findings from a number of epidemiological studies have indicated that motor vehicle accidents are responsible for a significant, but smaller proportion of cases (Brink, Imbus, & Woo-Sam, 1980; Bruce et al., 1979; Craft, Shaw, & Cartlidge, 1972; Goldstein & Levin, 1987; Rowbotham, MacIver, Dickson, & Bousfield, 1954; Rutter, Chadwick, Schaffer, & Brown, 1980). In most instances the child has been injured as a pedestrian, rather than as a passenger. There are many other common causes of TBI in childhood, and these vary across different age groups. In preschool age children (0–4 years), accidents in the home, many of which are falls, account for a large proportion of cases. The frequency of child abuse as a cause of head injury in young children has only recently been recognised, but at present it is not possible to obtain reliable statistics regarding the incidence of such injuries. In school-aged children a higher proportion of injuries result from accidents outside the home, such as falls, moving objects such as a bat or a ball striking the head, and automobile accidents where the child was a cyclist or a pedestrian. In adolescents there is a dramatic increase in head injuries where the adolescent was a driver or passenger, and alcohol or drugs are involved (Chorazy, 1985). As in adults, the number of male children and adolescents who sustain head injuries consistently and significantly outweighs the number of females (Chorazy, 1985).

PATHOPHYSIOLOGY

There are also pathophysiological differences in the impact of TBI in children relative to adults. As Levin et al. (1982a) have pointed out, differences in aetiology may contribute to such variation. Falls or low speed accidents may result in less severe rotational acceleration than that which is associated with motor vehicle accidents. However, the skull of a child is less rigid than that of an adult and cerebral convolutions are relatively shallow (Gurdjian & Webster, 1958; Jennett, 1972). This may provide a cushioning effect, but it has been suggested that the greater flexibility of the skull leads to increased deformation of the skull and more generalised shearing within the cortex (Gurdjian & Webster 1958; Jennett, 1972). There is evidence of differences in the sites of intracranial haemorrhage with age (Jamieson & Yelland, cited in Oddy, 1984b). Bruce, Schut, Bruno, Wood, and Sutton (1978) found a relatively lower incidence of mass lesions and a higher incidence of diffuse cerebral swelling in children.

PREDISPOSING FACTORS

Some studies have found that children who sustain TBI tend to come from socially disadvantaged families and to have premorbid emotional, behavioural and/or learning difficulties (Klonoff, 1971; Rutter et al., 1980). On the other hand, a more recent study conducted in Australia by Pelco, Sawyer, Duffield, Prior, and Kinsella (1992) did not confirm this finding. The implications of the presence of pre-existing difficulties are somewhat more complex for children than they are in adults. These will be explored in a later section of this chapter.

RECOVERY

It was, for many years, believed that children recover better from TBI than adults. Indeed mortality rates following paediatric head injury are lower than in adults (Bruce et al., 1978). Children may also show more impressive resolution of focal motor and sensory deficits (Bruce et al., 1979; Nici & Logue, 1984). Variations in aetiology may contribute to such differences. However, these differences cannot necessarily be assumed to be true for cognitive functions.

Some research on early versus late brain injury in animals by Kennard (1936, 1938, 1940) has suggested that the immature brain exhibits greater potential for recovery. On the other hand, it is also known that immature organs and those undergoing development are the most susceptible to damage (Dobbing, 1968; Johnson & Almli, 1978). More recent studies have shown the principle of greater plasticity for the young brain to be an oversimplification of the complex interaction of variables that must be considered. Damage to the young, as opposed to the mature brain, may disrupt the future acquisition of abilities. Goldman (1971, 1974) researched early versus late-appearing deficits following brain injury in young and old animals. She suggested that some of the apparent recovery in young animals immediately following brain injury may be the result of the functional immaturity of that brain area. Behavioural deficits may not appear until a later age, when those areas would normally become functional. Even Kennard's research did show late-developing deficits in infant-lesioned monkeys. This issue may be particularly pertinent in the case of TBI, where injury to the frontal lobes is particularly common. Since some frontal lobe functions may develop relatively later than other functions, deficits in frontal lobe function might not manifest themselves immediately following injury, but may develop over time.

Goldman (1971, 1974) hypothesised that the young animal brain has areas that are not yet "committed" to a specific function. These areas can sometimes take over the functions usually performed by an area that has been damaged. In humans this process has been explored most extensively with regard to the capacity of the right cerebral hemisphere to subsume language functions following early damage to the left hemisphere (Basser, 1962; Landsell, 1969; Milner, 1974; all cited in Nici & Logue, 1984). However, in instances where language seems to have been taken over by the right cerebral hemisphere in children, such a development has been accomplished at the expense of some other normally right hemisphere functions (Teuber, 1975; Woods & Teuber, 1973). These children's overall abilities are also compromised (Milner, 1974; Woods & Teuber, 1973).

Many studies have now demonstrated long-term neuropsychological deficits following severe TBI in children (Black, Blumer, Wellner, & Walker, 1971; Brink, Garrett, Hale, Woo-Sam, & Nickel, 1970; Chadwick, Rutter, Brown, Shaffer, & Traub, 1981; Heiskanen & Kaste, 1974; Jaffe et al., 1992, 1993; Klonoff, Low, & Clark, 1977; Knights et al., 1991; Levin & Eisenberg, 1979a; Levin, Eisenberg, Wigg, & Kobayashi, 1982b; Prior, Kinsella, Sawyer, Bryan, & Anderson, 1994). There have, however, been methodological problems in many of the follow-up studies conducted to date. These include a lack of longitudinal research, a failure to consistently measure and integrate indices of severity, a lack of appropriate screening criteria for premorbid emotional and learning difficulties and previous head injury, inadequate premorbid measures of intellectual functioning and academic achievement, excessive use of IQ tests, rather than more sensitive measures of specific cognitive functions, and a failure to use matched control groups. Whilst such problems limit the conclusions which may be drawn from some studies, there are several lines of evidence suggesting a causal link between brain injury and cognitive impairment in children. The presence of a recovery curve adds support to this link. A number of studies have shown substantial improvement in cognitive functions, particularly during the first one to two years post-injury (Black et al., 1971; Chadwick et al., 1981; Jaffe et al., 1993; Klonoff & Paris, 1974), but continuing up to five years after injury (Klonoff et al., 1977).

There is also evidence of a relationship between severity of injury and degree of neuropsychological impairment. Duration of coma has shown a moderate relationship with residual intellectual performance (Brink et al., 1970; Klonoff & Paris, 1974; Klonoff et al., 1977; Levin & Eisenberg, 1979a; Levin et al., 1982a; Winogron, Knights, & Bawden, 1984), children with the briefest periods of impaired consciousness having higher IQs. Jaffe et al. (1992, 1993) demonstrated a significant correlation between severity of injury, as determined by initial Glasgow Coma Scale scores, and performance on a range of cognitive measures. Other studies have reported a direct relationship between duration of post-traumatic amnesia (PTA) and outcome. Chadwick et al. (1981) found some degree of cognitive impairment was common following injuries giving rise to a PTA of at least 2 weeks, and that impairment tended to be lasting if the duration of PTA was greater than 3 weeks. Conversely, they concluded that no cognitive sequelae, transient or permanent, were present when the PTA was less than 24 hours.

COGNITIVE SEQUELAE OF MILD TBI IN CHILDREN

Results of studies of children with mild TBI have revealed little evidence of permanent cognitive sequelae. Jordan, Cannon, and Murdoch (1992) found no deficits in language competence or naming ability in mildly injured children studied up to 10 years post-injury. Knights et al. (1991), Fay et al. (1993) and Prior et al. (1994) also reported no ongoing impairments on a broad range of cognitive tests following mild paediatric TBI. Chadwick et al. (1981) concluded that no cognitive sequelae, transient or permanent, were present when the PTA was less than 24 hours. However, a careful examination of the results of this study did reveal a transient but significant deficit in the so-called "mildly" injured group (PTA less than seven days) on the WISC-R Coding subtest.

A significant issue in assessing the presence or otherwise of cognitive impairments following mild TBI is that of the sensitivity of the tests used to measure such impairments. The use of more specific tests of attention and speed of information processing, similar to those which have proved sensitive to deficits following mild head injury in adults, may be necessary to demonstrate the presence of cognitive impairment. The evidence of a transient impairment on the WISC-R Coding subtest in the study by Chadwick et al. (1981) exemplifies this. Chadwick et al. also used a version of the Paced Auditory Serial Addition Test (PASAT), based on the test devised by Gronwall and Sampson (1974) for testing adults. Unfortunately, however, they administered this test only once, 27 months after injury and found no significant deficits at this stage. There is a need for further research using such tests, before definitive conclusions can be drawn regarding the presence or otherwise of cognitive deficits following mild TBI in children. It remains possible that, as in adults, mild TBI results in transient deficits in attention, psychomotor speed and memory.

COGNITIVE DEFICITS DISPLAYED BY CHILDREN
FOLLOWING MODERATE OR SEVERE TBI

Unfortunately many of the follow-up studies in children have looked only at changes in IQ scores following TBI, and these tell us little about the specific nature of the deficits. As has been noted in Chapter 1, the use of such global measures may mask the presence of subtle problems, especially in areas such as attention, memory and executive function. There is certainly a need for further development and use of tests sensitive to these difficulties. It may be for this reason that there has been a widely held assumption that TBI results in more generalised impairment of intelligence in children, as opposed to the specific deficits seen in adults, namely problems with attention, memory, planning and problem-solving. A close examination of the evidence now available actually suggests that children with moderate and severe TBI show many deficits similar to those seen in adults.

Levin and Eisenberg (1979b) found that memory impairment was the most common cognitive deficit following TBI in children. Almost half of the group of subjects, who had injuries of varying severity, showed memory dysfunction. Levin et al. (1982b) examined the recovery of verbal and visual memory at least six months post-injury in matched groups of children and adolescents. Severe TBI resulted in residual impairment in the retrieval of verbal information from long-term storage in both age groups, and this was of comparable severity. Visual recognition memory was impaired in the children, but not the adolescents. The nature of the children's errors suggested a difficulty in inhibiting responses during continuous recall, noted to be associated with attentional problems on vigilance tasks. Jaffe et al. (1992) also found a consistent decline in verbal learning performance with increasing levels of injury severity. The injured children performed most poorly on free recall, but were able to benefit from cues. It seems clear that learning and memory skills are significantly impaired following severe TBI in children.

Although attentional difficulties are reported anecdotally with great frequency following TBI in children, there have, unfortunately, been relatively few attempts to study attentional deficits in brain-injured children. This is partly due to problems in the definition of attention and its multidimensional nature. Following from this, there are few well-developed tools to measure aspects of attention in children. Measures of attention most commonly used with children have included digit span tasks, continuous performance/vigilance measures and direct reinforcement of latency tasks. Kaufmann, Fletcher, and Levin (1994) reported persistent disturbance of attention one year after severe TBI

(Kaufmann, 1989, cited by Kaufmann et al., 1994). Children with severe injuries had difficulty inhibiting responses to distracting stimuli (Hannay, 1989, cited by Kaufmann et al., 1994). Younger children with comparable injuries performed more poorly on a continuous performance test, after the removal of normal developmental differences. The findings suggested that this difficulty contributed significantly to observed variability of performance on a memory task. It is important to be aware that attentional problems may contribute to difficulties with memory tests. The results obtained by Levin and Eisenberg (1979b) using the visual recognition memory task would support this contention. There is, however, a need for more comprehensive studies of attentional deficits and their impact on other cognitive functions following TBI in children.

Numerous studies have shown reduced speed of performance after paediatric head injury across a broad range of injury severity. As van Zomeren and his colleagues (van Zomeren, Brouwer, & Deelman, 1984) and Ponsford and Kinsella (1992) have shown, reduced speed of information processing may contribute to attentional difficulties. In children, reduced speed of performance has been especially apparent on visuomotor tasks. Chadwick et al. (1981), Winogron et al. (1984), Knights et al. (1991), and Jaffe et al. (1992, 1993) found reduced speed on tests such as Coding, Manual Dexterity, Finger Tapping, Purdue Pegboard, the Trail Making Test, and the Tactual Performance Test, to be amongst the most salient deficits in children with severe TBI.

Whilst verbal functions have been reported to be less affected than other abilities, there is evidence of linguistic impairment following severe TBI. Ewing-Cobbs, Fletcher, and Levin (1985) reported impaired performances on visual confrontation naming, object description, verbal fluency and writing to dictation in children with moderate to severe TBI. In more recent studies of a severely injured group of children, Jordan and colleagues (Jordan & Murdoch, 1990; Jordan, Ozanne, & Murdoch, 1988, 1990) also reported the presence of reduced performance scores on overall measures of language competence and measures of naming ability. Dennis (1992) found evidence of word-finding difficulties, whilst Chapman et al. (1992) revealed the presence of impaired information structure in the discourse of severe TBI children and adolescents. Winogron et al. (1984) also found significant deficits in verbal fluency in severely head-injured children. Chadwick et al. (1981) noted residual impairment on the WISC-R Similarities subtest, a test of the ability to deal with abstract verbal concepts, at one year post-injury.

These tests of higher language skills also tap executive functions attributed to the frontal lobes. It is quite possible that poor self-monitoring and reduced abstract thinking abilities contributed to the poor performances on tasks such as verbal fluency and Similarities. Impaired planning and problem-solving skills may have led to lowered scores on WISC-R Performance subtests. Wishart et al. (cited by Oddy, 1993) have also reported poor performances of children on tests commonly associated with frontal lobe function, namely, Verbal Fluency, Category Test, Part B of the Trail Making Test, and Picture Arrangement. Moreover, Chadwick et al. (1981) found significant residual impairment on the Matching Familiar Figures Test, a test of impulsivity.

In one of the best controlled studies conducted to date, Jaffe et al. (1992) found a marked decline in performance in severely injured children on what they classified as adaptive problem-solving tasks involving mental flexibility and speed, namely Progressive Figures and Colour Form (used for younger children) and Trail Making Part B (for older children), as well as, to a lesser extent, the Category Test. Prior et al. (1994) reported significantly more perseverative errors on the Wisconsin Card Sorting Test and greater difficulty in solving the Austin Maze in children with moderate and severe injuries relative to those with mild TBI. Levin (1994) reported significant deficits on the Tower of London task in children with severe TBI aged 6–16 years. There was evidence of increased rule-breaking and greater difficulty in planning the solution to more complex tasks, particularly in children with frontal lobe lesions.

Mateer and Williams (1991) carried out a series of single-case studies involving two children who had sustained severe TBI with evidence of frontal lobe injury in the third year of life, followed for at least five years. Another two children, injured between the ages of seven and nine, were followed for three to seven years post-injury. Mateer and Williams demonstrated consistent patterns of ongoing cognitive dysfunction, manifested in attentional problems, such as distractibility and disinhibition of response which affected memory performance, and inconsistencies in performances on measures of reading speed, writing efficiency and maths worksheets, as well as in school grades. No linguistic problems were apparent, but all children showed difficulties with pragmatic aspects of communication. Poor behavioural regulation, causing irritability, moodiness, impulsivity, and impaired social awareness were also common. Although it is not possible to speak with confidence about frontal lobe function in children, Diamond (1988) has suggested that the prefrontal cortex mediates the performance of behavioural tasks as early as the first year of life. This supports the contention that prefrontal zones may be partly functional at an earlier stage than has previously been assumed. From the evidence available there does seem to be a pattern of test performance which is suggestive of the presence of executive dysfunction in children with TBI. There is certainly a need for more comprehensive research in this area.

INTERACTION BETWEEN AGE AND RECOVERY

An issue which is debated in the literature is that of whether the age of the child affects potential for recovery. Do those who are younger show greater potential for recovery? Do younger children suffer more generalised cognitive impairment? Are those abilities which are most well-established at the time of injury (e.g. language) least likely to be affected? There are no clear answers to these questions provided by the studies conducted to date. Whilst Levin et al. (1982a) have reported evidence of more generalised impairment in children injured as infants or toddlers, Knights et al. (1991) found no significant differences in improvement on IQ scores between children aged under, and those over 10 years. Indeed, they felt the data suggested that the younger group made a more rapid and complete recovery. This was also the finding of Chadwick et al. (1981) and Klonoff et al. (1977). There is, at this point in time, no clear evidence that those who are younger suffer either more or less impairment than adults.

SCHOLASTIC PERFORMANCE FOLLOWING TBI

One very significant difference between children and adults is that children must go to school. In this setting they are expected to learn and acquire new skills, not just resume a familiar routine in the home or at work. Impairment of memory, attention and speed of thinking, so essential for the acquisition of new skills in the educational setting, may significantly affect progress at school, and thereby have lasting effects on the child's future. In this respect the impact of TBI in a child is potentially greater than that in an adult. There may be cumulative effects over time, leading to delays or even failure to acquire certain cognitive skills. Goldstein and Levin (1985) have suggested that preschoolers, in whom cognitive skills are developing rapidly, may be at risk for developing the most significant academic delays.

Several studies have shown persistent delays in reading, arithmetic performance and other school-related tasks in severely head-injured children with a PTA greater than three weeks (Chadwick et al., 1981; Jaffe et al., 1992, 1993; Knights et al., 1991; Prior et al., 1994; Schaffer, Bijur, Chadwick, & Rutter, 1980). A greater number of studies have found that a significant proportion of children with TBI have been considered by their teachers to be experiencing difficulties with schoolwork or have required placement in special classes (Brink et al., 1970; Chadwick et al., 1981; Flach & Malmros, 1972; Fuld & Fisher,

1977; Heiskanen & Kaste, 1974; Klonoff et al., 1977; Knights et al., 1991). In some of these studies, such as that of Klonoff et al. (1977), children with mild injuries were included, although the severity of injury of those experiencing ongoing difficulties in this study was not specifically reported. Chadwick et al. (1981) have cautioned against the conclusion that less severe head injuries do not affect scholastic performance. They pointed out that reduced speed of work performance and impaired learning abilities may lead to detrimental effects on scholastic attainment becoming apparent only gradually, as the child's increasing chronological age begins to outstrip the reduced rate of school progress. The finding of Jaffe et al. (1993) that, despite considerable recovery in cognitive test performance, there was a relative lack of growth in the injured students' academic attainment at one year after injury supports this contention. Further longitudinal studies may clarify this issue.

BEHAVIOURAL AND PSYCHIATRIC SEQUELAE

Methodological problems plagued many early studies of behaviour change following TBI in children. The issue is particularly complicated by the finding mentioned earlier that children who sustain TBI may tend to have behavioural or emotional disturbance prior to injury and to come from families in psychosocial adversity (Rutter et al., 1980). One of the most carefully controlled prospective studies in this area was conducted by Brown, Chadwick, Shaffer, Rutter, and Traub (1981). They studied two groups, one "mild" group of children whose PTA ranged from 1 hour to 7 days, and another group of "severe" injuries, whose PTA persisted for at least a week. These children were matched on a variety of social and demographic variables with a control group of children who had sustained orthopaedic injuries. The "mild" injury group had a higher rate of reported behavioural disturbance prior to injury than the control group, but the "severe" injury group did not.

Brown et al. (1981) examined the rate of psychiatric or behavioural disorder in children without evidence of premorbid problems. Although "mild" injury was not associated with an increased incidence of behavioural disturbance, severe injury was. Behavioural problems commonly reflected pre-injury behaviour, such that pre-existing difficulties were exacerbated after injury. Adverse social circumstances in the pre-injury environment were also related to the presence of behavioural disturbances following severe TBI. Brown et al. found that the degree of cognitive impairment had a weak relationship with post-injury behavioural sequelae. The relationship of behaviour disturbance with severity of injury was much weaker than the relationship between cognitive impairment and injury severity. These results suggested that the presence of behaviour problems after injury was influenced by factors other than severity, such as the children's pre-accident behaviour, cognitive level and psychosocial circumstances.

This finding of significant adaptive behavioural change following severe TBI in children has been replicated in subsequent studies by Fletcher, Ewing-Cobbs, Miner, Levin, and Eisenberg (1990) and Knights et al. (1991). Both of these studies employed standardised behavioural measures (Vineland Adaptive Behaviour Scales, Child Behaviour Checklist, Connors Parent and Teacher Questionnaires), as opposed to the structured clinical interview used by Brown et al. (1981). Fletcher et al. also screened out all children with pre-existing psychological problems. These studies, together with a more recent study by Fay et al. (1993), revealed no evidence of behavioural change following mild TBI. As Fletcher et al. (1990) concluded, if behaviour problems are reported following mild TBI, they may reflect pre-existing difficulties.

Examination of the nature of behaviour change in these studies reveals few consistencies. In Brown et al.'s (1981) study there was no single pattern of disrupted behaviour following injury, with the exception of a tendency towards marked social disinhibition in severely injured children. It would be reasonable to conclude that this pattern, which bears a close relationship to the so-called frontal lobe syndrome seen in adults, was a direct result of brain injury. However, the view that TBI leads to a characteristic behavioural syndrome in children, including impulsive, overactive, and hyperkinetic behaviour has not been supported in these recent studies. The nature of the behavioural changes appears to be more variable than in adults. There are a number of possible reasons for this.

According to Fletcher et al. (1990) and Fletcher and Ewing-Cobbs (1991), the lack of consistent findings may partly reflect the insensitivity in the methods of assessment used. Reports of change are largely subjective. The scope for reporting may be limited by the nature of the questions asked and the forced-choice response options on behaviour checklists. Furthermore, as Oddy (1993) has indicated, parents may attribute subtle changes in behaviour to normal age-related development, or tolerate behavioural alterations due to relief over the child's recovery, resulting in an underestimation of the degree of change. Whilst some of these criticisms may be applied to research on behaviour change in adults, it is clear that more objective measures of behaviour change should be developed.

Bearing in mind these methodological problems, it must be acknowledged that variability in behaviour patterns following paediatric TBI may also reflect the fact that children are more vulnerable emotionally and behaviourally, and their behaviour may be influenced by many factors other than the brain injury itself. Such factors include the child's pre-injury personality, social circumstances, and the way in which the family copes with the injury. The findings of Brown et al. (1981) support this, as do the more recent results of Rivara et al. (1993). They found that, in addition to injury severity, better overall pre-injury family functioning, a high level of family cohesion, positive family relationships and lower levels of "control" (family hierarchy and rules that are rigid) were significantly associated with good adaptive functioning, social competence and global functioning in the injured child at one year after injury.

Brown et al. (1981) found that changes in parental handling of children with TBI were common during the two years after injury. Parents may show a decreased use of discipline and be overprotective. Gaidolfi and Vignolo (1980) reported overprotective attitudes to be the most common response, particularly in families where the injury was severe. In exploring the stresses on families of children who have sustained TBI, Brown et al. noted that a decline in family relationships occurred in a significant proportion of families of severe TBI children. Such a decline appeared to result in a higher incidence of behavioural disturbance in the injured child. This finding supports the contention that injured children may be disproportionately affected by the stress on the family as a result of TBI. Jones (1987) found that children with TBI experience significantly increased levels of anxiety.

Children have particular emotional and psychological needs at different stages of development, and the injury may prevent these needs being met. Young children, forced to be in hospital for long periods, may experience separation anxiety and develop fears of death, medical procedures and pain. Feelings of helplessness in a child with TBI may lead to expresssions of violence (Barin, Hanchett, Jacob, & Scott, 1985). Older children and adolescents suffer from being different from their peers. Poor body image and social isolation can result in significant loss of self-esteem and depression. The process of becoming independent of parental support and influence, so central during adolescence, is significantly disrupted by TBI. Resultant "acting-out" behaviour may be exacerbated by a reduction in behavioural control resulting from frontal lobe injury. There is a significant need for further research into the environmental factors which influence children's behaviour following TBI.

SUMMARY OF DIFFERENCES BETWEEN TBI IN CHILDREN AND ADULTS

There are a number of differences between the impact of TBI in children and in adults. The causes of injury are more variable in children, and their pathophysiological responses to injury differ. Whilst there is some evidence to suggest that children have an increased probability of survival and show better motor–sensory recovery, it is clear that, like adults, children suffer ongoing impairment of cognitive function following severe TBI. From group studies there is, at this point in time, little evidence of lasting cognitive or behavioural impairment as a result of mild TBI, although this may occur in individual cases. The pattern of cognitive deficits following severe TBI depends to some extent on the age of the child and the level of premorbid cognitive development. It does resemble that seen in adults in certain respects, in that memory and speed of information processing appear to be particularly affected. There is also some evidence of impairment of attention, verbal fluency, abstract thinking and adaptive problem-solving abilities, although there is a need for further research in these areas. Behavioural changes are also common following severe TBI in children, but these follow a less predictable pattern than that seen in adults. They are influenced by pre-injury behaviour and psychosocial circumstances.

Both cognitive and behavioural deficits in children with TBI are more complex and variable than in adults, because they must be viewed within the context of a dynamic developmental process. Maturational, psychosocial and cognitive factors interact with injury far more in children than in adults. A child's deficits can only be viewed in relation to pretraumatic levels of development and behaviour. Infants and young children must not only regain former functions, but also continue to acquire new skills to set a foundation for further development. Thus, deficits might appear after a delay or accumulate over time. Finally, children may be more vulnerable emotionally, being disproportionately affected by the impact of their injuries on their families and on their social relationships.

THE *REAL* APPROACH TO ASSESSMENT AND REHABILITATION OF CHILDREN WITH TBI

It will be clear that the needs of children differ from those of adults in a number of ways, so that specialised assessment and rehabilitation services are extremely important. The need to follow the principles of the REAL approach to rehabilitation following TBI is possibly even greater in children than in adults. The complexity of the problems being confronted necessitates close teamwork across a broad range of disciplines. It is essential that family are involved at all levels of assessment and management. They need to provide a comprehensive understanding of the child's personality, behaviour patterns, and abilities prior to injury, to be active participants in the therapy process and to assist in planning for the child's future.

TBI children can be accurately assessed only within the context of their previous developmental stage and behaviour patterns. For social and emotional reasons it is particularly important to return children to their normal environment as early as possible. There is thus even greater pressure to conduct the rehabilitation process within the context of the child's everyday life. The fact that the child usually returns to the school environment, and potentially develops increasing scholastic difficulties over time, necessitates the provision of ongoing assistance extending into adulthood. Psychological support is also essential, since TBI children and adolescents may be particularly vulnerable emotionally. The following sections contain suggested guidelines for the implementation of the REAL approach as it applies to children with TBI, with particular emphasis on those aspects of assessment and rehabilitation which are unique to children and their families, and which have not been discussed in other chapters.

Assessment following paediatric TBI

The staff assessing and treating an acutely injured child should have special expertise in working with children. In particular, they need to be capable of understanding the child's developmental level physically, linguistically, cognitively, behaviourally and emotionally.

Given the clear relationship between indices of injury severity and outcome, there is, as with adults, a need to use objective measures of coma and PTA. However, these should be appropriate to the child's abilities. Some items from the Glasgow Coma Scale, such as the ability to obey commands or give an appropriate verbal response, are inappropriate as applied to young children, especially under the age of two years. If the Glasgow Coma Scale is to be used, the verbal response would need to be scored by giving the child a score of five if there is any vocalisation and zero if no crying occurs. The motor component of the scale may be applied after the first few months of life, leaving out the response to command. According to Bell and Britton (1989), the best motor response is a powerful predictor of outcome. Raimondi and Hirschauer (1984) developed the Children's Coma Scale to be used with infants and toddlers. The scale ranges from 3 to 11 points and includes such items as "cries" for the best verbal response and "flexes/extends" for the best motor response. Raimondi and Hirschauer found that scores on this scale correlated moderately well with global categories of outcome. A similar scale has been developed by Hahn, Chyng, Barthel, Bailes, Flannery, and McLone (1988). Although the usefulness of these Children's Coma Scales in understanding recovery patterns awaits further investigation, the development and use of age-appropriate scales is to be encouraged.

Similar problems apply with the use of adult measures of PTA to assess children. The Westmead PTA Scale has been validated for use in children over the age of seven years (Marosszeky, Batchelor, Shores, Marosszeky, Klein-Boonschate, & Fahey, 1993). Ewing-Cobbs, Levin, Fletcher, Miner, and Eisenberg (1990) have developed a children's version of the Galveston Orientation and Amnesia Test, known as the Children's Orientation and Amnesia Test (COAT). The COAT consists of a series of simple questions examining temporal orientation, recall of autobiographical information, and immediate and short-term memory. Norms are available which permit specification of the degree of PTA in children as young as 3 years. A recent study by Iverson, Iverson, and Barton (1994) has provided reference data for interpreting COAT scores of children with TBI who have learning disabilities.

Assessment of a child's feeding capacity and communication skills must also be appropriate to that child's developmental stage, as should any augmentative communication systems that are developed by the speech pathologist. Typical aphasia batteries and tests designed for children with congenital language impairments focus on knowledge of linguistic codes (syntax, morphology, lexicon). These are generally less useful for assessing the language disturbances of children with TBI than an assessment of the child's potential to learn language, as well as the ability to process, mentally manipulate and produce language in an efficient and organised manner (Baxter, Cohen, & Ylvisaker, 1985).

Following the principles of the REAL approach, the assessment of other cognitive deficits should also take place within the context of the child's premorbid level of ability. Statements that a child is functioning "within normal limits" on an IQ test do not reflect the degree of loss to a child who was previously functioning in the superior range. Conversely, the finding that a child who now demonstrates a borderline IQ was also borderline before the injury may suggest that the injury is less likely to interfere with school progress.

In the absence of a reliable measure of premorbid IQ, other information sources should be used to assess premorbid functioning. School records may offer an estimate of the child's previous scholastic performance in a variety of topic areas. Parental reports and checklists can also be useful sources of information, particularly for children who have not yet started school. Parental questionnaires should provide information about developmental milestones, educational history (e.g. remedial classes) and psychosocial factors. Interview formats such as the Vineland Adaptive Behaviour Scale (Sparrow, Balla, & Cicchetti, 1984) assess functioning in areas such as communication and daily living skills. Those such as the Connors Parent Questionnaire (Connors, 1973) and the Child Behaviour Checklist (Achenbach & Edelbrook, 1983) assess emotional/behavioural functioning.

Such questionnaires should be given as close as possible to the time of injury and use the same informant over serial administrations (Rutter et al., 1980). The limitations of these relatively subjective methods of reporting, as discussed earlier in relation to assessment of behaviour change, need to be borne in mind. Parents may over-rate the child's premorbid ability, under-rate problems after injury, or fail to report on problems not covered on a checklist or questionnaire. Teacher checklists can offer a measure of behaviours, such as attention and peer interaction, both pre- and post-injury, although, once again, there are limitations in the use of subjective reports.

There is a need for the development of better tests of specific cognitive abilities relevant to TBI in children, rather than the tendency to rely on IQ tests. Areas needing careful assessment include aspects of attention, speed of information processing, learning and memory, verbal expression, reading speed and comprehension, writing, arithmetic skills, auditory processing, visual and perceptual organisation, judgement, self-monitoring, planning, and problem-solving skills.

Consistent with the REAL philosophy, the assessment process should extend beyond the structured one-to-one test situation, which may not elicit distractibility and other attentional problems, organisational and adaptive difficulties, subtle problems with memory, information processing and communication, or the effects of fatigue. Furthermore, many cognitive tests assess skills or knowledge acquired prior to the injury, rather than the child's capacity to learn new information or skills. It is essential that therapists and teachers work together systematically to assess skills in these and other areas, particularly the child's ability to cope with increasing demands in terms of speed and complexity of information to be absorbed, distractions, organisational and adaptive functions and initiative. As Ylvisaker (1988) points out, identification of strengths and weaknesses within the classroom setting provides a structure for classroom-based intervention. This may involve task modification, cueing and/or compensatory strategies. It is also vital that reassessment be conducted at regular intervals over a number of years, so that relevant changes can be made as the child develops and recovers. Skills which fail to develop or be acquired at a later stage may be detected and appropriate support given.

In assessing behaviour, it is important to take careful account of the child's developmental level. Behavioural assessment should be based on observation, together with reports from parents, teachers and any others involved with the child. Because of the possibility of pre-existing behaviour problems, a careful history needs to be taken. An assessment should also be made of the child's emotional state, to detect changes in mood or self-esteem, anxiety, and depression.

Developmental considerations also influence the assessment and treatment of motor dysfunction. Infants and young children must not only regain former developmental and motor functions, but also develop additional motor skills to set a foundation for further development. Older children, on the other hand, must relearn previously integrated movements. Children's motivation in treatment will vary with chronological and developmental age. A seven-year-old child, for instance, may be interested only in getting back on a bike, whereas an adolescent may be concerned primarily with physical appearance.

Rehabilitation

Being in hospital can be very frightening for a child. Every effort should be made to surround the child with familiar pictures and toys and have family members present and involved in all aspects of the child's care. Parents will be extremely anxious, so that staff need to take every opportunity to explain what is going on and answer questions. Further discussion of issues pertaining to the families of TBI children is contained in a later section of this chapter. Other issues of relevance to management in the acute stages of recovery have been explored in detail in Chapter 2.

It is in the injured child's interests socially and emotionally to return home as soon as possible, and every attempt should be made to achieve this. However, children with severe TBI should not be discharged before the family understands how to manage them and appropriate arrangements have been made for ongoing therapy and other necessary support services. Discharge may not be appropriate if the child is still in PTA. Having a child who is in PTA at home places a very heavy burden on families, may lead to overstimulation of the child and the development of behaviour problems, which might have been avoided. Like adults, children in PTA need a quiet, familiar and well-structured environment, which can be manipulated to minimise agitation and the potential development of maladaptive behaviours. If this can be arranged in the home, this will be desirable, but it is not always possible.

In planning for discharge there is a need to seek out facilities for rehabilitation in the home and/or in outpatient settings nearby. Given the general lack of specialised paediatric rehabilitation facilities catering to children with TBI, this is likely to be difficult. However, it is not appropriate to mix children with adults in a rehabilitation setting. Children need far more structure and should be able to mix with their peers, rather than adults with TBI. Paediatric rehabilitation facilities should also provide for play therapy and educational assessment. Where specialised community-based facilities do not exist, services from a number of sources will need to be co-ordinated. These may include medical, nursing and therapy services, psychological assessment and guidance, normal school services, special education assistance and integration support. Given the lack of specialised paediatric rehabilitation facilities suitable for children with TBI, the "Whatever it Takes" model of Willer and Corrigan (1994), discussed in Chapter 7, is likely to be particularly applicable. Good case management is seen to be an essential component to the provision of a co-ordinated service. It is acknowledged that the guidelines suggested in this chapter represent the ideal, and that in many cases hospitals and families will need to seek out whatever services are available to fulfil the injured child's needs.

Parents should be provided with detailed information regarding progress, play an active role in the choices made regarding the rehabilitation of their child, and be involved in the therapy process. They will be the most important therapists for the child in the years to come. As with adults, some families may place unrealistic or inappropriate demands on the injured child and others may be overprotective. Such situations need to be handled carefully and tactfully, as it is extremely important to maintain open communication and a sense of trust. As Waaland and Kreutzer (1988) have pointed out, in view of the established association between parenting, family coping and other environmental factors, and the development of ongoing behavioural and psychiatric sequelae, early family intervention will hopefully minimise the development of such problems.

Guidance and support should be given in the appropriate management of behaviour, following the principles outlined in Chapter 6. Parents may also require assistance in dealing with the emotional responses of the injured child. It is important that families gain an understanding of the ways in which the child's behaviour and emotions may be influenced by the injury, as well as changes in circumstances and the nature of interactions of others. The structured routine which was present in the hospital needs, as far as possible, to be maintained in the home. Siblings, teachers, and any others having frequent contact with the child should also be involved in this process.

Suggested guidelines for return to school

Because of the unique demands of a learning environment, the consequences of inadequate preparation for, or inappropriate timing of, return to school can be quite disastrous. Teachers are usually extremely busy, having many different demands placed upon them. They may not spontaneously ask questions about what to expect from a TBI child or adolescent, or how to handle forthcoming problems. This may reflect a lack of understanding of such injuries, particularly where there has been a good physical recovery, or a reluctance to reveal uncertainty about managing the educational domain. Where there has been inadequate preparation for school reentry, problems that develop may be presented more in the form of complaints about the TBI student's failure to carry out tasks or comply with school rules, rather than as problems the staff might have in understanding the needs of the student.

Early contact should be made with the school to establish good communication and encourage the involvement of teachers and fellow students in the rehabilitation process. They should be encouraged to visit the injured student in hospital to provide a network of support, and to gain an understanding of the injury and the recovery process. Together with family members, they will be crucial in assisting the injured student's adaptation. It is helpful to hold a meeting involving teachers, therapists and the family early in the rehabilitation phase. This provides an opportunity to convey information regarding the nature of injuries and the possible time frame of the rehabilitation process. However, more importantly, it provides a forum in which the rehabilitation team can learn more about the student, and all parties can participate in setting goals and planning how these are to be achieved. Teachers may be asked to provide a profile of the student's previous strengths and weaknesses, together with samples of work completed prior to injury.

When it is felt that the injured child or adolescent is ready, a visiting teacher may, in close liaison with the school, begin to assess the student's ability to cope with schoolwork and at what level. If no visiting teacher is available, therapists will need to do this in liaison with the child's teacher. Appropriate tasks may then be introduced within the therapy setting. It is usually best to begin with schoolwork which the student has performed some time prior to injury, to maximise the possibility of success. It is likely to be very stressful for the student to experience failure with work which had previously presented little difficulty. Therefore this process needs to be taken very gradually.

Returning to the school environment

For children and adolescents, school meets many needs for socialisation and peer-group identification, as well as education. It is therefore particularly important that plans for return to the school environment be made as soon as it is felt that the student will cope in some capacity. This needs to be prepared for carefully. If it is possible, members of the rehabilitation team should visit the school, carefully assessing the injured student's ability to manage aspects such as the physical environment, timetable, subject content, and transportation. This enables potential problem areas to be pinpointed, so that therapists can work with teachers, fellow students, the family and the injured student to devise solutions to these. The student should also have opportunities to visit the school prior to returning. An attempt should be made to identify sources of support for the student, such as a school chaplain or counsellor.

Rehabilitation staff, as well as the visiting teacher need to meet with teachers involved with the student, providing information regarding the injured student's current strengths and weaknesses, and what specific problems are anticipated. They may work with the teachers to develop ways in which these can be circumvented or overcome, and plan an appropriate schedule of classes. It may be helpful for therapists to observe the child in the classroom to offer further practical advice. However, it is important not to go into the school environment with an attitude of superiority, issuing instructions to teachers and others at the school. Wherever possible the skills and experience of the teachers need to be harnessed to solve problems. Nevertheless, in some schools teachers will be stressed and under-resourced, having little additional time or energy available to give to an injured student. The approach taken to school reintegration will need to take account of this.

Classmates can also prove invaluable in the rehabilitation process, and they should be involved, along with the TBI student, as much as possible. They will usually be able to make suggestions or provide practical assistance in solving a range of problems. "Buddies" may help carry books, make sure the TBI student doesn't forget things, or get lost around the school, and has someone to sit with at lunch breaks. Such a network of support from classmates is particularly important for the TBI student, who usually feels different from everyone else, due to prolonged absence and newly acquired scars or disabilities. For older students, the establishment of a "Circle of Support", along the lines suggested by Willer et al. (1993a), and outlined in detail in Chapter 8, is likely to be particularly helpful in meeting this aim.

Most TBI students will need to return to school gradually, because of limited concentration and a tendency to fatigue. The school, therefore, needs to be prepared to be flexible, and to reduce demands on the student. This may involve reducing the number of subjects a student studies, or changing them to suit new limitations. Subjects initially studied should be selected based on an analysis of the cognitive demands they make. For example, it would not be wise for a student with memory and executive difficulties to initially attempt a subject where there is a large amount of material to be learned and significant demands are made upon organisational and conceptual abilities.

For TBI students with planning difficulties, there will be an increased need for structure. Returning to school, with its inherent schedule of classes, to some extent provides this. However, activities and assignments within classes may need additional structuring. For example, TBI students may have particular difficulty in writing an essay without some assistance as to how to plan and structure it, and they may not be able to utilise free time effectively. During instruction, the teacher's directions need to be specific, and clear expectations about the task are required. Instructions may need to be written down in a step-by-step fashion, or presented pictorially for those with reading difficulties. Problems in integrating material through specific modalities, such as reading, could be overcome through the use of other modalities, such as audiotapes. Oral tests may be given. Where memory is a problem, material will need to be simplified, repeated and written down, so that the student can review it. The student may benefit from the use of a diary, although diary use would need to be trained. Teachers should avoid using rote memory tasks to measure learning. For older students, help may be given to organise material and develop ways of enhancing storage and recall of material using mnemonics or cues along the lines discussed in Chapter 4.

Above all, TBI students need accommodation and time—time to make up what has been missed, extended time in testing and completion of assignments, time taken by teachers for repetition of directions and additional assistance, time to get from one place to another, time to recover. The provision of all this support to the TBI student is likely to place an impossible burden on the classroom teacher. If funding can be procured, this burden will be substantially relieved by the provision of an integration aide to assist the student in the classroom. Such an aide, who might be funded either through the educational system, or an insurer, can perform a similar role to that of a job coach in the employment setting. The integration aide, whether appointed by the school, the insurer or the rehabilitation team, will require input from the rehabilitation team along the lines of that given to an attendant carer. The aide should have a comprehensive understanding of the student's cognitive strengths and weaknesses, and appropriate ways of handling problems with mobility, communication and behaviour.

The integration aide may need to be present in the classroom at all times, actively facilitating the student's participation in lessons. Alternatively, the aide may give the student additional coaching or present what is being taught in a way in which it is more likely to be understood or remembered. A well-trained integration aide can be a very useful source of guidance to fellow students and teachers as to how best to manage behaviour problems. The aide can also act as an advocate for the student. Some brain-injured students, particularly adolescents, feel very self-conscious about having an integration aide with them in the classroom. This needs to be given careful consideration, as it is important not to further lower the student's self-esteem. In such cases the aide may have to work with the student outside the classroom.

As with return to work programmes, frequent contact between all those involved in the process of return to school is important. If possible, regular meetings need to be held between the teachers, the integration aide, and rehabilitation staff, as well as the parents, with the TBI student present if appropriate. The aim of such meetings should be to review progress and make necessary adjustments, as well as address any problems. Parental feedback is particularly important. A student may appear to be coping whilst at school, but be exhausted, irritable, and moody at home. This is generally an indication that too many demands are being made on the injured student.

Over time many brain-injured students will be able to cope with increased demands, and will no longer require therapy. Adjustments to the curriculum should be made accordingly. Later, decisions may need to be made as to whether the student should progress to the next level. Such decisions should always be given very careful consideration, weighing the advantages of peer group support against the impact of increasing demands on the student's self-esteem.

Whilst every effort should be made to return and maintain TBI students at their previous school, in a minority of cases, where there is very severe physical disability and a need for ongoing therapy, it may be necessary to move to a "special" school. Just as much care needs to be taken in the integration of TBI students into special schools as into regular schools. Whilst special schools may be geared to cope with the needs of disabled students, the teachers do not necessarily have any greater understanding of the impact of TBI, or how to manage the unique problems associated with TBI, particularly those of a behavioural nature. Ongoing support from the rehabilitation team is very important.

CASE REPORT—SALLY

Sally was aged seven years when she was hit by a car as she ran to retrieve a ball from the road. She was the youngest of three children. Her parents had separated a year before her injury. This had resulted in the onset of some attention-seeking behaviour and bed-wetting at home. Sally had started school the previous year, and had been making progress in learning to read and write, and developing mathematical concepts. Following the accident, in which Sally sustained a severe head injury, she was unconscious for three days. A CT scan revealed no abnormality. Sally remained confused and disoriented for three weeks. She was in the acute hospital throughout this period, her bed being placed in a quiet area. Her mother stayed with her, whilst her grandparents minded the other children. Her father also visited regularly. Her mother was initially distraught. When seen by the social worker she expressed considerable guilt over the fact that she had not been supervising Sally at the time the accident happened, compounding the guilt she already felt over the emotional effects of the marital breakdown on Sally. She was extremely anxious as to what the future would hold.

During her hospital stay, Sally was visited by therapists, but no cognitive or language assessment was conducted. Physically, Sally had some balance problems and clumsiness, but was otherwise recovering satisfactorily. She also made quite rapid gains cognitively after her emergence from PTA. However, it was apparent that she lacked concentration, was forgetful, and somewhat impulsive and irritable. Sally was discharged home shortly after emerging from PTA. Arrangements had been made for her to attend a rehabilitation centre with paediatric facilities for ongoing assessment and therapy on an outpatient basis.

Sally underwent physiotherapy, occupational therapy, speech therapy, and neuropsychological assessment. Interviews were conducted with her mother regarding her developmental history, her behaviour and cognitive abilities prior to and since the injury. Sally's mother noted that Sally was coping well at home from a physical point of view, and could feed and dress herself as before. However, she had become extremely irritable, and the bed-wetting and attention-seeking behaviour already present had worsened. Uncontrollable temper tantrums had become a frequent occurrence in response to the slightest frustration. Her mother also reported that Sally was more active than she had been, and could not sit and concentrate on an activity for any length of time.

Assessment by the physiotherapist revealed that Sally's balance problems were resolving. Neuropsychological assessment showed that Sally was of average ability, and most skills were at or near expected age levels. However, marked attentional difficulties were noted. She performed relatively poorly on verbal learning and memory tasks and the WISC-R Digit Span subtest, showed moderately reduced speed of thinking on the Coding subtest, demonstrated impulsivity on the Block Design and Mazes subtests, and she showed poor attention to detail on Picture Arrangement. She lacked persistence with difficult tasks. Assessment by the visiting teacher established that Sally's academic skills were generally age-appropriate. However, she demonstrated a short attention span, distractibility and slowness in performing school-related tasks.

A meeting was held, involving Sally's class teacher, mother and father, therapists, the neuropsychologist, and the visiting teacher. Her teacher commented that although Sally appeared to have suffered emotionally over her parents' separation, she had been coping well academically. An explanation of TBI and Sally's current strengths and weaknesses was given by the therapists. Some time was spent formulating goals, which were to return to school, deal with Sally's behaviour problems at home and assist her mother to deal with her emotional response. Arrangements were made for Sally to visit the school with her mother, so she could see her school friends again and familiarise herself with the classroom.

The visiting teacher and Sally's therapists introduced some schoolwork into her therapy sessions at the rehabilitation centre. They ascertained that she could only concentrate on tasks for up to 10 minutes at a time. Her concentration was best when she was in a room with no distractions. They were able to gradually extend the period of her concentration to 30 minutes by instituting a chart for recording how long she persisted with tasks, and a reward system, in which she was given smarties every time she extended her period of concentration. A behaviour programme was also set up in consultation with Sally's mother to manage her attention-seeking behaviour and temper tantrums at home.

Sally's mother had counselling to assist her in dealing with her guilt and the day-to-day problems of coping with Sally. Some sessions were also conducted involving Sally's elder sister and brother, to enable them to discuss the impact of Sally's injury on the family and attain an understanding of the nature and effects of Sally's injury.

Six weeks after her injury, Sally returned to school, initially for 2 hours per day in the mornings, followed by a rest, and a further 2 hours at the rehabilitation centre in the afternoon. Her class teacher was given guidelines for managing Sally's restless behaviour. She noted that Sally was slow to complete work, was distractible and at times seemed overwhelmed in the classroom setting. Arrangements were made for her to have an integration aide for two hours each day at the school, replacing the time at the rehabilitation centre. She went over the maths and reading work Sally had been doing in class in a quiet, one-to-one setting. Over the next three months, Sally's time at school was slowly increased, until she attended full-time. Her restless behaviour gradually decreased. Her integration aide was cut back to one hour per day.

At the end of the school year, Sally had fallen behind academically. It was apparent that she was still slow to learn, although she had made some progress with the assistance of her integration aide. Because it was very important to her to remain with her friends, it was decided to allow her to move up to the next grade. The integration support was maintained for the whole of the following year.

It is now three years since Sally's injury. Her progress at school has been slow and she has repeated one grade. She still receives tutoring on a twice-weekly basis. Her mother reports that she is not the same child as before the injury, both behaviourally and academically. She remains irritable in the evenings, being obviously very tired at the end of the day. Her mother has frequent battles with her over the smallest matters. Sally fights with her brother and sister constantly, as they have become intolerant of her unpredictable behaviour. She has also suffered emotionally, having lost confidence in her ability to learn at school. She has become a loner. Some days she does not want to go to school. Clearly, Sally and her family will require follow-up monitoring, assessment, and support for the duration of her education.

CASE REPORT—ROBERT

Robert was 14 when injured in a motor car accident. In addition to multiple orthopaedic injuries, he sustained an extremely severe head injury. He was comatose for approximately seven weeks and had a period of PTA lasting several months. Prior to his injury he had been doing Year Nine at a Technical School. He was described by his mother as a mature, bright, quick-witted, and outgoing lad, who was an accomplished sportsman. Although he did not apply himself very well at school, his ambition was to become a journalist, and he had already been writing some articles for the local newspaper. At the time of the accident, he lived at home in a country town with his mother and stepfather.

Robert had a period of inpatient hospitalisation and rehabilitation in the city about two hours' drive from his home. This lasted 15 months. He was severely disabled. Physically he had a significant tremor and balance problems and was confined to a wheelchair, although he learned to use a walking frame for short distances. Cognitively he was assessed as having been of above average intelligence, but he had slowed information processing, affecting his comprehension at times, memory difficulties and a limited capacity for planning and organisation. He showed good perseverance, and was able to recognise errors he made, but needed structure and guidance to use feedback from errors to improve task performance. He also showed difficulty in generalising or adapting to novel situations. Whilst aware of his problems to some extent, Robert underestimated their severity and implications. Robert's greatest strength, in addition to his intelligence, motivation and willingness to acknowledge problems, was his personable and generally happy nature.

Robert's friends were encouraged to visit him throughout the rehabilitation phase. It was unfortunate in this respect that he was such a distance from his home town, as this did limit opportunities for visiting. Early in the rehabilitation phase, contact was made with Robert's school to explain the nature of his injuries and the plans for his rehabilitation and return to school, although the time frame of this was somewhat uncertain at this stage. Four months prior to his return to school, Robert's speech pathologist, occupational therapist and psychologist visited the school. They went on a tour of the school with Robert, his mother and the school's integration co-ordinator in order to assess any modifications which would be needed to enable Robert to move around.

They later met to discuss plans for his return to the school. It was decided that, given his interest in pursuing a writing career, Robert would initially attempt Year 10 English. He would require one-to-one assistance from an integration aide for 10 hours per week in order to do this. Application was made to the Education Department for this assistance. Alterations needed to be made to the entrances to classrooms in order to improve accessibility, and application was made to the Education Department for these also. He could use a motorised scooter to get around between classrooms and a frame within classrooms, but would need assistance to enter and leave classrooms as he could not use steps or open doors. It was decided to recruit buddies from amongst his schoolfriends to provide this help. Robert could manage existing disabled toilet facilities. As a major aim of returning to school was to provide socialisation, Robert would remain in the school over lunch breaks and his buddies would assist him at these times.

In preparation for his return home, it was decided to reduce Robert's inpatient therapy programme to three days per week, so he could spend more time at home. A local occupational therapist was recruited to help structure Robert's days at home. She continued to work with him after he had returned to school. An attendant carer was also recruited two months before school started. In addition to attending school, Robert would have ongoing physiotherapy, speech therapy and occupational therapy in his local town. His attendant assisted him in his writing activities and in becoming involved in a number of other local activities of a recreational nature. He attended a gymnasium three times weekly, played billiards, watched sport with friends, and went out socially.

The content of Robert's therapy had for some time been geared towards helping him to work on his reading comprehension, and written and oral communication skills, as these would be required for him to study English. He was highly motivated in this area. A lap-top computer was purchased in order to facilitate Robert's writing, and a considerable period was spent teaching him to use this effectively.

The week before term commenced, the therapists visited the school again and checked that Robert could move around satisfactorily. They met with all of the staff and students who would be involved with Robert. They outlined Robert's strengths and weaknesses and the areas in which he would need assistance, and called for suggestions and volunteers. Robert was also involved in this meeting. Further educational sessions were conducted by the local occupational therapist. Additional time was spent training the integration aide, who was already working at the school, and discussing with her and Robert the ways in which she could most productively assist him. Because Robert could not listen and take notes in class, it was decided that she would sit with him in the classroom and take notes while he listened. She did this for two hours three times per week, and subsequently spent two additional 2-hour sessions reviewing the lessons and assisting Robert with his writing and comprehension work.

Robert's return to school proceeded quite smoothly. He had always been very popular and retained his ability to entertain his friends, thus he was never short of company. The local occupational therapist maintained regular contact, and organised a meeting of all involved parties six weeks after Robert had started school. His English teacher reported she had been working with him on critical analysis work, as he was having difficulty presenting more than one argument or critical evaluation. He also required encouragement to think laterally and answer unstructured questions. His confidence in talking in front of the class was increasing.

Robert was formally reviewed on a regular basis by the rehabilitation centre also. He went on to pass English at Years 10, 11, and 12 levels. In his final year of school he pursued his interest in writing by contributing to the sporting section of the local newspaper. He began to write his autobiography. He subsequently did a course in creative writing. Whilst continuing to require considerable support and assistance, Robert had managed to complete his education to his satisfaction, and in such a manner as to give him every opportunity to pursue his goals. He wrote the following progress report several months after returning to school:

"I am going well in physio and I'm on two crutches, and I'm doing swimming twice a week. Memory and mobility are still my major problems, but I feel I'm getting pretty independent. School is going well and I'm enjoying it and in the long run I'm sure it will be beneficial to my progress because it must be helping the brain somewhere along the line. I'm fitting in pretty well and the kids are helping me and I'm making a few friends too. I'm going to the local gym and that too is going great and I'm really enjoying going. I go three days per week and I'm up to two circuits. I'm also feeling stronger. I'm fitting in everywhere with recreational time. I've gone along to indoor cricket but find it too frustrating. I also watch a lot of sport and play billiards. Rachel (his attendant) is coming 30 hours per week and she is also going terrific, and I'm really enjoying her company."

FAMILY NEEDS

Although there have been many studies investigating the impact of TBI in adolescents and adults on the family, there has been little research on family reactions to the occurrence of TBI in a child. Martin (1988) and Waaland and Kreutzer (1988) have postulated that families of young children who are injured experience similar emotional reactions, and pass through similar phases of adjustment to relatives of TBI adults. These reactions have been discussed in detail in Chapter 9. The findings of Rivara et al. (1993) suggest that families who function well prior to injury cope best with the trauma, and this, in turn, leads to a better outcome in the injured child. There are some ways, however, in which the needs and stresses of parents of young children may differ from those of the relatives of adults who have sustained TBI.

As the natural caregivers, parents of TBI children must, in the acute stage, relinquish the care of their child to the treatment team. This is composed of strangers, who assume control over the child, and in whom parents have to place their trust. Parents must stand by as their child is subjected to a bewildering set of high technology procedures. While being given complex information about the child's injury, treatment and prognosis, parents are likely to be wrestling with feelings of loss, fear, denial, and anger. They may have difficulty understanding the information and explanation given by doctors, who can usually spare only limited time while the injured child is in danger. As with adults, empathic listening, repetition, clarification of information, and reassurance need to be available to parents at this and all stages of recovery. Every effort should be made to involve parents in the care of their child at all stages of recovery.

As Martin (1988) has indicated, although many of the emotions and stages experienced by families of adults who are injured are also experienced by the parents of children who sustain TBI, in some respects these are heightened. Initially, parents are likely to wish only that the child will survive, but may ask key questions that contain elements of their own hopes for the child, such as going to university or becoming an athlete. Parents of children with lasting disabilities will never see their child grow up to fulfil their dreams and have to adjust their ambitions. Instead of hoping for a professional career for their child, there may only be hope that the child will live independently. Many hopes may be replaced by fears. Under these circumstances there can be an enormous sense of grief over unfulfilled potential. Guilt is another common reaction. As a parent's role includes nurturance and protection, injury to a child may indicate to the parents that they have failed in this role, whatever the circumstances of the accident. Such emotional responses may accentuate denial and anger and prolong the adjustment process.

In addition to dealing with the injured child and their own emotional responses, parents have the stresses of responsibilities to the rest of the family. After the child's survival is ensured, members of the extended family gradually resume their usual activities, and healthy siblings return to school. One parent, usually the mother, tends to spend more time with the injured child. But the family remains in crisis. Siblings, having experienced the trauma of seeing their injured brother or sister in hospital, may harbour fantasies and fears which create anxiety for them. There tends to be a significant and lengthy disruption to normal family functioning. Siblings receive less attention from their parents and may develop feelings of jealousy. In younger children, loss of parental contact can lead to regressive behaviour, acting out, or rejection of absent parents. In older children, anxiety may cause a reduction in school performance, resentment of increased household responsibilities and avoidance of the home.

Siblings of children who sustain TBI need to be given opportunities to discuss their perceptions and feelings about the injured brother or sister, and the impact of the injury on the family and themselves. Siblings are frequently remarkably ill-informed regarding the nature of the injury and prognosis. Whilst parents and rehabilitation staff may feel this is protecting them, it can actually engender anxiety. Time needs to be taken to answer questions clearly and simply. Individual therapy time spent with siblings may be supplemented by attendance at a support group for the siblings of injured children. If such a group can be organised, it provides an invaluable opportunity for siblings to share their experiences and receive peer support. An effort should also be made to preserve the routine of siblings as much as possible. Parents need to be encouraged and given the necessary support to set aside time with them.

The greatest victim of disrupted family life under these circumstances is usually the parents' time to themselves, both as a couple and individually. Other children and family business are cared for at the expense of the couple's personal needs. Marital stress is common, particularly in troubled marriages, but also in healthy ones. Resentment may develop when parents have differing perceptions of the injured child's disabilities and needs. Counselling should be made available to emphasise the importance of ongoing communication and mutual support. Discussion with other parents of injured children may also prove helpful. Parents need to hear that it is both necessary and important for them to take care of themselves, and to fulfil needs other than simply eating and sleeping. For many parents this is very difficult, as time away from the injured child may be very painful, at least in the early stages of recovery.

As discussed in Chapter 9, counselling or family therapy may be necessary to assist the family as a whole to grieve effectively, and to redefine and restructure family relationships and roles. In view of the vulnerability of injured children behaviourally and emotionally, the importance of maximising family coping after injury cannot be overemphasised. Apart from the work of Singer et al. (1994), described in Chapter 9, which demonstrated the benefits of a psychoeducational stress management programme for parents of brain-injured children, there have been no research studies that have systematically investigated the impact of different approaches to facilitate family coping and adjustment following paediatric TBI. There is a great need for such studies, as effective family intervention is likely to maximise the child's psychosocial adjustment.

Families of children who sustain TBI are likely to face even greater stresses than those of adults with TBI in obtaining adequate services for the injured child. Appropriate rehabilitation services for children who sustain TBI are few and far between. Due to a relative lack of knowledge regarding TBI in children, the quality of therapy and educational services available tends to be limited. Moreover, as Waaland and Kreutzer (1988) have pointed out, the needs of the child will change significantly over time. Each developmental level will bring with it the potential emergence of new cognitive deficiencies, and behavioural and emotional changes. As time passes, vocational, avocational, social, and relationship issues will become more important than educational issues. There will be concern over the future care of a severely disabled child, should the parents be no longer able to provide this.

Ideally, assistance in dealing with behavioural, emotional, educational, vocational, financial, and legal problems needs to be available to families throughout the lifespan of the injured child. In the case of severe disability, there will also be a need to provide access to respite care, in addition to attendant care. It is vital to link families of injured children with a network of ongoing social and emotional supports. In many respects the long-term needs of children who sustain TBI and their families remain unclear. There is a significant need for further, well-controlled, longitudinal research, which documents not only the long-term problems, but also the impact of different family coping styles on outcome, and the effectiveness of interventions focusing on the child in the home and educational setting, the siblings and the family as a whole.

CONCLUSIONS

The impact of TBI is somewhat different in children from that in adults. Whilst children appear to have a lower mortality and show a better motor–sensory recovery, there is clear evidence of lasting impairment in the domains of memory, attention, speed of performance, abstract thinking, and executive function. These have long-term effects on academic attainment. Behaviour problems are also common following severe TBI, but they follow a less predictable pattern, being associated with premorbid behavioural patterns and family functioning, as well as the injury and emotional factors. There is a need for skilled and careful assessment in all these areas, including a comprehensive assessment of the child's physical, linguistic, cognitive, academic, and behavioural functioning prior to injury, as well as social and family functioning. Rehabilitation facilities need to cater specifically to children, and have the flexibility to work in the community. Attention should be paid to the child's social and emotional adjustment throughout the rehabilitation process. Return to school must be carefully planned, with follow-up support available over many years, as the demands on the child change. Given the impact of family functioning on outcome following paediatric TBI, ongoing family support is also vital.

References

Abrams, D., Barker, L.T., Haffey, W., & Nelson, H. (1993). The economics of return to work for survivors of traumatic brain injury: Vocational services are worth the investment. *Journal of Head Trauma Rehabilitation, 8*(4), 59–76.

Achenbach, T.M., & Edelbrook, C. (1983). *Manual for the Child Behaviour Checklist and Revised Behaviour Profile.* Burlington, VT: University of Vermont.

Acker, M.B. (1986). Relationships between test scores and everyday life functioning. In B. Uzzell & Y. Gross (Eds.), *Clinical neuropsychology of intervention* (pp. 85–111). Boston, MA: Martinus Nijhoff.

Acker, M.B. (1990). A review of the ecological validity of neuropsychological tests. In D.E. Tupper & K.D. Cicerone (Eds.), *The neuropsychology of everyday life: Assessment and basic competencies* (pp. 19–55). Boston, MA: Kluwer Academic Publishers.

Acker, M.B., & Davis, J.R. (1989). Psychology test scores as predictors of late outcome in brain injury. *Neuropsychology, 3,* 101–111.

Adams, J.H. (1988). The autopsy in fatal non–missile head injuries. In C.L. Berry (Ed.), *Neuropathology (Current Topics in Pathology, 76,* pp.1–22). Berlin: Springer-Verlag.

Adams, J.H., Doyle, D., Graham, D.I., Lawrence, A.E., & McLellan, D.R. (1986). Gliding contusions in nonmissile head injury in humans. *Archives of Pathology and Laboratory Medicine, 110,* 485–488.

Adams, J.H., Doyle, D., Graham, D.I., Lawrence, A.E., McLellan, D.R., Gennarelli, T.A., Pastusko, M., & Sakamoto, T. (1985). The contusion index: A reappraisal in human and experimental non-missile head injury. *Neuropathology and Applied Neurobiology, 11,* 299–308.

Adams, J.H., Mitchell, D.E., Graham, D.I., & Doyle, D. (1977). Diffuse brain damage of immediate impact type: Its relationship to "primary brain-stem damage" in head injury, *Brain, 100*, 489–502.

Alderman, N. (1991). The treatment of avoidance behaviour following severe brain injury by satiation through negative practice. *Brain Injury, 5*, 77–86.

Alderman, N., & Ward, A. (1991). Behavioural treatment of the dysexecutive syndrome: Reduction of repetitive speech using response cost and cognitive overlearning. *Neuropsychological Rehabilitation, 1*, 65–80.

Allen, C.K. (1985). *Occupational therapy for psychiatric diseases: Measurement and management of cognitive disabilities.* Boston, MA: Little Brown.

Allen, C.C., & Ruff, R.M. (1990). Self–rating versus neuropsychological performance of moderate versus severe head injured patients. *Brain Injury, 4*, 7–17.

Almli, C.R., & Finger, S. (1992). Brain injury and recovery of function: Theories and mechanisms of functional reorganization. *Journal of Head Trauma Rehabilitation, 7*(2), 70–77

Alter, I., John, E.R., & Ransohoff, J. (1990). Computer analysis of cortical evoked potentials following severe head injury. *Brain Injury, 4*, 19–26.

Anderson, D.W., & McLaurin, R.L. (Eds.), (1980). Report on the national head and spinal cord injury survey. *Journal of Neurosurgery, 53* (Supplement).

Andrews, K. (1990). Medical management. *Physical Medicine and Rehabilitation: State of the Art Reviews, 4*, 495–515.

Andrews, K. (1993). Should PVS patients be treated? *Neuropsychological Rehabilitation, 3*, 109–119.

Ansell, B.J. (1993). Slow–to–recover patients: Improvement to rehabilitation readiness. *Journal of Head Trauma Rehabilitation, 8*(3), 88–98.

Ansell, B.J., & Keenan, J.E. (1989). The Western Neuro Sensory Stimulation Profile: A tool for assessing slow-to-recover head-injured patients. *Archives of Physical Medicine and Rehabilitation, 70*, 104–108.

Artiola i Fortuny, L., Briggs, M., Newcombe, F., Ratcliff, G., & Thomas, C. (1980). Measuring the duration of post-traumatic amnesia. *Journal of Neurology, Neurosurgery, and Psychiatry, 43*, 377–379.

Baddeley, A.D. (1986). *Working memory.* Oxford: Clarendon Press.

Baddeley, A., Harris, J., Sunderland, A., Watts, K., & Wilson, B.A. (1987). Closed head injury and memory. In H.S. Levin, J. Grafman, & H.M. Eisenberg (Eds.), *Neurobehavioural recovery from head injury* (pp. 295–317). New York: Oxford University Press.

Baker, J. (1988). Explaining coma arousal therapy. *Australian Nurses Journal, 17*(11), 8–11.

Barin, J.J., Hanchett, J.M., Jacob, W.L., & Scott, M.B. (1985). Counselling the head-injured patient. In M. Ylvisaker (Ed.), *Head injury rehabilitation: Children and adolescents* (pp. 361–382). Philadelphia: Taylor & Francis.

Bates, D. (1993). The management of medical coma. *Journal of Neurology, Neurosurgery, and Psychiatry, 56*, 589–598.

Baxter, R., Cohen, S.B., & Ylvisaker, M. (1985). Comprehensive cognitive assessment. In M. Ylvisaker (Ed.), *Head injury rehabilitation: Children and adolescents* (pp. 247–274). Boston, MA: College Hill Press

Beck, A.T., Rush, A.J., Shaw, B.F., & Emery, G. (1979). *Cognitive therapy of depression.* New York: The Guilford Press.

Bell, B.A., & Britton, J. (1989). Mechanisms of trauma. In D.A. Johnson, D. Uttley & M. Wyke (Eds.), *Children's head injury: who cares?* (pp. 1–11). London: Taylor & Francis.

Bellack, A.S. (1983). Recurrent problems in the behavioural assessment of social skill. *Behavioural Research and Therapy, 21*(1), 29–41.

Benedict, H.B., Brandt, J., & Bergey, G. (1993). An attempt at memory retraining in severe amnesia: An experimental single-case study. *Neuropsychological Rehabilitation, 3*, 37–51.

Benjamin, L., Debinski, A., Fletcher, D., Hedger, C., Mealings, M. & Stewart–Scott, A. (1989). The use of the Bethesda Conversational Skills Profile in closed head injury. In V. Anderson & M. Bailey (Eds.), *Theory and function: Bridging the gap: Proceedings of the fourteenth annual Brain Impairment Conference* (pp. 57–64). Melbourne: Australian Society for the Study of Brain Impairment.

Bennett–Levy, J., & Powell, G.E. (1980). The Subjective Memory Questionnaire (SMQ). An investigation into the self-reporting of real-life memory skills. *British Journal of Social and Clinical Psychology, 19*, 177–188.

Benson, D.F., & Geschwind, N. (1967). Shrinking retrograde amnesia. *Journal of Neurology, Neurosurgery, and Psychiatry, 30*, 539–544.

Benton, A.L., & Hamsher, K.deS. (1989). *Mutilingual aphasia examination* (2nd edition). San Antonio, TX: The Psychological Corporation.

Ben-Yishay, Y. Lakin, P., Ross, B., Rattok, J., Cohen, J., & Diller, L. (1980). Developing a core "curriculum" for group-exercises designed for head trauma patients who are undergoing rehabilitation. In *Working approaches to remediation of cognitive deficits in brain damaged persons* (Rehabilitation Monograph No. 61) (pp.175–234). New York: New York University Medical Center, Institute of Rehabilitation Medicine.

Ben-Yishay, Y., Piasetsky, E.B., & Rattock, J. (1987). A systematic method for ameliorating disorders in basic attention. In M.J. Meier, A.L. Benton, & L. Diller (Eds.), *Neuropsychological rehabilitation* (pp. 165–181). New York: Churchill Livingstone.

Berg, I.J., Koning-Haanstra, M., & Deelman, B.G. (1991). Long-term effects of memory rehabilitation: A controlled study. *Neuropsychological Rehabilitation, 1*, 97–111.

Bergman, M.M. (1991). Computer enhanced self-sufficiency: Part 1. Creation and implementation of a text writer for an individual with traumatic brain injury. *Neuropsychology, 5*, 17–23.

Bergman, M.M., & Kemmerer, A.G. (1991). Computer enhanced self-sufficiency: Part 2. Uses and subjective benefits of a text writer for an individual with traumatic brain injury. *Neuropsychology, 5*, 25–28.

Berrol, S. (1986). Evolution and the persistent vegetative state. *Journal of Head Trauma Rehabilitation, 1*(1), 7–13.

Berrol, S. (1990). Persistent vegetative state. *Physical Medicine and Rehabilitation: State of the Art Reviews, 4* (3), 559–567.

Beukelman, D.R., Yorkston, K.M. & Lossing, C.A. (1984). Functional communication assessment of adults with neurogenic disorders. In: A.S. Halpern & M.J. Fuhrer (Eds.), *Functional assessment in rehabilitation* (pp. 101–115). Baltimore, MD: Paul H. Brookes Publishing Co.

Binder, L.M., & Schreiber, V. (1980). Visual imagery and verbal mediation as memory aids in recovering alcoholics. *Journal of Clinical Neuropsychology, 2*, 71–74.

Bishara, S.N., Partridge, F.M., Godfrey, H., & Knight, R.G. (1992). Post-traumatic amnesia and Glasgow Coma Scale related to outcome in survivors in a consecutive series of patients with severe closed-head injury. *Brain Injury, 6*, 373–380.

Bishop, D., & Miller, I.W. (1988). Traumatic brain injury: Empirical family assessment techniques. *Journal of Head Trauma Rehabilitation, 3*(4), 16–30.

Black, P., Blumer, D., Wellner, A., & Walker, A.E. (1971). The head-injured child: Time course of recovery, with implications for rehabilitation. *Proceedings of an International Symposium on Head Injuries* (pp. 131–137). Edinburgh: Churchill Livingstone.

Black, P., Markowitz, R.S., & Cianci, S. (1975). Recovery of motor function after lesions in motor cortex of monkey. In *Ciba Foundation Symposium No. 34, outcome of severe damage to the central nervous system* (pp. 65–84). Amsterdam: Elsevier.

Blackerby, W.F. (1990). A treatment model for sexuality disturbance following brain injury. *Journal of Head Trauma Rehabilitation, 5*(2), 73–82.

Bloomer, J. S., & Williams, S. K. (1979). *The Bay Area Functional Performance Evaluation (research edition)*. Palo Alto, CA: Consulting Psychologists Press.

Blumbergs, P.C., Jones, N.R., & North, J.B. (1989). Diffuse axonal injury in head trauma. *Journal of Neurology, Neurosurgery, and Psychiatry, 52*, 838–841.

Boake, C. (1991). Social skills training following head injury. In J.S. Kreutzer & P.S. Wehman (Eds.), *Cognitive rehabilitation for persons with traumatic brain injury* (pp. 181–189). Baltimore, MD: Paul Brookes Publishing Co.

Bond, M. (1975). Assessment of psychosocial outcome after severe head injury. In R. Porter & D.W. Fitzsimmons (Eds.), Outcome of severe damage to the central nervous system. *Ciba Foundation Symposium 34* (new series, pp. 141–157). Amsterdam: Elsevier.

Bond, M. (1976). Assessment of the psychosocial outcome of severe head injury. *Acta Neurochirurgica, 34*, 57–70.

Bond, M. (1984). The psychiatry of closed head injury. In N. Brooks (Ed.), *Closed head injury. Psychological, social and family consequences* (pp. 148–178). London: Oxford University Press.

Bontke, C.F., Baize, C.M., & Boake, C. (1992). Coma management and sensory stimulation. *Physical Medicine and Rehabilitation Clinics of North America, 3*, 259–272.

Bowers, S.A., & Marshall, L.F. (1980). Outcome in 200 consecutive cases of severe head injury treated in San Diego County: A prospective analysis. *Neurosurgery, 6*, 237–242.

Bowie, V. (1989). *Coping with violence. A guide for the human services*. Sydney: Karibuni Press.

Bragg, R.M., Klockars, A.J., & Berninger, V.W. (1992). Comparison of families with and without adolescents with traumatic brain injury. *Journal of Head Trauma Rehabilitation, 7*(4), 94–108.

Braun, C.M.J., Lussier, F., Baribeau, J.M.C., & Ethier, M. (1989). Does severe traumatic closed head injury impair sense of humour? *Brain Injury, 3*, 345–354.

Braunling-McMorrow, D., Lloyd, K., & Fralish, K. (1986). Teaching social skills to head injured adults. *Journal of Rehabilitation, Jan/Feb/Mar*, 39–44.

Bricolo, A., Turazzi, S., & Feriotti, G. (1980). Prolonged posttraumatic unconsciousness. Therapeutic assets and liabilities. *Journal of Neurosurgery, 52*, 625–634.

Brink, J.D., Garrett, A.L., Hale, W.R., Woo-Sam, J., & Nickel, V.L. (1970). Recovery of motor and intellectual function in children sustaining severe head injuries. *Developmental Medicine and Child Neurology, 12*, 565–571.

Brink, J.D., Imbus, C., & Woo-Sam, J. (1980). Physical recovery after severe head trauma in children and adolescents. *Journal of Paediatrics, 97*, 721–727.

Broe, G.A., Tate, R.L., Ross, G., Tregeagle, S., & Lulham, J. (1981). The nature and effects of brain damage following severe head injury in young subjects. In T.A.R. Dinning & T.J. Connelly (Eds.), *Head injuries. An integrated approach* (pp. 92–97). Brisbane: John Wiley & Sons.

Brooke, M.M., Patterson, D.R., Quested, K.A., Cardenas, D., & Farrel-Roberts, L. (1992). The treatment of agitation during initial hospitalization after traumatic brain injury. *Archives of Physical Medicine and Rehabilitation, 73*, 917–921.

Brooke, M.M., Quested, K.A., Patterson, D.R., & Valois, T.A. (1992). Driving evaluation after traumatic brain injury. *American Journal of Physical Medicine and Rehabilitation, 71*, 177–182.

Brooks, D.N. (1975). Long- and short-term memory in head-injured patients. *Cortex, 11*, 329–340.

Brooks, D.N. (1976). Wechsler Memory Scale performance and its relationship to brain damage after severe closed head injury. *Journal of Neurology, Neurosurgery, and Psychiatry, 39*, 593.

Brooks, N. (1984a). Cognitive deficits after head injury. In N. Brooks (Ed.), *Closed head injury: Psychological, social, and family consequences* (pp. 44–73). Oxford: Oxford University Press.

Brooks, N. (1984b). Head injury and the family. In N. Brooks (Ed.), *Closed head injury: Psychological, social, and family consequences* (pp. 123–147). Oxford: Oxford University Press.

Brooks, D.N., & Aughton, M.E. (1979). Psychological consequences of blunt head injury. *International Rehabilitation Medicine, 1*, 160–165.

Brooks, D.N., Campsie, L., Symington, C., Beattie, A., & McKinlay, W. (1986). The five-year outcome of severe blunt head injury: A relative's view. *Journal of Neurology, Neurosurgery, and Psychiatry, 49*, 764–770.

Brooks, N., Campsie, L., Symington, C., Beattie, A., & McKinlay, W. (1987a). The effects of severe head injury on patient and relative within seven years of injury. *Journal of Head Trauma Rehabilitation, 2*(3), 1–13.

Brooks, D.N., & McKinlay, W. (1983). Personality and behavioural change after severe blunt head injury—a relative's view. *Journal of Neurology, Neurosurgery, and Psychiatry, 46*, 336–344.

Brooks, D.N., McKinlay, W., Symington, C., Beattie, A., & Campsie, L. (1987b). Return to work within the first seven years of head injury. *Brain Injury, 1*, 5–19.

Brotherton, F.A., Thomas, L.L., Wisotzek, I.E., & Milan, M.A. (1988). Social skills training in the rehabilitation of patients with traumatic closed head injury. *Archives of Physical Medicine and Rehabilitation, 69*, 827–832.

Brouwer, W.H., & Van Wolffelaar, P.C. (1985). Sustained attention and sustained effort after closed head injury. *Cortex, 21*, 111–119.

Brown, D.S.O., & Nell, V. (1992). Recovery from diffuse traumatic brain injury in Johannesburg: A concurrent prospective study. *Archives of Physical Medicine and Rehabilitation, 73*, 758–770.

Brown, G., Chadwick, O., Shaffer, D., Rutter, M., & Traub, M. (1981). A prospective study of children with head injuries. III. Psychiatric sequelae. *Psychological Medicine, 11*, 63–78.

Bruce, D.A., Raphaely, R.C., Goldberg, A.I., Zimmerman, R.A., Bilaniuk, L.T., Schut, L., & Kuhl, D.E. (1979). Pathophysiology, treatment and outcome following severe head injury in children. *Child's Brain, 5*, 174–191.

Bruce, D.A., Schut, L., Bruno, L.A., Wood, J.H., & Sutton, L.N. (1978). Outcome following severe head injuries in children. *Journal of Neurosurgery, 48*, 679–688.

Burke, J.M., Danick, J.A., Bemis, B., & Durgin, C.J. (1994). A process approach to memory book training for neurological patients. *Brain Injury, 8*, 71–81.

Burke, W. (1988). *Head injury rehabilitation: Developing social skills*. Houston, TX: HDI Publishers.

Burke, W.H., Wesolowski, M.D., & Guth, M.L. (1988). Comprehensive head injury rehabilitation: an outcome evaluation. *Brain Injury, 2*, 313–322

Burke, W.H., Zenicus, A.H., Wesolowski, M.D., & Doubleday, F. (1991). Improving executive function disorders in brain-injured clients. *Brain Injury, 5*, 241–252.

Buschke, H., & Fuld, P.A. (1974). Evaluating storage, retention, and retrieval in disordered memory and learning. *Neurology, 24*, 1019–1025.

Campbell, T.F., & Dollaghan, C.A. (1992). A method for obtaining listener judgements of spontaneously produced language: Social validation through direct magnitude estimation. *Topics in Language Disorders, 12*(2), 42–55.

Casanova, J.S., & Ferber, J. (1976). Comprehensive evaluation of basic living skills. *The American Journal of Occupational Therapy, 76*, 101–105.

Cermak, L. (1975). Imagery as an aid to retrieval for Korsakoff patients. *Cortex, 11*, 163–169.

Chadwick, O., Rutter, M., Brown, G., Shaffer, D., & Traub, M. (1981). A prospective study of children with head injuries. II. Cognitive sequelae. *Psychological Medicine, 11*, 49–61.

Chapman, S.B., Culhane, K.A., Levin, H.S., Harwood, H., Mendelsohn, D., Ewing-Cobbs, L., Fletcher, J.M., & Bruce, D. (1992). Narrative discourse after closed head injury in children and adolescents. *Brain & Language, 43*, 42–65.

Chorazy, A.L. (1985). Introduction: Head injury rehabilitation: Children and adolescents. In M. Ylvisaker (Ed.), *Head injury rehabilitation: Children and adolescents* (pp. xix–xxii). Philadelphia: Taylor & Francis.

Christensen, A. (1984). *Luria's Neuropsychological investigation* (2nd edition). Bogtrykker, Vojens: P.J. Schmidts.

Christiansen, C. (1993). Continuing challenges of functional assessment in rehabilitiation: Recommended changes. *The American Journal of Occupational Therapy, 47*, 258–259.

Cicerone, K.D. (1991). Psychotherapy after mild traumatic brain injury: Relation to the nature and severity of subjective complaints. *Journal of Head Trauma Rehabilitation, 6*(4), 30–43.

Cicerone, K.D., & Tupper, D.E. (1990). Neuropsychological rehabilitation: Treatment of errors in everyday functioning. In D.E. Tupper & K.D. Cicerone (Eds.), *The neuropsychology of everyday life: Issues in development and rehabilitation* (pp. 271–291). Boston, MA: Kluwer Academic Publishers.

Cicerone, K.D., & Wood, J. C. (1987). Planning disorder after closed head injury: A case study. *Archives of Physical Medicine and Rehabilitation, 68*, 111–115.

Connors, C. (1973). Rating scales for use in drug studies in children. *Psychopharmacology Bulletin, 9* (Special Supplement), 24–84.

Cook, J. (1991). Higher education: An attainable goal for students who have sustained head injuries. *Journal of Head Trauma Rehabilitation, 6*(1), 64–72.

Cope, D.N. (1987). Psychopharmacologic considerations in the treatment of traumatic brain injury. *Journal of Head Trauma Rehabilitation, 2*(4), 1–5.

Cope, D.N., Cole, J.R., Hall, K.M., & Barkan, H. (1991a). Brain injury: Analysis of outcome in a post-acute rehabilitation system. Part 1: General analysis. *Brain Injury, 5*, 111–125.

Cope, D.N., Cole, J.R., Hall, K.M., & Barkan, H. (1991b). Brain injury: Analysis of outcome in a post-acute rehabilitation system. Part 2: Subanalyses. *Brain Injury, 5*, 127–139.

Cope, D.N., & Hall, K. (1982). Head injury rehabilitation: Benefit of early intervention. *Archives of Physical Medicine and Rehabilitation, 63*, 433–437.

Corrigan, J.D., Arnett, J.A., Houck, L.J., & Jackson, R.D. (1985). Reality orientation for brain injured patients: Group treatment and monitoring of recovery. *Archives of Physical Medicine and Rehabilitation, 66*, 626–630.

Corrigan, J.D., & Mysiw, W.J. (1988). Agitation following traumatic brain injury: Equivocal evidence for a discrete stage of cognitive recovery. *Archives of Physical Medicine and Rehabilitation, 69*, 487–492.

Cottle, R. (1988, February). *Psychosocial aspects of head injury*. Paper presented at a seminar on the Management of Head Injury, Bethesda Hospital, Melbourne, Australia.

Corrigan, J.D., Mysiw, W.J., Gribble, M.W., & Chock, S.K.L. (1992). Agitation, cognition and amnesia during post-traumatic amnesia. *Brain Injury, 6*, 155–160.

Craft, A.W., Shaw, D.A., & Cartlidge, N. (1972). Head injuries in children. *British Medical Journal, 4*, 200–203.

Cranford, R.E. (1988). The persistent vegetative state: the medical reality (Getting the facts straight). *Hastings Center Report, Feb/Mar*, 27–32.

Cranford, R., & Zasler, N. (1994). *Vegetative state: Challenges, controversies, and caveats. An interactive dialogue*. Fourth IASTBI Conference, St. Louis, MO.

Crepeau, F., & Scherzer, P. (1993). Predictors and indicators of work status after traumatic brain injury: A meta-analysis. *Neuropsychological Rehabilitation, 3*, 5–35.

Crook, T.H., & Larrabee, G.J. (1992). Normative data on a self-rating scale for evaluating memory in everyday life. *Archives of Clinical Neuropsychology, 7*, 41–51.

Crosson, B. (1987). Treatment of interpersonal deficits for head-trauma patients in inpatient rehabilitation settings. *The Clinical Neuropsychologist, 1*, 335–352.

Crosson, B., Barco, P.P., Velozo, CA., Bolesta, M.M., Cooper, P.V., Werts, D., & Brobeck, T.C. (1989). Awareness and compensation in post-acute head injury rehabilitation. *Journal of Head Trauma Rehabilitation, 4*(3), 46–54.

Crovitz, H.F. (1979). Memory retraining in brain damaged patients: The airplane list. *Cortex, 15*, 131–134

Damasio, A.R. (1985). The frontal lobes. In K. M. Heilman & E. Valenstein (Eds.), *Clinical neuropsychology*. New York: Oxford University Press.

Damico, J.S. (1985). Clinical discourse analysis: A functional approach to language assessment. In C.S. Simon (Ed.), *Communication skills and classroom success* (pp. 165–203). London: Taylor & Francis. (1991 edn.: Eau Claire, WI: Thinking Publications.)

Davis, A., Davis, S., Moss, N., Marks, J., McGrath, J., Hovard, L., Axon, J., & Wade, D. (1992). First steps towards an interdisciplinary approach to rehabilitation. *Clinical Rehabilitation, 6*, 237–244.

Davis, D.L., & Schneider, L.K. (1990). Ramifications of traumatic brain injury for sexuality. *Journal of Head Trauma Rehabilitation, 5*(2), 31–37.

Davis G.A., & Wilcox, M.J. (1985). *Adult aphasia rehabilitation. Applied pragmatics*. San Diego, CA: College Hill.

Deacon, D., & Campbell K. (1991). Decision-making following closed head injury: Can response speed be retrained? *Journal of Clinical and Experimental Neuropsychology, 13*, 639–651.

Deitz, J. (1992). Self-psychological approach to posttraumatic stress disorder: Neurobiological aspects of transmuting internalization. *Journal of the American Academy of Psychoanalysis, 20*, 277–293.

Delis, D.C., Kramer, J.H., Kaplan, E., & Ober, B.A. (1987). *California Verbal Learning Test*. San Antonio, TX: The Psychological Corporation.

Dennis, M. (1992). Word finding in children and adolescents with a history of brain injury. *Topics in Language Disorders, Nov.*, 66–82.

Diamond, A. (1988). Differences between adult and infant cognition: Is the crucial variable presence or absence of language? In L. Weiskrantz (Ed.), *Thought without language* (pp. 337–370). New York: Oxford University Press

Dikmen, S., Machamer, J., & Temkin, N. (1993). Psychosocial outcome in patients with moderate to severe head injury: 2-year follow-up. *Brain Injury, 7*, 113–124.

Dikmen, S., McLean, A., & Temkin, N. (1986). Neuropsychological and psychosocial consequences of minor head injury. *Journal of Neurology, Neurosurgery, and Psychiatry, 49*, 1227–1232.

Diller, L., Ben-Yishay, Y., Gerstman, L., Goodkin, R., Gordon, W., & Weinberg, J. (1974). *Studies in cognition and rehabilitation in hemiplegia* (Rehabilitation Monograph No. 50). New York: New York University Medical Center, Institute of Rehabilitation Medicine.

Dobbing, J. (1968). Vulnerable periods in developing brain. In A.N. Davison & J. Dobbing (Eds.), *Applied neurochemistry*. Oxford: Blackwell.

Dolan, M.P., & Norton, J.C. (1977). A programmed training technique that uses reinforcement to facilitate acquisition and retention in brain damaged patients. *Journal of Clinical Psychology, 33*, 496–501.

Douglas, M.J. (1987). *Perceptions of family environment among severely head-injured patients and their relatives*. Unpublished master's thesis, University of Victoria, BC, Canada.

Douglas, M.J. (1990). *Traumatic brain injury and the family*. Paper presented at the N.Z.S.T.A. Biennial Conference, Christchurch.

Douglas, M.J. (1994). *Indicators of long-term family functioning following severe TBI*. Unpublished PhD thesis, University of Victoria, BC, Canada.

Duncan, J.S., Trimble, M.R., & Shovon, S.D. (1989). The effects of phenytoin, carbamazepine and valproate withdrawal on cognitive function (abstract). *Neurology, 39*, 149.

Eames, P. (1988). Behavior disorders after severe head injury: Their nature and causes and strategies for management. *Journal of Head Trauma Rehabilitation, 3*(3), 1–6.

Eames, P., & Wood, R.L. (1985). Rehabilitation after severe brain injury: A special-unit approach to behaviour disorders. *International Rehabilitation Medicine, 7*, 130–133.

Ehrlich, J., & Sipes, A. (1985) Group treatment of communication skills for head trauma patients. *Cognitive Rehabilitation, 3*, 32–37.

Elsass, L., & Kinsella, G. (1987). Social interaction after severe closed head injury. *Psychological Medicine, 17*, 67–78.

Eisenberg, H.M., Weiner, R.L., & Tabaddor, K. (1987). Emergency care and initial evaluation. In P.R. Cooper (Ed.), *Head injury* (2nd edition, pp. 20–23). Baltimore, MD: Williams and Wilkins.

Ewert, J., Levin, H.S., Watson, M.G., & Kalisky, Z. (1989). Procedural memory during post-traumatic amnesia in survivors of severe closed head injury. *Archives of Neurology, 46*, 911–916.

Ewing-Cobbs, L., Fletcher, J., J.M., & Levin, H.S. (1985). Neuropsychological sequelae following paediatric head injury. In M. Ylvisaker (Ed.), *Head injury rehabilitation: Children and adolescents* (pp. 71–89). Philadelphia: Taylor & Francis.

Ewing-Cobbs, L., Levin, H., Fletcher, J., Miner, M., & Eisenberg, H. (1990). The Children's Orientation and Amnesia test: Relationship to acute severity and to recovery of memory. *Neurosurgery, 27*, 683–691.

Ezrachi, O., Ben-Yishay, Y., Kay, T., Diller, L., & Rattok, J. (1991). Predicting employment in traumatic brain injury following neuropsychological rehabilitation. *Journal of Head Trauma Rehabilitation, 6*(3), 71–84.

Fahy, T.J., Irving, M.H., & Millac, P. (1967). Severe head injuries – A six-year follow-up. *Lancet, 2*, 475–479.

Fay, G.C., Jaffe, K.M., Polissar, N.L., Liao, S., Martin, K.M., Shurtleff, H.A., Rivara, J.B., & Winn, R. (1993). Mild paediatric traumatic brain injury: A cohort study. *Archives of Physical Medicine and Rehabilitation, 74*, 895–901.

Feeney, D.M., Gonzalez, A., & Law, W.A. (1982). Amphetamine, haloperidol, and experience interact to affect rate of recovery after motor cortex injury. *Science, 217*, 855–857.

Finger, S., & Stein, D.G. (1982). *Brain damage and recovery.* New York: Academic Press.

Flach, J., & Malmros, R. (1972). A long-term follow-up study of children with severe head injury. *Scandinavian Journal of Rehabilitation Medicine, 4*, 9–15.

Fletcher, J.M., & Ewing-Cobbs, L. (1991). Head injury in children. Editorial. *Brain Injury, 5*, 337–338.

Fletcher, J.M., Ewing-Cobbs, L., Miner, M.E., Levin, H.S., & Eisenberg, H.M. (1990). Behavioral changes after closed head injury in children. *Journal of Consulting and Clinical Psychology, 58*, 93–98.

Fordyce, D.J., Roueche, J.R., & Prigatano, G.P. (1983). Enhanced emotional reactions in chronic head trauma patients. *Journal of Neurology, Neurosurgery, and Psychiatry, 46*, 620–624.

Forrester, G., Encel, J.C., & Geffen, G. (1994). Measuring post-traumatic amnesia (PTA): An historical review. *Brain Injury, 8*, 175–184.

Fox, G.M., Bashford, G,M., & Caust, S.L. (1992). Identifying safe versus unsafe drivers following brain impairment: The Coorabel Programme. *Disability and Rehabilitation, 14*, 140–145.

Freeman, E.A. (1987). *The catastrophe of coma. A way back*. Queensland, Australia: David Bateman.

Freeman, E.A. (1991). Coma arousal therapy. *Clinical Rehabilitation, 5*, 241–249.

Fryer, J. (1989). Adolescent community integration. In P. Bach-y-Rita (Ed.), *Traumatic brain injury* (pp. 255–286). New York: Demos Publications.

Fryer, L.J., & Haffey, W.J. (1987). Cognitive rehabilitation and community readaptation: Outcomes from two program models. *Journal of Head Trauma Rehabilitation, 2*(3), 51–63.

Fuld, P.A., & Fisher, P. (1977). Recovery of intellectual ability after closed head injury. *Developmental Medicine and Child Neurology, 19*, 708–716.

Gaidolfi, E., & Vignolo, L.A. (1980). Closed head injuries in school-aged children: Neuropsychological sequelae in early adulthood. *Italian Journal of Neurological Science, 1*, 65–73.

Gajar, A., Schloss, P.J., Schloss, C.N., & Thompson, C.K. (1984) Effects of feedback and self-monitoring on head trauma youths' conversation skills. *Journal of Applied Behaviour Analysis, 17*, 353–358.

Ganes, T., & Lundar, T. (1988). EEG and evoked potentials in comatose patients with severe brain damage. *Electroencephalography and Clinical Neurophysiology, 69*, 6–13.

Gardos, G. (1980). Disinhibition of behavior by antianxiety drugs. *Psychosomatics, 21*, 1025–1026.

Gasparrini, B., & Satz, P. (1979). A treatment for memory problems in left hemisphere CVA patients. *Journal of Clinical Neuropsychology, 1*, 137–150.

Gasquoine, P.G. (1991). Learning in post-traumatic amnesia following extremely severe closed head injury. *Brain Injury, 5*, 169–175.

Gazzaniga, M.S. (1978). Is seeing believing: notes on clinical recovery. In S. Finger (Ed.), *Recovery from brain damage* (pp. 410–414). New York: Plenum Press.

Gennarelli, T.A., Thibault, L.E., Adams, J.H., Graham, D.I., Thompson, C.J., & Marcincin, R.P. (1982). Diffuse axonal injury and traumatic coma in the primate. *Annals of Neurology, 12*, 564–574.

Gentile, A.M., Green, S., Nieburgs, A., Schmelzer, W., & Stein, D.G. (1978). Disruption and recovery of locomotor and manipulatory behaviour following cortical lesions in rats. *Behavioural Biology, 22*, 417–455.

Giacino, J.T., Kezmarsky, M.A., DeLuca, J., & Cicerone, K.D. (1991). Monitoring rate of recovery to predict outcome in minimally responsive patients. *Archives of Physical Medicine and Rehabilitation, 72*, 897–901.

Giles, G.M., & Clarke-Wilson, J. (1988). The use of behavioral techniques in functional skills training after severe brain injury. *The American Journal of Occupational Therapy, 42*, 658–665.

Giles, G.M., Fussey, I., & Burgess, P. (1988). The behavioural treatment of verbal interaction skills following severe head injury: A single case study. *Brain Injury, 2*, 75–79.

Glasgow, R.E., Zeiss, R.A., Barrera, M., & Lewinsohn, P.M. (1977). Case studies on remediating memory deficits in brain damaged individuals. *Journal of Clinical Psychology, 33*, 1049–1054.

Godfrey, H.P.D., & Knight, R.G. (1988). Memory training and behavioral rehabilitation of a severely head-injured adult. *Archives of Physical Medicine and Rehabilitation, 69*, 458–460.

Goldman, P.S. (1971). Functional development of the prefrontal cortex in early life and the problem of neuronal plasticity. *Experimental Neurology, 32*, 366–387.

Goldman, P.S. (1974). An alternative to developmental plasticity: Heterogeneity of C.N.S. structures in infants and adults. In D.G. Stein, J.J. Rosen, & N. Butters (Eds.), *Plasticity and recovery of function in the central nervous system* (pp. 149–174). New York: Academic Press.

Goldstein, A.P. (1976). *Skill training for community living: Applying structured learning therapy.* New York: Pergamon Press.

Goldstein, A.P., Sprafkin, R.P., Gershaw, N.J., & Klein, P. (1980). *Skill-streaming the adolescent. A structured learning approach to teaching prosocial skills.* Illinois: Research Press Co.

Goldstein, F., & Levin, H.S. (1985). Intellectual and academic outcome following closed head injury in children and adolescents: Research strategies and empirical findings. *Developmental Neuropsychology, 1*, 215–229.

Goldstein, F., & Levin, H.S. (1987). Epidemiology of paediatric closed head injury: Incidence, clinical characterisitics and risk factors. *Journal of Learning Disabilities, 20*, 518–525.

Goodglass, H., & Kaplan, E. (1972). *The assessment of aphasia and related disorders.* Philadelphia: Lea & Febiger.

Gouvier, W.D., Cubic, B., Jones, G., Brantley, P., & Cutlip, Q. (1992). Postconcussion symptoms and daily stress in normal and head-injured college populations. *Archives of Clinical Neuropsychology, 7*, 193–211.

Graham, D.I., Adams, J.H., & Doyle, D. (1978). Ischaemic brain damage in fatal non-missile head injuries. *Journal of Neurological Science, 39*, 213–234.

Graham, D.I., Ford, I., Adams, J.H., Doyle, D., Teasdale, G.M., Lawrence, A.E., & McLellan, D.R. (1989). Ischaemic brain damage is still common in fatal non-missile head injury. *Journal of Neurology, Neurosurgery, and Psychiatry, 52*, 346–350.

Graham, D.I., Lawrence, A.E., Adams, J.H., Doyle, D., & McLellan, D.R. (1987). Brain damage in non-missile head injury secondary to high intracranial pressure. *Neuropathology and Applied Neurobiology, 13*, 207–217.

Granger, C.V., Albrecht, G.L., & Hamilton, B.B. (1979). Outcome of comprehensive medical rehabilitation: Measurement by PULSES Profile and the Barthel Index. *Archives of Physical Medicine and Rehabilitation, 60*, 145–154.

Granger, C.V., & Hamilton, B.B. (1987). *Uniform data set for medical rehabilitation.* Buffalo, NY: Research Foundation, State University of New York.

Granholm, L., & Svendgaard, N. (1972). Hydrocephalus following traumatic head injuries. *Scandinavian Journal of Rehabilitation Medicine, 4*, 31–34.

Gray, J.M., & Robertson, I. (1989). Remediation of attentional difficulties following brain injury: Three experimental case studies. *Brain Injury, 3*, 163–170.

Gray, J.M., Robertson, I., Pentland, B., & Anderson, S. (1992). Microcomputer-based attentional retraining after brain damage: A randomised group controlled trial. *Neuropsychological Rehabilitation, 2*, 97–115.

Grice, H.P. (1975). Logic in conversation. In P. Cole & J. Morgan (Eds.), *Studies in syntax and semantics* (vol. 3. pp. 41–58). New York: Academic Press.

Groher, M. (1977). Language and memory disorders following closed head trauma. *Journal of Speech and Hearing Research, 20*, 212–223.

Gronwall, D.M. (1976). Performance changes during recovery from closed head injury. *Proceedings of the Australian Association of Neurologists, 13*, 143–147.

Gronwall, D.M. (1986). Rehabilitation programs for patients with mild head injury: Components, problems and evaluation. *Journal of Head Trauma Rehabilitation, 1*(2), 53–62.

Gronwall, D.M. (1989). Cumulative and persisting effects of concussion on attention and cognition. In H. Levin & A. Benton (Eds.), *Mild head injury.* New York: Oxford University Press.

Gronwall, D.M (1991). Minor head injury. *Neuropsychology, 5*, 253–265.

Gronwall, D.M., & Sampson, H. (1974). *The psychological effects of concussion.* Auckland: Auckland University Press/Oxford University Press.

Gronwall, D.M., & Wrightson, P. (1974). Delayed recovery of intellectual function after minor head injury. *Lancet, 2*, 995–997.

Gronwall, D.M., & Wrightson, P. (1980). Duration of post-traumatic amnesia after mild head injury. *Journal of Clinical Neuropsychology, 2*, 51–60.

Groswasser, Z., Mendelson, L., Stern, M., Schecter, I., & Najenson, T. (1977). Re-evaluation of prognostic factors in rehabilitation after severe head injury. *Scandinavian Journal of Rehabilitation Medicine, 9*, 147.

Gurdjian, E.S., & Webster, J.E. (1958). *Head injuries: Mechanisms, diagnosis and management.* Boston, MA: Little, Brown and Co.

Haas, J.F., Cope, D.N., & Hall, K. (1987). Premorbid prevalence of poor academic performance in severe head injury. *Journal of Neurology, Neurosurgery, and Psychiatry, 50*, 52–56.

Haffey, W.J., & Abrams, D.L. (1991). Employment outcomes for participants in a brain injury work reentry program: Preliminary findings. *Journal of Head Trauma Rehabilitation, 6*(3), 24–34.

Haffey, W.J., & Johnston, M.V. (1990). A functional assessment system for real-world rehabilitation outcomes. In D.E. Tupper & K.D. Cicerone (Eds.), *The neuropsychology of everyday life: Assessment and basic competencies* (pp. 99–123). Boston, MA: Kluwer Academic Publishers.

Hagen, C. (1982). Language-cognitive disorganization following closed head injury: A conceptualisation. In L.E. Trexler (Ed.), *Cognitive rehabilitation. Conceptualization and intervention* (pp. 131–151). New York: Plenum Press.

Hagen, C. (1984). Language disorders in head trauma. In A. Holland (Ed.), *Language disorders in adults* (pp. 245–280). San Diego, CA: College-Hill Press.

Hahn, Y.S., Chyng, C., Barthel, M.J., Bailes, J., Flannery, A.M., McLone, D.G. (1988). Head injuries in children under 36 months of age. Demography and outcome. *Child's Nervous System, 4*, 34–40.

Hall, D.E., & DePompei, R. (1986). Implications for the head injured reentering higher education. *Cognitive Rehabilitation, May/June, 6*–8.

Hall, K.M., Karsmark, P., Stevens, M., Englander, J., O'Hare, P., & Wright, J. (1994). Family stressors in traumatic brain injury: A two-year follow-up. *Archives of Physical Medicine and Rehabilitation, 75*, 876–884.

Hall, M.E., Macdonald, S., & Young, G.C. (1992). The effectiveness of directed multisensory stimulation versus non-directed stimulation in comatose CHI patients: a pilot study of a single subject design. *Brain Injury, 6*, 435–445.

Harrick, L., Krefting, L., Johnston, J., Carlson, P., & Minnes, P. (1994). Stability of functional outcomes following transitional living programme participation: 3-year follow-up. *Brain Injury, 8*, 439–447.

Hart, T., & Hayden, M.E. (1986). The ecological validity of neuropsychological assessment and remediation. In B. Uzzell & Y. Gross (Eds.), *Clinical neuropsychology of intervention* (pp. 21–50). Boston, MA: Martinus Nijhoff.

Hartley, L.L. (1990). Assessment of functional communication. In D.E. Tupper & K.D. Cicerone (Eds.), *The neuropsychology of everyday life. Assessment and basic competencies* (pp 125–167). Boston, MA: Kluver Academic Publishers.

Hartley, L.L., & Griffith, A. (1989). A functional approach to the cognitive-communication deficits of closed head injured clients. *Journal of Speech–Language Pathology and Audiology, 13*(2), 51–57.

Hartley, L.L., & Levin, H.S. (1990). Linguistic deficits after closed head injury: a current appraisal. *Aphasiology, 4*, 353–370.

Haynes, M.K.M. (1992). Nutrition in the severely head-injured patient. *Clinical Rehabilitation, 6*, 153–158.

Health Department of Victoria, Community Services Victoria and Transport Accident Commission (1991). *Report of Head Injury Impact Study.* Melbourne: Health Department of Victoria.

Heaton, R.K., & Pendleton, M.G. (1981). Use of neuropsychological tests to predict adult patients' everyday functioning. *Journal of Consulting and Clinical Psychology, 49*, 807–821.

Heilman, K., Safran, X., & Geschwind, N. (1971). Closed head trauma and aphasia. *Journal of Neurology, Neurosurgery and Psychiatry, 34*, 265–269.

Heiskanen, O., & Kaste, M. (1974). Late prognosis of severe brain injury in children. *Developmental Medicine and Child Neurology, 16*, 11–14.

Helffenstein, D.A., & Wechsler, F.S. (1982). The use of Interpersonal Process Recall (I.P.R.) in the remediation of interpersonal and communication skill deficits in the newly brain-injured. *Clinical Neuropsychology, 4*, 139–143.

Hersh, N., & Treadgold, L. (1994). NeuroPage: The rehabilitation of memory dysfunction by prosthetic memory and cueing. *NeuroRehabilitation, 4*, 187–197.

Higashi, K., Sakata, Y., Hatano, M., Abiko, S., Ihara, K., Katayama, S., Wakuta, Y., Okamura, T., Ueda, H., Zenke, M., & Aoki, H. (1977). Epidemiological studies on patients with a persistent vegetative state. *Journal of Neurology, Neurosurgery and Psychiatry, 40*, 876–885.

Hinkeldey, N.S., & Corrigan, J.D. (1990) The structure of head-injured patients' neurobehavioural complaints: A preliminary study. *Brain Injury, 4*, 115–133.

Holbourn, A.H.S. (1943). Mechanics of head injuries. *Lancet, 2*, 438–441.

Holbrook, M., & Skilbeck, C.E. (1983). An activities index for use with stroke patients. *Age and Ageing, 12*, 166–170.

Holland, A.L. (1980). *Communicative abilities in daily living.* Baltimore, MD: University Park Press.

Holland, A.L. (1982a). Observing functional communication of aphasic patients. *Journal of Speech and Hearing Disorders, 47*, 50–56.

Holland, A.L. (1982b). When is aphasia aphasia? The problem of closed head injury. In R.H. Brookshire (Ed.), *Clinical aphasiology conference proceedings* (pp. 345–349). Minneapolis, MN: BRK Publishers.

Hopewell, C.A., Burke, W.H., Weslowski, M., & Zawlocki, R. (1990). Behavioural learning therapies for the traumatically brain-injured patient. In R.L. Wood & I. Fussey (Eds.), *Cognitive rehabilitation in perspective* (pp. 229–245). London: Taylor & Francis.

Hopewell, C.A., & Price, R.J. (1985). Driving after head injury. *Journal of Clinical and Experimental Neuropsychology, 7*, 148.

Horn, L.J., & Zasler, N.D. (1990). Neuroanatomy and neurophysiology of sexual function. *Journal of Head Trauma Rehabilitation, 5*(2), 1–13.

Horn, S., Shiel, A., McLellan, L., Campbell, M., Watson, M., & Wilson, B. (1993). A review of behavioural assessment scales for monitoring recovery in and after coma with pilot data on a new scale of visual awareness. *Neuropsychological Rehabilitation, 3*, 121–137.

Horne, D.J.deL. (1994). The psychology of working with victims of traumatic accidents. In R. Watts & D.J.deL. Horne (Eds.), *Coping with trauma: The victim and the helper* (pp. 85–99). Brisbane: Australian Academic Press.

Horton, A.M. (1979). Behavioural neuropsychology: Rationale and research. *Clinical Neuropsychology, 1*(2), 20–23.

Houston, D., Williams, S.L., Bloomer, J., & Mann, W.C. (1989). The Bay Area Functional Performance Evaluation: Development and standardization. *The American Journal of Occupational Therapy, 43*, 170–183.

Hudson, R.A. (1980). *Sociolinguistics*. Cambridge: Cambridge University Press.

Hughes, J.R., (1978). Limitations of the EEG in coma and brain death. *Annals of the New York Academy of Sciences, 315*, 121–136.

Iverson, G.L., Iverson, A.M., & Barton, E.A. (1994). The Children's Orientation and Amnesia Test: Educational status is a moderator variable in tracking recovery from TBI. *Brain Injury, 8*, 685–688.

Jacobs, H.E. (1988). The Los Angeles Head Injury Survey: Procedures and preliminary findings. *Archives of Physical Medicine and Rehabilitation, 69*, 425–431.

Jacobs, H.E. (1989). Adult community integration. In P. Bach-y-Rita (Ed.), *Traumatic brain injury* (pp. 287–318). New York: Demos Publications.

Jacobs, H.E., Blatnick, M., & Sandhorst, J.V. (1990). What is lifelong living, and how does it relate to quality of life? *Journal of Head Trauma Rehabilitation, 5*(1), 1–8.

Jaffe, K.M., Fay, G.C., Polissar, N.L., Martin, K.M., Shurtleff, H.A., Rivara, J.B., & Winn, R. (1992). Severity of paediatric traumatic brain injury and early neurobehavioral outcome: A cohort study. *Archives of Physical Medicine and Rehabilitation, 73*, 540–547.

Jaffe, K.M., Fay, G.C., Polissar, N.L., Martin, K.M., Shurtleff, H.A., Rivara, J.B., & Winn, R. (1993). Severity of paediatric traumatic brain injury and neurobehavioral recovery at one year—a cohort study. *Archives of Physical Medicine and Rehabilitation, 74*, 587–595.

Jennett, B. (1976). Assessment of severity of head injury. *Journal of Neurology, Neurosurgery, and Psychiatry, 39*, 647–655.

Jennett, B. (1972). Head injuries in children. *Developmental Medicine and Child Neurology, 14*, 137–147.

Jennett, B. (1979). Posttraumatic epilepsy. *Advances in Neurology, 22*, 137–147.

Jennett, B. (1992). Letting vegetative patients die. *British Medical Journal, 305*, 1305–1306.

Jennett, B., & Bond, M. (1975). Assessment of outcome after severe brain damage. *Lancet, 1*, 480–487.

Jennett, B., & MacMillan, R. (1981). Epidemiology of head injury. *British Medical Journal, 282*, 101–104.

Jennett, B., & Plum, F. (1972). Persistent vegetative state after brain damage. A syndrome in search of a name. *Lancet, 1*, 734–737.

Jennett, B., Snoek, J., Bond, M., & Brooks, N. (1981). Disability after severe head injury: Observations on the use of the Glasgow Outcome Scale. *Journal of Neurology, Neurosurgery, and Psychiatry, 44*, 285–293.

Jennett, B., & Teasdale, G. (1981). *Management of head injuries.* Philadelphia: Davis.

Jennett, B., Teasdale, G., Galbraith, S., Pickard, J., Grant, H., Braakman, C., Avelaat, C., Maas, A., Minderhoud, J., Vecht, C.J., Heiden, J., Small, R., Caton, W., & Kurze, T. (1977). Severe head injuries in three countries. *Journal of Neurology, Neurosurgery, and Psychiatry, 44*, 285–293.

Johnson, D., & Almli, C.R. (1978). Age, brain damage, and performance. In S. Finger (Ed.), *Recovery from brain damage* (pp. 115–134). New York: Plenum Press.

Johnson, D.A., & Roethig-Johnson, K. (1989). Early rehabilitation of head-injured patients. *Nursing Times, 85*(4), 25–28.

Johnson, R. (1987). Return to work after severe head injury. *Disability Studies, 9*, 49–54.

Johnston, M.V. (1991). Outcomes of community re-entry programmes for brain injury survivors. Part 2: Further investigations. *Brain Injury, 5*, 155–168.

Johnston, M.V., & Lewis, F.D. (1991). Outcomes of community re-entry programmes for brain injury survivors. Part 1: Independent living and productive activities. *Brain Injury, 5*, 141–154.

Jones, D. (1987). *Neuropsychological and psychosocial outcome following closed head injuries in children.* Unpublished master's thesis, LaTrobe University, Melbourne, Australia.

Jones, M.K. (1974). Imagery as a mnemonic aid after left temporal lobectomy: Contrast between material specific and generalised memory disorders. *Neuropsychologia, 12*, 21–30.

Jordan, F.M., Cannon, A., & Murdoch, B.E. (1992). Language abilities of mildly closed head injured children (CHI) 10 years post-injury. *Brain Injury, 6*, 39–44.

Jordan, F., & Murdoch, B. (1990). A comparison of the conversational skills of closed head injured children and normal children. *Australian Journal of Human Communication Disorders, 18*(1), 69–82.

Jordan, F.M., Ozanne, A.E., & Murdoch, B.E. (1988). Long term speech and language disorders subsequent to closed head injury in children. *Brain Injury, 2*, 179–185.

Jordan, F.M., Ozanne, A.E., & Murdoch, B.E. (1990). Performance of closed head injured children on a naming task. *Brain Injury, 4*, 147–154.

Josman, N., & Katz, N. (1991). A problem-solving version of the Allen Cognitive Level Test. *The American Journal of Occupational Therapy, 45*, 331–338.

Kaplan, E., Goodglass, H., Weintraub, S., & Segal, O. (1983). *Boston Naming Test.* Philadelphia: Lea & Febiger.

Katz, S., Ford, A., Moskowitz, R., Jackson, B., & Jaffe, M. (1963). Studies of illness in aged: Index of ADL: Standardized measure of biological and psychosocial function. *Journal of the American Medical Association, 185*, 914–919.

Kaufmann, P.M., Fletcher, J.M., & Levin, H.S. (1994). *The role of attention in learning and memory function following paediatric traumatic brain injury.* Paper presented at the Twenty-Second Annual INS Meeting, Cincinnati, OH, February.

Kay, T. (1992). Neuropsychological diagnosis: Disentangling the multiple determinants of functional disability after mild traumatic brain injury. In L. Horn & N. Zasler (Eds.), Rehabilitation of post-concussive disorders. *Physical Medicine and Rehabilitation, 6*, 109–128. Philadelphia: Hanley & Belfus Inc.

Kearns, K.J. (1990). Procedures and measures. In L.B. Olswang, C.K. Thompson, S.F. Warren, & N.J. Minghetti (Eds.), *Treatment efficacy research in communication disorders* (pp.79–90). Rockville, Maryland: American Speech–Language–Hearing Foundation.

Kendal, P.C., & Wilcox, L.E. (1979). Self-control in children: Development of a rating scale. *Consulting and Clinical Psychology, 47*, 1020–1030.

Kennard, M.A. (1936). Age and other factors in motor recovery from precentral lesions in monkeys. *American Journal of Physiology, 115*, 138–146.

Kennard, M.A. (1938). Reorganization of motor function in the cerebral cortex of monkeys deprived of motor and pre-motor areas in infancy. *Journal of Neurophysiology, 1*, 477–496.

Kennard, M.A. (1940). Relation of age to motor impairment in man and in subhuman primates. *Archives of Neurology and Psychiatry, 44*, 377–397.

Kertesz, A. (1982). *Western Aphasia Battery*. New York: Grune & Stratton.

Kewman, D.G., Seigerman, C., Kintner, H., Chu, S., Henson, D., & Reeder, C. (1985). Simulation training of psychomotor skills: Teaching the brain-damaged to drive. *Rehabilitation Psychology, 30*, 11–27.

Kinsella, G., Moran, C., Ford, B., & Ponsford, J. (1988). Emotional disorder and its assessment within the severe head injured population. *Psychological Medicine, 18*, 57–63.

Kirsch, N.L., Levine, S.P., Fallon-Krueger, M., & Jaros, L. (1987). The microcomputer as an "orthotic" device for patients with cognitive deficits. *Journal of Head Trauma Rehabilitation, 2*(4), 77–86.

Klein, R. M., & Bell, B. (1982). Self-care skills: Behavioral measurement with Klein-Bell ADL Scale. *Archives of Physical Medicine and Rehabilitation, 63*, 335–338.

Klonoff, H. (1971). Head injuries in children: Predisposing factors. *American Journal of Public Health, 61*, 2404–2417.

Klonoff, H., Low, M.D., & Clark, C. (1977). Head injuries in children: A prospective five-year follow-up. *Journal of Neurology, Neurosurgery, and Psychiatry, 40*, 1211–1219.

Klonoff, H., & Paris, R. (1974). Immediate, short-term and residual effects of acute head injuries in children. Neuropsychological and neurological correlates. In R.M. Reitan & L.A. Davidson (Eds.), *Clinical neuropsychology: Current status and applications* (pp. 179–210). Washington: John Wiley.

Klonoff, P.S., Costa, L.D., & Snow, W.G. (1986a). Predictors and indicators of quality of life in patients with closed head injury. *Journal of Clinical and Experimental Neuropsychology, 8*, 469–485.

Klonoff, P.S., Snow, W.G., & Costa, L.D. (1986b). Quality of life in patients 2 to 4 years after closed head injury. *Neurosurgery, 19*, 735–743.

Knights, R.M., Ivan, L.P., Ventureyra, E.C.G., Bentivoglio, C., Stoddart, C., Winogron, W., & Bawden, H.N. (1991). The effects of head injury in children on neuropsychological and behavioural functioning, *Brain Injury, 5*, 339–351.

Kovacs, F. (1995). *Time pressure management for head injured patients: Strategy training to compensate for mental slowness*. Unpublished PhD thesis, University of Nijmegen, The Netherlands.

Kovacs, F., Fasotti, L., Eling, P., & Brouwer, W. (1993, March–April). *Strategy training to compensate for mental slowness in head injured patients.* Poster presented at the International Brain Injury Forum: The quest for better outcomes, Oxford.

Kozloff, R. (1987). Networks of social support and outcome from severe head injury. *Journal of Head Trauma Rehabilitation, 2*(3), 14–23.

Kreutzer, J.S., Gervasio, A.H., & Camplair, P.S. (1994a). Patient correlates of caregivers' distress and family functioning after traumatic brain injury. *Brain Injury, 8,* 211–230.

Kreutzer, J.S., Gervasio, A.H., & Camplair, P.S. (1994b). Primary caregivers' psychological status and family functioning after traumatic brain injury. *Brain Injury, 8,* 197–210.

Kreutzer, J.S., Leininger, B.E., Sherron, P., & Groah, C. (1989). Management of psychosocial dysfunction following traumatic brain injury to improve employment outcome. In P. Wehman and J. Kreutzer (Eds.), *Vocational rehabilitation after traumatic brain injury.* Rockville, MD: Aspen Publishers.

Kreutzer, J.S., & Morton, M.V. (1988). Traumatic brain injury: Supported employment and compensatory strategies for enhancing vocational outcomes. In P. Wehman & S. Moon (Eds.), *Vocational rehabilitation and supported employment* (pp. 291–311). Baltimore, MD: Paul H. Brookes Publishing Company.

Kreutzer, J.S., & Zasler, N.D. (1989). Psychosexual consequences of traumatic brain injury: methodology and preliminary findings. *Brain Injury, 3,* 177–186.

Lam, C.S., McMahon, B.T., Priddy, D.A., & Gehred-Schultz, A. (1988). Deficit awareness and treatment performance among traumatic head injury adults. *Brain Injury, 2,* 235–242.

Lamont, M. (1993). *Stress in caregivers of head-injured persons.* Unpublished Master's thesis, LaTrobe University, Melbourne, Australia.

Langer, K.G., & Padrone, F.J. (1992). Psychotherapeutic treatment of awareness in acute rehabilitation of traumatic brain injury. *Neuropsychological Rehabilitation, 2,* 59–70.

Langfitt, T.W., Obrist, W.D., Alavi, A., Grossman, R., Zimmerman, R., Jaggi, J., Uzzell, B., Reivich, M., & Patton, D. (1987). Regional structure and function in head-injured patients: Correlation of CT, MRI, PET, CBF, and neuropsychological assessment. In H.S. Levin, J. Grafman, & H.M. Eisenberg (Eds.), *Neurobehavioural recovery from head injury* (pp. 30–42). New York: Oxford University Press.

Laurence, S, & Stein, D. (1978). Recovery after brain damage and the concept of localization of function. In S. Finger (Ed.), *Recovery from brain damage: Research and theory* (pp. 369–407). New York: Plenum Press.

Law, M. (1993). Evaluating activities of daily living: Directions for the future. *The Americian Journal of Occupational Therapy, 47,* 233–237.

Law, M., Baptiste, S., McColl, M., Opzoomer, A., Polatajko, H., & Pollock, N. (1990). The Canadian Occupational Performance Measure: An outcome measure for occupational therapy. *Canadian Journal of Occupational Therapy, 57,* 82–87.

Lawson, M.J., & Rice, D.N. (1989). Effects of training in use of executive strategies on a verbal memory problem resulting from closed head injury. *Journal of Experimental and Clinical Neuropsychology, 11,* 842–854.

Leach, L.R., Frank, R.G., Bouman, D.E., & Farmer, J. (1994). Family functioning, social support and depression after traumatic brain injury. *Brain Injury, 8*, 599–606.

Levin, H.S. (1994). *Neurobehavioural outcome in children and its relationship to MRI*. Paper presented at the Fourth Conference of the International Association for the Study of Traumatic Brain Injury, St Louis, MO, September.

Levin, H.S., Amparo, E., Eisenberg, H.M., Williams, D.H., High, W.M., Jr., McArdle, C.B., & Weiner, R.L. (1987a). Magnetic resonance imaging and computerised tomography in relation to the neurobehavioral sequelae of mild and moderate head injuries. *Journal of Neurosurgery, 66*, 706–713.

Levin, H.S., Benton, A.L., & Grossman, R.G. (1982a). *Neurobehavioral consequences of closed head injury*. New York: Oxford University Press.

Levin, H.S., & Eisenberg, H.M. (1979a). Neuropsychological impairment after closed head injury in children and adolescents. *Journal of Paediatric Psychology, 4*, 389–402.

Levin, H.S., & Eisenberg, H.M. (1979b). Neuropsychological outcome of closed head injury in children and adolescents. *Child's Brain, 5*, 281–292.

Levin, H.S., Eisenberg, H.M, & Benton, A.L. (Eds.) (1991). *Frontal lobe function and dysfunction*. New York: Oxford University Press.

Levin, H.S., Eisenberg, H.M., Wigg, N.R., & Kobayashi, K. (1982b). Memory and intellectual ability after head injury in children and adolescents. *Neurosurgery, 11*, 668–673.

Levin, H.S., & Grossman, R.G. (1978). Behavioural sequelae of closed head injury: A quantitative study. *Archives of Neurology, 35*, 720–727.

Levin, H., Grossman, R., & Kelly, P. (1976). Aphasia disorder in patients with closed head injury. *Journal of Neurology, Neurosurgery, and Psychiatry, 39*, 1062–1070.

Levin, H., Grossman, R.G., Sawar, M., & Meyers, C.A. (1981). Linguistic recovery after closed head injury. *Brain and Language, 12*, 360–374.

Levin, H.S., High, W.M., Goethe, K.E., Sisson, R.E., Overall, J.E., Rhoades, H.M., Eisenberg, H.M., Kalisky, Z., & Gary, H.E. (1987b). The Neurobehavioural Rating Scale: Assessment of the behavioural sequelae of head injury by the clinician. *Journal of Neurology, Neurosurgery, and Psychiatry, 50*, 183–193.

Levin, H.S., Mattis, S., Ruff, R.M., Eisenberg, H.M., Marshall, L.F., Tabbador, K., High, W.M., Jr., & Frankowski, R.F. (1987c). Neurobehavioral outcome following minor head injury: A three-center study. *Journal of Neurosurgery, 66*, 234–243.

Levin, H.S., O'Donnell, V.M., & Grossman, R.G. (1979). The Galveston Orientation and Amnesia Test. *Journal of Nervous and Mental Disease, 167*, 675–684.

Levy, D.E., Sidtis, J.J., Rottenberg, D.A., Jarden, J.O., Strother, S.C., Dhawan, V., Ginos, J.Z., Tramo, M.J., Evans, A.C., & Plum, F. (1987). Differences in cerebral blood flow and glucose utilization in vegetative versus locked-in patients. *Annals of Neurology, 22*, 673–682.

Lewinsohn, P.M., Danaher, G.B., & Kikel, S. (1977). Visual imagery as a mnemonic aid for brain injured persons. *Journal of Consulting and Clinical Psychology, 45*, 717–723.

Lewis, F.D., Nelson, J., Nelson, C., & Reusink, P. (1988). Effects of three feedback contingencies on the socially inappropriate talk of a brain injured adult. *Behaviour Therapy, 19*, 203–211.

Lezak, M.D. (1978). Living with the characterologically altered brain injured patient. *Journal of Clinical Psychiatry, 39,* 592–598.

Lezak, M.D. (1982). Assessing initiative, planning, and executive capabilities. In G.A. Broe & R.L. Tate (Eds.), *Proceedings of the Fifth Annual Brain Impairment Conference* (pp. 53–58). Supplement to the Bulletin of the Postgraduate Committee in Medicine, University of Sydney.

Lezak, M.D. (1983). *Neuropsychological assessment* (2nd edition). New York: Oxford University Press.

Lezak, M.D. (1994). *Neuropsychological assessment* (3rd edition). New York: Oxford University Press.

Lezak, M. (1987). Relationships between personality disorders, social disorders, social disturbances, and physical disability following traumatic brain injury. *Journal of Head Trauma Rehabilitation, 2*(1), 57–69.

Lira, F.T., Carne, W., & Masri, A.M. (1983). Treatment of anger and impulsivity in a brain damaged patient: A case study applying stress inoculation. *Clinical Neuropsychology, 5,* 159–160.

Little, M.M., Williams, J.M., & Long, C.J. (1986). Clinical memory tests and everyday life. *Archives of Clinical Neuropsychology, 1,* 323–333.

Livingston, M.G., & Brooks, D.N. (1988). The burden on families of the brain-injured: A review. *Journal of Head Trauma Rehabilitation, 3*(4), 6–15.

Lohman, T., Ziggas, D., & Pierce, R.S. (1989). Word fluency performance on common categories by subjects with closed head injuries. *Aphasiology, 3*(8), 685–693.

Long, C.S., & Webb, W.L., Jr. (1983). Psychological sequelae of head trauma, *Psychiatric Medicine, 1,* 35–77.

Luria, A.R. (1963). *Recovery of function after brain injury.* New York: Macmillan.

Luria, A.R. (1973). The frontal lobes and the regulation of behaviour. In K.H. Pribram & A.R. Luria (Eds.), *Psychophysiology of the frontal lobes* (pp. 3–26). New York: Academic Press.

Lysaght, R., & Bodenhamer, E. (1990). The use of relaxation training to enhance functional outcomes in adults with traumatic head injuries. *American Journal of Occupational Therapy, 44,* 797–802.

MacFlynn, G., Montgomery, E.A., Fenton, G.W., & Rutherford, W. (1984). Measurement of reaction time following minor head injury. *Journal of Neurology, Neurosurgery, and Psychiatry, 47,* 1326–1331.

Maddocks, D., & Sloan, S. (1993). Issues concerning the sensitivity of neuropsychological tests of executive dysfunction. *Proceedings of the Seventeenth Annual Brain Impairment Conference,* pp. 109–113. Canberra, August. Bowen Hills: Australian Academic Press.

Maguire, T.J., Hodges, D.L., Medhat, M.A., & Redford, J.B. (1986). Transient locked-in syndrome and phenobarbitol. *Archives of Physical Medicine and Rehabilitation, 68,* 566–567.

Mahoney, F.I., & Barthel, D.W. (1965). Functional evaluation: The Barthel Index. *Maryland State Medical Journal, 14,* 61–65.

Malec, J., Jones, R., Rao, N., & Stubbs, K. (1984). Video-game practice effects on sustained attention in patients with cranio-cerebral trauma. *Cognitive Rehabilitation, 2*(4), 18–23

Malec, J.F., Smigielski, J.S., DePompolo, R.W., & Thompson, J.M. (1993). Outcome evaluation and prediction in a comprehensive-integrated post-acute outpatient brain injury rehabilitation programme. *Brain Injury, 7,* 15–29.

Malkmus, D. (1989). Community reentry: Cognitive-communicative intervention within a social skill context. *Topics in Language Disorders, 9*(2), 50–66.

Mandleberg, I.A. (1975). Cognitive recovery after severe head injury: 2. Wechsler Adult Intelligence Scale during post-traumatic amnesia. *Journal of Neurology, Neurosurgery, and Psychiatry, 38*, 1127–1132.

Marosszeky, N.E.V., Batchelor, J., Shores, E.A., Marosszeky, J.E., Klein-Boonschate, M., & Fahey, P.P. (1993). The performance of hospitalised, non head-injured children on the Westmead PTA Scale. *The Clinical Neuropsychologist, 7*(1), 85–95.

Marsh, N.V., & Knight, R.G. (1991a). Behavioural assessment of social competence following severe head injury. *Journal of Clinical and Experimental Neuropsychology, 13*, 729–740.

Marsh, N.V., & Knight, R.G. (1991b). Relationship between cognitive deficits and social skill after head injury. *Neuropsychology, 5*, 107–117.

Marshall, J.F. (1984). Brain function: Neural adaptations and recovery from injury. *Annual Review of Psychology, 32*, 277–308.

Marshall, L.F., Becker, D.P., Bowers, S.A., Cayard, C., Eisenberg, H., Gross, C.R., Grossman, R.G., Jane, J.A., Kunitz, S.C., Rimel, R., Tabaddor, K., & Warren, J. (1983). The National Traumatic Coma Data Bank. Part 1: Design, purpose, goals, and results. *Journal of Neurosurgery, 59*, 276–284.

Martin, D.A. (1988). Children and adolescents with traumatic brain injury: Impact on the family. *Journal of Learning Disabilities, 21*, 464–470.

Mateer, C. (1992). Systems of care for post-concussive syndrome. In L. Horn & N. Zasler (Eds.), Rehabilitation of post-concussive disorders. *Physical Medicine and Rehabilitation, 6*, 143–160. Philadelphia: Hanley & Belfus Inc.

Mateer, C.A., & Sohlberg, M.M. (1988). A paradigm shift in memory rehabilitation. In H.A. Whitaker (Ed.), *Neuropsychological studies of nonfocal brain damage* (pp. 202–225). New York: Springer-Verlag.

Mateer, C.A., Sohlberg, M.M., & Youngman, P.K. (1990). The management of acquired attention and memory deficits. In Wood, R.L. & Fussey, I. (Eds.), *Cognitive rehabilitation in perspective* (pp. 68–95). London: Taylor & Francis.

Mateer, C.A., & Williams, D. (1991). Effects of frontal lobe injury in childhood. *Developmental Neuropsychology, 7*, 359–376.

Mayer, N.H., Keating, D.J., & Rapp, D. (1986). Skills, routines, and activity patterns of daily living: A functional nested approach. In B. Uzzell & Y. Gross (Eds.), *Clinical neuropsychology of intervention*, (pp. 205–221). Boston: Martinus Nijhoff.

McCarthy, R.A. & Warrington, E.K. (1990). *Cognitive neuropsychology: A clinical introduction.* San Diego, CA: Academic Press.

McDonald, S. & van Sommers, P. (1993). Pragmatic language skills after closed head injury: Ability to negotiate requests. *Cognitive Neuropsychology, 10*(4), 297–315.

McGrath, J.R., & Davis, A.M. (1992). Rehabilitation: Where are we going and how do we get there? *Clinical Rehabilitation, 6*, 225–235.

McKinlay, W.W., & Brooks, D.N. (1984). Methodological problems in assessing psychosocial recovery following severe head injury. *Journal of Clinical Neuropsychology, 6*, 87–99.

McKinlay, W.W., Brooks, D.N., & Bond, M.R. (1983). Post-concussional symptoms, financial compensation and outcome of severe blunt head injury. *Journal of Neurology, Neurosurgery, and Psychiatry, 46*, 1084–1091.

McKinlay, W.W., Brooks, D.N., Bond, M.R., Martinage, D.P., & Marshall, M.M. (1981). The short-term outcome of severe blunt head injury as reported by relatives of the injured persons. *Journal of Neurology, Neurosurgery, and Psychiatry, 44*, 527–533.

McKinlay, W., & Hickox, A. (1988). How can families help in the rehabilitation of the head injured? *Journal of Head Trauma Rehabilitation, 3*(4), 64–72.

McLellan, D.R. (1990). The structural basis of coma and recovery. *Physical Medicine and Rehabilitation: State of the Art Reviews, 4*, 389–407.

McNeny, R. (1990). Daily living skills. The foundation of community living. In J.S. Kreutzer & P. Wehman (Eds.), *Community integration following traumatic brain injury* (pp. 105–113). Baltimore, MD: Paul H. Brookes Publishing Company.

McSweeny, A.J. (1990). Quality-of-life assessment in neuropsychology. In D.E. Tupper & K.D. Cicerone (Eds.), *The neuropsychology of everyday life: Assessment and basic competencies* (pp. 185–218). Boston, MA: Kluwer Academic Publishers.

Medlar, T., & Medlar, J. (1990). Nursing management of sexuality issues. *Journal of Head Trauma Rehabilitation, 5*(2), 46–51.

Melamed, S., Groswasser, Z., & Stern, M.J. (1992). Acceptance of disability, work involvement and subjective rehabilitation status of traumatic brain-injured (TBI) patients. *Brain Injury, 6*, 233–243.

Miller, E. (1984). *Recovery and management of neuropsychological impairments*. Chichester: John Wiley & Sons.

Miller, E. (1994). Recovery and management of neuropsychological disorders. In S. Touyz, D. Byrne, & A. Gilandis (Eds.), *Neuropsychology in clinical practice* (pp. 329–342). Sydney: Academic Press.

Miller, H. (1961). Accident neurosis: Lecture 1. *British Medical Journal, 243*, 919–925.

Miller, H. (1966). Mental after-effects of head injury. *Proceedings of the Royal Society of Medicine, 59*, 257–261.

Miller, L. (1993). The "trauma" of head trauma: Clinical, neuropsychological, and forensic aspects of posttraumatic stress syndromes in brain injury. *The Journal of Cognitive Rehabilitation, July / August*, 18–29.

Miller, W.G., & Berenguer, E. (1994). Neuropsychological assessment of the traumatic head-injured patient. In S. Touyz, D. Byrne, & A. Gilandis (Eds.), *Neuropsychology in clinical practice* (pp. 79–106). Sydney: Academic Press.

Mills, V.M., Nesbeda, T., Katz, D.I., & Alexander, M.P. (1992). Outcomes for traumatically brain-injured patients following post-acute rehabilitation programmes. *Brain Injury, 6*, 219–228.

Milner, B. (1963). Effects of brain lesions on card sorting. *Archives of Neurology, 9*, 90–100.

Milner, B. (1974). Hemispheric specialisation: Scope and limits. In F.O. Schmitt & G.G. Worden (Eds.), *The neurosciences: Third study program*. Cambridge, MA: MIT Press.

Milton, S.B., Prutting, C.A., & Binder, G.M. (1984). Appraisal of communicative competence in head injured adults. In R.H. Brookshire (Ed.). *Proceedings of the Clinical Aphasiology Conference* (pp. 114–123). Minneapolis, MN: BRK Publishers.

Milton, S.B., & Wertz, R.T. (1986). Management of persisting communication deficits in patients with traumatic brain injury. In: B.P. Uzzell & Y. Gross (Eds), *Clinical neuropsychology of intervention* (pp. 223–282). Boston, MA: Martinus Nijhoff.

Mitchell, S., Bradley, V.A., Welch, J.L., & Britton, P.G. (1990). Coma arousal procedure: A therapeutic intervention in the treatment of head injury. *Brain Injury, 4*, 273–279.

Moffat, N. (1984). Strategies of memory therapy. In B.A. Wilson & N. Moffat (Eds.), *Clinical management of memory problems* (pp. 63–88). London: Croom Helm.

Molloy, M.P. (1994). Computer-enhanced rehabilitation in the private practice setting. In S. Touyz, D. Byrne, & A. Gilandas (Eds.), *Neuropsychology in clinical practice* (pp. 359–370). Sydney: Academic Press, Inc.

Moore, A., Stambrook, M., & Peters, L. (1993). Centripetal and centrifugal family life cycle factors in long-term outcome following traumatic brain injury. *Brain Injury, 7*, 247–256.

Moore, A.D., Stambrook, M., Peters, L.C., Cardoses, E.R., & Kassum, P.A. (1990). Long-term multidimensional outcome following isolated traumatic brain injuries and traumatic brain injuries associated with multiple trauma. *Brain Injury, 4*, 379–389.

Moore, B.E., & Ruesch, J. (1944). Prolonged disturbances of consciousness following head injury. *The New England Journal of Medicine, 230*, 445–452.

Moos, R.H., & Moos, B.S. (1981). *Family environment scale*. Palo Alto, CA: Consulting Psychologists Press.

Montgomery, B., & Evans, L. (1983). *Living and loving together*. Melbourne, Australia: Nelson Publishers.

Montgomery, B., & Evans, L. (1984). *You and stress*. Melbourne, Australia: Nelson Publishers.

Morse, P.A., & Montgomery, C.E. (1992). Neuropsychological evaluation of traumatic brain injury. In R. F. White (Ed.), *Clinical syndromes in adult neuropsychology: The practitioner's handbook*. Amsterdam: Elsievier Science Publishers.

Morse, P.A., & Morse, A.R. (1988). Functional living skills: Promoting the interaction between neuropsychology and occupational therapy. *Journal of Head Trauma Rehabilitation, 3*, 33–44.

Multi-Society Task Force on PVS, Part One. (1994). Medical aspects of the persistent vegetative state (First of two parts). *The New England Journal of Medicine, May 26*, 1499–1508.

Multi-Society Task Force on PVS, Part Two. (1994). Medical aspects of the persistent vegetative state (Second of two parts). *The New England Journal of Medicine, June 2*, 1572–1579.

Naugle, R.I., & Chelune, G.J. (1990). Integrating neuropsychological and "real-life" data: A neuropsychological model for assessing everyday functioning. In D.E. Tupper & K.D. Cicerone (Eds.), *The neuropsychology of everyday life: Assessment and basic competencies* (pp. 57–73). Boston, MA: Kluwer Academic Publishers.

Nedd, K., Sfakianakis, G., Ganz, W., Urricchio, B., Vernberg, D., Villanueva, P., Jabir, A.M., Bartlett, J., & Keena, J. (1993). 99m Tc-HMPAQ SPECT of the brain in mild to moderate traumatic brain injury patients: Compared with CT-a prospective study. *Brain Injury, 7*, 469–479.

Nelson, H.E., & O'Connell, A. (1978). Dementia: The estimation of premorbid intelligence levels using the new adult reading test. *Cortex, 14*, 234–244.

Newcombe, F. (1982). The psychological consequences of closed head injury: Assessment and rehabilitation. Injury: *The British Journal of Accident Surgery, 14*, 111–136.

Newton, M.R., Greenwood, R.J., Britton, K.E., Charlesworth, M., Nimmon, C.C., Carroll, M.J., & Dolke, G. (1992). A study comparing SPECT with CT and MRI after closed head injury. *Journal of Neurology, Neurosurgery and Psychiatry, 55*, 92–94.

NHIF (National Head Injury Foundation). (1984). *The silent epidemic.* Framingham, MA: NHIF.

NHIF (National Head Injury Foundation) Task Force on Special Education. (1989). *An educator's manual: What educators need to know about students with traumatic brain injury.* Southborough, MA: NHIF.

Nici, J., & Logue, P. (1984). Neuropsychological consequences of head injuries. In R.A. Hock (Ed.), *The rehabilitation of the child with a traumatic brain injury* (pp. 177–206). Springfield, IL: Charles C. Thomas.

Niemann, H., Ruff, R.M., & Baser, C.A. (1990). Computer-assisted attention retraining in head-injured individuals: A controlled efficacy study of an outpatient program. *Journal of Consulting and Clinical Psychology, 58*, 811–817.

Novack, T.A. (1993, February). Some thoughts on family coping after traumatic brain injury. *Headway Victoria Newsletter*, p.6.

Novaco, R. (1975). *Anger control: The development and evaluation of an experimental treatment.* Lexington, MA: Lexington Books.

Oboler, S.K. (1986). Brain death and persistent vegetative states. *Clinics in Geriatric Medicine, 2*, 547–576.

O'Connor, M., & Cermak, L. (1987). Rehabilitation of organic memory disorders. In M.J. Meier, A.L. Benton, & L. Diller (Eds.), *Neuropsychological rehabilitation* (pp. 260–279). New York: Churchill Livingstone.

Oddy, M. (1984a). Head injury and social adjustment. In N. Brooks (Ed.), *Closed head injury: Psychological, social and family consequences* (pp. 108–122). London: Oxford University Press.

Oddy, M. (1984b). Head injury during childhood: The psychological implications. In N. Brooks (Ed.), *Closed head injury: Psychological, social and family consequences* (pp. 179–194).

Oddy, M. (1993). Head injury during childhood. *Neuropsychological Rehabilitation, 3*, 301–320.

Oddy, M., Coughlan, T., Tyerman, A., & Jenkins, D. (1985). Social adjustment after closed head injury: A further follow-up seven years after injury. *Journal of Neurology, Neurosurgery, and Psychiatry, 48*, 564–568.

Oddy, M., & Humphrey, M. (1980). Social recovery during the year following severe head injury. *Journal of Neurology, Neurosurgery, and Psychiatry, 43*, 798–802.

Oddy, M., Humphrey, M., & Uttley, D. (1978a). Subjective impairment and social recovery after closed head injury. *Journal of Neurology, Neurosurgery, and Psychiatry, 41*, 611–616.

Oddy, M., Humphrey, M., & Uttley, D. (1978b). Stresses upon the relatives of head-injured patients. *British Journal of Psychiatry, 133*, 507–513.

Olver, J. (1991). Towards community re-entry. Preliminary evaluation of Bethesda Hospital's Transitional Living Program. *Think Magazine, June*, 28–29.

Ommaya, A.K., & Gennarelli, T.A. (1974). Cerebral concussion and traumatic unconsciousness: Correlation of experimental and clinical observations on blunt head injuries. *Brain, 97*, 633–654.

Osterreith, P.A. (1944). Le test de copie d'une figure complexe. *Archives of Psychology, 30*, 206–353.

Pang, D. (1985). Pathophysiologic correlates of neurobehavioural syndromes following closed head injury. In M. Ylvisaker (Ed.), *Head injury rehabilitation: Children and adolescents* (pp. 3–70). Boston, MA: College-Hill Press.

Panikoff, L. B. (1983). Recovery trends of functional skills in the head-injured adult. *The American Journal of Occupational Therapy, 37*, 735–743.

Panting, A., & Merry, P. (1972). The long-term rehabilitation of severe head injuries with particular reference to the need for social and medical support for the patient's family. *Rehabilitation, 38*, 33–37.

Papanicolaou, A.C. (1987). Electrophysiological methods for the study of attentional deficits in head injury. In H.S. Levin, J. Grafman, & H.M. Eisenberg (Eds.), *Neurobehavioural recovery from head injury*. New York: Oxford University Press.

Papanicolaou, A.C., Loring, D.W., Eisenberg, H.M., Raz, N., & Contreras, F.L. (1986). Auditory brain stem evoked responses in comatose head injured patients. *Neurosurgery, 18*(2), 173–175.

Parente, R., Stapleton, M.C., & Wheatley, C.J. (1991). Practical strategies for vocational reentry after traumatic brain injury. *Journal of Head Trauma Rehabilitation, 6*(3), 35–45.

Parry, A. (1985). *Head injury: Factors related to the adjustment of family members*. Unpublished Master's thesis, LaTrobe University, Melbourne, Australia.

Patten, B.M. (1972). The ancient art of memory: Usefulness in treatment. *Archives of Neurology, 26*, 25–31.

Pearce, J.M.S. (1987). The locked in syndrome. *British Medical Journal, 294*, 198–199.

Pedretti, L.W. (1985). *Occupational therapy, practice skills for physical dysfunction*. St Louis, MO: The C.V. Mosby Company.

Pelco, L., Sawyer, M., Duffield, G., Prior, M., & Kinsella, G. (1992) Premorbid emotional and behavioural adjustment in children with mild head injuries. *Brain Injury, 6*(1), 29–37.

Penn, C. (1985). The profile of communicative appropriateness: A clinical tool for the assessment of pragmatics. *The South African Journal of Communication Disorders, 32*, 18–23.

Perlesz, A., Furlong, M., & McLachlan, D. (1989). Family-centred rehabilitation: Family therapy for the head injured and their relatives. In R. Harris, R. Burns, & R. Rees (Eds.), *Recovery from brain injury: Expectations, needs and processes* (pp. 180–191). Adelaide: Institute for the Study of Learning Difficulties.

Pessar, L.F., Coad, M.L., Linn, R.T., & Willer, B.S. (1993). The effects of parental traumatic brain injury on the behaviour of parents and children. *Brain Injury, 7*, 231–240.

Peters, L., Stambrook, M., Moore, A., & Esses, L. (1990). Psychosocial sequelae of head injury: Effects on the marital relationship. *Brain Injury, 4*, 39–47.

Phillips, M., Ponsford, J., Saling, M., Sloan, S., Benjamin, L., & Currie, D. (1991). Management of memory impairment following closed head injury: Evaluation of an external memory aid (Abstract). *Journal of Clinical and Experimental Neuropsychology, 13*, 439.

Pierce, J.P., Lyle, D.M., Quine, S., Evans, N.J., Morris, J., & Fearnside, M.R. (1990). The effectiveness of coma arousal intervention. *Brain Injury, 4,* 191–197.

Pilz, P. (1983). Axonal injury in head injury. *Acta Neurochirurgie (Wien)* (Supplement 32), 119–123.

Plum, F., & Posner, J.B. (1972). Diagnosis of stupor and coma. *Contemporary Neurology Series* (2nd edition). Philadelphia: F.A. Davis & Co.

Ponsford, J.L. (1990). Editorial: Psychological sequelae of closed head injury: time to redress the imbalance. *Brain Injury, 4,* 111–114.

Ponsford, J.L., & Kinsella, G. (1988). Evaluation of a remedial programme for attentional deficits following closed head injury. *Journal of Clinical and Experimental Neuropsychology, 10,* 693–708.

Ponsford, J.L., & Kinsella, G. (1991). The use of a rating scale of attentional behaviour. *Neuropsychological Rehabilitation, 1,* 241–257.

Ponsford, J.L., & Kinsella, G. (1992). Attentional deficits following closed-head injury. *Journal of Clinical and Experimental Neuropsychology, 14,* 822–838.

Ponsford, J.L., Olver, J.H., & Curran, C. (1994). *Outcome following TBI: A comparison between two and five years after injury.* Paper presented at the Fourth Conference of the International Association for the Study of Traumatic Brain Injury, St. Louis, Missouri, September.

Ponsford, J.L., Olver, J.H., & Curran, C. (1995a). A profile of outcome two years following traumatic brain injury, *Brain Injury, 9,* 1–10.

Ponsford, J.L., Olver, J.H., Curran, C., & Ng, K. (1995b). Prediction of employment status two years after traumatic brain injury. *Brain Injury, 9,* 11–20.

Porteus, S. (1965). *Porteus Maze Test: Fifty years' application.* Palo Alto, CA: Pacific.

Powell, G.E. (1981). *Brain function therapy.* London: Gower.

Power, P.W. (1985). Family coping behaviours in chronic illness: A rehabilitation perspective. *Rehabilitation Literature, 46,* 78–83.

Prigatano, G. (1986). A patient competency rating. In G.P. Prigatano and others, *Neuropsychological rehabilitation after brain injury* (pp. 143–151). Baltimore, MD: Johns Hopkins University Press.

Prigatano, G.P. (1991). Disturbances of self-awareness of deficit after traumatic brain injury. In G.P. Prigatano & D.L. Schacter (Eds.), *Awareness of deficit after brain injury* (pp. 111–126). New York: Oxford University Press.

Prigatano, G., & Altman, I. (1990). Impaired awareness of behavioural limitations after traumatic brain injury. *Archives of Physical Medicine and Rehabilitation, 71,* 1058–1064.

Prigatano, G.P., & Fordyce, D.J. (1986). Cognitive dysfunction and psychosocial adjustment after brain injury. In Prigatano, G.P. and others, *Neuropsychological rehabilitation after brain injury* (pp. 1–17). Baltimore, MD: Johns Hopkins University Press.

Prigatano, G.P., O'Brien, K.P., & Klonoff, P.S. (1988). The clinical management of delusions in post acute traumatic brain injured patients. *Journal of Head Trauma Rehabilitation, 3*(3), 23–32.

Prigatano, G.P., Roueche, J.R., & Fordyce, D.J. (1985). Nonaphasic language disturbances after closed head injury. *Language Sciences, 1,* 217–229.

Prior, M., Kinsella, G., Sawyer, M., Bryan, D., & Anderson, V. (1994). Cognitive and psychosocial outcome after head injury in children. *Australian Psychologist, 29*(2), 116–123.

Prutting, C., & Kirchner, D. (1983). Applied pragmatics. In T. Gallagher & C. Prutting (Eds.), *Pragmatic assessment and intervention issues in language* (pp. 29–64). San Diego, CA: College-Hill Press.

Rader, M.A., Alston, J.B., & Ellis, D.W. (1989). Sensory stimulation of severely brain injured patients. *Brain Injury, 3*, 141–147.

Rader, M.A., & Ellis, D.W. (1989). *Sensory stimulation assessment measure: Manual for administration*. Camden, NJ: Institute of Brain Injury Research and Teaching.

Raimondi, A.J., & Hirschauer, J. (1984). Head injury in the infant and toddler. *Child's Brain, 11*, 12–35.

Randt, C., & Brown, E. (1983). *Randt Memory Test*. New York: Life Science Associates.

Rappaport, M. (1986). Brain evoked potentials in coma and the vegetative state. *Journal of Head Trauma Rehabilitation, 1*(1), 15–29.

Rappaport, M., Dougherty, A.M., & Kelting, D. L. (1992). Evaluation of coma and vegetative states. *Archives of Physical Medicine and Rehabilitation, 73*, 628–634.

Rappaport, M., Hall, K.M., Hopkins, K., Belleza, T., & Cope, D.N. (1982). Disability rating scale for severe head trauma: Coma to community. *Archives of Physical Medicine and Rehabilitation, 63*, 118–123.

Rappaport, M., Herrero-Backe, C., Rappaport, M.L., & Winterfield, K.M. (1989). Head injury outcome up to ten years later. *Archives of Physical Medicine and Rehabilitation, 70*, 885–892.

Rattok, J., Ben-Yishay, Y., Ezrachi. O., Larkin, P., Piasetsky, E., Ross, B., Silver, S., Vakil, E., Zide, E., & Diller, L. (1992). Outcome of different treatment mixes in a multidimensional neuropsychological rehabilitation program. *Neuropsychology, 6*, 395–415.

Reitan, R.M., & Wolfson, D. (1985). *The Halstead–Reitan Neuropsychological Test Battery*. Tucson, AZ: Neuropsychology Press.

Rey, A. (1959). *Le test de copie de figure complexe*. Paris: Editions centre de psychologie appliquée.

Rey, A. (1964). *L'Examen clinique en psychologie*. Paris: Presses Universitaires de France.

Richardson, J.T.E. (1990). *Clinical and neuropsychological aspects of closed head injury*. Hove, UK: Lawrence Erlbaum Associates Ltd.

Richardson, J.T.E., & Barry, C. (1985). The effects of minor closed head injury upon human memory: Further evidence on the role of mental imagery. *Cognitive Neuropsychology, 2*, 149–168.

Rimel, R.W., Giordani, B., Barth, J.T., Boll, T.J., & Jane, J.A. (1981). Disability caused by minor head injury. *Neurosurgery, 9*, 221–228.

Rimel, R.W., & Jane, J.A. (1984). Patient characteristics. In M. Rosenthal, E.R. Griffith, M.R. Bond, & J.D. Miller (Eds.), *Rehabilitation of the head injured adult* (pp. 9–20). Philadelphia: Davis.

Rivara, J.B., Jaffe, K., Fay, G.C., Polissar, N.L., Martin, K.M., Shurtleff, H.A., & Liao, S. (1993). Family functioning and injury severity as predictors of child functioning one year following traumatic brain injury. *Archives of Physical Medicine and Rehabilitation, 74*, 1047–1055.

Robertson, I., Gray, J.M., & McKenzie, S. (1988). Microcomputer-based cognitive rehabilitation of visual neglect: Three multiple-baseline single-case studies. *Brain Injury, 2,* 151–163.

Robertson, I.H., Ward, T., Ridgeway, V., & Nimmo-Smith, I. (1994). *The Test of Everyday Attention.* Flempton, Bury St Edmunds, Suffolk: Thames Valley Test Company.

Romano, M.D. (1974). Family response to traumatic head injury. *Scandinavian Journal of Rehabilitation Medicine, 6,* 1–4.

Rosenbaum, M., & Najenson, T. (1976). Changes in life patterns and symptoms of low mood as reported by wives of severely brain-injured soldiers. *Journal of Consulting and Clinical Psychology, 44,* 881–888.

Rosenthal, M., & Young, T. (1988). Effective family intervention after traumatic brain injury: Theory and practice. *Journal of Head Trauma Rehabilitation, 3*(4), 42–50.

Rowbotham, G.F., MacIver, I.N., Dickson, J., & Bousfield, N.E. (1954). Analysis of 1,400 cases of acute injury to the head. *British Medical Journal, 1,* 726–730.

Rowley, G., & Fielding, K. (1991). Reliability and accuracy of the Glasgow Coma Scale with experienced and inexperienced users. *Lancet, 337,* 535–538.

Ruff, R. M., Baser, C. A., Johnson, J. W., Marshall, L. F., Klauber, S. K., Klauber, M. R., & Minteer, M. (1989). Neuropsychological rehabilitation: An experimental study with head-injured patients. *Journal of Head Trauma Rehabilitation, 4*(3), 20–36.

Ruff, R.M, Marshall, L.F., Crouch, J., Klauber, M.R., Levin, H.S., Barth, J., Kreutzer, J., Blunt, B.A., Foulkes, M.A., Eisenberg, H.M., Jane, J.A., & Marmarou, A. (1993). Predictors of outcome following severe head trauma: Follow-up data from the Traumatic Coma Data Bank. *Brain Injury, 7,* 101–111.

Russell, W.R., & Nathan, P.W. (1946). Traumatic amnesia. *Brain, 69,* 280–300.

Russell, W.R., & Smith, A. (1961). Post-traumatic amnesia in closed head injury. *Archives of Neurology, 5,* 16–29.

Rutter, M., Chadwick, O., Shaffer, D., & Brown, G. (1980). A prospective study of children with head injuries: I. Design and methods. *Psychological Medicine, 10,* 633–646.

Ryan, T.V., & Ruff, R.M. (1988). The efficacy of structured memory retraining in a group comparison of head trauma patients. *Archives of Clinical Neuropsychology, 3,* 165–179.

Sale, P., West, M., Sherron, P., & Wehman, P. (1991). Exploratory analysis of job separations from supported employment for persons with traumatic brain injury. *Journal of Head Trauma Rehabilitation, 6*(3), 1–11.

Saling, M. (1994). Neuropsychology beyond 2001: The future of diagnostic expertise. In S. Touyz, D. Byrne, & A. Gilandis (Eds.), *Neuropsychology in clinical practice* (pp. 3–14). Sydney: Academic Press.

Sandel, M.E., Olive, D.A., & Rader, M.A. (1993). Chlorpromazine-induced psychosis after brain injury. Case Study. *Brain Injury, 7,* 77–83.

Saneda, D.L., & Corrigan, J.D. (1992). Predicting clearing of post-traumatic amnesia following closed-head injury. *Brain Injury, 6,* 167–174.

Sarno, M.T. (1969). *Functional Communication Profile: Manual of directions* (Rehabilitation Monograph No. 42). New York: New York University Medical Center, Institute of Rehabilitation Medicine.

Sarno, M.T., Buonaguro, A., & Levita, E. (1986). Characteristics of verbal impairment in closed head injured patients. *Archives of Physical Medicine and Rehabilitation, 67*, 400–405.

Sarno, M.T., Buonaguro, A., & Levita, E. (1987). Aphasia in closed head injury and stroke. *Aphasiology, 1*, 331–338.

Sarno, J. E., Sarno, M. T., & Levita, E. (1973). The Functional Life Scale. *Archives of Physical Medicine and Rehabilitation, 54*, 214–220.

Sazbon, L., Costeff, H., & Groswasser, Z. (1992). Epidemiological findings in traumatic post-comatose unawareness. *Brain Injury, 6*, 359–362.

Schacter, D.L., & Crovitz, H.F. (1977). Memory function after closed head injury: a review of quantitative research. *Cortex, 13*, 150–176.

Schacter, D.L., & Glisky, E.L. (1986). Memory remediation: Restoration, alleviation, and the acquisition of domain specific knowledge. In B. Uzzell & Y. Gross (Eds.), *Clinical neuropsychology of intervention* (pp. 257–282). Boston, MA: Martinus Nijhoff.

Schacter, D.L., Glisky, E.L., & McGlynn, S.M. (1990). Impact of memory disorder in everyday life: Awareness of deficits and return to work. In D. Tupper & K. Cicerone (Eds.), *The neuropsychology of everyday life: Assessment and basic competencies* (pp. 231–258). Boston, MA: Kluwer Academic Publishers.

Schacter, D.L., Rich, S.A., & Stampp, M.S. (1985). Remediation of memory disorders: experimental evaluation of the spaced retrieval technique. *Journal of Experimental and Clinical Neuropsychology, 7*, 79–96.

Schoenfeld, T.A., & Hamilton, L.W. (1977). Secondary brain changes following lesions: A new paradigm for lesion experimentation. *Physiology and Behaviour, 18*, 951–967.

Schoening, H. A., Anderegg, L., Bergstrom, D., Fonda, M., Steinke, N., & Ulrich, P. (1965). Numerical scoring of self-care status of patients. *Archives of Physical Medicine and Rehabilitiation, 46*, 689–697.

Schwartz, L., & McKinley, N.L. (1984). *Daily communication. Strategies for the language disordered adolescent.* Eau Claire, Wisconsin: Thinking Publications.

Searight, H. R., Dunn, E. J., Grisso, T., Margolis, R. B., & Gibbons, J. L. (1989). The relation of the Halstead–Reitan neuropsychological battery to ratings of everyday functioning in a geriatric sample. *Neuropsychology, 3*, 135–145.

Shaffer, D., Bijur, P., Chadwick, O., & Rutter, M. (1980). Head injury and later reading disability. *Journal of the American Academy of Child Psychiatry, 19*, 592–610.

Shallice, T. (1982). Specific impairments of planning. In D.E. Broadbent & L. Weiskrantz (Eds.), *The neuropsychology of cognitive function* (pp. 199–209). London: The Royal Society.

Shallice, T., & Burgess, P.W. (1991). Deficits in strategy application following frontal lobe damage in man. *Brain, 114*, 727–741.

Shiel, A., Wilson, B.A., Horn, S., Watson, M., & McLellan, D.L. (1994, June). *A scale to identify and evaluate cognitive behaviours after severe head injury.* Paper presented at the Sixteenth European Conference of the International Neuropsychological Society, Angers, France.

Shimamura, A.P., Janowsky, J.S., & Squire, L.R. (1991). What is the role of frontal lobe damage in memory disorders? In H. Levin, H. Eisenberg, & A. Benton (Eds.), *Frontal lobe functions and dysfunctions* (pp. 173–198). New York: Oxford University Press.

Shores, E.A., Marosszeky, J.E., Sandanam, J., & Batchelor, J. (1986). Preliminary validation of a scale for measuring the duration of post-traumatic amnesia. *Medical Journal of Australia, 144*, 569–572.

Siegel, A., & Alavi, A. (1990). Brain imaging techniques. Physical medicine and rehabilitation. *State of the Art Reviews, 4*, 433–446.

Singer, G.H.S., Glang, A., Nixon, C., Cooley, E., Kerns, K.A., Williams, D., & Powers, L.E. (1994). A comparison of two psychosocial interventions for parents of children with acquired brain injury: An exploratory study. *Journal of Head Trauma Rehabilitation, 9*(4), 38–49.

Sivak, M., Hill, C.S., Henson, D.L., Butler, B.P., Silber, S.M., & Olson, P.L. (1984). Improved driving performance following perceptual training in persons with brain damage. *Archives of Physical Medicine and Rehabilitation, 65*, 163–167.

Sivak, M., Hill, C.S., & Olson, P.L. (1984). Computerized video tasks as training techniques for driving-related perceptual deficits of persons with brain damage: A pilot evaluation. *International Journal of Rehabilitation Research, 7*, 389–398.

Sloan, S., Benjamin, L., & Hawkins, W. (1989). Group treatment of memory problems following closed head injury. In V. Anderson & M. Bailey (Eds.), *Theory and Function: Bridging the Gap*. Proceedings of the Fourteenth Annual Brain Impairment Conference (pp. 36–42). Melbourne: ASSBI.

Smith, A. (1973). *Symbol Digit Modalities Test*. Los Angeles: Western Psychological Services.

Snaith, R.P., Bridge, G.W., & Hamilton, M. (1976). *The Leeds Scales for the Self Assessment of Anxiety and Depression*. London: Psychological Test Publications.

Snow, P., Douglas, J., & Ponsford, J. (1995). Discourse assessment following traumatic brain injury: A pilot study examining some demographic and methodological issues. *Aphasiology, 9*, 365–380.

Snow, P., Lambier, J., Parsons, C., Mooney, L., Couch, D., & Russell, J. (1987). Conversational skills following closed head injury: Some preliminary findings. In: C.D. Field, A.C. Kneebone, & M.W. Reid (Eds.), *Brain Impairment: Proceedings of the Eleventh Annual Brain Impairment Conference* (pp. 87–97). Melbourne: ASSBI.

Snow, R.B., Zimmerman, R.D., Gandy, S.E., & Deck, M.D.F. (1986). Comparison of magnetic resonance imaging and computed tomography in the evaluation of head injury. *Neurosurgery, 18*, 45–52.

Soderback, I. (1988). A housework-based assessment of intellectual functions in patients with acquired brain damage. *Scandinavian Journal of Rehabilitation Medicine, 20*, 57–69.

Sohlberg, M.M., & Mateer, C.A. (1987). Effectiveness of an attention-training program. *Journal of Clinical and Experimental Neuropsychology, 9*, 117–130.

Sohlberg, M.M., & Mateer, C.A. (1989). Training use of compensatory memory books: A three stage behavioral approach. *Journal of Clinical and Experimental Neuropsychology, 11*, 871–891.

Sohlberg, M.M., & Mateer, C.A. (1990). Evaluation and treatment of communicative skills. In: J. Kreutzer and P. Wehman (Eds.), *Community integration following traumatic brain injury* (pp. 67–83). Baltimore, MD: Paul H. Brooks Publishing Co.

Sohlberg, M.M., Mateer, C.A., & Stuss, D.T. (1993). Contemporary approaches to the management of executive control dysfunction. *Journal of Head Trauma Rehabilitation, 8*(1), 45–58.

Sohlberg, M.M., Sprunk, H., & Metzelaar, K. (1988). Efficacy of an external cuing system in an individual with severe frontal lobe damage. *Cognitive Rehabilitation, July/August*, 36–40.

Sohlberg, M.M., White, O., Evans, E., & Mateer, C. (1992a). Background and initial case studies into the effects of prospective memory training. *Brain Injury, 6*, 129–138.

Sohlberg, M.M., White, O., Evans, E., & Mateer, C. (1992b). An investigation of the effects of prospective memory training. *Brain Injury, 6*, 139–154.

Sparrow, S., Balla, D., & Cicchetti, D. (1984). *Vineland Adaptive Behaviour Scales*. Circle Pines, MN: American Guidance Service.

Spettell, C.M., Ellis, D.W., Ross, S.E., Sandel, M.E., O'Malley, K.F., Stein, S.C., Spivack, G., & Hurley, K.E. (1991). Time of rehabilitation admission and severity of trauma: Effect on brain injury outcome. *Archives of Physical Medicine and Rehabilitation, 72*, 320–325.

Spielberger, C.D., Gorsuch, R.L., Lushene, R., Vagg, P.R., & Jacobs, G.A. (1983). *Self-evaluation questionnaire*. Palo Alto, CA: Consulting Psychologists Press.

Spreen, O., & Benton, A. (1969). *Neurosensory Centre Comprehensive Examination for Aphasia*. Victoria, BC: Neuropsychological Laboratory, Department of Psychology, University of Victoria.

Stern, J.M., & Stern, B. (1989). Visual imagery as a cognitive means of compensation for brain injury. *Brain Injury, 3*, 413–419.

Steward, O. (1989). Reorganization of neuronal connections following CNS trauma: Principles and experimental paradigms. *Journal of Neurotrauma, 6*(2), 99–152.

Strich, S.J. (1956). Diffuse degeneration of the cerebral white matter in severe dementia following head injury. *Journal of Neurology, Neurosurgery, and Psychiatry, 19*, 163–185.

Stroop, J.R. (1935). Studies of interference in serial verbal reactions. *Journal of Experimental Psychology, 18*, 643–662.

Stubbs, M. (1983). *Discourse analysis. The sociolinguistic analysis of natural language*. Oxford: Basil Blackwell.

Stuss, D.T., & Benson, D.F. (1986). *The frontal lobes*. New York: Raven Press.

Stuss, D.T., Ely, P., Hugenholtz, H., Richard, M.T., Larochelle, S., Poirier, C.A., & Bell, I. (1985). Subtle neuropsychological deficits in patients with good recovery after closed head injury. *Neurosurgery, 17*, 41–47.

Stuss, D.T., Stethem, L.L., Hugenholtz, H., Picton, T., Pivik, J., & Richard, M.T. (1989). Reaction time after head injury: Fatigue, divided and focused attention, and consistency of performance. *Journal of Neurology, Neurosurgery, and Psychiatry, 52*, 742–748.

Sunderland, A., Harris, J.E., & Baddeley, A.D. (1983). Do laboratory tests predict everyday memory? A neuropsychological study. *Journal of Verbal Learning and Verbal Behaviour, 22*, 341–357.

Sunderland, A., Harris, J., & Gleave, J. (1984). Memory failures in everyday life following severe head injury. *Journal of Clinical Neuropsychology, 6*, 127–142.

Swindell, C.S., Pashek, G.V., & Holland, A.L. (1982). A questionnaire for surveying personal and communicative style. In R.H. Brookshire (Ed.), *Clinical Aphasiology Conference Proceedings* (pp. 50–63). Minneapolis, MN: BRK Publishers.

Swonger, A.K., & Constantine, L.L. (1983). *Drugs and therapy: A handbook of psychotropic drugs* (pp. 305–311). Boston, MA: Little, Brown.

Symonds, C.P. (1937). Mental disorder following head injury. *Proceedings of the Royal Society of Medicine, 30*, 1081–1094.

Symonds, C.P. (1940). Concussion and contusion of the brain and their sequelae. In S. Brock (Ed.), *Injuries of the skull, brain and spinal cord: Neuro-psychiatric, surgical, and medico-legal aspects* (pp. 69–111). London: Bailliere, Tindall and Cox.

Symonds, C.P. (1942). Discussion of the differential diagnosis and treatment of post-contusional states. *Proceedings of the Royal Society of Medicine, 35*, 601–607.

Symonds, C.P., & Russell, W.R. (1943). Accidental head injuries: Prognosis in Service Patients. *Lancet, 1*, 7–10.

Tabbador, K., Mattis, S., & Zazula, T. (1983). Cognitive recovery after moderate and severe head injury (Abstract). *Archives of Physical Medicine and Rehabilitation, 64*, 489.

Tate, R.L., Lulham, J.M., Broe, G.A., Strettles, B., & Pfaff, A. (1989). Psychosocial outcome for the survivors of severe blunt head injury: The results from a consecutive series of 100 patients. *Journal of Neurology, Neurosurgery, and Psychiatry, 52*, 117–126.

Teasdale, G., & Jennett, B. (1974). Assessment of coma and impaired consciousness: A practical scale. *Lancet, 2*, 81–84.

Teasdale, G., & Jennett, B. (1976). Assessment and prognosis of coma after head injury. *Acta Neurochirurgica, 34*, 45–55.

Teasdale, G., & Mendelow, D. (1984). Pathophysiology of head injuries. In Brooks, N. (Ed.), *Closed head injury: Psychological, social and family consequences* (pp. 4–36). Oxford: Oxford University Press.

Teuber, H.L. (1975). Recovery of function after brain injury in man. In *Ciba Foundation Symposium no. 34, Outcome of severe damage to the central nervous system* (pp. 159–190). Amsterdam: Elsevier.

Thoene, A.I.T., & Glisky, E.L. (1995). Learning of name–face associations in memory impaired patients: A comparison of different training procedures. *Journal of the International Neuropsychological Society, 1*, 29–38.

Thompson, P.J., & Trimble, M.R. (1983). Anticonvulsant serum levels: Relationship to impairments of cognitive functioning. *Journal of Neurology, Neurosurgery, and Psychiatry, 46*, 227–233.

Thompson, J. (1992). Stress theory and therapeutic practice. *Stress Medicine, 8*, 147–150.

Thomsen, I.V. (1975). Evaluation and outcome of aphasia in patients with severe closed head trauma. *Journal of Neurology, Neurosurgery and Psychiatry, 38*, 713–718.

Thomsen, I.V. (1984). Late outcome of very severe blunt head injury: A ten to fifteen year second follow-up. *Journal of Neurology, Neurosurgery, and Psychiatry, 47*, 260–268.

Trexler, L., & Zappala, G. (1988). Neuropathological determinants of acquired attention disorders in traumatic brain injury. *Brain and Cognition, 8*, 291–302.

Tromp, E., & Mulder, T. (1991). Slowness of information processing after traumatic head injury. *Journal of Clinical and Experimental Neuropsychology, 13*, 821–830.

Tuel, S.M., Presty, S.K., Meythaler, J.M., Heinemann, A.W., & Katz, R.T. (1992). Functional improvement in severe head injury after readmission for rehabilitation. *Brain Injury, 6*, 363–372.

Tupper, D.E., & Cicerone, K.D. (1990). An introduction to the neurpsychology of everyday life. In D.E. Tupper & K.D. Cicerone (Eds.), *The neuropsychology of everyday life: Assessment and basic competencies* (pp. 3–18). Boston, MA: Kluwer Academic Publishers.

Tyerman, A., & Humphrey, M. (1984). Changes in self concept following severe head injury. *International Journal of Rehabilitation Research, 7*, 11–23.

Tyerman, A., Young, K., & Booth, J. (1994). *Change in family roles after severe traumatic brain injury.* Paper presented at the Fourth Conference of the International Association for the Study of Traumatic Brain Injury, St Louis, MO: September.

Uomoto, J.M., & Brockway, J.A. (1992). Anger management training for brain injured patients and their family members. *Archives of Physical Medicine and Rehabilitation, 73*, 674–679.

Vander Schaaf, S. (1990). An operational model of lifelong living. *Journal of Head Trauma Rehabilitation, 5*(1), 40–46.

van Zomeren, A.H. (1981). *Reaction time and attention after closed head injury.* Lisse, The Netherlands: Swets and Zeitlinger, B.V.

van Zomeren, A.H., & Brouwer, W.H. (1994). *Clinical neuropsychology of attention.* New York: Oxford University Press.

van Zomeren, A.H., & Brouwer, W.H. (1987). Head injury and concepts of attention. In H.S. Levin, J. Grafman, & H.M. Eisenberg (Eds.), *Neurobehavioral recovery from head injury* (pp. 398–415). Oxford: Oxford University Press.

van Zomeren, A.H., Brouwer, W.H., & Deelman, B.G. (1984). Attentional deficits: The riddles of selectivity, speed and alertness. In N. Brooks (Ed.), *Closed head injury: Psychological, social, and family consequences* (pp. 74–107). Oxford: Oxford University Press.

van Zomeren, A.H., Brouwer, W.H., & Minderhoud, J.M. (1987). Acquired brain damage and car driving: A review. *Archives of Physical Medicine and Rehabilitation, 68*, 697–705.

van Zomeren, A.H., Brouwer, W.H., Rothengatter, J.A., & Snoek, J.W. (1988). Fitness to drive a car after recovery from very severe head injury. *Archives of Physical Medicine and Rehabilitation, 69*, 92–96.

van Zomeren, A.H., & van den Burg, W. (1985). Residual complaints of patients two years after severe head injury. *Journal of Neurology, Neurosurgery, and Psychiatry, 48*, 21–28.

Vogenthaler, D.R. (1987). An overview of head injury: Its consequences and rehabilitation. *Brain Injury, 1*, 113–127.

Vogenthaler, D.R., Smith, K.R. Jr, & Goldfader, P. (1989). Head injury, an empirical study: Describing long-term productivity and independent living outcome. *Brain Injury, 3*, 355–368.

von Cramon, D.Y., & Matthes-von Cramon, G. (1994). Back to work with a chronic dysexecutive syndrome? (A case report). *Neuropsychological Rehabilitation, 4*, 399–417.

von Cramon, D.Y., Matthes-von Cramon, G., & Mai, N. (1991). Problem-solving deficits in brain-injured patients: A therapeutic approach. *Neuropsychological Rehabilitation, 1*, 45–64.

Waaland, P.K., & Kreutzer, J.S. (1988). Family response to childhood traumatic brain injury. *Journal of Head Trauma Rehabilitation, 3*(4), 51–63.

Wade, D.T., Legh-Smith, J., & Hewer, R.L. (1985). Social activities after stroke. *International Rehabilitation Medicine, 7*, 176–181.

Walsh, K.W. (1991). *Understanding brain damage: A primer of neuropsychological evaluation* (2nd edition). Edinburgh: Churchill Livingstone.

Walsh, K. (1994). Neuropsychological assessment of patients with memory disorders. In S. Touyz, D. Byrne, & A. Gilandas (Eds.), *Neuropsychology in clinical practice* (pp. 107–127). Sydney: Academic Press.

Warnock, H., Northin, D., Carberry, S., Ward, E., Hughes, D., Tennant, A., & Chamberlain, M. A. (1992). Head injury: Developing community occupational therapy to meet the challenge. *British Journal of Occupational Therapy, 55*, 99–102.

Watson, M., & Horn, S. (1991). The "ten pound note test": Suggestions for eliciting improved responses in the severely brain injured patient. *Brain Injury, 5*, 421–424.

Weber, M. (1990). A practical clinical approach to understanding and treating attentional problems. *Journal of Head Trauma Rehabilitation, 5*(2), 73–85.

Wechsler, D. (1981). *Wechsler Adult Intelligence Scale—Revised.* San Antonio, TX: The Psychological Corporation.

Wechsler, D. (1987). *Wechsler Memory Scale—Revised.* San Antonio. TX: The Psychological Corporation.

Weddell, R., Oddy, M., & Jenkins, D. (1980). Social adjustment after rehabilitation: A 2-year follow-up of patients with severe head injury. *Psychological Medicine, 10*, 257–263.

Wehman, P., Kregel, J., Sherron, P., Nguyen, S., Kreutzer, J., Fry, R., & Zasler, N. (1993). Critical factors associated with the successful supported employment placement of patients with severe traumatic brain injury. *Brain Injury, 7*, 31–44.

Wehman, P., Kregel, J., West, M., & Cifu, D. (1994). Return to work for patients with traumatic brain jnjury. Analysis of costs. *American Journal of Physical Medicine and Rehabilitation, 73*, 280–282.

Wehman, P., Kreutzer, J.S., Stonnington, H.H., Wood, W., Sherron, P., Diambra, J., Fry, R., & Groah, C. (1988). Supported employment for persons with traumatic brain injury: A preliminary report. *Journal of Head Trauma Rehabilitation, 3*(4), 82–94.

Wehman, P.H., & Kreutzer, J.S. (1994). *Return to work for patients with TBI: Six years of outcome data and program guidelines.* Paper presented at the Fourth Conference of the International Association for the Study of Traumatic Brain Injury, St Louis, MO, September.

Wehman, P., Kreutzer, J., West, M., Sherron, P. Zasler, N., Groah, C. Stonnington, H.H., Burns, C., & Sale, P. (1990). Return to work for persons with traumatic brain injury: A supported employment approach. *Archives of Physical Medicine and Rehabilitation, 71*, 1047–1052.

West, M., Wehman, P., Kregel, J., Kreutzer, J., Sherron, P., & Zasler, N. (1991). Costs of operating a supported work program for traumatically brain-injured individuals. *Archives of Physical Medicine and Rehabilitation, 72*, 127–131.

Whiteneck, G.G., Charlifue, S.W., Gerhart, K.A., Overholser, D., & Richardson, G.N. (1992). Quantifying handicap: A new measure of long-term rehabilitation outcomes. *Archives of Physical Medicine and Rehabilitation, 73*, 519–526.

WHO (World Health Organization) (1980). *International classification of impairments, disabilities, and handicaps: A manual of classification relating to the consequences of disease.* Geneva, Switzerland.

Whyte J., & Glenn, M.B. (1986). The care and rehabilitation of the patient in a persistent vegetative state. *Journal of Head Trauma Rehabilitation, 1*(1), 39–53.

Whyte, J., Polansky, M., Cavallucci, C., Fleming, M., & Coslett, H.B. (submitted). Clinical inattention after traumatic brain injury.

Wiig, E.H. (1982). *Let's talk: Developing prosocial communication skills.* Columbus, OH: Merrill.

Wiig, E. H., Alexander, E.W., & Secord, W. (1988). Linguistic competence and level of cognitive functioning in adults with traumatic closed head injury. In H.A. Whitaker (Ed.), *Neuropsychological studies of non-focal brain damage: Dementia and trauma* (pp. 186–201). New York: Springer-Verlag.

Wiig, E.H., & Secord, W. (1989). *Test of Language Competence for Adults.* San Antonio, TX: Psychological Corporation.

Wiig, E.H., & Semel, E.M. (1976). *Language disabilities in children and adolescents.* Columbus, OH: Merrill.

Willer, B.S., Allen, K., Anthony, J., & Cowlan, G. (1993a). *Circles of support for individuals with acquired brain injury. Manual.* State University of New York at Buffalo, Buffalo, New York: Rehabilitation Research and Training Center on Community Integration of Persons with Traumatic Brain Injury.

Willer, B.S., Allen, K.M., Liss, M., & Zicht, M.S. (1991). Problems and coping strategies of individuals with traumatic brain injury and their spouses. *Archives of Physical Medicine and Rehabilitation, 72*, 460–468.

Willer, B., & Corrigan, J.D. (1994). Whatever it takes: A model for community-based services. *Brain Injury, 8*, 647–659.

Willer, B., Linn, R., & Allen, K. (1993b). Community integration and barriers to integration for individuals with brain injury. In M.A.J. Finlayson & S. Garner (Eds.), *Brain injury rehabilitation: Clinical considerations* (pp. 355–375). Baltimore, MD: Williams & Wilkins.

Willer, B., Ottenbacher, K., & Coad, M. (1994). The Community Integration Questionnaire: A comparative examination. *American Journal of Physical Medicine and Rehabilitation, 73*, 103–111.

Wilson, B.A. (1984). Memory therapy in practice. In B.A. Wilson & N. Moffat (Eds.), *Clinical management of memory problems* (pp. 89–111). London: Croom Helm.

Wilson, B.A. (1987a). *Rehabilitation of memory.* New York: Guilford Press.

Wilson, B.A. (1987b). Single-case experimental designs in neuropsychological rehabilitation. *Journal of Clinical and Experimental Neuropsychology, 9*, 527–544.

Wilson, B.A. (1991). Long-term prognosis of patients with severe memory disorders. *Neuropsychological Rehabilitation, 1*, 117–134.

Wilson, B.A. (1993). Ecological validity of neuropsychological assessment: Do neuropsychological indices predict performance in everyday activities? *Applied and Preventive Psychology, 2*, 209–215.

Wilson, B.A., Baddeley, A.D., Evans, J.J., & Shiel, A. (1994). Errorless learning in the rehabilitation of memory impaired people. *Neuropsychological Rehabilitation, 4*, 307–326.

Wilson, B.A., Baddeley, A., Shiel, A., Patton, G. (1992a). How does post-traumatic amnesia differ from the amnesic syndrome and from chronic memory impairment? *Neuropsychological Rehabilitation, 2*, 169–256.

Wilson, B.A., Cockburn, J., & Baddeley, A.D. (1985). *The Rivermead Behavioural Memory Test Manual*. Flempton, Bury St. Edmunds, Suffolk: Thames Valley Test Company.

Wilson, B.A., Cockburn, J., & Halligan, P. (1987). *The Behavioural Inattention Test*. Flempton, Bury St. Edmunds, Suffolk: Thames Valley Test Company.

Wilson, C., & Robertson, I.H. (1992). A home-based intervention for attentional slips during reading following head injury: A single case study. *Neuropsychological Rehabilitation, 2*, 193–205.

Wilson, J.T.L., & Wyper, D. (1992). Neuroimaging and neuropsychological functioning following closed head injury: CT, MRI, and SPECT. *Journal of Head Trauma Rehabilitation, 7*(4), 29–39.

Wilson, R.S., Rosenbaum, G. Brown, G., Rourke, D., Whitman, D., & Grisell, J. (1978). An index of premorbid intelligence. *Journal of Consulting and Clinical Psychology, 46*, 1554–1555.

Wilson, S.L., McCranny, S.M., & Andrews, K. (1992b). The efficacy of music stimulation in prolonged coma—four single case experiments. *Clinical Rehabilitation, 6*, 181–187.

Wilson, S.L., Powell, G., Elliot, K., & Thwaites, H. (1991). Sensory stimulation in prolonged coma: Four single case studies. *Brain Injury, 5*, 393–400.

Winogron, H.W., Knights, R.M., & Bawden, H.N. (1984). Neuropsychological deficits following head injury in children. *Journal of Clinical Neuropsychology, 6*, 269–286.

Wood, R.L. (1984). Behaviour disorders following severe brain injury: their presentation and psychological management. In N. Brooks (Ed.), *Closed head injury: Psychological, social and family consequences* (pp. 195–219). Oxford: Oxford University Press.

Wood, R.L. (1986). Rehabilitation of patients with disorders of attention. *Journal of Head Trauma Rehabiltation, 1*, 43–53.

Wood, R.L. (1987). *Brain injury rehabilitation: A neurobehavioural approach*. London: Croom Helm.

Wood, R.L. (1990). Towards a model of cognitive rehabilitation. In R.L. Wood & I. Fussey (Eds.), *Cognitive rehabilitation in perspective* (pp. 3–25). Hove, UK: Lawrence Erlbaum Associates Ltd.

Wood, R.L. (1991). Critical analysis of the concept of sensory stimulation for patients in vegetative states. *Brain Injury, 5*, 401–409.

Wood, R.L., & Fussey, I. (1987). Computer-based cognitive retraining: A controlled study. *International Disability Studies, 9*, 149–154.

Wood, R.L., Winkowski, T., & Miller, J. (1993). Sensory regulation as a method to promote recovery in patients with altered states of consciousness. *Neuropsychological Rehabilitation, 3*, 177–190.

Wood, R.L., Winkowski, T.B., Miller, J.L., Tierney, L., & Goldman, L. (1992). Evaluating sensory regulation as a method to improve awareness in vegetative patients with altered states of consciousness: A pilot study. *Brain Injury, 6*, 411–418.

Woods, B.T., & Teuber, H.L. (1973). Early onset of complementary specialisation of cerebral hemispheres in man. *Transactions of the American Neurological Association, 98*, 113–117.

Wrightson, P., & Gronwall, D. (1981). Time off work and symptoms after minor head injury. *Injury, 12*, 445–454.

Yarnell, P.R., & Lynch, S. (1970). Retrograde memory immediately after concussion. *Lancet, 1*, 863–864.

Ying, Z,., Schmid, J., Schmid, J., & Hess, C.W. (1992). Motor and somatosensory evoked potentials in coma: analysis and relation to clinical status and outcome. *Journal of Neurology, Neurosurgery, and Psychiatry, 55*, 470–474.

Ylvisaker, M. (1988). *Head injury rehabilitation: Head injury rehabilitation with children and adolescents.* HDI professional series on traumatic brain injury, vol. 12. Houston, TX: HDI Publishers.

Ylvisaker, M., Hartwick, P., & Stevens, M. (1991). School reentry following head injury: Managing the transition from hospital to school. *Journal of Head Trauma Rehabilitation, 6*(1), 10–22.

Ylvisaker, M.S., & Holland, A.L. (1985). Coaching, self-coaching, and rehabilitation of head injury. In D.F. Johns (Ed.), *Clinical management of neurogenic communicative disorders* (pp. 243–257). Boston, MA: Little, Brown & Co.

Yorkston, K.M., & Beukelman, D.R. (1980). Analysis of connected speech samples of aphasic and normal speakers. *Journal of Speech and Hearing Disorders, 45*, 27–36.

Yorkston, K.M., Zeches, J., Farrier, L., & Uomoto, J. (1993). Lexical pitch as a measure of word choice in narratives of traumatically brain injured and control subjects. In M.L. Lemme (Ed.), *Clinical Aphasiology* (vol. 21, pp. 165–172). Austin, TX: Pro-Ed.

Youngjohn, J. R., Larrabee, G. J., & Crook, T. H. (1991). First–last names and the grocery list selective reminding test: Two computerized measures of everyday verbal learning. *Archives of Clinical Neuropsychology, 6*, 287–300.

Yudofsky, S., Silver, J.M., & Hales, R.E. (1990). Pharmacologic management of aggression in the elderly. *Journal of Clinical Psychiatry, 51*, 22–28.

Yudofsky, S., Williams, N., & Groman, J. (1981). Propranolol in the treatment of rage and violent behaviour in patients with chronic brain syndrome. *American Journal of Psychiatry, 138*, 218–220.

Zarski, J.J., DePompei, R., & Zook, A. (1988). Traumatic head injury: Dimensions of family responsivity. *Journal of Head Trauma Rehabilitation, 3*(4), 31–41.

Zasler, N.D., & Horn, L.J. (1990). Rehabilitative management of sexual dysfunction. *Journal of Head Trauma Rehabilitation, 5*(2), 14–24.

Zencius, A., Wesolowski, M.D., & Burke, W.H. (1990). A comparison of four memory strategies with traumatically brain-injured clients. *Brain Injury, 4*, 33–38.

Zencius, A., Wesolowski, M.D., Krankowski, T., & Burke, W.H. (1991). Memory notebook training with traumatically brain-injured clients. *Brain Injury, 5*, 321–325.

Zimmerman, R.A., Bilaniuk, L.T., & Gennarelli, T. (1978). Computed tomography of shearing injuries of the cerebral white matter. *Radiology, 127*, 393–396.

Author index

Subject index